# LEADERSHIP AND ORGANIZATION:

## A Behavioral Science Approach

McGRAW-HILL SERIES IN MANAGEMENT
Keith Davis, *Consulting Editor*

WITH THE RESEARCH AND
WRITING COLLABORATION OF

PAULA BROWN, Department of Anthropology, The Australian National University, Canberra, Australia

MURRAY KAHANE, Clinical Psychologist, Beverly Hills, California

VERNE J. KALLEJIAN, Psychologist, Los Angeles, California

MARVIN A. KLEMES, Assistant Clinical Professor, Department of Psychiatry, University of California, Los Angeles; and Private Practice, Beverly Hills, California

JEROME REISEL, Acting Assistant Professor of Business Administration, University of California, Los Angeles; and Clinical Psychologist, Arcadia, California

WARREN H. SCHMIDT, State-wide Director of Conferences and Community Services, University Extension; and Lecturer in Business Administration, University of California, Los Angeles

CLOVIS SHEPHERD, Assistant Professor of Sociology, University of California, Santa Barbara, California

EUGENE TALBOT, Staff Psychologist, Austen Riggs Center, Inc., Stockbridge, Massachusetts

JOHN H. ZENGER, Coordinator, Management Development and Training, Pacific Finance Corporation, Los Angeles, California

AND WITH COMMENTARIES
ON THE CONTENTS OF THIS BOOK BY

GEORGE R. BACH, Director, Institute of Group Psychotherapy, Beverly Hills, California; and Lecturer in Psychology, Claremont Graduate School, Claremont, California

ROBERT DUBIN, Research Professor of Sociology, University of Oregon, Eugene, Oregon

LYNDALL F. URWICK, Author, Lecturer, and Management Consultant, Urwick, Orr, and Partners, Ltd., London, England

# LEADERSHIP AND ORGANIZATION:

## A Behavioral Science Approach

Robert Tannenbaum

Irving R. Weschler

Fred Massarik

Graduate School of Business Administration
and Institute of Industrial Relations
University of California, Los Angeles

McGRAW-HILL BOOK COMPANY, INC.    1961

New York    Toronto    London

HM
141
·T35

LEADERSHIP AND ORGANIZATION

II

62845

THE MAPLE PRESS COMPANY, YORK, PA.

# Preface

In recent years the areas of leadership, training, and organization have increasingly challenged theorists, researchers, and practitioners. Evidence of this has been a growing literature from many disciplines and approaches. Without self-consciously determining the long-range directions of our work, we have found ourselves challenged by these issues and contributing to this literature.

This book represents a selected collection of the writings, from 1950 to 1960, of members of the Human Relations Research Group (HRRG), Institute of Industrial Relations and Graduate School of Business Administration, University of California, Los Angeles. The writings are followed by independent comments and appraisal from different viewpoints, prepared by distinguished experts in management theory, group psychotherapy and psychology, and sociology.

Joining together more than a decade ago, we,[1] as members of the HRRG, originally defined our general research orientation as the identification and measurement of variables associated with effective group

---

[1] To attain some consistency in style in the expository portions of this book, the "we" form is variously used when referring to the Human Relations Research Group, to any one or more of its members, and to a few collaborators of some HRRG members. Authorship of specific articles is indicated in a starred footnote at the beginning of each chapter. The "we" form should not imply that either the three authors or the HRRG members and collaborators always found themselves in a state of unanimity. Still, as much of the HRRG work was—and is—the product of team effort, concepts of senior authorship, the pinpointing of a specific idea to a given person, and other matters of particularizing credits are often meaningless or impossible.

The three authors are coequal in their responsibility for the contents of this volume. All we can do is hope that this assumption of "we-ness"—with all its current, frequently negative connotations of "togetherness"—does communicate a sense of sharing in the explorations at hand without doing violence to the feelings and ideas of too many of our associates and collaborators.

vii

functioning. As time passed, we became more specifically interested in the range of personality, group, organizational, and cultural variables having bearing on the exercise of leadership or interpersonal influence. We have not attempted to build a single "grand theory." Indeed, our ideas have undergone change as each of us has variously engaged in the tasks of empirical researchers, conceptualizers, classroom teachers, and human relations trainers.

Initially located exclusively within the Institute of Industrial Relations, in recent years the HRRG has been sponsored jointly by the Institute and by the Graduate School of Business Administration. From its beginning, the HRRG has been administratively headed by Robert Tannenbaum; but in its research and writing tasks it has most often functioned as a group of peers. Major financial support in the early 1950s came from the U.S. Office of Naval Research, which provided a three-year grant for a project entitled "Motivational Factors in Productivity" (Grant Nonr-233 [09]). Subsequently, a special program within the framework of the HRRG concerning "Interpersonal Influence and the Nursing Function" was supported by a three-year grant from the U.S. Public Health Service (Grant GN-4552). This research, conducted with the additional sponsorship of the UCLA School of Nursing, entailed a comprehensive program whose scope is beyond the limits of this volume. Its methods and findings are reported in a separate monograph, principally authored by Dr. Genevieve R. Meyer.[2]

In recent years, much of the HRRG effort has been devoted to the description and evaluation of a type of human relations training program that we have designated as "sensitivity training." This work has been supported financially by the Division of Research of the Graduate School of Business Administration.

From the very beginning, the HRRG has been interdisciplinary in outlook and practice. Inevitably, the problems that interested us could be examined from a variety of vantage points. Even our relatively small nucleus of three researchers embodied a range of disciplinary orientations, including psychology, sociology, cultural anthropology, business administration, and economics. The three of us were joined through the years by other collaborators—graduate students as well as mature researchers. These collaborators likewise had their roots in a variety of scientific disciplines.

[2] *Tenderness and Technique: Nursing Values in Transition,* Institute of Industrial Relations, University of California, Los Angeles, Industrial Relations Monograph no. 6, 1960.

In addition to Dr. Meyer, those associated with the nursing project were Craig MacAndrew, Jo Eleanor Elliott, Miriam Horowitz, Louise Marlene Kincaid, Bruce Gordon, Hannah Sprowls, Joan Butler, Jeanne Quint, Phyllis Nie, Martha Adams, and Marilyn Folck.

As we came to work together, we did indeed have our ups and downs, our moments of disagreement, and our conceptual and semantic barriers. But, all in all, we have felt a general internal cohesiveness—rich in intellectual give and take, and providing a fruitful setting for exploration and learning that, to us, at any rate, has been consistently exciting.

The nature of our philosophy and organization has been such that we have had available a grab bag of social science tools for use in tackling research problems. For some, the insights of the clinical psychologist proved to be particularly helpful. For others, the social anthropologist provided a base from which the statistically trained sociologist could make his contribution. We have had occasion to use the rigorous, model-building skill of the economist, the practical outlook of the organizational consultant, the experimental know-how of the industrial psychologist. While the term did not have currency when we began our work, we have, in effect, been operating from the framework of the behavioral sciences, rather than from a highly specific, rigidly circumscribed theoretical position. Our choice of problems and of techniques for solving them has been limited by time, competence, and resources rather than by a particular, fixed theoretical predilection.

We have been fortunate to be working in times that academically have been ripe with ferment and stimulation. Clearly, it is impossible to trace or to detail all the major influences under whose impact our ideas have taken shape. The towering notions of dynamic psychology, as originally developed by Freud and his disciples, undoubtedly made their mark. So did the brilliant writings of Kurt Lewin and of his students, whose formulations concerning relations between individual and group no doubt can be traced in our work. We have been strongly influenced by the thinking of Carl Rogers, particularly with respect to the concepts of client-centeredness, acceptance, and listening; by J. L. Moreno, in the areas of sociometry and psychodrama; by the pioneering contributions of Elton Mayo and of his associates, in enriching our understanding of the industrial civilization that provides the broad context for our research. The approaches of the National and Western Training Laboratories in Group Development have interacted with many other approaches to human relations training in the evolution of sensitivity training. Vast areas of practice and experimentation, such as group psychotherapy, classic and "modern" organization theory, group dynamics—these and many more have been significant sources of ideas.

In our intellectually formative years, in our formal and informal academic education, great teachers made their impact. Once more, a complete listing is impossible, but of special significance were men such as Frank H. Knight, Raleigh W. Stone, and Frederick H. Harbison, of the University of Chicago; Franklin Fearing, William S. Robinson, and

Abraham Kaplan, of the University of California, Los Angeles; Paul F. Lazarsfeld, of Columbia University; and Milton L. Blum and John Hastings, of the City College of New York.

Throughout the years, the HRRG has served as a useful research training laboratory for graduate students working for degrees in some of the social science departments and the Graduate School of Business Administration of the University of California. Within the framework of our research activities, these students have often developed concepts and methods that have become integral parts of the HRRG formulations. Norman B. Henderson, Verne J. Kallejian, Arnold S. Gebel, Jerome Reisel, Eugene Talbot, Murray Kahane, Clovis Shepherd, and Carolyn K. Staats are those who completed their doctoral dissertations during or after HRRG membership. Gary Carlson, Kaj Lohmann, Robert C. Dorn, Gertrude Peterson, John H. Zenger, Henri Tieleman, Gerald B. Fogelson, and Iris Tan either are still working on their dissertations or have left academic life for positions in industry, government, or education.

The present volume is designed as an overview of HRRG work from its inception to the present.[3] As such, it is a collection of articles, research papers, excerpts from monographs, and the like. These writings are presented in the first three of the four major parts of this book: 1. Leadership and the Influence Process; 2. Sensitivity Training: A Personal Approach to the Development of Leaders; 3. Studies in Organization. The initial part presents some general reflections on the human relations area and a number of theoretical and practical statements concerning concepts and processes basic to leadership. The second part deals with our approach to the development of leadership effectiveness—sensitivity training. It includes chapters focusing on the purposes and functions of this training method, as well as some consideration of concepts such as trainer role and group development. The third part develops some theoretical notions pertaining to formal organization, examines the operation of a particular organization—a government research laboratory, addresses itself to the matters of organizational objectives and performance evaluation, and presents the results of some empirical explorations in the organization area.

The investigations and theoretical statements presented in the chapters of this volume do, of course, reflect thinking at different stages in the development of the HRRG. Further, when written they were addressed to different audiences, from knowledgeable professional colleagues to hardware-oriented practicing executives. Some chapters are concerned with fairly "heavy" theory or detailed quantitative research. Others are more broadly speculative, interpretative, or discursive. Thus, it is likely that the present reader will find the pattern of the book somewhat uneven.[4] Re-

---

[3] With the previously noted exception of the nursing research project.

[4] The "present reader" is, of course, always an abstraction. In order to serve as a kind of rough guide for the actual reader, one may classify the chapters according

gardless, it was our decision to rest, with minor editing (except for some chapters in Part 2), on the principal content of the original writings. Though some of our ideas and terminologies have changed through the years, in most instances we felt that substantial rewriting would defeat the purpose of presenting the realities of the work as it actually came to be. Indeed, we hope that we have moved in a direction that the reader may judge to be growth, as one compares more recent publications with earlier ones.

The organization of the book does not follow a chronological pattern. Rather, it seeks to present various concepts and methods within a logical framework, as briefly sketched above, and as will be elaborated in introductory notes preceding Parts 1, 2, and 3.

Part 4 of the book presents commentaries on HRRG theory, concepts, and methods prepared at our request by three leading experts in cognate fields. These discussants were asked to evaluate our work from the vantage point of their own frame of reference, considering particularly the broader implications of the concepts and methods as proposed by HRRG. The discussants were assured that their comments would be subject solely to normal, routine editing and that no change in substance whatsoever would be made. Further, it was stressed that the discussants would have complete freedom in the specifics of their approach to the appraisal and that we would seek no rebuttal.

In connection with this task, we are most fortunate to have obtained the cooperation of the following: Dr. George Bach, of the Institute of Group Psychotherapy, Beverly Hills, California; Prof. Robert Dubin, of the Department of Sociology, University of Oregon; and Col. Lyndall Urwick, of the consulting firm Urwick, Orr, and Partners, Ltd., England.

The book concludes with two bibliographies. The first lists all publications of the HRRG from its beginning to the present. The second is a

---

to four categories or levels: theoretical, empirical, descriptive, and interpretative. Theoretical articles are those which develop conceptual frameworks usually in a fairly technical manner. Empirical articles are those reporting specific research conducted by the HRRG, often providing statistical data and quantitative results. Descriptive articles provide, as the term denotes, descriptions of research, training methods, or other phases of HRRG work; they are not oriented in a quantitative direction but rather provide an over-all picture of some endeavor. Interpretative articles seek to explain, often in popular and discursive terms, issues, concepts, areas of investigation, etc., that have been of interest to the HRRG. Some articles indeed share several of these four characteristics.

The theoretical and empirical chapters are likely to be of special concern to the graduate student and research scholar, whereas those with an interpretative and descriptive orientation are appropriate for the general administrator and interested nonacademic reader as well as for student and scholar: Chapter 1, interpretative; 2, theoretical; 3, 4, 5, and 6, interpretative; 7, theoretical; 8, interpretative; 9, 10, 11, and 12, descriptive; 13, theoretical and empirical; 14, interpretative and descriptive; 15 and 16, theoretical; 17 and 18, descriptive; 19, 20, and 21, empirical; 22, empirical and theoretical; 23 and 24, interpretative.

selected, annotated bibliography, which presents some relevant works written by others. This bibliography is designed to update, complement, supplement, and extend notions presented in this book. It is our hope that such a bibliography will be of value to those readers who might want to use this book as a point of departure for further investigation into the many human relations areas with which it deals.

We are grateful—with no strings attached—to the discussants for having taken on their assignments. We wish to thank the grantors, foundations, and other sources of financing that directly and indirectly have made possible our efforts. A special note of appreciation is due to the U.S. Naval Ordnance Test Station, Pasadena, California, which provided us with a particularly hospitable setting for much of our early field research. We wish to express our gratitude to the journals and their editors who gave permission to reprint material that originally appeared elsewhere. Of course, we wish to make special mention of our collaborators through the years. Under Deans Neil H. Jacoby and George W. Robbins, of the Graduate School of Business Administration, and Directors George H. Hildebrand and Benjamin Aaron, of the Institute of Industrial Relations, our group found a hospitable setting and ready support. The warmth and understanding of the late Edgar L. Warren, director of the Institute of Industrial Relations (1947–1956), meant more to the HRRG and to each of us personally than we can express.

This book cannot be put to press without some credit being given to our little group of secretaries, who in times of stress, as well as in rare moments of relative serenity, have taken us under their protective wings. Not only have they given us technical assistance of high quality, but, perhaps of equal importance, they have been sources of friendship and counsel when most needed. We are grateful to all of them: Louise Lett, Jacqueline Gordon, Lois Smallwood, Pat Shepherd, Joyce Hertzberg, Ethel Davis, Barbara Rigby, Jo Ann Woods, Lucille R. Moss, Judy O'Hara, and Florence Orman. Mrs. Orman has served and suffered far beyond the call of duty in the final preparation of the manuscript. Mrs. Shepherd prepared competently both the subject-matter and author indexes. The wise counsel of our Institute editor, Anne P. Cook, has been, as always, invaluable.

Finally, for reasons that are personally meaningful to us, we want to mention our wives—Edith Tannenbaum, Franzi Weschler, Estelle Massarik—and our children—Judy and Debbie Tannenbaum; Lawrence, Robert, Toni Ellen, and Raymond Philippe Weschler; and Michael Massarik.

*Robert Tannenbaum*
*Irving R. Weschler*
*Fred Massarik*

# Contents

# Contents

### PART FOUR. COMMENTARIES

### BIBLIOGRAPHIES

# PART ONE

# Leadership and the Influence Process

Our designation as the Human Relations Research Group has had its advantages and limitations. At the time we chose the name, we could think of none better to characterize the interdisciplinary, people-oriented character of our group and its research interests. The term *human relations* was a relatively new one, but it was being widely used; the term *behavioral sciences*, with its present connotations, was not then employed extensively.

In the years which have followed, "human relations" has taken on a variety of meanings, an outcome which has confused discourse rather than clarified it. To some, the term came to designate a "new movement" of significance; to others, it appeared a miraculous panacea. For others still (perhaps for many) the term acquired negative connotations. Inevitably such negative affect may have some impact, small or great, on the mental set which our readers bring to this book.

We therefore feel it appropriate to introduce not only Part 1 but also the book with a chapter (Chapter 1) which attempts to clarify the use of the term "human relations," to make explicit what we mean by it, and to face head-on the major expressed reasons for the negative affect. It is our hope that the reader will view our work in a context of this expression of meaning and of values.

Central to the work of our group since its formation has been the notion of *leadership and the influence process.* Implicitly in our early years, and explicitly in more recent years, this notion has provided a framework which has guided much of our work; no doubt, it will continue to do so.

We have found this framework to be a most useful one. The social process by which one person attempts to influence one or more other persons is encountered in a large variety of interpersonal relationships;

1

e.g., the superior-subordinate, the staff-line, the consultant-client, the salesman-customer, the teacher-student, the counselor-counselee, the husband-wife, and the parent-child. These relationships always occur in, are affected by, and in turn affect a context of groups, organizations, and cultures. Thus, a more adequate understanding of leadership must depend upon increased insight into the nature of many personality, group, organizational, and cultural variables and their interrelationship and interaction in a system of influence.

Our framework, presented in Chapter 2, has provided the common thread which has loosely bound together our separate studies and our attempts at concept formulation. It has also helped us in our continuing efforts to integrate the findings of others with our own.

Two elements contained in our leadership framework have entered strongly into our formulations, research, and practice in recent years. These are *social sensitivity* (or *empathy*) and *action flexibility* (or *behavioral flexibility*). We consider both of these variables as being of key importance in contributing to leadership effectiveness. Our research work to date has given primary attention to the former, while our formulations and practice have leaned heavily on both.

The meaning of social sensitivity in the cultural context of today is presented in Chapter 3. An explanation is offered as to why the notion has become important and of considerable interest to many. At the same time, limits to the application of the concept are presented. In Chapter 4, the process of social perception is examined with reference to its three basic aspects: the perceiver, the perceived, and the situation or total setting within which perception occurs. Major barriers and aids to one's accuracy of social perception (or social sensitivity) are then considered and illustrated.

The challenging issue of choosing from among alternative leadership styles is presented and analyzed in Chapter 5. Types of behavior available to the leader are described, and criteria are presented to guide the leader in his choice from among these. Two major implications are drawn: the successful leader is one who is keenly aware of the forces which are most relevant to his behavior at any given time; *and* he is one who is able to behave appropriately in the light of such understanding. Thus, once again, these are the notions of social sensitivity and action flexibility.

Broadly speaking, the objective of all leadership attempts is change—change in motivation, in attitudes, in behavior, etc., whether at the level of the individual or of the group. Chapters 6 and 7 present different facets of the problem of change. Chapter 6 analyzes key elements underlying the effective introduction of change in an organizational context. Symptoms of resistance to change are described, and the causes of such resistance are considered. A conclusion is drawn that the resistance of managers themselves to the adoption of new methods of management may represent one of the most serious barriers to the introduction of change in organizations. Chapter 7 views participation by subordinates in the managerial decision-making process as a means for the introduction of change. Participation is defined, the advantages of participation as a managerial device are considered, and many conditions essential to effective participation are analyzed.

This part concludes with Chapter 8, in which an increasingly critical leadership problem is diagnosed—the problem of managing differences, whether within the individual or between individuals, groups, or organizations. The leader is often threatened by the existence (present or potential) of such differences and, as a result, deals with them ineffectively. But differences can be utilized constructively in the attainment of leadership objectives. Alternative methods for dealing with differences are presented, and the conditions for their use are considered.

CHAPTER 1

## Some Basic Issues in Human Relations*

Human relations today has its iconoclasts and believers, critics and supporters, detractors and zealots. This is not surprising; for during the past twenty years, numerous research groups have burgeoned, and many individual investigators have become most active in the field.

There has been a fantastic outpouring of professional and popular books and articles, untold new or revised college and university offerings, a plethora of in-plant training courses, a growing number of training laboratories and seminars, and a seemingly ever-increasing schedule of meetings and speeches—all concerned, in whole or in part, with "human relations."

It is to be expected that such a rapid and extensive development—involving persons with widely disparate education and experience, and carrying with it numerous challenges to contemporary ideas and practice—should become a focal point for controversy. In the face of such controversy, excesses (whether pro or con) have been inevitable and confusion rampant. Little wonder, then, that the innocent bystander has increasingly been asking: "What is this 'human relations' all about?"

Quite recently, and appropriately, a number of evaluative articles have appeared, each attempting to appraise this new development.[1]

* This chapter is based upon the following publications: "Some Basic Issues in Human Relations," by Robert Tannenbaum, appearing in Robert D. Gray (ed.), *The Frontiers of Industrial Relations* [Pasadena, Calif.: Industrial Relations Section, California Institute of Technology (copyrighted), 1959] (also published as "Some Current Issues in Human Relations," *California Management Review*, vol. II, no. 1, pp. 49–58, Fall, 1959); and *An Evaluative Focus on Human Relations* by Robert Tannenbaum, miscellaneous publication (mimeo) of the Institute of Industrial Relations, University of California, Los Angeles (1954).

[1] See, for example, William Gomberg, "The Use of Psychology in Industry: A Trade Union Point of View," *Management Science*, vol. 3, no. 4, pp. 348–370, July, 1957; William H. Knowles, "Human Relations in Industry: Research and Concepts,"

5

Some of them have been written by partisans; nevertheless, each makes a valuable contribution by highlighting trends, clarifying principal issues, or raising basic questions.

The present chapter represents an effort to make a further contribution to current discussion. For a number of years, we have thought extensively about, done research in, taught, and practiced in the area of human relations. With this background of experience as a base, an attempt will be made to bring some order out of the chaos which often surrounds the use of the term "human relations" and to indicate what the term now means to us. We will then present and react to some of the most frequently recurring criticisms directed at this new field.

## WHAT IS "HUMAN RELATIONS"?

Writing in 1950, John W. McConnell stated: "Facetiously, someone has remarked that human relations are whatever those interested in human relations study. If one may judge by the divergent approaches of a number of research groups, no single definition is at present possible."[2] Not only have the approaches of research groups diverged, but so have the usages of teachers, speakers, writers, practitioners, and the lay public. In the decade since McConnell wrote his article, little has occurred to dispel the confusion.

Often the key source of difficulty in professional and public discourse on human relations is a semantic rather than a substantive one. Certainly the term "human relations" means different things to different men; as a result, adversaries talk about different things, frequently without knowing it. Certainly, if the term is to continue in use, greater precision in its employment will be needed.

Four principal denotations of "human relations" have developed in usage during recent decades. The term has variously referred to inter- and intrapersonal phenomena, to a tool kit for practitioners, to an ethical orientation, and to an emerging scientific discipline.

### Human Relations as Inter- and Intrapersonal Phenomena

The term is most frequently employed to refer to *inter*personal phenomena. These phenomena may be involved in the relations between

---

*California Management Review*, vol. 1, no. 1, pp. 87–105, Fall, 1958; Malcolm P. McNair, "What Price Human Relations?," *Harvard Business Review*, vol. 35, no. 2, pp. 15 ff., March-April, 1957; Malcolm P. McNair, "Too Much 'Human Relations'?," *Look*, Oct. 20, 1958, pp. 47–48; Donald R. Schoen, "Human Relations: Boon or Bogle?," *Harvard Business Review*, vol. 35, no. 6 pp. 41–47, November-December, 1957; William Foote Whyte, "Human Relations Theory—A Progress Report," *Harvard Business Review*, vol. 34, no. 5, pp. 125–132, September-October, 1956.

[2] "Problems of Method in the Study of Human Relations," *Industrial and Labor Relations Review*, vol. 3, no. 4, p. 549, July, 1950.

one person and another; among the members of a group; between one group and another; among the persons and groups in an organization; between one organization and another; among the persons, groups, and organizations in a culture; and between cultures.

The individual often strives to improve his human relations. The manager refers to human relations in his plant. Municipal and community commissions on human relations concern themselves with the relations among various religious and ethnic groups. And so it goes. True, some more specific terms have emerged to denote certain relations—for example, personnel relations; group dynamics; union-management relations, or industrial relations; public relations; and international relations—and yet the term "human relations" continues to be used at times to refer to each.

The term has been used less frequently to refer to *intra*personal phenomena—variables involved in the relationship of an individual with himself. These factors have been of concern to therapists, clinicians, counselors, and educators. Illustrative of these phenomena are the characteristics of a person's internal communication network, including the relationship between his conscious and unconscious selves.

## Human Relations as a Tool Kit for Practitioners

The term is often used to denote a variously conceived collection of methods and techniques for dealing with problems arising out of inter- and intrapersonal relations. In some instances, these have procedural implications, as in role playing, buzz grouping, T-group training, the use of consultants and of panels, consultative supervision, participative management, and brainstorming. In other instances, these have behavioral implications, as in listening, conveying acceptance, and avoiding defensiveness and aggressiveness. The purpose of many human relations courses, seminars, and programs offered by industrial organizations, schools, and others is to make available to the participant some new human relations devices. And these are often expectantly sought as "open sesames" to increased interpersonal effectiveness.

## Human Relations as an Ethical Orientation

The term often suggests values. It implies both "good" practice in the use of the tool kit and a "high" quality of interpersonal relations. For example, human relations is "an ethical system emphasizing the positive good that may result from the right kind of interrelationships among people." It is "a spirit of cooperation and understanding among individuals and groups at all levels of the organization"; "the attitude of one human being toward another"; "the dignity, the sense of satisfaction, the feeling of security, or the lack of it that individuals have in an organization"; "how well people get along with one another, showing ethical regard for each other"; "liking and disliking"; "considerate behavior"; "good manners"; "decencies of relationships."[3] In this usage, human relations is both a guide for behavior and a desirable end to be sought.

## Human Relations as a Scientific Discipline

Finally, the term "human relations" is being used to denote a field of inquiry—one which cuts across the jurisdictional boundaries of the traditional social sciences in an effort to avoid fragmented, compartmentalized, or partial approaches to human problems.

In an important sense, this field meets an often-expressed need for a more unified approach. As early as 1928, Max Scheler felt that " . . . we no longer possess any clear and consistent idea of man. The ever-growing multiplicity of the particular sciences that are engaged in the study of men has much more confused and obscured than elucidated our concept of man."[4] Twenty years later, in a context of research in industrial relations, Professor E. Wight Bakke made this closely related observation:[5]

It is obvious that the problem of human behavior with which we are dealing can not be understood in terms of psychology or any one of the social sciences alone. Is it not possible, therefore, that in attempting to follow the problem wherever it leads us, and employing whatever concepts and research techniques are relevant, we shall be able to define the problem in such a way and develop concepts and a theoretical framework of such a nature that a major contribution will be made to the foundation for an integrated social and psychological science? Whether or not this result appears possible or attractive to present scholars in these fields, we who are studying industrial relations are forced to work in this direction. It is not a case of choice alone, but of necessity, for we can not get results satisfactory to ourselves and applicable to the solution of practical problems by employing the concepts, theories, and methods of any one science.

In recent years, there has been a growing recognition of the rich insights to be gained through approaching problems of inter- and intrapersonal relations holistically rather than partially through the more narrow orientations of any one of the traditional social sciences. Individual researchers are increasingly incorporating the theories and meth-

[3] The statements in quotes are taken from responses to a questionnaire used in preparation for the writing of the evaluative article by Robert Tannenbaum cited in footnote 1.

[4] Quoted in Rollo May, Ernest Angel, and Henri F. Ellenberger (eds.), *Existence* (New York: Basic Books, Inc., 1958), p. 22.

[5] "Industrial Relations Research," *Proceedings of the American Philosophical Society,* vol. 92, no. 5, p. 379, November, 1948.

ods of disciplines other than their own into their work. There are research groups comprised of individuals from many disciplines who are attempting in one way or another to pool their respective competencies in the work that they do. Some universities are encouraging interdepartmental collaboration and occasionally establishing new, integrated departments. And publications are appearing which effectively bring together methods developed in different disciplines.

Observing these and related trends, we see a scientific discipline emerging—a discipline which will ultimately integrate many of the social sciences. There are those who refer to this emerging discipline as "human relations." Others are calling it "the behavioral sciences." What is important here is not the term itself (some other more appropriate one may in time evolve and gain general acceptance), but that to which the term refers.

This emerging discipline will bring to bear existing and newly developed theories, methods, and techniques of the relevant social sciences upon the study of inter- and intrapersonal phenomena, ranging fully from the personality dynamics of individuals at one extreme to the relations between cultures at the other. This discipline will be a field of study focusing upon definable phenomena and yielding a body of knowledge relevant to human behavior. It will have its applied branch, which will use knowledge emerging from basic research in the solution of particular problems for specified purposes. Associated with the latter branch will be researchers, who will use existing knowledge to provide a systematic basis for later implementation, and practitioners, who will diagnose situations and take action which they deem appropriate in terms of objectives to be achieved. It would be hazardous to guess how long it might take for this new discipline to emerge full-blown, but the current trend in this direction is apparent and the ultimate outcome, inevitable.[6]

## WHAT ABOUT "HUMAN RELATIONS"?

In considering the most frequently recurring questions raised about "human relations," it seems important to keep in mind the diversity of meanings attached to the term. Too often of late, criticisms which in reality are aimed at but one aspect of "human relations" tend to be perceived by many as damning the entire field. Most typically, questions are raised about the practice of human relations—about the tool

[6] This assessment of trends and prediction was first stated by Robert Tannenbaum in essentially the above form in the evaluative article cited in footnote 1. In light of developments during the five years since that writing, we are now even more strongly convinced of the outcome predicted.

kit, about the applicability of the tools, or about the ethics guiding the use of the tools. Much less frequently are questions raised about human relations as a scientific discipline or about the phenomena upon which the discipline focuses.[7]

The questions recently raised about human relations can challenge partisans to reexamine their basic assumptions, their values, and their practices. They can make a real contribution to the development of the broad field of human relations by dampening excesses and eliminating unsound elements from thought and practice. A closer look at these criticisms is therefore in order.

## Is "Human Relations" Here to Stay?

With the emergence of any new thought or mode which commands enthusiastic camp followers and wide public attention, the question inevitably arises as to whether or not this is a "here today—gone tomorrow" phenomenon. With respect to human relations, for example, Professor McNair in his two articles uses such descriptive terms as "vogue," "fashion," "fad," and "cult." To some persons, at least, it is a passing fancy whose principal adherents are essentially blind partisans placing their bets on the wrong horse.

*Human Relations as a Kit of Tools.* This charge does have merit with respect to some of the contents of the human relations tool kit. It is not unusual for a particular method—such as buzz grouping or brainstorming (methods which are most valuable when appropriately employed) —to be oversold by some proponents and to be ineptly used by some practitioners. Both overselling and improper usage can lead first to wariness and then to rejection. As a result, the good is often discarded with the bad.

The unstructured training group, evolved by the National Training Laboratory in Group Development and later utilized with modifications by other training laboratories and in sensitivity training (see Part 2), is a case in point. The unstructured group—which minimizes or eliminates the use of such conventional means as formal leadership, prescribed member roles, and agenda—is a potent device for the generation of certain types of learning experiences. When used for this purpose by artful trainers, worthwhile ends can be attained. However, there have been those who, having experienced such training, assume that the device of the unstructured group is universally applicable (even, for example, to *ad hoc,* short-lived, decision-making groups) or

---

[7] One major exception to this observation needs mention. Many professionals active in the social sciences disagree as to whether or not there is a trend toward the integration of these sciences and whether, even though the trend may be present, this is a desirable direction.

that one experience in such a group qualifies them as expert practitioners in this area. As a result, the device itself is rejected by some, when in fact their criticism should be directed at the misuse of the device.

It is the excesses and the deficient practices which most often lead individuals to doubt the permanency of any innovation. Fortunately, human relations devices (as well as all others) must, in order to survive, pay off in practice. If they do not, they will fall by the wayside or be adapted until they do pay off. And most nonprofessional practitioners are sooner or later found out.

*Human Relations as a Scientific Discipline.* When we view human relations as a scientific discipline, with both basic and applied branches, there is little reason to doubt that it is here to stay. Rather than being a fad or fashion, it is as fundamental as man's relationship to man.

The nature of the points at issue here can perhaps be well illustrated with reference to a controversy currently taking place in many professional schools of business administration. There are those who argue that human relations (or the behavioral sciences) has no place in such a school because it has little if any relevance to business management, and that the current interest in such schools in the subject is but a passing fancy.

Many who take this view see business units as essentially economic and technological entities (which certainly they are) but not important as social organizations (which certainly they also are). To them, people are not unique human beings in unique social groupings, but rather names on organization charts whose on-the-job behavior is primarily determined (or ought to be) by job descriptions and the desires of their bosses.

An increasing number of scholars, however, are becoming aware of and able to accept the fact that people (with all their really human qualities) are a fundamental part of any business organization. They are there as individuals with their particular personalities; they are there as members of many types of groups; they are units in the total organization; and they are affected by the culture that surrounds them.

While the effective manager must, without question, be able to understand and deal with economic and technological phenomena, he must *also* be able to understand and deal with interpersonal phenomena. Managerial problems involving motivation, morale, teamwork, creativity, introduction of change, demand creation, public relations, etc., can adequately be solved only through a keen understanding of relevant human relations variables and an ability to behave appropriately in light of such understanding.

Because the manager's need for understanding and skill in the human area is so basic and pervasive and because the emerging science of human relations has presently and potentially so very much to offer him in the direction of meeting this need, it seems quite clear that human relations (as a scientific discipline) is bound to be accepted as a basic teaching and research area in professional schools of business administration.

What is apparent in this one illustrative instance is equally apparent in others. Man's relationship to man has posed problems for as long as he can remember. Until fairly recently, he has typically "played it by ear" in facing these problems. Now, the evolving discipline, although still young and often immature, increasingly offers a better insight into the problems and ways for dealing with them. However, much remains to be done. The following problem areas are illustrative of those requiring additional emphasis as the scientific discipline of human relations faces the future:

GAINING A BETTER UNDERSTANDING OF THE VARIABLES UNDERLYING INTERPERSONAL EFFECTIVENESS. Interpersonal effectiveness is influenced by three types of variables: personality variables, interpersonal variables, and situational variables. Much recent research has arrived at broad statistical generalizations about groups of individuals, types of relations, and varieties of situations. These generalizations represent good beginnings. However, work must rapidly proceed to the point where individual predictions can be made; that is, where it can be predicted how a specific individual with a given personality involved in a given interpersonal relation in a given situation will behave.[8]

Progress here depends on concentrated research on numerous exciting problems. For example, there is the problem involving the relation between deeper personality variables and overt behavior. Researchers have milked dry the "superficial" trait approach, in which overt behavior has been explained in terms of such generalities as the need for status, security, and recognition. The experiential insights gained by psychotherapists, added to the numerous recent research findings relating to the authoritarian personality syndrome, social perception, social sensitivity, and flexibility, provide an indication of the deeper roots which must be explored.

FACILITATING ATTITUDINAL AND BEHAVIORAL CHANGE. In this connection, we need a better understanding of the dynamics of resistance to change. Most of what is now done by practitioners in dealing with such resistance represents distillations from experience, and certainly

[8] For one example of work aimed in this direction, see Jeanne Watson, "The Application of Psychoanalytic Measures of Personality to the Study of Social Behavior," paper presented at the 61st Annual Convention of the American Psychological Association, 1953. Mimeographed, available from Research Center for Group Dynamics, University of Michigan.

much experience has already been gained. However, there is a paucity of findings from research to give the practitioner a sound foundation against which to validate and to improve his art.

ESTABLISHING APPROPRIATE CRITERIA FOR THE EVALUATION OF PERFORM- ANCE. Most researchers who have been working in the industrial setting have been plagued by the problem of criteria. This is also of consider- able importance to the operating man. Researchers are often interested in discovering variables associated with effectiveness, but what is effec- tiveness in any given setting? Is it profitability, maximum output, in- dividual satisfaction, development of the individual, or what?[9] The variables related to effectiveness may very well be different depending upon the criterion (or criteria) of effectiveness chosen. But just select- ing the appropriate criterion is not enough. Once chosen, how is the criterion operationally defined? And if there is in fact more than one criterion, how can they best be combined? Finally, the problem remains of evaluating performance (whether individual or group) with refer- ence to the criterion or of relating the variables under study to the criterion. These unsolved problems are at present critical barriers to useful progress in the area of human relations research.

THE AREA OF INTERGROUP RELATIONS. One of the major unsolved prob- lems concerns the roles of conflict and cooperation in the relations be- tween groups. Is cooperation always desirable and always possible? What happens when the objectives of two groups are diametrically opposed? What about the process of accommodation, which is often the feasible middle ground between the two extremes? There is also here the problem of the individual—the person caught between two or more groups. This problem of dual loyalty presents challenging questions for research.

RECOGNIZING THE IMPORTANCE OF CULTURE VARIABLES. Not long ago, a psychologist stated: "Perhaps one of the outstanding weaknesses of contemporary psychological theory is the relative neglect of the en- vironment by many of the most influential theoretical viewpoints."[10] Researchers have often neglected the subcultures of the plant or union in which their research has been carried on as well as the broader cul- ture of which the plant or union forms a part. What are, for example, the cultural boundaries of conclusions such as the one that says that effective leaders are those who are employee-oriented rather than work-

[9] See Bernard M. Bass, "Ultimate Criteria of Organizational Worth," *Personnel Psychology*, vol. 5, no. 3, pp. 157–173, Autumn, 1952, in which he suggests that an organization be evaluated in terms of (1) the degree to which it is productive, profitable, and self-maintaining; (2) the degree to which it is of value to its mem- bers; and (3) the degree to which it and its members are of value to society.
[10] Isidor Chein, "The Environment as a Determinant of Behavior," *Journal of Social Psychology*, vol. 39, p. 115, 1954.

oriented? Such boundaries are rarely made explicit in the published reports of research. Likewise, problems of intrapersonal role conflict arising from membership in different reference groups have often been neglected.[11]

There remains the problem of how best to take culture into account. In the area of industrial relations, William F. Whyte has dealt with the question in this way:[12]

Whether we shall consider the environment is not, I believe, the central issue. . . . The problem is to discover the most effective ways of taking the environmental factors into account. I am simply proposing that we take the social systems of union and management as the central items for study. I am suggesting that we will make progress faster if we study small, manageable units, even when they are parts of large organizations. The influences flowing down from top management and top union can be noted as they are manifested in the behavior of the people under observation. Similarly, the community influences must be noted in exactly the same way; as they come out in specific items of behavior within the social system.

A differing emphasis in approach is suggested by Conrad M. Arensberg, who stated:[13]

Much of the individual behavior social psychology seeks to explain is a by-product of changes in the larger organization—themselves networks of interpersonal role adaptation—of which the small groups so far studied are but minute parts. Small-group dynamics is a dependent, not an independent variable.

THE INDIVIDUAL IN THE ORGANIZATION. According to Dorwin Cartwright, one of the questions men of practical affairs ask about groups is: "How do you keep a group from destroying the individuality and personal freedom of its members?"[14] The question is one which haunts researchers as well.[15]

[11] The kinds of problems we have in mind here are well illustrated in Melvin E. Seeman, "Role Conflict and Ambivalence in Leadership," *American Sociological Review*, vol. 18, no. 4, pp. 373–380, August, 1953.

[12] In Part II of John T. Dunlop and William Foote Whyte, "Framework for the Analysis of Industrial Relations: Two Views," *Industrial and Labor Relations Review*, vol. 3, no. 3, p. 410, April, 1950.

[13] Conrad M. Arensberg, "Behavior and Organization: Industrial Studies," in John H. Rohrer and Muzafer Sherif (eds.), *Social Psychology at the Crossroads* (New York: Harper & Brothers, 1951), chap. 14.

[14] D. Cartwright, "Toward a Social Psychology of Groups: The Concept of Power," presidential address delivered before the Society for the Psychological Study of Social Issues, Cleveland, Ohio, Sept. 5, 1953. Mimeographed.

[15] Chris Argyris, in his recent research, has devoted much attention to this and closely related questions. See his *Personality and Organization* (New York: Harper & Brothers, 1957).

First, the individual brings to the organization a number of personal needs, some of which, at least, must be satisfied in the organizational context; at the same time, he is expected to behave in a way which will make possible the attainment of an organizational goal. Sometimes the satisfaction of personal needs and the attainment of organizational goals are congruent, but often they are not.

A second phase of the problem involves the relationship of the so-called informal to the formal aspects of organization. There is a growing body of research about the informal aspects, and certainly for a number of years much attention has been given to the formal aspects. What we need to know more about is the optimum interlinkage of the two. Just to cite one example, of what relevance to the attainment of organizational objectives is the grapevine as a means of communication (a means which is closely associated with the satisfaction of personal needs)?[16]

A third aspect of the problem is one which poses the conflict between democracy and authority associated with formal hierarchies. Daniel Bell has stated that "ultimately, the problem of leadership is shaped by the fact that while we live in a society of political democracy, almost all basic social patterns are authoritarian and tend to instill feelings of helplessness and dependence. . . . Our factories, hierarchical in structure, are, for all the talk of human relations programs, still places where certain men exercise arbitrary authority over others."[17]

As the democratic value orientation becomes more deeply embedded in our social fabric, we are being forced increasingly to examine the extent to which democratic principles have applicability within bureaucracies. Perhaps the problem is not essentially one involving a choice between two extremes, democracy *or* authority; but, as William F. Whyte has said, "It is a problem of weaving authority and participation effectively together."[18] As we see it, the problem involves the definition of appropriate limits by authority and the exercise of freedom or democracy within these limits. The questions of how the limits should be defined and how democracy can best be implemented within them require much additional research.

Closely related here is the notion of power. All kinds of key questions remain to be answered with respect to this construct, but these

[16] See, for example, Keith Davis, "A Method of Studying Communication Patterns in Organizations," *Personnel Psychology,* vol. 6, pp. 301–312, Autumn, 1953, and "Management Communication and the Grapevine," *Harvard Business Review,* vol. 31, pp. 43–49, September-October, 1953.

[17] " 'Screening' Leaders in a Democracy," *Commentary,* vol. 5, no. 4, p. 375, April, 1948.

[18] "Leadership and Group Participation," New York State School of Industrial and Labor Relations, Cornell University, Bulletin 24, May, 1953, p. 40. See also Chap. 5.

have already been well pointed up by Dorwin Cartwright in his presidential address to the Society for the Psychological Study of Social Issues.[19]

## Does Applied Human Relations Implement Legitimate Organizational Objectives?

There are certainly those who would answer this question with a resounding negative; in fact, some would maintain that applied human relations actually interferes with the attainment of such objectives.

Once again Professor McNair provides the phrases which best capture the flavor of this point of view. Americans "cannot afford the pampering luxury of 'human relations' . . . the cult of human relations is but part and parcel of the sloppy sentimentalism characterizing the world today." He feels that we can devote "too much effort in business in trying to keep everybody happy," and he points out that "without friction it is possible to go too far in the direction of sweetness and light, harmony, and the avoidance of all irritation. The present day emphasis on 'bringing everybody along' can easily lead to a deadly level of mediocrity."

One group of human relations specialists have been referred to frequently by their colleagues as "the happiness boys." A university professor of industrial relations with a national reputation once wrote one of us that human relations has a connotation for him of "back-slapping and fanny-patting." And only recently a management consultant has written: "It's time to debunk human relations! Why? Because we've come to believe that it's only an employee's relationship to his fellow workers that matters and the better this relationship, the happier he will be."[20]

One charge suggested by many of these statements is that the principal objective of human relations practitioners is to keep people happy, regardless of the price. Employee happiness becomes an end in itself—even in organizational contexts. It is felt that human relations practitioners are often "bleeding hearts," soft (lacking in tough-mindedness), and that they would "give the company away" if they were but given the chance.

No doubt there are many persons in positions of responsibility in formal organizations who act as if happiness were always the ultimate organizational value or who blindly make the assumption that happiness leads to the attainment of other goals. But any professional human relations practitioner worth his salt is not this naive.

He knows that organizations are guided by different short- and long-

---

[19] Cartwright, *op. cit.*

[20] Bernard Davis, "It's Time to Debunk Human Relations!," *Sales Management*, Mar. 7, 1959, p. 82.

run objectives. Almost always some notions of profit maximization, of service maximization, and/or of organizational survival are included. Employee happiness might even be one of the goals. But whatever objectives the organization defines for itself, its concern is to discover (through applied research, if at all possible) which human variables are significantly related to the attainment of these objectives. The manager can then use the resulting knowledge reasonably to ensure an optimum utilization of the human resources available to his organization in the attainment of its chosen objectives.

A related charge is that human relations stands for "sweetness and light" and for "peace at any price." Human relations specialists, it is suggested, hold to the view that good comes only from harmony and bad from conflict.

On the contrary, professionals in the field have as their principal concerns the *understanding* of harmony and of conflict as social phenomena; the discovery of those individual, group, and situational variables most responsible for harmony and conflict; and the determination of possible relationships between harmony and conflict on the one hand and the achievement of organizational objectives on the other.

It is becoming increasingly clear from research and practice that conflict—whether within the individual or between individuals, groups, organizations, or cultures—in addition to being a destructive force, can also be a most constructive force.[21] It may, for example, be positively related to such factors as individual and group growth or development, creativity, high motivation, and organizational flexibility. Discovering and implementing such relationships has in the past represented and will continue to represent a challenge to the human relations specialist —whether researcher or practitioner.

## Is Human Relations Destroying the Individual?

One of the most frequently recurring charges aimed at human relations is that its values and practices result in a sacrificing of the individual to the group. No longer are we very concerned, so the argument goes, with the development of independent, inner-directed persons. Instead, all important values derive from the group. Group-think, conformity, togetherness, adjustment, other-directedness—these are the gods of the day. Many competent observers confirm the existence of considerable power of the group over the individual in their descriptions of our current social order.[22] Have human relations theory and practice

---

[21] This matter is explored in Chap. 8.
[22] See, for example, Erich Fromm, *Escape From Freedom* (New York: Rinehart & Company, Inc., 1941); David Riesman et al., *The Lonely Crowd* (New Haven, Conn.: Yale University Press, 1950); and William H. Whyte, Jr., *The Organization Man* (New York: Simon and Schuster, Inc., 1956).

contributed to this trend? At issue here are questions primarily of values and of methods.

Indeed, many persons with varying motives have used methods associated with human relations to inhibit individuality. For example, devices for dealing with conflict, for gaining consensus, and for building group identification and loyalty have been used to serve such a purpose. However, the predominant values of the vast majority of professional specialists in human relations are oriented toward the individual, and their practice has strongly reflected this value orientation.

Human relations researchers in study after study have made contributions toward a better understanding of the variables related to conformity. Personality, group, organizational, and cultural factors which either inhibit or enhance the expression of individuality have been isolated and described. In recent years, considerable research attention has been devoted to gaining insights into creativity—individual, group, and organizational.

At the same time, human relations practitioners in their various activities have reflected deep concern for the individual. At the many laboratories in group development, it is true that much attention is devoted to group variables. But these are experienced and analyzed in order to determine (among other things) their inhibiting or enhancing effect on the individual. An implicit, if not explicit, question guiding all these laboratories is: "What can be done in a group to facilitate the maximum contribution and development of each member of the group?"

There has been increasing emphasis on listening and on empathy (or social sensitivity)—processes for better understanding another person from *his* point of view (seeing things as *he* sees them, and feeling things as *he* feels them). The trend in management-development programs reflects a deep concern not only for the manager's specialized development as a manager, but also for his broader development as a human being. Growing utilization of a wide variety of participational methods is also evidence of a greater awareness of the individual and a desire more fully to utilize his full knowledge and experience.

Most human relations researchers and professional practitioners, it seems to us, have made quite extensive and valuable contributions in the direction of the enhancement of the individual, and these contributions are beginning to be felt in spite of rather strong societal pressures being exerted in the other direction.

## Is Human Relations Primarily a Device for Manipulation?

Professor McNair expresses his own conviction on this matter, as follows: " . . . I am essentially disturbed at the combination of *skill* with *human relations*. For me, 'human relations skill' has a cold-blooded connotation of proficiency, technical expertness, calculated effect." (The italics are his.) Erich Fromm states a similar point of view in these words: "Beyond 'market psychology' another new field of psychology has arisen, based on the wish to understand and manipulate the employee. This is called 'human relations' . . . what Taylor did for the rationalization of physical work the psychologists do for the mental and emotional aspect of the worker. He is made into a *thing*, treated and manipulated like a thing, and so-called 'human relations' are the most inhuman ones, because they are 'reified' and alienated relations."[23]

Here is one of the most crucial issues confronting human relations. Individuals *can* skillfully get others to do what they want them to do, and often without the others being aware of what is going on. They do use others as instruments to attain their own selfish ends, without having any other concern for them. Such use is an everyday fact.

Once again, a question of individual values is posed. The findings of human relations research and the tool kit of the practitioner can be utilized for the attainment of a variety of ends—both good and bad. The fact that this is true should not be allowed to cast clouds of suspicion and of rejection over the findings and the tools per se. The issue here is similar to that in the field of atomic physics. Atomic power, too, can be used for both socially desirable and undesirable ends. Because thousands of persons can be annihilated by one well-placed bomb, the basic validity of the knowledge and skills underlying its construction and detonation should not thereby be called into question.

What needs to be attacked is the ethical orientation of those who pervert the growing body of human relations knowledge and skills to undesirable ends. A wider dissemination of information would be desirable with respect to the knowledge and skills that are presently available and how these can be used in constructive ways. By this means, not only might the welfare of mankind be enhanced, but also the individual's ability to detect and to resist manipulative efforts, however these might be directed at him.

## Should Human Relations Concern Itself with Below-surface Attributes of Individuals?

Professor McNair, in his two articles, speaks of "amateur psychiatry," of "plumbing the hidden thoughts of everybody," of the "unwarranted invasion of the privacy of individuals," of "undue preoccupation with human relations," and of "dubious ('morbid') introspection." He feels that human relations training encourages people "to pick at the scabs of their psychic wounds." And he argues that "we should be able to take

---

[23] Erich Fromm, "Man Is Not a Thing," *The Saturday Review*, Mar. 16, 1957, p. 9. The italics are his.

a man at face value and not always fret about what he really means. Too many of us are trying to be little tin Freuds." The concern here seems to be with both the inappropriateness of and the dangers involved in getting below the surface of others or of ourselves.

When others are involved, perhaps the ethical orientation of the practitioner is again of prime importance. His basic values and attitudes with respect to other people are key determinants of his behavior. If he is guided by a deep regard for others, if he sees them as valued human beings instead of as puppets, if he has a strong desire to be of help to them in ways that *they* perceive as helpful, and if he feels it important to respect whatever limits *they* deem appropriate for themselves, his behavior will most likely be appropriate and not harmful to others. The practitioner's behavior is likely also to be influenced by his own level of emotional maturity. To the degree that he is free from (or at least in control of) drives whose expression is reflected in such behavior as aggression and domination which can be destructive of another person, he is more likely to be able behaviorally to implement the values and attitudes just mentioned.

The presence of malpractice in society should not block us from pursuing through competent research and an ethical, mature practice the many beneficial goals that are within reach. A few examples may be of help in illustrating the nature of these goals.

¶ Knowing or understanding another person deeply and accurately is of great importance in many human relationships. Managers often pride themselves in trying to get "all the facts" before making decisions. And yet, in decisions involving people, "taking a man at face value" typically results in a walling-off of many facts crucially relevant to the decision. For example, a man might be fired because he "appears lazy," although the "laziness" may mask an inhibited talent whose expression could be of considerable value, not only to the company, but also to the well-being of the individual himself. Greater understanding *can* enrich human relationships, making them more productive and satisfying for all parties involved.

¶ Dealing with another person with reference solely to his surface self (or his façade) often involves dealing with him as a robot. For him to be motivated, creative, loyal, etc., his feelings or emotions must be reached. Not to tap the mainsprings of men involves a cost both to society and to the men themselves.

¶ The so-called helping relationship—found, for example, in teaching, training, management development, consulting, counseling, and psychotherapy—must of necessity involve "getting below the surface." The objective of such a relationship is the enhancement of the other—his growth and development in some direction desired by him. If such a relationship dealt only with that on the surface, nothing of value could be accomplished; the client would remain in dead center. But there is a growing body of evidence to indicate that important growth goals can be attained through appropriate processes of depth exploration.

¶ The process of getting to know one's self is often, if not always, difficult and painful, because it entails getting behind defenses and dealing with deeper elements which one may have been avoiding for years. But this process is an essential one in any individual's striving for greater personal adequacy.

In each of these examples, worthwhile ends (as seen by the parties involved) can be attained by dealing with below-surface attributes of individuals without doing harm to them. Human relations research and clinical experience have contributed much to our understanding of personality in all its complexity and of the processes involved in "depth" relationships such as those illustrated and, from research and practice, have evolved devices which can be used beneficially in attaining the goals of such relationships.

## AN EPILOGUE

We have tried in the preceding to convey to the reader our own position on some basic issues in human relations. The positions we have taken are admittedly not those of a disinterested observer, but the hope is that they are at least informed and that they are meaningful to the reader.

We have been troubled by the confusion surrounding the various uses of the term "human relations" and have attempted to bring some order out of this confusion. We are convinced that an integrated behavioral-science discipline is emerging (call it what you will) and that this development is highly desirable.

We have been challenged by the frequent charges aimed at various aspects of this evolving discipline and have tried to give our reaction to each. These charges, if squarely met, will help us to remove the excesses and the irrelevancies that have inevitably been a by-product of a rapidly developing field. They will help us to be clearer on the organizational and social relevancy of what we do. But perhaps more importantly they will keep us focused on those values which reflect respect for the dignity and the individual worth of the human beings who are the subjects of our research and the objects of our practice.

The emerging scientific discipline of human relations can only gain through seriously heeding the charges directed its way, through conscientious self-examination, and through a willingness to take corrective action where appropriate.

# CHAPTER 2

# Leadership: A Frame of Reference*

## INTRODUCTION

The word *leadership* has been widely used. Political orators, business executives, social workers, and scholars employ it in speech and writing. Yet, there is widespread disagreement as to its meaning. Among social scientists, the theoretical formulations of the leadership concept have continued to shift, focusing first upon one aspect and then upon another. Much still needs to be done to develop a basic, systematic theory. The time seems ripe for attempting a careful statement of a frame of reference which may serve to make available research more meaningful, and which may guide future research and practice.[1] Specifically, such a frame of reference can perform the useful function of pointing to the variables which need to be measured. It can help us to state hypotheses concerning the key variables underlying leadership effectiveness. It can also provide meaningful objectives for the development of more adequate leaders.

## A BRIEF HISTORICAL VIEW

The history of the "leadership" concept highlights the shifting focus in theoretical orientation. Early leadership research focused on the *leader* himself, to the virtual exclusion of other variables. It was as-

---

* This chapter is a slightly modified version of an article under the same title by Robert Tannenbaum and Fred Massarik, *Management Science*, vol. 4, no. 1, pp. 1–19, October, 1957.

[1] The evolution of the frame of reference proposed in this chapter cannot be attributed to any one individual; rather, most persons who have been members of the Human Relations Research Group, Institute of Industrial Relations and School of Business Administration, UCLA, during the past few years have played a significant role in its development. These persons, in addition to the present authors, are Paula Brown, Raymond Ezekiel, Arnold Gebel, Murray Kahane, Verne Kallejian, Gertrude Peterson, Clovis and Pat Shepherd, Eugene Talbot, and Irving R. Weschler.

sumed that leadership effectiveness could be explained by isolating psychological and physical characteristics, or traits, which were presumed to differentiate the leader from other members of his group. Studies guided by this assumption generally proved none too fruitful. Almost without exception universal traits proved elusive, and there was little agreement as to the most useful traits. Gouldner reviews some of the empirical and conservatively interpreted evidence relating to "universal traits," such as intelligence and psychosexual appeal. However, he concludes: "At this time there is no reliable evidence concerning the existence of universal leadership traits."[2] It does not now seem surprising that this approach proved rather sterile. Leaders do not function in isolation. They must deal with followers within a cultural, social, and physical context.

With the fall from grace of the trait approach, the emphasis swung away from the leader as an entity complete unto himself. Instead, the *situationist* approach came to the fore. The situationists do not necessarily abandon the search for significant leader characteristics, but they attempt to look for them in situations containing common elements. Stogdill, after examining a large number of leadership studies aimed at isolating the traits of effective leaders, comes to the following conclusion: "The qualities, characteristics and skills required in a leader are determined to a large extent by the demands of the situation in which he is to function as a leader."[3]

More recently the *follower* has been systematically considered as a major variable in leadership research. This approach focuses on personal needs, assuming that the most effective leader is the one who most nearly satisfies the needs of his followers.[4]

There have been many attempts to assess recent developments in leadership theory. The trait approach, the situationist approach, and the follower-oriented approach have variously been discussed and evaluated by a number of authors including Stogdill, Jenkins, Gouldner, and Sanford.[5] On the basis of their work, it has become increasingly clear that, in the words of Sanford,[6]

[2] Alvin W. Gouldner (ed.): *Studies in Leadership* (New York: Harper & Brothers, 1950), pp. 31–35, especially p. 34.
[3] See Ralph M. Stogdill, "Personal Factors Associated with Leadership: A Survey of the Literature," *Journal of Psychology*, vol. 25, p. 63, January, 1948.
[4] For example, see Fillmore H. Sanford, *Authoritarianism and Leadership* (Philadelphia: Institute for Research in Human Relations, 1950), chap. 1.
[5] See Stogdill, *op. cit.;* Gouldner, *op. cit.* (Introduction); William D. Jenkins, "A Review of Leadership Studies with Particular Reference to Military Problems," *Psychological Bulletin*, vol. 44, pp. 54–79, January, 1947; Fillmore H. Sanford, "Research in Military Leadership," in his *Current Trends: Psychology in the World Emergency* (Pittsburgh: University of Pittsburgh Press, 1952), pp. 45–59.
[6] Sanford, "Research in Military Leadership," p. 60.

It now looks as if any comprehensive theory of leadership will have to find a way of dealing, in terms of one consistent set of rubrics, with the three delineable facets of the leadership phenomenon:

1. the leader and his psychological attributes
2. the follower with his problems, attitudes and needs, and
3. the group situation in which followers and leaders relate with one another.

To concentrate on any one of these facets of the problem represents oversimplification of an intricate phenomenon.

Consequently, the frame of reference which we present is an attempt to take into account these three facets.

## A BASIC DEFINITION OF LEADERSHIP

We define leadership as *interpersonal influence, exercised in situation and directed, through the communication process, toward the attainment of a specified goal or goals.*[7] Leadership always involves attempts on the part of a *leader* (influencer) to affect (influence) the behavior of a *follower* (influencee) or followers in *situation*.

This definition has the virtue of generality. It does not limit the leadership concept to formally appointed functionaries or to individuals whose influence potential rests upon the voluntary consent of others. Rather, it is applicable to *all* interpersonal relationships in which influence attempts are involved. Relationships as apparently diverse as the superior-subordinate, the staff-line, the consultant-client, the salesman-customer, the teacher-student, the counselor-counselee, the husband-wife, or the parent-child are all seen as involving leadership. Thus, our proposed frame of reference, based on the definition and given continuing substance through a flow of relevant research findings from many disciplines, can be useful in understanding a wide range of social phenomena.

[7] Essentially, our definition subsumes definitions 1B, 1C, and 1E in the Ohio State "Paradigm for the Study of Leadership," all of which have to do with influence. The Ohio State definitions follow.

"1B. (The leader is the) individual who exercises positive influence acts upon others.

"1C. (The leader is the) individual who exercises more, or more important, positive influence acts than any other member in the group.

"1E. (The leader is the) individual who exercises most influence in goal-setting and goal-achievement."

See Richard T. Morris and Melvin Seeman, "The Problem of Leadership: An Interdisciplinary Approach," *American Journal of Sociology*, vol. 56, no. 2, p. 151, September, 1950. Reasons for our use of *situation* rather than *a situation* are presented on page 26.

One way of characterizing our definition of leadership is to say that it treats leadership as a *process* or *function* rather than as an exclusive attribute of a *prescribed role*. The subordinate often influences the superior; the customer, the salesman; and the group member, the chairman. In any given relationship, the roles of the influencer and the influencee often shift from one person to the other. Conceptually, the influence process or function is present even though the specific individuals taking the roles of influencer and influencee may vary. Thus, the leader role is one which is rarely taken continuously by one individual, even under specific conditions with the same persons. Instead, it is one that is taken at one time or another by each individual.

One criticism of our definition is that it unrealistically focuses on what appears to be a two-person relationship to the exclusion of group phenomena. For a number of reasons, we find this criticism unconvincing. First, the influencee at any given time may be more than one individual; an entire group may be considered to be the "follower." Second, since the leader role is not restricted to a formally prescribed person, the notion of shared leadership is consistent with our view. Finally, the presence of other persons—with their values, beliefs, and customary modes of behavior—in the context of any given (and often momentary) interpersonal relationship represents a complex of variables which we take into account as a part of the situation. Our focus is on a relationship which is often transitory and always affected by situational contexts.

## THE COMPONENTS OF LEADERSHIP

Having made these general observations about the definition, we will now discuss in greater detail some considerations that arise in connection with its major components.

### Interpersonal Influence

The essence of leadership is interpersonal influence, involving the influencer in an attempt to affect the behavior of the influencee through communication. We use the word *attempt* advisedly, in order to draw a distinction between influence efforts and influence effects.

To many, an act of leadership has occurred only if specified goals have been achieved. Under this interpretation, whether or not an individual may be called a leader in a given influence instance depends upon whether or not he is successful. If he is not, no leadership has occurred. Were we to accept this notion of leadership, we would be faced with the necessity of finding a satisfactory term for labeling unsuccessful influence efforts. It is our preference to let leadership refer

to influence attempts and to treat the assessment of leadership effectiveness as a separate matter. Thus a person who attempts to influence
others but is unsuccessful is still a leader in our view, although a
highly ineffective one.

It is useful to draw a distinction between power and leadership.
Power is potential for influence. However, even though an individual
may possess considerable power in relationship to another, he may for
a number of reasons (his personal values, apparent lack of necessity to
do so, misjudgment) not use all of the power available to him. A leadership act reflects that portion of the power available to an individual
which he chooses to employ at the time.[8]

It should be noted, in contrast to the above view, that the concept
*power* frequently connotes a potential for coercion, based, for example,
upon physical force, informal social pressure, law, and authority. In
actuality, a given leader typically has available not only these external
sources providing him with power, but also power derived from such
inner resources as understanding and flexibility.

## Exercised in Situation

The concept *situation* is to be found in much of the recent writing on
leadership. An analysis of this literature indicates that the term has
been variously used to denote an activity or a particular set of activities
engaged in by a group; group characteristics, including interpersonal
relationships; group goals or needs; and the cultural context.[9]

It seems appropriate to us to define *situation* as including only those
aspects of the objective context which, at any given moment, have an
attitudinal or behavioral impact (whether consciously or unconsciously)
on the individuals in the influence relationship, and to recognize that
the situation of the leader and that of the follower may differ from
each other in many respects. Both the phenomenological field and unconscious modes of response to external stimuli are relevant here.
Stimuli having independent empirical reality, but having no impact on
one or the other of the individuals, cannot be viewed as components of
their respective situations. It is thus important to know, though not al-

[8] For a relevant discussion of power, see D. Cartwright, *Toward a Social Psychology of Groups: The Concept of Power,* presidential address delivered before the
Society for the Psychological Study of Social Issues, Cleveland, Ohio, Sept. 5, 1953,
p. 19. Mimeographed.

[9] For varying views of "situation," see Daniel Bell, " 'Screening' Leaders in a
Democracy," *Commentary,* vol. 5, no. 4, pp. 368–375, April, 1948; Gouldner, *op.
cit.;* J. K. Hemphill, *Situational Factors in Leadership,* The Ohio State University
Studies, Bureau of Educational Research Monograph no. 32 (Columbus: The Ohio
State University, 1949); Jenkins, *op. cit.;* Paul Pigors, *Leadership or Domination*
(Boston: Houghton Mifflin Company, 1935); Sanford, *Authoritarianism and Leader-
ship;* Melvin Seeman, "Role Conflict and Ambivalence in Leadership," *American
Sociological Review,* vol. 18, pp. 373–380, August, 1953; Stogdill, *op. cit.*

ways easy operationally to ascertain, which stimuli external to the leader and to the follower affect each as they interact in the influence relationship.

The objective context of any influence relationship might include any or all of the following:

1. Physical phenomena (noise, light, table and chair arrangement, etc.)
2. Other individuals, including the members of the specific group of which the leader and follower are a part
3. The organization
4. The broader culture, including social norms, role prescriptions, stereotypes, etc.
5. Goals, including personal goals, group goals, and organizational goals

In reality, goals are an essential part of the concepts of group, organization, and culture. However, because of their special importance to the study of leadership, we here treat them separately.

An individual may influence the behavior of others by manipulating elements of their environment (situation). Thus, placing physical facilities in close proximity so that people can work near each other rather than in isolation may promote higher levels of productivity and/or job satisfaction. Since our definition limits leadership to interpersonal influence exercised through the communication process, we would not associate manipulation of situational components with leadership except in a special case—that in which such manipulation is intended by the leader as a communication symbol per se, carrying with it such implications as "this is a good place to work," "they always have our interests at heart," and the like.

## The Communication Process

Our definition of leadership concerns only that interpersonal influence which is exercised through the communication process. We thus exclude, for example, the direct physical manipulation of another person, since such coercion, in its pure form, does not utilize symbolic means. On the other hand, we include threats and other coercive devices which can be imparted only by means of communication.

There are many problems involved in differentiating conceptually between the communication[10] and the leadership processes. We view

---

[10] For two excellent discussions of the communication process, see Franklin Fearing, "Toward a Psychological Theory of Human Communication," *Journal of Personality*, vol. 22, pp. 71–88, September, 1953; Wendell Johnson, "The Fateful Process of Mr. A. Talking to Mr. B.," *Harvard Business Review*, vol. 31, pp. 49–56, January-February, 1953.

communication as the sole process through which a leader, as leader, can function. The objective of a communicator, as communicator, is to transmit a message from himself to a communicatee which the latter will interpret as the former desires. The communicator's goal is to convey meanings, or ideas, without distortion.

The leader is interested in more than simply conveying ideas for their own sake. With rare exceptions, the leader's final objective is not solely to bring about attitude change. Rather, the leader makes use of communication as the medium through which he tries to affect the follower's attitudes so that the follower will be ready to move or will actually move in the direction of the specified goal. Of course, there is often a time lag between a change in the follower's attitude and the actual or potential goal movement.

An individual may communicate effectively without being an effective leader. He may desire, for example, that another individual leave the room, and he tells him so. The other individual may say, "I understand you want me to leave the room," and yet remain seated. The leader has been understood, the meaning he has transmitted presumably has been received without distortion, and effective communication has taken place. However, the leader has not succeeded in changing the follower's attitudes in such a way that this follower has been motivated to behave in accordance with the specified goal (overt behavior involving leaving the room). Thus, the leadership attempt has been ineffective.

As our later discussion will suggest, a leader, in order to be effective, needs to select those communication behaviors from his repertory which are likely to "strike the right chord" in the follower's personality make-up, resulting in changed attitudes and behavior in line with the desired goal.

### Directed toward the Attainment of a Specified Goal or Goals

All leadership acts are goal-oriented. The leader uses his influence to achieve some desired (although often unconscious) goal or goals. These goals toward which individuals exert their influence fall into four categories, whose differences have considerable relevance for leadership theory. The following classification should not suggest that any given influence effort is necessarily aimed exclusively at one single goal. Often a complex of goals is involved, as when a leader brings about the attainment of organizational goals and at the same time satisfies some of his own needs.

1. *Organizational Goals.* In formal organizations, managers (as leaders) are those who are held responsible by their superiors for influencing others (subordinates) toward the attainment of organizational

goals.[11] These goals are the rationally contrived purposes of the organizational entity. Since these goals often have little or no direct motivational import to the followers, the manager's task of leadership often requires him to use other inducements which do have relevance to the need systems of the followers.

2. *Group Goals.* In small, informal, face-to-face groups the relevant goals are those which evolve through the interaction of the members of the group. They reflect (although not necessarily unanimously) "what the group wants to do." In such a situation, the leader is anyone who uses his influence to facilitate the group's attainment of its own goals. The achievement of a position of effective influence in such groups depends upon an individual's sensitivity to the group's objectives and upon his skill in bringing about their realization.

3. *Personal Goals of the Follower.* In such activities as teaching, training, counseling, therapy, and consulting, the leader often uses his influence to assist the follower in attaining his own (the follower's) personal goals.[12] For example, through the establishment of an atmosphere of warmth, security, and acceptance and through the use of facilitative methods, the leader aids another person to reach ends he has not been able to reach by himself.

4. *Personal Goals of the Leader.* Leaders also use their influence primarily to meet their own needs. At times such personal motives are at the level of consciousness and can be made explicit, but often they lie at the unconscious level where they are hidden from the leader. A teacher may think that he lectures to a class because "this is the best way to teach," without realizing that in so doing he feels more secure because the students never have a chance to "show him up." Likewise, a supervisor may harshly discipline a subordinate because "it is important to keep people in line," although a deep-felt need to express hostility receives some satisfaction through his behavior.

The issue of conscious and unconscious intent poses some knotty problems for both leadership theory and research. Should we be concerned only with objectives that can be made explicit by the leader, or should we admit unconscious motives? If we attempt the latter, by what operational methods do we define the hidden purposes? Unconscious purposes frequently do motivate the leader even though, with the exception of projective techniques, we have few methods available for operationalizing such hidden motives.

---

[11] See Chap. 15.

[12] See, for example, Carl R. Rogers, *Client-centered Therapy* (Boston: Houghton Mifflin Company, 1951); and Thomas Gordon, *Group-centered Leadership* (Boston: Houghton Mifflin Company, 1955). No selflessness on the part of the leader is implied. His need satisfaction comes through remuneration for his services and/or gratification from serving others.

LEADERSHIP EFFECTIVENESS

Our definition of leadership focuses on influence efforts rather than upon influence effects. However, once leadership has been exercised, it becomes appropriate to raise questions about the effectiveness of such leadership.

The effectiveness of any influence attempt must always be assessed with reference to the leader's intended goal or goals. This again points up the crucial nature of the conscious-unconscious intent issue discussed above. No leadership act is inherently effective or ineffective; it might be either, depending upon the goals with reference to which it is assessed. Further, regardless of the leader's intended purpose, a given act of a leader might be seen as effective when viewed by his superior in terms of organizational goals, and at the same time be seen as ineffective when viewed by his subordinates in terms of informal-group goals.

Many operational problems are involved in assessing leadership effectiveness. The very multiplicity of coexisting goals encountered in most real-life situations makes clear-cut measurement difficult. Further, the usual goal clusters contain elements that have differential weight in the attainment of still "higher" goals in a hierarchy. An industrial organization, for example, may have many goals: high employee morale, labor peace, high productivity, contribution to community welfare, etc. These several goals may all contribute to a more inclusive goal, as culturally or organizationally espoused: increased profits. High productivity and labor peace may be viewed as "more important" subgoals for the attainment of profits than employee morale or community welfare. Or, indeed, the opposite may be the case.

Specific leadership acts may also assist the attainment of certain goals while retarding the attainment of others. Finally, all leadership acts are in fact intertwined with numerous nonleadership acts (involving perhaps such factors as accounting procedures, production control, and technological progress), all of which may contribute to organizational success. Therefore, one often encounters real difficulty in the assessment of leadership effectiveness per se.

Our concept of leadership effectiveness is nonmoral in that it implies nothing about the goodness or badness of the goals of influence, nor, for that matter, about the influence methods used to achieve these goals. The ethical evaluation involves factors different from those involved in effectiveness evaluation. For example, a gangster's effort—involving lies and coercion—to lead a teen-ager into a life of crime may prove to be a highly effective, although repugnant, leadership act.

Perhaps the most challenging question relating to leadership effectiveness is the one which focuses upon the variables most closely associated with such effectiveness. What can be said about the leadership process which may help us better to understand that which makes for leadership effectiveness?

Consistent with our definition of leadership, we feel that effectiveness in leadership is a function of the dynamic interrelationship of the personality characteristics of the leader, the personality characteristics of the follower, and the characteristics of the situation within the field of each individual.

We have already pointed out that the *situation* has a differential impact on both the leader and the follower as they interact. The *personality of the follower* (as it manifests itself in a given situation) becomes a key variable with which the leader must deal. The needs, attitudes, values, and feelings of the follower determine the kinds of stimuli produced by the leader to which the follower will respond. The *personality of the leader* (also manifesting itself in a situation) influences his range of perception of follower and situation, his judgment of what is relevant among these perceptions, and thence his sensitivity to the personality of the follower and to the situation. The leader's personality also has impact on his behavioral repertory (action flexibility) and on his skill in selecting appropriate communication behaviors.

In the sections which follow, we will examine in greater detail the interrelationship of these elements of the leadership process for the purpose of better answering the question: "What makes for leadership effectiveness?"

## THE DYNAMICS OF LEADERSHIP

The principal dramatis personae of the leadership process, it has been noted, are the leader, who wishes to initiate interpersonal influence through communication, and the follower, whose attitudes and behavior are to be influenced toward the attainment of a specified goal. The complete leadership process, shown in Figure 2-1, is subsequently discussed, and a brief summary is presented in the next few paragraphs.

In order to understand the leadership process, it becomes necessary to consider the *personality of the leader* in relation to the *personality of the follower* and to the *characteristics of situation* as appropriate starting points. We shall speak primarily of the leader, recognizing the shifting nature of the leadership role.

The leader's *needs* and his related *perceptual capacities* (potential for responding to a variety of external stimuli) affect his response to the many stimuli which confront him. These stimuli are received from the follower and from the situation (physical phenomena, other individuals, groups, organizations, the broader cultural context, and goals). His

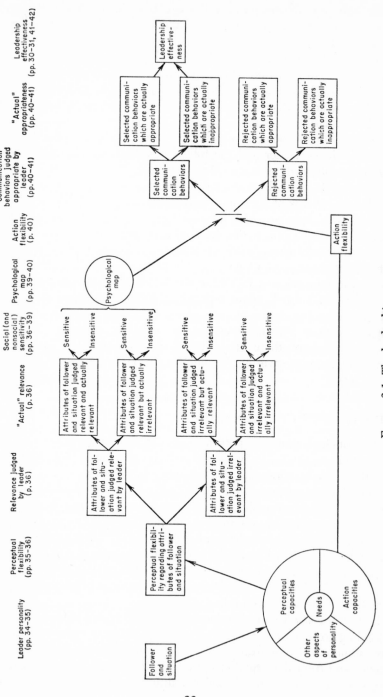

FIGURE 2-1. The leadership process.

needs and perceptual capacities in relation to the quality and quantity of available stimuli determine his *perceptual flexibility* (the range of perceptions), which provides him with a basis for influence attempts.

A mere range of perceptions is not all that is necessary. The leader must distinguish those perceptions which he believes to be *relevant* to the attainment of the specified goal from those which he considers *irrelevant*. He may, of course, err in making this distinction, as defined by some external, "actual" criterion of relevance.

Further, not all perceptions may be accurate or "correct" in the sense that they agree with a stipulated criterion of "reality." When such agreement does exist in the leader's perception, one may speak of *sensitivity* (here used as a synonym for accuracy of perception)—*social sensitivity* in re follower, other individuals, groups, organizations, and cultures; *nonsocial sensitivity* in re physical phenomena. When no such agreement exists, one may speak of *insensitivity*.

The perceptual preliminaries that we have described thus far do not necessarily proceed in a logical, conscious, or rational sequence. Nor are perceptions equivalent in the sense that one accurate perception is as good as another, if "goodness" is measured by the extent to which a perception may lay the groundwork for subsequent effective influence attempts.

Once the leader has taken a look at the "buzzing, blooming confusion" which initially may confront him, and once he has sized up the factors which he deems to be goal-relevant, he has available his *psychological map*, which may provide a basis for action. It is at this point that his personality once more comes into play. His *needs* and his related *action capacities* (capacities for behavior) determine his *action flexibility* (range of available communication behaviors).

Communication serves as the process through which influence is exerted.[13] It aims to bring about coincidence between the meaning of information transmitted by the communicator (the information input) and the meaning of information received by the communicatee (the information output). The leader uses communication stimuli as tools by which he may affect the perceptual-cognitive structure of the follower. He attempts to select from his alternative communication behaviors those which he believes will appropriately affect the follower

---

[13] Consistent with our definition of leadership, influence in the present context is limited to influence exercised through communication. Like a manager, the more comprehensive concept, the individual here viewed as leader may also engage in actions, limited by his action capacities, which may constitute influence efforts of a noncommunication type: physical manipulations, redesign of plant layout, development of new office systems, etc. Ultimately, managerial effectiveness is a resultant of the effectiveness of leadership actions and of other goal-oriented actions which are of a nonleadership character and which do not involve communication.

so that the desired attitude changes may in turn result in the desired behavioral changes. Certain *communication behaviors* are therefore *judged appropriate* by the leader and *selected,* and others are *judged inappropriate* and *rejected.* The selected behaviors may, may not, or may partially attain the specified goal. The degree to which the leader-selected behaviors are actually appropriate, i.e., succeed in moving the follower toward attainment of the specified goal, is a measure of *leadership effectiveness.*

The series of events just described may be viewed as a particular sequence in an ongoing cycle. Events at any one step of the series may be "fed back" to the leader, resulting in modifications in his behavior and altering other parts of the sequence. The leadership process, although analyzable in terms of discrete events, is not a mechanical addition of such events, but a process involving the principle of feedback.

We now discuss in more detail each of these aspects of the leadership process.

## Leader Personality: Needs, Perceptual Capacities, Action Capacities

Past attempts to define leadership in terms of leader characteristics were generally fruitless; however, the topic of leader personality can not be ignored. Two attributes of the leader's needs are of particular importance. First, his needs significantly determine what he can see or do in the course of his influence attempts. His fear of rejection may cause him to suspect rejection when in fact he has acceptance. This fear may also prevent him, for example, from disciplining a subordinate when this is in order. Second, his needs, by affecting other aspects of his personality structure, have impact on how he is perceived by the follower. In many subtle respects these reciprocal perceptions condition the follower's responses to influence attempts.

Perceptual capacities and action capacities, as aspects of leader personality, are conceptually analogous to personality variables such as intelligence and emotional stability. They are viewed as "internal" bases for subsequent behavior, characterized by some stability and generality.

Conceivably, tests developed for the measurement of perceptual and action capacities should provide some probability indication of actual behavior that may be expected under real-life conditions. Under the stresses of reality, effective intelligence may not correspond to intelligence as abstractly predicted by a test. There may be a gap between the leader's perceptual and action capacities and his actual perceptions and behaviors under a given set of real circumstances. The development of adequate operational tests for perceptual and action capacities is a task which needs to be undertaken.

Perceptual capacity is viewed as a potential for responding to a variety of external stimuli. Action capacity is viewed analogously as a potential for responding behaviorally under a variety of conditions. However, not all action capacities can be utilized in the exertion of interpersonal influence. In our view, communication capacities are the exclusive focus. They are seen as potential skills for the production of symbolic stimuli, including verbal behavior, facial expression, gestures, etc.

## Perceptual Flexibility

*Perceptual flexibility* is defined as the range of stimuli of which the leader is cognitively aware in an actual leadership situation. It constitutes the *realized potential* for perception (as defined by perceptual capacities); it is what a person in fact is aware of under a given set of circumstances. The perceptual flexibility concept implies nothing about the correctness or incorrectness of the leader's perceptions. It deals solely with the range of perceptions which he may have available as he seeks understanding of follower and situation.

The range of perceptions which the leader may have is typically a function of the quantity of stimuli available. However, the relationship certainly need not involve a one-to-one correspondence between stimuli and the perceptual response to them. In some cases, a particular leader may have available only a few stimuli about the follower, but by means of his personality resources (e.g., experience in presumably similar situations), he may give evidence of considerable perceptual flexibility. One might distinguish pathological conditions of perceptual flexibility involving cases in which a person gives evidence of a wide range of perceptions, none of which have a consensually significant relation to reality. Certain types of schizophrenics might exemplify this extreme, which undoubtedly has many milder counterparts found in ordinary leadership situations.

In line with the distinction between follower and situation, as entities toward which the leader must respond, we may distinguish *perceptual flexibility regarding attributes of the follower* and *perceptual flexibility regarding attributes of the situation.*

How does perceptual flexibility fit within the frame of the leadership process? The leadership process begins with a wide variety of stimuli impinging upon the leader. Some of these stimuli may have no discernible perceptual impact upon him. Others are received by him at various points of the conscious-unconscious continuum. The distinction between stimuli having no impact and those having impact at an unconscious level is, of course, difficult to make in operational terms, although it seems to be conceptually necessary.

The perceptual processes concerning follower and situation are complex. For instance, with respect to perceptual flexibility regarding follower attributes, the leader may seek to share cognitively the follower's total phenomenological field—to see things from the latter's point of view. He may seek to assess the impact upon the follower of stimuli derived from the various elements of the situation. And the leader may wish to predict how he himself is perceived by the follower. Thus, as the leader responds to the follower, the former deals not simply with the latter's relatively stable personality characteristics, but rather with the interaction of these characteristics with stimuli emitted by the leader and by elements in the follower's situation.

### Relevance Judged by Leader and "Actual" Relevance

The processes of "structuring the situation" and of "understanding the follower" imply that the leader has some purpose in mind. Ordinarily, he does not make a total or comprehensive attempt to make explicit *all* possible perceptions, i.e., to make fully explicit all available perceptual flexibility. Perhaps intuitively and automatically he does not even bother with certain perceptions because they do not seem to hold much promise as guidelines to the actions which he contemplates.

Whether it occurs as a result of careful thinking, or whether it happens spontaneously, the leader makes some kind of judgment, sorting perceptions which he judges to be relevant from those he believes irrelevant. The notion of relevancy clearly stipulates a link in the mind of the leader between the stimulus perceived and the goal desired. No perception is intrinsically relevant, nor is a given perception equally relevant for the attainment of all goals. Further, it is possible to distinguish those perceptions which the leader holds relevant or irrelevant from those which are "actually" relevant or irrelevant as judged by an external third party.

The ability of the leader to ignore or quickly discard actually irrelevant stimuli may be a correlate of leadership effectiveness. In routine leadership acts the leader habitually judges certain stimuli as relevant and disregards others. The skill to see relevancy in stimuli which on prior occasions were irrelevant may facilitate the leader's task under changing conditions of follower and situation. A leader's skill in judging relevancy probably varies for different judgmental tasks, e.g., judging relevance re follower attributes and re attributes of situation.

### Social (and Nonsocial) Sensitivity

*General Considerations.* As soon as the explicit or implicit judgment of relevancy has been made by the leader, the question arises as to whether the perceptions that are believed to be relevant are also correct. All perceptions which agree with a specified criterion of "reality" are classified as correct, or sensitive; those which do not, as insensitive.

The leader obviously seeks to maximize those perceptions which are both relevant and correct. Sensitivity to irrelevant items, insensitivity to relevant items, and, of course, insensitive perceptions of irrelevant items contribute nothing toward providing the leader with an accurate psychological map with which to guide his choice of influence efforts.

It is probably most important for the leader to be socially sensitive to relevant dynamics of the follower whom he seeks to influence, including the follower's needs, feelings, and motivations, although sensitivity alone is not necessarily a guarantee of leadership effectiveness. His sensitivity to other entities is also important. One may consider, for example, social sensitivity to particular groups, organizations, and cultures, as well as sensitivity to the various goals, as discussed in the section "Directed toward the Attainment of a Specified Goal or Goals." In addition, nonsocial sensitivity to physical aspects frequently is necessary for the leader.

*The Types of Social Sensitivity.* Much current research has been concerned with a detailed explication of the social sensitivity concept. While detailed treatment can not be given here, a few observations may suggest the scope and complexity of this concept (see Chapter 4).[14]

Social sensitivity (here used synonymously with social perceptual accuracy) covers a wide variety of processes. We have already indicated that the content of the perceptions may vary, and that in this sense one may distinguish numerous social sensitivities, ranging from interpersonal sensitivity toward individuals to sensitivity for broad cultures. A sensitivity toward self ("insight" into self) also has been investigated as a possible correlate of sensitivity toward others and as a correlate of interpersonal effectiveness.

Social sensitivity as a generic concept has been studied under a number of headings, some of which have referred to fully synonymous phenomena while others have involved somewhat diverse nuances of meaning. These headings include "empathy," "diagnostic skill," "understanding others," etc. The leader's attempt to "understand" the follower involves a type of social sensitivity, containing a number of components which cause it to be a complex concept.

There are many aspects of the follower's personality and of the follower's situation which the leader may need to understand. Empirical

---

[14] As noted earlier, current usage sometimes views social sensitivity as a particular skill and social perceptual accuracy as a resultant, including all accurate social perceptions regardless of their origin. For relevant theory, see, for instance, F. Massarik, "Socio-perceptual Accuracy in Two Contrasting Group Settings," unpublished doctoral dissertation, University of California, Los Angeles, 1957; N. L. Gage and L. J. Cronbach, "Conceptual and Methodological Problems in Interpersonal Perception," *Psychological Review*, vol. 62, pp. 411–422, November, 1955; American Psychological Association, "The Status of Empathy as a Hypothetical Construct in Psychology Today," a symposium at the Convention of the American Psychological Association, Cleveland, Ohio, 1953.

research has reflected this by requiring various subjects in the many experiments to make predictions regarding such diverse attributes of other persons as their self descriptions, their perceptions of others, their attitudes toward social issues, and their views of group characteristics. A leader may have a particular reason for maximizing his social sensitivity to the follower's self concept and motivations, to the follower's perception of other individuals (including the follower's perception of the leader), to the follower's perception of social relationships, and to the follower's perception of his own situation.

Frequently, a leader is concerned with predicting the social characteristics of groups or organizations.[15] His concern may be with eventual influence efforts directed toward these groups and organizations, or else he may wish to be socially sensitive to them as an aid to assessing their impact on individual followers. The functions of political leaders and the activities of anthropologists may require comprehension of broad cultural entities as well as the understanding of groups and organizations. It is probable that the psychological attributes facilitating social sensitivity to groups, organizations, and cultural entities differ from those necessary for interpersonal sensitivity.

*Levels of Difficulty in Social Sensitivity.* For each of the various types of social sensitivity, one may distinguish various "levels of depth" which affect the accuracy with which particular predictions can be made. On the whole, certain judgments are easier to make than others. The average leader, for example, may have a better "batting average" in making a rough estimate of a follower's age, or an approximate judgment on the size of a group of subordinates, than he has with respect to a follower's unconscious dynamics, or a group's state of interpersonal tension. The determination of level of difficulty undoubtedly is statistical and empirical in nature. In individual instances, it certainly is a function of (1) the psychological attributes of the leader which determine his skills in social perception (his perceptual capacities) and (2) the quantity and quality of stimuli, or cues, available to the leader.

With respect to prediction, it may be that superficial behavioral characteristics, public attitudes, feelings and attitudes privately held, and unconscious processes represent increasing degrees of depth and therefore of difficulty. Further, the task of prediction becomes increasingly difficult as the leader is required to make many and complex extrapolations from available stimuli to the desired judgment.

*The Effect of Assumed Similarity.* If a leader closely resembles a follower in relevant attributes, the dynamic of "assuming similarity" (sometimes called "naive projection") may prove to be a boon in

[15] For example, see K. Chowdry and T. M. Newcomb, "The Relative Abilities of Leaders and Non-leaders to Estimate Opinions of Their Own Groups," *Journal of Abnormal and Social Psychology,* vol. 47, pp. 51–57, January, 1952.

achieving social sensitivity.[16] If the leader does not resemble the follower, this same dynamic may prove to be a burden. If the leader assumes that the follower whom he is trying to understand is essentially a "carbon copy" of himself, the leader may be tempted to attribute all his own feelings and attitudes to this follower. Of course, if this "carbon-copy hypothesis" is borne out, such naive projection may make for a condition resembling successful understanding of the follower. Unfortunately from the standpoint of ease of social perception, the hypothesis is seldom fully correct, and often it is quite false. As a result, more than a naive faith in the similarity between himself and others is necessary if the leader wishes to increase his social sensitivity toward the follower, particularly in view of the usual changing and heterogeneous nature of interpersonal relationships.

While it is self-evident that followers are not exact replicas of the leader, nor replicas of each other, there are, of course, important similarities among people. Certain groups may preselect their members by numerous explicit and implicit criteria. The formation of subcultures creates conformity to various norms, and thence varying degrees of homogeneity. This suggests that the leader needs to be skillful in assessing similarities between himself and a follower, and among followers, in addition to being skillful in the assessment of individual differences.

*Other Variables Affecting Social Sensitivity.* Many unanswered questions remain regarding the processes themselves that help or hinder social sensitivity, and regarding the attributes and dynamics of the socially sensitive individual. Factors associated with the total organization of personality, the leader's ego involvement with the follower, and his affective relationships with the follower are among other variables that may affect these processes.

### *The Psychological Map*

The point now has been reached in our analysis of the leadership process at which we may assume that the leader has completed the cognitive perceptual structuring of follower and situation. The end result of this structuring process may be called the *psychological map.*[17] The leader assesses follower and situation as a preliminary to action. In doing so, he forms a mental image of the barriers and facilitating circumstances that bear on the desired goals of his leadership behavior. He further visualizes (sometimes explicitly and sometimes implicitly) those action pathways open to him which he believes will lead to leadership effectiveness. However, the psychological map that is available to

[16] See A. H. Hastorf and I. E. Bender, "A Caution Respecting the Measurement of Empathic Ability," *Journal of Abnormal and Social Psychology,* vol. 47, pp. 574–576, April, 1952.

[17] For an explication of an earlier, related concept, see E. C. Tolman, "Cognitive Maps in Rats and Men," *Psychological Review,* vol. 55, pp. 189–208, July, 1948.

him undoubtedly is a combination of accurate and inaccurate notions regarding relevant and irrelevant items. Whatever the nature of its components, this map provides the basis for the course which the leader follows in his attempt to exert influence through communication.

## Action Flexibility

At any given time, a person has available a repertory of behaviors which, singly or in combination, he may bring into play in his attempt to deal with his environment. The scope of this repertory, the range of behaviors of which the person sees himself as capable, is defined as his *action flexibility*. It constitutes the realized potential for action (as defined by action capacities) under a given set of circumstances. By the present definition of leadership, we are concerned solely with the communication aspect of action flexibility. Therefore, our emphasis is upon the leader's repertory in communication, his skills in transmitting meanings through the use of symbols. The context in which communication occurs involves more than "sending" *verbal messages;* it includes also the leader's behaviors which affect the follower's receptivity or blocking of the meanings which the leader transmits. For example, *listening* by the leader to the follower may facilitate the extent to which the latter subsequently lends himself to "hearing" or "understanding" the former's messages. Nonverbal communication is clearly relevant.[18]

Action flexibility is related to the leader's personality resources, particularly to his action capacities. Rigidities in the personality structure, lack of experience and training, and similar impediments may restrict the leader's capacities for behavior, and thence his flexibility in communicating.

Construction of operational tests for action flexibility (as, indeed, also for perceptual flexibility) involves a host of difficulties. Mere verbal, conscious answers by the leader to the inquiry "What can you do or say to influence the follower?" are likely to give an incomplete picture, to say the least. More searching approaches may be required involving exploration of the leader's underlying dynamics and inferred capacities for richness of behavior.

## Selection of Communication Behaviors Judged Appropriate by Leader and "Actual" Appropriateness

The very fact that the leader seeks to exert influence on a follower presupposes that some communication behaviors, though available, are quickly and automatically judged by the leader to be inappropriate to the task at hand. Some may be so clearly inappropriate that they are not

[18] See J. Ruesch and W. Kees, *Nonverbal Communication* (Berkeley and Los Angeles: University of California Press, 1956).

even perceived. Other communication behaviors, however, may not lend themselves to such quick and automatic choice or to such facile disregard. In this latter case, the leader may need to make explicit his attempt to study his psychological map of follower and situation which is the end result of the perceptual preliminaries (perceptual flexibility, judging relevance, sensitivity). Having evaluated the information provided by this map, the leader may seek to select communication behaviors which he judges to be most appropriate in the light of available information. He seeks to exert influence toward the attainment of a specified goal by the follower, and one may assume that an adequate psychological map, which contains actually relevant and accurate information, will facilitate his endeavors.

Misinformation in varying quantities and of varying significance is also likely to be contained in the map. The leader may discard (judge as inappropriate) some communication behaviors which actually are appropriate, as externally defined, while in turn he may select some actually inappropriate ones which should have been discarded. The ultimate test, of course, is the degree to which the behaviors chosen prove actually appropriate, i.e., effective, as measured by the criterion of goal attainment. For instance, if a sharp command motivates an employee quickly to perform a defined task, this command-giving behavior is judged as appropriate. On the other hand, if the same behavior causes an altercation and subsequent hostility, the behavior, at least in the short run, is inappropriate.

### Some Final Thoughts about Leadership Effectiveness

Finally, we wish to highlight some key variables, suggested by the preceding analysis, that may underlie leadership effectiveness.

Though still vaguely defined, some attributes of leader personality appear to be associated with leadership effectiveness. These attributes are the leader's needs, perceptual capacities, and action capacities. They are of importance only (1) to the extent to which they affect what the leader sees in his attempt to understand follower and situation and (2) to the extent to which they have impact on his communication skills. Needs that reduce the leader's perceptual capacities, that impair his perceptual flexibility, that mar his judgments of relevance, and that reduce his sensitivities are likely to be negatively associated with leadership effectiveness. Similarly, needs that adversely affect his action capacities, action flexibility, and selection of appropriate communication behaviors are also likely to hinder leadership effectiveness.

The follower is an important variable in the psychological map that forms the basis for the leader's communication behaviors. It is of crucial importance that the leader be sensitive to relevant attributes of the follower. The relevant attributes seldom will be of a superficial kind, such as the follower's appearance or his publicly held attitudes. Rather, the leader needs to assess correctly attributes such as the follower's feelings, his motives, and his perceptions of others. As there are many types of social sensitivity, leaders whose followers are entire groups may need to develop different perceptual skills than leaders dealing principally with individuals.

While social sensitivity (and perhaps accuracy in the psychological map generally) is assumed to facilitate leadership effectiveness, such facilitation does not necessarily proceed in a linear fashion. "Too much" social sensitivity, for example, may pose a threat to the follower, thus potentially impeding leadership effectiveness, unless the leader finds appropriate behavioral skills by means of which to offset the possible threat. Constant preoccupation with "understanding the follower" conceivably may prove paralyzing and may interfere with the development of an adequate psychological map.

An adequate psychological map is economical in the sense that it is confined to the minimum pattern of relevant and correct perceptions. This implies that the effective leader is skillful in ignoring or discarding irrelevant and incorrect perceptions.

The leader needs to utilize his psychological map as a guideline for the exertion of interpersonal influence. In this connection, the effective leader clearly recognizes, or has fully internalized at an unconscious level, the goals toward which he wishes to direct influence.

Further, the effective leader has available an adequate repertory of communication behaviors (as part of his action flexibility). In the utilization of this repertory, the effective leader will be skillful in selecting those behaviors which are most appropriate for the accomplishment of the goals which he seeks. There may be some cases in which unconscious internalization of goals by the leader is so complete that he selects appropriate behaviors even though the psychological map is not accurate or clear.

Some researchable questions generated by this frame of reference can focus on the leader as a component within an interacting system whose ends are the attainment of specified goals. It then becomes possible to examine the variance of goal attainment (leadership effectiveness) accounted for by the various parts of the system as spelled out in this frame of reference. Also, our experience has indicated that the frame of reference can provide a basis for and facilitate a systematic analysis of the sensitivity training process. This is a process through which members of unstructured training groups can gain increased social sensitivity and action flexibility.[19]

[19] See Part 2.

CHAPTER 3

## Cultural Perspectives
## on Understanding People*

"People should understand people."
This admonition is implicit in much human relations training and in current approaches to supervision. Indeed, in various guises, the value of interpersonal understanding permeates the fabric of contemporary culture. If science, too, is to be regarded as an activity with roots in the spirit of the culture, then the recent upsurge of scientific interest in accuracy of social perception, social sensitivity, or empathy,[1] may be one more manifestation of a pervasive, contemporary social value.

Considering this popular and academic concern with understanding people, one may wonder how it all came to be. While one cannot neatly trace the tributaries to the trend, some rough assessments of the present role of interpersonal understanding and an exploration of its antecedents may be in order.

In essence, understanding others today is viewed as a prerequisite par excellence—as a most expedient steppingstone to success. This position may be paraphrased somewhat as follows: "If I learn to figure what makes people tick, I'll know better what they need and want. This will help me to do the *right* thing. I'll get along better. I'll be able to make other people do what I want them to do. So, naturally, this ought to make it possible for me to become successful in whatever I'm doing."

---

* This chapter is based on a portion of an unpublished doctoral dissertation, "Socio-perceptual Accuracy in Two Contrasting Group Settings," by Fred Massarik, University of California, Los Angeles, June, 1957, and part of it has been especially prepared for this book.
[1] The terms noted are treated as synonymous in the present discourse, although technical distinctions are sometimes made among them in the professional literature.

Fundamentally, this is a pragmatic position. Understanding others is not an abstract ethical value; rather, it is to be desired because of its actual or imputed uses. However, it may serve various ends. For instance, to some, understanding people may be but one more method to increase industrial productivity. To others, it may be an aid in manipulation of subordinates for the sake of satisfying personal power needs. To still others it may be a means for avoiding threatening interpersonal situations.

But in a different context, some may find that accurate social perception is a powerful tool in the tasks of helping and teaching. The instructor who correctly assesses the strengths and limitations of his student, the supervisor who grasps the potentialities of the employee, the social worker who truly empathizes with his client's problems, the psychotherapist who senses the labyrinthine paths of the neurotic personality—all these use their knowledge of people as a basis for helping others to learn and to grow. In this fashion, the sensitivity trainer, too, seeks to aid the trainee in the quest for heightened personal awareness and social effectiveness.

## CLUES IN PERSONALITY

The concern for understanding others may well be linked with personality configurations flourishing in the cultural milieu of the mid-twentieth century. Such configurations are described, for example, by David Riesman and collaborators in discussing the concept of the "other-directed personality." To quote from their work, *The Lonely Crowd*:[2]

What is common to all the other-directed people is that their contemporaries are the source of direction for the individual—either those known to him, or those with whom he is indirectly acquainted. . . . The goals toward which the other-directed person strives shift with [guidance from others]; it is only the process of striving itself and the process of paying close attention to the signals from others that remain unaltered throughout life.

Here is the credo that people behave as they do because they search for an understanding of the wishes of others; it is this understanding that becomes the guide for action.

A variation of this theme appeared in somewhat earlier writing by Erich Fromm,[3] in his analysis of the "marketing orientation." Fromm

    [2] David Riesman, with Nathan Glazer and Reuel Denney, *The Lonely Crowd: A Study of the Changing American Character* (New Haven: Yale University Press, 1950; abridged edition, New York: Doubleday Anchor Books, 1953), p. 37 of the abridged edition.
    [3] Erich Fromm, *Man for Himself: An Inquiry in the Psychology of Ethics* (New York: Rinehart & Company, Inc., 1947), pp. 67–72.

suggests that there exists a relationship between understanding others and success: such understanding provides a basis for being better able to "sell oneself," the latter being a necessary precondition for eventual rewards and attainments. Thus, Fromm describes a culturally rooted personality dynamic that places a high premium on the capacity for correctly assessing the reactions and attributes of people. Indeed, nothing less than "success"—financial, personal, or otherwise—ultimately depends on interpersonal insight.

But it is not merely *overt* success that is at stake. Fromm further proposes that the integration of personality itself, the individual's self-identity, hinges upon an assessment of the reactions of others. Says Fromm:[4] "Since man cannot live doubting his identity, he must, in the marketing orientation, find the conviction in identity not in reference to himself and his powers, but in the opinion of others about him."

Louis Kronenberger, a literary critic with a bent for insightful cultural analysis, adds a further dimension. Kronenberger notes that the peculiar shifting character of conformity in American life necessitates a constant concern with the effective diagnosis of the reactions of others. "The correct thing to do," the way to be "hep" to the latest subtle variations of approved behavior requires constant vigilance. The cultural key slogan, Kronenberger proposes,[5] " . . . is no longer 'playing the game'; it is 'knowing the score.' And of course the catch is that the score is always changing and that in the end one must spend not less time but more in order to be *au courant*."

And how does one learn how to stay *au courant?* At the level of the individual, it may involve the continuing "tuning in" on what one's contemporaries think and say. It may take the form of training programs concerned with the gathering of insight into the behavior of other people. Or, perhaps more naively, it may be the ingesting of the welter of books whose jacket blurbs promise that after three easy chapters the reader will know nearly all that matters about the complexities of human nature.

In the economic sphere, it becomes necessary to understand the wants of the consumer. No longer is it sufficient to produce cars that are merely mechanically adequate; it becomes crucial to respond to a vast congeries of detailed consumer wants and to seek out wants that can be stimulated and promoted. The personality of the consumer emerges as a kind of road map to guide production. If certain tail lights, seat covers, or exterior trims appeal to the woman car buyer, by all means let us know this and meet the demand. If a sufficient public col-

---

[4] *Ibid,* p. 73.
[5] Louis Kronenberger, *Company Manners: A Cultural Inquiry into American Life* (Indianapolis and New York: The Bobbs-Merrill Company, Inc., 1954), p. 184.

lective "personality" is ready to respond favorably to safety belts, to very small automobiles, or to very large, this is certainly worth knowing—here is a potential need that can be nurtured and brought to "maturity." And this "maturity" does indeed spell "success"—for producer and consumer alike. Thus market research, and the vogue of motivation research, are the systematic manifestations of this concern with consumer personality. But the concern permeates the institutional structure; it does not stop at the boundary of the advertising agency or at the door of the corporation's sales department.

## CLUES IN THE ROLE OF THE HERO

To probe the sweeping cultural influence of the value of understanding others, one may consider the character of the "heroes" of the culture —the figures that often epitomize the currents of social process. If the individualistic robber baron, the great statesman, or the empire-building magnate of the turn of the century was the American cultural hero of yesteryear, today's pattern is quite different. No longer is vast power, be it social or economic, seen as a universal end in itself. A Henry Ford I, for example, or a William Randolph Hearst or a John D. Rockefeller was viewed rather differently than today's giants of industry or journalism. Once, an individual's power was admired for its intrinsic significance and for the self-sufficiency that it implied. The stress was on the apparently single-handed creation of economic holdings and on the hero's accumulation of material wealth. The actual and perceived gap between rich and poor was abysmal. But, as the mass-production function came to be established, and as the distribution function came to assume increasing significance, "personality," as used in the popular sense, rather than power as such, rose to be a key cultural value.

Thus, today the heroes are no longer towering monolithic figures, viewed with substantially equal respect by a vast majority of members of society. Rather, there appear *many* heroes, each in a sense catering to members of a distinguishable subculture. Heroes, too, must compete in the market place. Diversification, and the forming of allegiances around specific and even subtly different orientations, becomes the pattern. e. e. cummings may be a hero to some, but to others the hero is Dylan Thomas, or Jack Kerouac, or a contemporary version of the Renaissance man. Davy Crockett may have had his momentary virtue, but he is soon replaced by Tom Corbett, Space Cadet, who in turn must give way to a brand new luminary.

The very system of American government supports this instability, this constant need for reorientation. Officials are elected periodically and for limited periods of time. To be elected the candidates must "sell" something like an over-all positive impression, a "good personality." Campaign issues and promises have their impact, but perhaps more crucial still is a trust in the candidate's "integrity," a belief in his "sincerity," etc.—all responses to "personality." And as a new election takes place, the new hero stands ready to supersede the old.

Thus, it seems that today's hero, perhaps in highest measure, must be an expert in the assessment of reactions of people. His position is intimately affected by his skill in this ubiquitous realm of social perception. Indeed, he must be able to *act* on the basis of what he sees, but accurate perception surely raises the odds in his favor.

CLUES IN RESPONSE TO THE HERO

For the grass-roots member of society, acceptance may well depend upon his willingness to agree with his peers in the choice of the "right" hero. The public of Elvis Presley may not overlap heavily with the public of Van Cliburn. Nor is a Van Cliburn admirer likely to find a particularly cordial reception among Presley fans by strongly derogating the virtues of the rock-and-roll idol, while lauding the merits of the pianist. The price of deviation is the unleashing of hurtful devices of social control—ridicule, ostracism, rejection—devices serving the ends of conformity to the ever-shifting but powerful norms.

To be successful (as, for example, the hero is successful), one must "sell one's personality" to a public. In order to do this effectively, understanding the demands of this public is crucial. In turn, the members of this public must acquire the skill for understanding how their peers feel—for instance, how they regard the cultural heroes—for social acceptance may hinge upon sharing the appropriate perceptions with one's fellows.

There is little novelty in the observation that a considerable technology has grown around the need for the hero to understand his public and the desire of the public to understand the hero. The field of public opinion research, similar to market and motivation research in the economic sphere, perhaps is the illustration par excellence of the feed-back mechanism, by which the hero seeks cues about the characteristics of his public, and particularly about how this public responds to his own "personality." If not the exclusive technique, at least it has become the epitome of "making rational" the pervasive desire to tune in on the reactions of others to the self. Social sensitivity in its day-by-day import shares the same logical root, although in ordinary face-to-face interactions the cues that form its basis are more dynamic, unsystematic, and personalized.

The public's desire to learn about the intimate details of the hero's life sometimes has been deemed a special form of voyeurism. This it may be, but perhaps it is more than this. As the inside reporter, the gossip columnist, the intimate interviewer lays bare to public gaze the real or imagined idiosyncrasies of the hero, he produces a significant reservoir of cues. These cues become the public's raw material around which it may structure its "understanding" of the hero. The social distance between hero and public shrinks; he becomes comprehensible as a human being: he emerges like you and me, only more so. This is the stuff of which loyalties are made. Thus, for a while anyway, the hero *holds his public by being (presumably) understood.* In turn, the public maintains its character as an in-group, its integrity, by being "in the know" about the hero, *by (presumably) understanding him.*

It must be clear, of course, that the accuracy—the actuality—of the understanding in question is a presumption, nothing more. The public's image of the hero, perhaps even more than the hero's image of the public, may not—and, indeed, typically does not—conform to empirical fact. The public relations counsellor often is regarded as the "bogey man," who obfuscates facts about people for the sake of greater palatability and acceptability. But, in addition, the hero consciously selects the cues that he reveals in his outward appearances. And the public selectively perceives and wishfully distorts these cues in forming an impression of the hero. Thus a superficial image results—a pasteboard façade, quite incongruent with the deeply rooted, real, and fundamental aspects of the human personality.

OPPOSING VALUES

Perhaps, understanding others—however important—is not a universal cultural value. Lack of responsibility, lack of concern with realistic assessment of the contemporary social scene represent values of an opposing sort. Such contravening values are implicitly attributed to key decision-making mechanisms in American society by C. Wright Mills, in *The Power Elite.*[6] Mills hypothesizes that, in spite of traditional lip service to democracy, military, corporate, and political elites in America can find refuge in superficiality, functioning without making serious efforts to appraise, morally and conscientiously, the responses and needs of those ultimately affected by the elites' decisions.

However, one may assume that the elites—as leaders generally, including dictators—at least require broad guides that set limits within which the resultant decisions must be tolerable to the affected publics. These guides do demand some level of understanding of others. And

[6] C. Wright Mills, *The Power Elite* (New York: Oxford University Press, 1956), especially pp. 343–361.

intramurally, among the elite members themselves, understanding at the interpersonal level clearly affects the decision-making process.

Whether or not one agrees with Mills' hypothesis, his argument lends credence to the concept that understanding others is *differentially* important at various levels of the status and power hierarchy. Perhaps he who lacks power seeks security through a better understanding of those who have a surfeit of power.

The quest for security, it has been pointed out, typically involves pressure toward conformity. The 1950s have brought forth a welter of writings concerning the role of conformity in American society. The popular version of these perhaps is best exemplified by William H. Whyte, Jr.'s *The Organization Man,*[7] and by the attack on the forces tending the individual away from the classic pioneer spirit into the seductive arms of "groupy" adjustment. Here, in somewhat different guise, is Riesman's other-directed personality and Fromm's marketing orientation, both noted previously.

There can be little doubt that pressures toward conformity often are responded to by the individual's attempt to understand fully what others expect of him. This is an approach to mimicry. Ultimately, one will need to consider whether this kind of "blending in" with the characteristics of the enveloping social group must be inherently destructive of individual uniqueness.

## SEARCH FOR SELF-UNDERSTANDING

It may be that the crucially important concept of *self-understanding* may prove to be a significant antidote to the more deleterious consequences of conformity. Now, simultaneously with the unabated concern with understanding others, we witness the emergence of a revitalized search for true knowledge of the self. This search grows from within a broader stream of inward-oriented philosophic strivings, which Erich Kahler, in *The Tower and the Abyss,*[8] refers to as "the new sensibility." He traces this new sensibility to three sources: (1) a deep uneasiness —a generalized feeling of malaise, a revolt against mechanical rationalism, and a search for inner meaning, stemming from the historical events of the eighteenth century; (2) a steady growth of man's self-reflection and psychological introspection, the roots of which reach back into the Renaissance, but whose contemporary products have taken the form of systematic psychoanalysis; and (3) the autonomous

[7] William H. Whyte, Jr., *The Organization Man* (New York: Simon and Schuster, Inc., 1958).
[8] Erich Kahler, *The Tower and the Abyss: An Inquiry into the Transformation of the Individual* (New York: Braziller, 1957), especially pp. 138–144.

proliferation of artistic techniques and of modes of expression fostering enhanced susceptibility to impression. It is the second of these three sources, the new rise of self-reflection and psychological introspection, that relates most clearly to self-understanding (and thence to understanding of others) as significant concepts for current inquiry.

Kahler quotes Sénancour's *Oberman*, in what may be the essence of the renewed quest for self-understanding: " . . . *de nous maintenir semblables à nous-mêmes*" (to maintain ourselves identical with ourselves). Here is the battle cry of man's need to become truly attuned to what he really is. Here is the core of the search behind the façades of the social front, the quest for the attainment of internal congruence with its resultant reduction of anxiety and its potential freeing of creative capacity.

A central thesis underlying the scientific concern with social sensitivity in present sociopsychological theory—including leadership theory and sensitivity training—revolves about the relationship between social sensitivity and self-understanding. It is suggested that heightened levels of self-insight, stemming from fully understood emotional processes, will facilitate understanding of others. Indeed, the elimination of internal blockages and aberrations and the attainment of internal congruence may be crucial in making possible more accurate perception of people. While the "marketing orientation" and the "other-directed personality" seek personal integration by meticulous attention to responses of the other persons in the environment, it is more probable that personal integration is the keystone upon which accurate social perception rests.

Efforts directed toward understanding others are not inherently wedded to the cause of changing one's behavior to conform slavishly to the wishes of others. Rather, an accurate perception of the responses of others can aid positive, healthful personality growth. For instance, the reactions of others toward aspects of one's personality that lie below the level of one's awareness can open avenues of self-understanding that otherwise might have remained forever closed. Certainly, as a predictor or precondition of effective behavior and personality functioning, accuracy of social perception is a construct of theoretical and practical importance.

## SOCIAL SENSITIVITY AS A CONCEPT

Much more remains to be learned about social sensitivity as a scientific concept. Its prehistory no doubt reaches into ancient times. In more modern days, at the German University of Halle about the turn of this century, it was the philosopher-psychologist Husserl who popularized and elaborated the concept of phenomenology, with its stress on the "mental facts" of immediate experience. Within the same current of development came the work of Lipps. It was he who introduced the notion of *Einfühlung*, the concept of "empathy," to the armamentarium of psychology.[9] But consistent empirical research in the area of social perception did not get under way until after World War II, particularly with the work of Dymond and Cottrell.[10] In the years that followed, many writers of sociological and psychological persuasion joined the fray,[11] and lively controversy occasionally rose to testify to the vitality of the quest.

Still a somewhat neglected area of research is the explicit, theoretical specification of exactly what aspects of the other's personality and behavior are the target of understanding. Obviously, it is one thing to interpret accurately a brief spoken sentence about the weather and quite another to grasp fully the subtlety of a lover's smile for his beloved.

In its relatively brief modern history the construct of social sensitivity has run the gamut from mystic intuitionism to extreme operationalism, from analytic sterility to clinical richness. Its status as a scientific tool remains in flux, but the direction of its development is encouraging. On the broader cultural scene, it would appear that the reaching out for an understanding of other people, as represented by social sensitivity, inherently is neither to be commended nor condemned. It is a part of our time. It may focus on neurotic needs of seeking salvation and identity by response to the wishes of others. Or it may be a source of deeper learning by illuminating through the eyes of those we love and trust the cavernous complexities of innermost personality. Alike for researcher, man of affairs, and social philosopher, understanding others continues to pose an intellectually and emotionally provocative challenge.

[9] For treatment of the early modern history of the empathy concept and its antecedents, particularly phenomenology, see Edwin G. Boring, *A History of Experimental Psychology* (2d ed.; New York: Appleton-Century-Crofts, Inc., 1950), especially pp. 367–369, p. 455.

[10] Rosalind F. Dymond, "A Preliminary Investigation of the Relationship of Insight and Empathy," *Journal of Consulting Psychology*, vol. 12, pp. 228–233, 1948; Rosalind F. Dymond, "A Scale for the Measurement of Empathic Ability," *Journal of Consulting Psychology*, vol. 13, pp. 127–133, 1949; L. S. Cottrell, Jr., and Rosalind F. Dymond, "The Empathic Responses: A Neglected Field for Research," *Psychiatry*, vol. 12, pp. 355–359, 1949.

[11] For a representative view of recent approaches to the study of social perception, see Renato Tagiuri and Luigi Petrullo, *Person Perception and Interpersonal Behavior* (Stanford, Calif.: Stanford University Press, 1958); Urie Bronfenbrenner, John Harding, and Mary Gallwey, "The Measurement of Skill in Social Perception," in D. C. McClelland et al., *Talent and Society* (Princeton, N.J.: D. Van Nostrand Company, Inc., 1958), pp. 29–111; Ronald Taft, "The Ability to Judge People," *Psychological Bulletin*, vol. 52, pp. 1–21, 1955; David A. Stewart, *Preface to Empathy* (New York: Philosophical Library, Inc., 1956).

CHAPTER 4

## *The Process of Understanding People*\*

Mike Corey walked into his office, fifteen minutes behind schedule. Through the glass partition Mike caught a glimpse of his boss. Arthur Blick looked up briefly as Mike slid into his chair. A number of signs obscured the full view: "Tomorrow We Finally Have to Get Organized," "THIMK," "Wait Till Next Time—You Have Done Enough Damage for Now." Mike tried to look inconspicuous, though his mind was working rapidly. He was late for the third straight day. Oh, there were good reasons all right . . . one day his wife needed to be driven downtown and *she* wasn't ready—one day he had a terrible headache . . . and then . . . today. . . . His thoughts shifted abruptly—it really didn't matter as long as Blick was in a good mood. Mike had some very definite ideas about what kind of guy his boss was. Usually he wasn't a bad sort; businesslike, but human too. If you had a big problem, he probably would listen. Still he was so darn changeable, and you had to hit him "just right" if you wanted to get along. This morning Blick seemed preoccupied . . . he looked up as if he hardly saw you, yet the way he spun back to his desk telegraphed "bad news."

This was Jean Krugmeier's first day on her job. She liked being an employment interviewer. People were interesting, and it would be a novel experience to sit behind a desk all day. The initial two interviews proceeded uneventfully. The third applicant wanted to be foreman of the shipping gang. He was a young, burly 250-pounder who said that he used to work in the steel mills near Gary. He spoke loudly, with much self-assurance. "Some sort of a bully—a leering Casanova of the hot-rod set," Jean thought. Jean always did dislike guys like this, especially this sort of massive redhead. Just like her kid brother used to be—"a real pest!" The more he bragged about his qualifica-

---

\* This chapter is a slightly modified version of "Empathy Revisited: The Process of Understanding People," by Fred Massarik and Irving R. Weschler, reproduced from the *California Management Review*, vol. 1, no. 2, pp. 36–46, Winter, 1959. (Copyright by The Regents of the University of California.)

52

tions, the more Jean became annoyed. It wouldn't do to let her feelings show; interviewers are supposed to be friendly and objective. She smiled sweetly, even if she did have a mild suspicion that her antagonism might be coming through. "I am sorry, we cannot use you just now," she said. "You don't seem to have the kind of experience we are looking for. But we'll be sure to keep your application in the active file and call you as soon as something comes up. Thank you for thinking of applying with us."

## LOOKING AT SOCIAL PERCEPTION

These anecdotes serve to illustrate the all-pervasive role that *social perception* plays in our lives. Forming impressions of people is a part of our daily experience, yet we rarely single out the process for explicit consideration.[1]

Mike Corey was very much concerned with making the correct perceptual assessment of Arthur Blick's mood for the morning. Of course, he reacted without specifically worrying about his *empathy*.[2] He did what came naturally. The physical obstructions in the glass partition between the two offices were not the only barriers between these men. Mike's own views, attitudes, and feelings contributed to the difficulties, and so in turn did Blick's behavior, which provided Mike with only a limited amount of information (or *cues*). The fact that the entire relationship was set in the context of a given office situation both aided and impeded the extent to which Mike Corey could accurately perceive the relevant aspects of his boss's personality.

Jean Krugmeier probably does not think of herself as a prejudiced person. She may associate the term "prejudice" primarily with racial intolerance. She argues vociferously that people must have an "open mind." Still, like all of us, she too has "blind spots" and uses "short-cut thinking," which gives her a distorted picture of reality. Her feelings about burly redheaded men are very much like any other prejudice. They are supported by a *stereotype* that, in essence, says: "All of them

[1] The area covered by this chapter has been subject to systematic study only in very recent years. It is still much in flux, and few findings of certainty are as yet available. As we seek to lay out some of the problems, methods, and results with which this research is concerned, we are much aware of the tentative nature of our comments. The technically inclined reader is urged to examine R. Tagiui and L. Petrullo, *Person Perception and Interpersonal Behavior* (Stanford, Calif.: Stanford University Press, 1958); F. Heider, *Psychology of Interpersonal Relations* (New York: John Wiley and Sons, Inc., 1958); and Urie Bronfenbrenner, John Harding, and Mary Gallwey, "The Measurement of Skill in Social Perception," in D. C. McClelland et al., *Talent and Society* (Princeton, N.J.: D. Van Nostrand Company, Inc., 1958).

[2] In this context, we shall treat as synonymous the concepts *empathy, understanding of people, social sensitivity,* and *accuracy in social perception.* For a fuller treatment of the concept *social sensitivity,* see Chaps. 2 and 3.

are alike!" Thus, Jean's feelings may be irrational, her mind may be closed, and her social perception less than accurate because she subconsciously prevents relevant information about people "of this sort" from reaching her.

## The Illusion of Objectivity

Most of us pride ourselves on our ability to look at people in a dispassionate, objective manner. Yet the psychological realities are that every time we have a personal contact we *do* form favorable or unfavorable impressions that influence our social behavior. We all have some positive or negative feeling in our interpersonal experiences. We *do* like or dislike in varying degrees, even if we are not always willing or able to recognize our true feelings.

*Social perception* is the means by which people form impressions of and, hopefully, understand one another. *Empathy, or social sensitivity,* is the extent to which they succeed in developing *accurate impressions,* or actual understanding, of others.[3] Social perception is not always rational or conscious; thus it follows that empathy is not necessarily the result of conscious, rational effort. For some, it may just seem to "happen," while others may develop it only after much training and living experience.

Three basic aspects of social perception must be considered: (1) *the perceiver,* the person who is "looking" and attempting to understand; (2) *the perceived,* the person who is being "looked at" or understood; and (3) *the situation,* the total setting of social and nonsocial forces within which the act of social perception is lodged.[4] We have already encountered "perceivers" Mike Corey and Jean Krugmeier, and their respective "perceived" counterparts, Arthur Blick and the burly job applicant.

## The Perceivers and the Perceived

Perceivers and perceived need not be single individuals. Entire *social groupings* may do the "looking" or may be "looked at." We can, for example, conceive of the social perceptions existing between two rival departments of a corporation, with each department viewing the other with possible hostility or competitive jealousy. Similarly, we may dis-

[3] Many complexities are involved in the actual measurement of social sensitivity. The definition given here is a kind of practical short cut, useful for most everyday applications. For a consideration of the conceptual issues, see, for example, N. L. Gage and L. J. Cronbach, "Conceptual and Methodological Problems in Interpersonal Perception," *Psychological Review,* vol. 62, pp. 411–422, 1955, and L. J. Cronbach, "Processes Affecting Scores on 'Understanding of Others' and 'Assumed Similarity,'" *Psychological Bulletin,* vol. 52, pp. 177–193, 1955.

[4] This approach is in harmony with the frame of reference presented in Chap. 2.

tinguish social perceptions among small work groups, among large companies, and even among nations. Indeed, any group of people, as well as any given person, can be a principal participant in the process of social perception.

The perceiver and perceived are not billiard balls on a flat table top. Their interactions do not usually produce obvious one-to-one cause-and-effect relations, for the perceived and the perceiver both possess personalities of great complexity. Social perception develops in the give and take among these *personalities in action.*

What is termed "personality" for the individual may be viewed as a unique pattern of "group characteristics" for the social grouping, be it work group, department, company, or nation. This pattern does not result from a simple addition of the personalities of individual members, although these individual personalities do have an impact. Rather, the social grouping's "personality" results from its formal and informal traditions, and from its accepted ways of "doing things." For example, some groups operate rigidly "according to the book"; others are more flexible and freewheeling. Some groups are highly integrated, with close and supportive relationships existing among their members; others are torn by antagonistic cliques and by intense rivalries. Some groups set high and constant standards for the admission of new members; others are more open and lax in their membership requirements.[5]

*Patterns of Perceiving*

The process of social perception can be graphically portrayed in a variety of ways. If I stands for "individual," and G for any "grouping" of individuals (and if the arrow stands for the act of perceiving), we may consider such relations as the following:

| Type | Perceiver to perceived |
|------|------------------------|
| A | I → I (individual to individual) |
| B | I → G (individual to grouping) |
| C | G → I (grouping to individual) |
| D | G → G (grouping to grouping) |

Our anecdotes were of the type A variety—one individual perceiving another individual. Jean Krugmeier's perception of the job applicant, however, was influenced by a type B perception, her view of all burly, red-headed men—a view that she as an individual held for a broader

[5] Among the better-known approaches to the analysis of the personality of a group is that of J. K. Hemphill and C. M. Westie, "The Measurement of Group Dimensions," *Journal of Psychology,* vol. 29, pp. 325–342, 1950. Many sociologists have also made important contributions in this area; see, for example, Robert Dubin, *The World of Work* (Englewood Cliffs, N.J.: Prentice-Hall, Inc., 1958), and Melville Dalton, *Men Who Manage* (New York: John Wiley and Sons, Inc., 1959).

(though tenuous) grouping of persons. Under conditions beyond those already described, Mike Corey may be perceived in a type C relationship by his fellow employees, a grouping that may view him with envy and anger because of his ability to get away with lateness without apparent untoward consequences.

Type D perceptions become important particularly in attempts to analyze the nature of complex organizations, such as large sections or departments, entire firms, or other entities composed of various subgroups. For instance, a management consultant may wish to assess the way in which the sales department views the credit department, how the research section sees the development branch, or how employee relations relate to wage and salary administration, and vice versa.

The four types of perceptual processes noted so far are relatively straightforward: type A, interindividual perception; type B, an individual's perception of a grouping; type C, a grouping's perception of an individual; and type D, intergroup perception. Yet in each type countless obvious as well as hidden distortions can and do occur which prevent the perceiver from obtaining a faithful image. These breakdowns in communications, which we shall need to explore further at a later point, magnify their effects when we consider what might be termed *higher-order perception.*

As Mike Corey, for instance, forms his perceptions of Arthur Blick, he also considers the way in which Blick reciprocates. In other words, Corey is very much concerned to know how Blick feels about him. Corey makes assumptions about Blick's view of him which may or may not be correct. He may "think" that Blick hardly saw him, when—if he were to probe Blick's true reaction—he might learn that Blick saw Corey very well indeed and was actively annoyed with his repeated tardiness. The extent to which one accurately recognizes someone else's reactions to oneself defines a special kind of social sensitivity—the ability to assess correctly what another person "thinks" about you.

Above, we are dealing with a "perception of a perception." We may conceive of a theoretically infinite series of social perceptions that begin as follows:

1. First-order perceptions: how the perceiver views the perceived (as illustrated by types A, B, C, and D)
2. Second-order perceptions: how the perceiver "thinks" the perceived views the perceiver
3. Third-order perceptions: how the perceiver "thinks" the perceived views "the perceiver's perception of the perceived," etc.

By the time we reach third-order perceptions, the pattern has become immensely problematical. Any further higher order adds to the complexity. Fortunately, most of our actual perceptions governing inter-actions with others probably do not get more involved than those defined by the first or second order.

## One Empathy—or Many?

There may be several different "empathies." Some perceivers seem more skillful in seeing beneath the surface and in ferreting out correct perceptions from vast networks of superficial psychological defenses. Others are more capable in hurdling the abyss that separates their actual observations of cues from the more remote recesses of behavior that they are seeking to understand. Some excel in painstakingly accumu-lating fragments of perceptual evidence and piecing them together. Others have a unique capacity for the elegant sweep that pulls together quickly and accurately a broad complexity of social phenomena.

Understanding social groupings rather than individuals involves unique problems and may require different skills of perception from those needed in understanding individuals. The talent for sizing up group opinion is probably different from the "diagnostic skills" needed for understanding a specific employee. An executive of a large corpora-tion, for instance, may excel in accurately assessing opinions and atti-tudes of union and work force, but he may need to sharpen his skills in empathizing with his fellow corporate officers.

The probable existence of several "empathies" is not surprising if we consider the diversity of the factors at work. We have available a tremendous variety of cues that we may draw on in order to understand how another person thinks or feels, and these make differential demands upon our skills to draw inferences that will yield accurate perceptions.

## Cues: Raw Material of Perceiving

Cues are often direct: through words, gestures, facial expressions, and specific behavioral acts, they are transmitted to the perceiver (inter-preter) directly by the perceived (communicator), sometimes con-sciously, sometimes subconsciously. At other times, the perceiver gets his insights secondhand—as by gossip, through reference letters, or by comments overheard during a coffee break.

Some cues are more obvious in their apparent meaning. A broad smile and a friendly hello usually reflect a clear expression of personal warmth, while a vague wave of the hand is considerably more ambiguous and thus more difficult to interpret.

Some cues are more clear-cut than others. A girl's approximate age—the beautician's art notwithstanding—is likely to be more easily assess-able than the meaning of a Mona Lisa–like smile; and despite best in-tentions, it may be virtually impossible to base an analysis of a person's basic psychological motivations on a casual martini-clouded social contact.

The psychological leap to be made from the cues available to what we seek to understand presents another consideration. As Mike Corey viewed his boss Blick, he had knowledge of Blick's customary office behavior. He had observed Blick before and under roughly similar conditions. Past cues provided a good base of present generalizations. On the other hand, Mike Corey might want to join Blick's country-club set. There he would need some insights into the latter's social behavior. Corey would search for some implicit theory, derived from Blick's on-the-job reactions, the only reactions with which he is actually familiar. He would try to extrapolate from Blick's available pattern of cues into a relatively distant and different situation, and risk empathic failure in the process.

## The Perceiver's Background

The perceiver brings to the task of understanding others two sets of interrelated characteristics: (1) his general background, *demographic characteristics;* and (2) his unique self, *personality characteristics.*

Demographic characteristics are those broad sociological aspects of the individual which, for the most part, are easily definable, specific, and outside the more subtle ebb and flow of personality as such. Age, sex, nationality, religion, number of siblings, occupation, and economic level are illustrative.

When the psychologist Ronald Taft[6] reviewed studies on the relation of certain demographic attributes to social perceptual skill (especially empathy for individuals rather than for social groupings), he formed conclusions such as the following: (1) ability to judge emotional expression in others increases with age in children, but does not seem to increase further with age in adulthood; (2) sex differences in empathy are negligible, but there may be a very slight edge in favor of women.

Thus it seems that when dealing with adults, such as those encountered in business, age alone provides no free ticket to social perceptual wisdom. Although—hopefully—age may bring increases in some areas of technical knowledge, the process of getting older in and of itself does not lead to heightened empathy. Further, there does not seem to be much substance to the widely held assumption that women are "better judges" of people than men; the controversy on this point is not fully resolved.

More significant relationships emerge from an analysis of dynamic personality characteristics. Taft's attempt to find common threads in

[6] See R. Taft, "The Ability to Judge People," *Psychological Bulletin,* vol. 52, pp. 1–23, 1955.

the web of available research leads him to postulate rather substantial association between emotional adjustment and empathy. A person's emotional adjustment hinges primarily on how he sees himself and how he feels about himself—it is closely linked to his *self concept.*

One's self concept provides a kind of psychological "base of operations" that inevitably affects relations with family, friends, business associates, and strangers. Some aspects of the self concept are at the surface of personality; these are the *publicly held attitudes*—the things we don't mind telling other people about ourselves and our views of the world. And there are some feelings about the self of which we are aware, but which we do not want to share with others—these are the *privately held attitudes* to the self. And buried still deeper are the *subconscious and unconscious aspects*—feelings about "who" we are and "what" we are that somehow we cannot face up to, even to ourselves. The theories of psychoanalysis and depth psychology deal at length with these "disassociated" parts of the self, which as subtly disturbing, often powerful sources of internal turmoil may affect and hinder a person's effective functioning.

## BARRIERS AND AIDS TO EMPATHY

The individual who has resolved most of his internal conflicts appears in a better position to direct his energies to the understanding of others. He is likely not to meet "booby traps" of his own unconscious devising that prevent accurate perception. The *healthy personality* is based upon a fundamental self-acceptance at all levels—public to unconscious. It relies on an openness to experience, a willingness to respond realistically to relevant cues; it exhibits a lack of dogmatism and a capacity for responding to the world flexibly and dynamically. When we are under pressure, or in a state of anxiety, we are less likely to perceive accurately the motives and actions of those about us. It is only when we have reached a fair give-and-take balance between ourselves and the world that we are in a secure position to venture important human relations judgments.

In light of this, is it likely that in a nirvana of perfect psychological equilibrium all social perceptions would be accurate? On the basis of what we know, the answer is no. In order to understand others, there must be some driving force, some motivation, some problem. Such cause or problem implies the existence of some tensions within the perceiver. In a fully tensionless state—in a hypothetical state of perfect adjustment —there could be no reason to care about understanding anything or anybody. As a result there would be little meaningful social perception or social interaction. As too many cooks are said to spoil the broth, too many tranquilizers seem to spoil the wellsprings of human understanding. While excess tension reduces empathy, its complete absence induces a state of apathy.

## The Special Case of Self-insight

Empathy and self-insight tend to go hand in hand, although the evidence is by no means all in.[7] Fortunate, they say, is the individual who knows how much or how little he truly knows about himself—who is aware of his own capacities, limitations, motivations, and attitudes.

The sole tool that we bring to the task of understanding others is our own personality. The cues we receive from the outside must be processed through the perceptual equipment that is "us"—through lenses of our own background and expectations. If we are to be successful in assessing the meaning of cues that impinge on us, we must become aware of the distortions that may be introduced by our "built-in" perceptual equipment.

A realistic view of our perceptual limitations, and of the kinds of aberrations we tend to introduce in what we see and hear, should help us to make allowances in interpreting the world around us. If, for instance, we are aware that people who seem to be weak and submissive make us irrationally angry, we may be able to develop safeguards against our own unreasonable anger and ultimately gain a more realistic understanding of the motivations of the other person.

Self-insight does not come easy. Many factors mitigate against it. Central among these is our system of *psychological defenses*—the ways in which we systematically and unconsciously protect ourselves from facing what might be real or imagined threats to our personal security.

These protective distortions—which frequently concern our perceptions of others—help us make reality more palatable. There is no human being alive who is without some pattern of psychological defenses. Unfortunately, the cost of excessive utilization of defenses is the progressive removal from reality. Without some controlled and mild forms of self-delusion, adjustment of the ordinary everyday sort may be difficult. Yet the defenses that we bring into play as we seek to understand ourselves and others seduce us into various states of unreality; they make us see that which is *not* there, and hide that which might be apparent.

In our illustrations of Mike Corey and Jean Krugmeier, not much may have been at stake. However, similar processes, affected by the distortions of psychological defenses, influence decisions of major importance: for example, the selection and promotion of top management personnel,

[7] See, for example, J. S. Bruner and R. Tagiuri, "The Perception of People," in G. Lindzey (ed.), *Handbook of Social Psychology* (Reading, Mass.: Addison-Wesley Publishing Company, 1954), vol. 2, pp. 645–646.

the establishment of budgetary commitments, the theme of advertising campaigns, or the assessment of company performance.

## The Force of Attitude

One particularly pervasive pattern of personal defenses found in industry, which interferes with the process of understanding others, is characterized by a high degree of *authoritarianism,* with concurrent *rigidity in perception* and *intolerance for ambiguity.* The authoritarian person seems to need to view the world in clearly defined segments, some strictly black, others strictly white. He does not make much room for gradations—things are clearly good or abominably bad, people friendly or hostile, nations with us or against us. Thus, the authoritarian unconsciously fails to recognize subtle but significant interpersonal phenomena, because he is unable to evaluate shades of gray for what they are.[8] Extreme nonauthoritarian personalities—"nothing is definite, all is a matter of shading"—also encounter difficulties in understanding others since they too have a singularly single-minded view of what the world and its inhabitants are like.

The attitudes with which we approach the task of understanding others, then, do a great deal to determine just what we will be able to see. Attitudes basically serve as organizing forces that order in some preliminary manner the potential chaos and complexity confronting us. They give meaning to what we are prepared to see and hear. As such, they serve a necessary and useful function.

## "Playing the Odds"

The question of whether the holding of stereotypes is necessarily detrimental to accurate social perception deserves consideration. If we define a "stereotype" as an *inaccurate perception* of a given grouping, it follows logically that stereotypes are hindrances. But, more generally, we *do* need to be able to type people by means of broad and flexible generalizations. In that sense, a realistic view of a group of individuals (a kind of "accurate stereotype") may increase the odds for accuracy in our perception of others. Thus we may make assumptions about the characteristics of a specific company's board of directors, about the honor graduates of a college, or about women secretaries. We frame enlightened guesses concerning the manner in which a directive will be interpreted by first-line supervision, the way in which a sales campaign on bottled beer will be received by the housewives in suburbia, or how the new profit-sharing plan suggested by the union's bargaining committee will strike the company attorney. This kind of "typing," while

[8] See T. W. Adorno, E. Frenkel-Brunswik, D. J. Levinson, and R. N. Sanford, *The Authoritarian Personality* (New York: Harper & Brothers, 1950).

based upon prior perceptions of individuals and groups, necessarily is a kind of oversimplification; still its use in a consciously wary manner is a constant necessity if we are to relate to people.

Since understanding people involves relative probabilities of being right, caution is always in order. We must ever attempt to remain open to a constant flow of new information which may help us alter our perceptions in the light of changing circumstances. It is the danger of fossilization—the pitfall of "hardening" perceptions irrationally—that needs to be avoided.

## Link between Perceiver and Perceived

The personality of the perceived also determines the success of social perception. Ultimately it is the relationship that emerges between perceiver and perceived which becomes crucial. *Communication* linking the two—the sending and receiving of messages (involving feelings as well as content)—becomes raw material underlying the process of understanding others. Cues are messages from the perceived to the perceiver. In each instance, the perceiver "samples" certain small units of behavior that come from the perceived. While these samples in a statistical sense are neither random nor necessarily representative, they form the basis for generalizations that constitute predictions about the behavior of others. As communications develop, a person becomes both perceiver and perceived—sending and receiving cues of great variety and with high speed.

In the relationship between perceiver and perceived it becomes important for the perceiver to elicit cues from the perceived which will do the most to reveal, on a sample basis, the relevant aspects of the perceived's feelings, thoughts, and potential behavior. This ability to break through a person's outer veneer, to penetrate false fronts, has two facets: (1) the perceiver's *skill in facilitating the sending of cues* by the perceived, and (2) the perceiver's *skill in picking up and interpreting properly* the cues that have been sent.

Jean Krugmeier, for example, by eliciting fully the attitudes and aspirations of her job applicant might have succeeded in bringing to the surface relevant cues that might have made possible a more sensible evaluation of his potential. She might have reduced the applicant's defensiveness by proving herself receptive to his comments and accepting of him as a person, by listening for his feelings as well as meaning, and by communicating to him her understanding of his point of view.

As we engage in the process of understanding people, our hope for ever-increasing accuracy rests partially with our ability to get *feedback* on how others view the accuracy of our perceptions. We must remain in tune with the reactions of others—not in order to become blind automata, but rather to double check and review the validity of our own perceptions.

## The Danger of Expertise

Usually we receive feedback from members of our own *reference groups*—our families, friends, and business associates. These are the people whose opinions about us usually matter to us. Parents and close relatives especially, who have provided us with experiences which make us what we are, often continue to give us, as Robert Burns so aptly put it, "the giftie . . . to see oorsels as ithers see us."

At times, the validity of our insights and understanding of people is assessed by experts, by psychiatrists or psychologists who have been trained in personality diagnosis and behavior prediction. Unfortunately, research has shown that some of these experts, in spite of their intellectual grasp of interpersonal relations, are rather inept judges of people. This startling paradox has some rather persuasive explanations to account for it. First, intellect alone—though a slight help—does not guarantee empathy. More importantly, for some people too much knowledge is a dangerous thing! For them, there exists the danger of *overreaching*. They are confronted with the ever-present temptation to read into cues complex "deeper" meanings which in reality may not be there at all. This is the pitfall of imagining psychological ghosts behind each casual remark, simply because of some intellectual predisposition to make interpretations at more esoteric levels.

For experienced clinicians, the process of feedback here again proves to be a partial safeguard. If all too often our views of others, though psychologically "sophisticated," find no confirmation, either by the subject of our perception or through the perceptions of other observers, we may suspect that we are overreaching in our search for perceptual accuracy.

## The Role of Feelings

Regardless of the specific situation in which social perception takes place, some positive feelings of varying intensity will be exchanged between perceiver and perceived. These feelings condition the process of social perception. They set up *halos,* which reduce the accuracy of empathic judgments. If we believe that some persons "can do no wrong," if we are enamored of their righteousness and virtue, if we blindly approve of everything they do—we will be unable accurately to assess their less desirable characteristics or behaviors. The inverse is equally true: pervasive hostility and prejudice also obliterate any chance for a realistic appraisal of people's positive characteristics.

A more subtle manifestation of the impact of feelings on perceptual accuracy can be found in the process of *naive projection* (assuming similarity), the attributing by the perceiver of his own characteristics to the perceived. If few cues are available to the perceiver, if he is unable to utilize those that are available, or if his feelings toward the other person are in fact similar to those he has about himself, projection may become his significant *modus operandi*. The vacuum that might be filled by meaningful cues is taken up by assumptions implying that the perceived resembles the perceiver.

Assuming similarity to another person is intrinsically neither a barrier nor a block to accurate social perception. If the perceived really *is* much like the perceiver with respect to the characteristics involved in the judgment, assuming similarity is clearly warranted. Although some unique psychological perceptual skill may or may not have been at work, accurate social perception will result.

One can visualize an extreme situation in which the major prerequisite for social perceptual accuracy is the knack for picking out associates who resemble us with regard to relevant personality dimensions. If we succeed in this selection, be our choice conscious or unconscious, all we may need in order to understand them is to assume that they are, more or less, replicas of ourselves. Obviously, reality rarely permits this uncritical, though convenient, approach. More likely we may find that we assume similarity where none exists, thus hindering social sensitivity by the unwarranted assumption.

A blind assumption, on the other hand, that we do *not* resemble others (or a particular "other") can also lead to misperception. In most cases, the perceiver and the perceived do share in common some attitudes, feelings, and similar personality characteristics. The challenge confronting us is to recognize those elements that we have in common with other individuals, while at the same time noting the differences that make us unique. Likewise, when dealing with many people, we need to learn to discriminate the relevant differences among them, while remaining aware of the similarities which they, as a group, share. Thus, as a particular boss considers a group of subordinates, he must ask—and answer—these four questions:

1. In what respects is each of these persons like me?
2. In what respects does each of these persons differ from me?
3. In what ways do all these people resemble one another?
4. In what ways is each of these people unique from every other?

Clearly, this is a large order.

The *relative stress* with which people relate to one another also influences their ultimate empathy toward each other. As superiors, for instance, we may find it relatively easy to size up properly the feelings and attitudes of our subordinates; as subordinates our anxieties may becloud our perceptions of our superiors' intent and attitudes. The well-known phenomenon of "seeing red" when angered and the notion that "love is blind" represent classic illustrations of the befogging effect of strong emotions on social perception. Most accurate social perception, it seems, occurs under conditions which do not involve extremely charged feelings.

Because each individual approaches the task of social perception in his own particular situation, his personal receptivity will be influenced by the nature of this situation. An executive who operates in an environment of "yes men" may come to be attuned to hearing "yes," even if the real sound is more like "maybe." An amusing cartoon series of medical specialists on vacation shows a plastic surgeon fascinated by the Sphinx in Egypt, a urologist intrigued by the shapes of swimming pools, and a gynecologist marveling at the fertile life in the farm's pigsty.

The *broader culture*, too, provides certain expectations and highlights specific types of cues. The "man in the gray flannel suit," the "rate buster," the "organization man," the "huckster," the "tycoon"—all these are cultural types which are readily found on the American business scene, and whose existence is typically recognized by those of us who share a common cultural heritage.

## Pay-off for Empathy

Whatever its correlates and roots, empathy provides a road map, defining properly the social world confronting the perceiver. There is no guarantee, however, that even the most understanding perceiver will be able to behave appropriately, even if his road map is clear and accurate. He further requires an adequate repertory of behaviors—*behavioral flexibility*—to provoke the kinds of action that will most effectively attain the goals he seeks.

Social sensitivity and social effectiveness do not necessarily go hand in hand. In *The Outsider*, Colin Wilson[9] draws the portrait of the cultural hero who sees too much, whose perceptions penetrate all too well, but who tragically lacks the customary social skills for functioning within the reality that he perceives.

"Seeing too much," if not buttressed by an appropriate range of available behaviors, can indeed prove a threat to self and others and thereby reduce ultimate social effectiveness. In terms of actual pay-off, having too much empathy may well be as detrimental as having too little. Seeing the surrounding social world in proper perspective is useful only if knowledge can be successfully implemented by action.

[9] Colin Wilson, *The Outsider* (Boston: Houghton Mifflin Company, 1956).

As an executive faces the myriad decisions he needs to make, it becomes quite clear that he must master two tasks: he must learn to see accurately the human, as well as the inanimate, factors of the total scene; and he must acquire the skills of action which, while based upon accurate perception, tap wellsprings of behavior that ultimately lead to the successful attainment of personal and organizational goals.

Social effectiveness can be developed. For some people, dealing with feelings is as easy as recognizing and manipulating facts. For others, the world of emotions is mysterious indeed. The improvement of social skills is a many-sided challenge. Neither intellectual learning nor emotional experience alone suffice. Nor is the heightening of social sensitivity the sole sacrosanct cure-all. Experiences are needed that reach the full personality. Increased social effectiveness depends on a "tool kit" of appropriate behaviors, in addition to enhanced understanding of social situations. Special clinically oriented training experiences[10] hold promise to bring about integrated intellectual, emotional, and behavioral learnings that can make for greater effectiveness in dealing with others.

[10] Sensitivity training is one approach designed to improve a person's social sensitivity and behavioral flexibility. For a full discussion, see the chapters in Part 2. Similar programs sponsored by the National Training Laboratories in Group Development are described in numerous publications, especially those by Leland P. Bradford.

CHAPTER 5

## *How to Choose a Leadership Pattern*[*]

¶ "I put most problems into my group's hands and leave it to them to carry the ball from there. I serve merely as a catalyst, mirroring back the people's thoughts and feelings so that they can better understand them."

¶ "It's foolish to make decisions oneself on matters that affect people. I always talk things over with my subordinates, but I make it clear to them that I'm the one who has to have the final say."

¶ "Once I have decided on a course of action, I do my best to sell my ideas to my employees."

¶ "I'm being paid to lead. If I let a lot of other people make the decisions I should be making, then I'm not worth my salt."

¶ "I believe in getting things done. I can't waste time calling meetings. Someone has to call the shots around here, and I think it should be me."

Each of these statements represents a point of view about "good leadership." Considerable experience, factual data, and theoretical principles could be cited to support each statement, even though they seem to be inconsistent when placed together. Such contradictions point up the dilemma in which the modern manager frequently finds himself.

### NEW PROBLEM

The problem of how the modern manager can be "democratic" in his relations with subordinates and at the same time maintain the necessary authority and control in the organization for which he is responsible has come into focus increasingly in recent years.

[*] This chapter is a slightly modified version of an article under the same title by Robert Tannenbaum and Warren H. Schmidt, appearing in the *Harvard Business Review*, vol. 36, no. 2, pp. 95–101, March-April, 1958.

Earlier in the century this problem was not so acutely felt. The successful executive was generally pictured as possessing intelligence, imagination, initiative, the capacity to make rapid (and generally wise) decisions, and the ability to inspire subordinates. People tended to think of the world as being divided into "leaders" and "followers."

*New Focus*

Gradually, however, from the social sciences emerged the concept of "group dynamics" with its focus on members of the group rather than solely on the leader. Research efforts of social scientists underscored the importance of employee involvement and participation in decision making. Evidence began to challenge the efficiency of highly directive leadership, and increasing attention was paid to problems of motivation and human relations.

Through training laboratories in group development that sprang up across the country, many of the newer notions of leadership began to exert an impact. These training laboratories were carefully designed to give people a firsthand experience in full participation and decision making. The designated "leaders" deliberately attempted to reduce their own power and to make group members as responsible as possible for setting their own goals and methods within the laboratory experience.

It was perhaps inevitable that some of the people who attended the training laboratories regarded this kind of leadership as being truly "democratic" and went home with the determination to build fully participative decision making into their own organizations. Whenever their bosses made a decision without convening a staff meeting, they tended to perceive this as authoritarian behavior. The true symbol of democratic leadership to some was the meeting—and the less directed from the top, the more democratic it was.

Some of the more enthusiastic alumni of these training laboratories began to get the habit of categorizing leader behavior as "democratic" *or* "authoritarian." The boss who made too many decisions himself was thought of as an authoritarian, and his directive behavior was often attributed solely to his personality.

*New Need*

The net result of the research findings and of the human relations training based upon them has been to call into question the stereotype of an effective leader. Consequently, the modern manager often finds himself in an uncomfortable state of mind.

Often he is not quite sure how to behave; there are times when he is torn between exerting "strong" leadership and "permissive" leadership. Sometimes new knowledge pushes him in one direction ("I should really get the group to help make this decision"), but at the same time his experience pushes him in another direction ("I really understand the problem better than the group, and therefore I should make the decision"). He is not sure when a group decision is really appropriate or when holding a staff meeting serves merely as a device for avoiding his own decision-making responsibility.

The purpose of this chapter is to suggest a framework which managers may find useful in grappling with this dilemma. First we shall look at the different patterns of leadership behavior that the manager can choose from in relating himself to his subordinates. Then we shall turn to some of the questions suggested by this range of patterns. For instance, how important is it for a manager's subordinates to know what type of leadership he is using in a situation? What factors should he consider in deciding on a leadership pattern? What difference do his long-run objectives make as compared with his immediate objectives?

## RANGE OF BEHAVIOR

Figure 5-1 presents the continuum or range of possible leadership behaviors available to a manager. Each type of action is related to the degree of authority used by the boss and to the amount of freedom

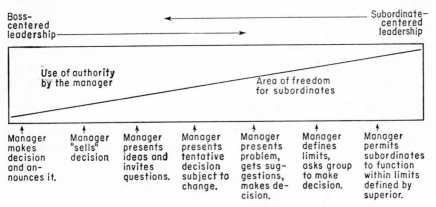

FIGURE 5-1. Continuum of leadership behavior.

available to his subordinates in reaching decisions. The actions seen on the extreme left characterize the manager who maintains a high degree of control, while those seen on the extreme right characterize the manager who releases a high degree of control. Neither extreme is absolute; authority and freedom are never without their limitations.

Now let us look more closely at each of the behavior points occurring along this continuum:

## The Manager Makes the Decision and Announces It

In this case the boss identifies a problem, considers alternative solutions, chooses one of them, and then reports this decision to his subordinates for implementation. He may or may not give consideration to what he believes his subordinates will think or feel about his decision; in any case, he provides no opportunity for them to participate directly in the decision-making process. Coercion may or may not be used or implied.

## The Manager "Sells" His Decision

Here the manager, as before, takes responsibility for identifying the problem and arriving at a decision. However, rather than simply announcing it, he takes the additional step of persuading his subordinates to accept it. In doing so, he recognizes the possibility of some resistance among those who will be faced with the decision, and he seeks to reduce this resistance by indicating, for example, what the employees have to gain from his decision.

## The Manager Presents His Ideas, Invites Questions

Here the boss who has arrived at a decision and who seeks acceptance of his ideas provides an opportunity for his subordinates to get a fuller explanation of his thinking and his intentions. After presenting the ideas, he invites questions so that his associates can better understand what he is trying to accomplish. This give and take also enables the manager and the subordinates to explore more fully the implications of the decision.

## The Manager Presents a Tentative Decision Subject to Change

This kind of behavior permits the subordinates to exert some influence on the decision. The initiative for identifying and diagnosing the problem remains with the boss. Before meeting with his staff, he has thought the problem through and arrived at a decision—but only a tentative one. Before finalizing it, he presents his proposed solution for the reaction of those who will be affected by it. He says in effect, "I'd like to hear what you have to say about this plan that I have developed. I'll appreciate your frank reactions, but will reserve for myself the final decision."

## The Manager Presents the Problem, Gets Suggestions, and Then Makes His Decision

Up to this point the boss has come before the group with a solution of his own. Not so in this case. The subordinates now get the first chance to suggest solutions. The manager's initial role involves identifying the problem. He might, for example, say something of this sort: "We are faced with a number of complaints from newspapers and the general public on our service policy. What is wrong here? What ideas do you have for coming to grips with this problem?"

The function of the group becomes one of increasing the manager's repertory of possible solutions to the problem. The purpose is to capitalize on the knowledge and experience of those who are on the "firing line." From the expanded list of alternatives developed by the manager and his subordinates, the manager then selects the solution that he regards as most promising.[1]

## The Manager Defines the Limits and Requests the Group to Make a Decision

At this point the manager passes to the group (possibly including himself as a member) the right to make decisions. Before doing so, however, he defines the problem to be solved and the boundaries within which the decision must be made.

An example might be the handling of a parking problem at a plant. The boss decides that this is something that should be worked on by the people involved, so he calls them together and points up the existence of the problem. Then he tells them:

There is the open field just north of the main plant which has been designated for additional employee parking. We can build underground or surface multi-level facilities as long as the cost does not exceed $100,000. Within these limits we are free to work out whatever solution makes sense to us. After we decide on a specific plan, the company will spend the available money in whatever way we indicate.

## The Manager Permits the Group to Make Decisions within Prescribed Limits

This represents an extreme degree of group freedom only occasionally encountered in formal organizations, as, for instance, in many research groups. Here the team of managers or engineers undertakes the identification and diagnosis of the problem, develops alternative procedures for solving it, and decides on one or more of these alternative solutions. The only limits directly imposed on the group by the organization are those specified by the superior of the team's boss. If the boss participates in the decision-making process, he attempts to do so with no more authority than any other member of the group. He commits

[1] For a fuller explanation of this approach, see Leo B. Moore, "Too Much Management, Too Little Change," *Harvard Business Review*, vol. 34, no. 1, pp. 41–48, January-February, 1956.

himself in advance to assist in implementing whatever decision the group makes.

## KEY QUESTIONS

As the continuum in Figure 5-1 demonstrates, there are a number of alternative ways in which a manager can relate himself to the group or individuals he is supervising. At the extreme left of the range, the emphasis is on the manager—on what *he* is interested in, how *he* sees things, how *he* feels about them. As we move toward the subordinate-centered end of the continuum, however, the focus is increasingly on the subordinates—on what *they* are interested in, how *they* look at things, how *they* feel about them.

When business leadership is regarded in this way, a number of questions arise. Let us take four of special importance:

1. Can a boss ever relinquish his responsibility by delegating it to someone else?

Our view is that the manager must expect to be held responsible by his superior for the quality of the decisions made, even though operationally these decisions may have been made on a group basis. He should, therefore, be ready to accept whatever risk is involved whenever he delegates decision-making power to his subordinates. Delegation is not a way of "passing the buck." Also, it should be emphasized that the amount of freedom the boss gives to his subordinates cannot be greater than the freedom which he himself has been given by his own superior.

2. Should the manager participate with his subordinates once he has delegated responsibility to them?

The manager should carefully think over this question and decide on his role prior to involving the subordinate group. He should ask if his presence will inhibit or facilitate the problem-solving process. There may be some instances when he should leave the group to let it solve the problem for itself. Typically, however, the boss has useful ideas to contribute, and should function as an additional member of the group. In the latter instance, it is important that he indicate clearly to the group that he sees himself in a *member role* rather than in an *authority role*.

3. How important is it for the group to recognize what kind of leadership behavior the boss is using?

It makes a great deal of difference. Many relationship problems between boss and subordinate occur because the boss fails to make clear how he plans to use his authority. If, for example, he actually intends to make a certain decision himself, but the subordinate group gets the impression that he has delegated this authority, considerable confusion and resentment are likely to follow. Problems may also occur when the boss uses a "democratic" façade to conceal the fact that he has already made a decision which he hopes the group will accept as its own. The attempt to "make them think it was their idea in the first place" is a risky one. We believe that it is highly important for the manager to be honest and clear in describing what authority he is keeping and what role he is asking his subordinates to assume in solving a particular problem.

4. Can you tell how "democratic" a manager is by the number of decisions his subordinates make?

The sheer *number* of decisions is not an accurate index of the amount of freedom that a subordinate group enjoys. More important is the *significance* of the decisions which the boss entrusts to his subordinates. Obviously a decision on how to arrange desks is of an entirely different order from a decision involving the introduction of new electronic data-processing equipment. Even though the widest possible limits are given in dealing with the first issue, the group will sense no particular degree of responsibility. For a boss to permit the group to decide equipment policy, even within rather narrow limits, would reflect a greater degree of confidence in them on his part.

DECIDING HOW TO LEAD

Now let us turn from the types of leadership that are possible in a company situation to the question of what types are *practical* and *desirable*. What factors or forces should a manager consider in deciding how to manage? Three are of particular importance:

¶ Forces in the manager
¶ Forces in the subordinates
¶ Forces in the situation

We should like briefly to describe these elements and indicate how they might influence a manager's action in a decision-making situation.[2] The strength of each of them will, of course, vary from instance to instance, but the manager who is sensitive to them can better assess the problems which face him and determine which mode of leadership behavior is most appropriate for him.

*Forces in the Manager*

The manager's behavior in any given instance will be influenced greatly by the many forces operating within his own personality. He will, of course, perceive his leadership problems in a unique way on

[2] See also Chap. 7.

the basis of his background, knowledge, and experience. Among the important internal forces affecting him will be the following:

*His Value System.* How strongly does he feel that individuals should have a share in making the decisions which affect them? Or, how convinced is he that the official who is paid to assume responsibility should personally carry the burden of decision making? The strength of his convictions on questions like these will tend to move the manager to one end or the other of the continuum shown in Figure 5-1. His behavior will also be influenced by the relative importance that he attaches to organizational efficiency, personal growth of subordinates, and company profits.[3]

*His Confidence in His Subordinates.* Managers differ greatly in the amount of trust they have in other people generally, and this carries over to the particular employees they supervise at a given time. In viewing his particular group of subordinates, the manager is likely to consider their knowledge and competence with respect to the problem. A central question he might ask himself is: "Who is best qualified to deal with this problem?" Often he may, justifiably or not, have more confidence in his own capabilities than in those of his subordinates.

*His Own Leadership Inclinations.* There are some managers who seem to function more comfortably and naturally as highly directive leaders. Resolving problems and issuing orders come easily to them. Other managers seem to operate more comfortably in a team role, where they are continually sharing many of their functions with their subordinates.

*His Feelings of Security in an Uncertain Situation.* The manager who releases control over the decision-making process thereby reduces the predictability of the outcome. Some managers have a greater need than others for predictability and stability in their environment. This "tolerance for ambiguity" is being viewed increasingly by psychologists as a key variable in a person's manner of dealing with problems.

The manager brings these and other highly personal variables to each situation he faces. If he can see them as forces which consciously or unconsciously influence his behavior, he can better understand what makes him prefer to act in a given way. Understanding this, he can often make himself more effective.

*Forces in the Subordinate*

Before deciding how to lead a certain group, the manager will also want to consider a number of forces affecting his subordinates' behavior. He will want to remember that each employee, like himself, is influenced by many personality variables. In addition, each subordinate

---

[3] See Chris Argyris, "Top Management Dilemma: Company Needs vs. Individual Development," *Personnel*, vol. 32, no. 2, pp. 123–134, September, 1955.

has a set of expectations about how the boss should act in relation to him (the phrase "expected behavior" is one we hear more and more often these days at discussions of leadership and teaching). The better the manager understands these factors, the more accurately he can determine what kind of behavior on his part will enable his subordinates to act most effectively.

Generally speaking, the manager can permit his subordinates greater freedom if the following essential conditions exist:

¶ If the subordinates have relatively high needs for independence. (As we all know, people differ greatly in the amount of direction that they desire.)

¶ If the subordinates have a readiness to assume responsibility for decision making. (Some see additional responsibility as a tribute to their ability; others see it as "passing the buck.")

¶ If they have a relatively high tolerance for ambiguity. (Some employees prefer to have clear-cut directives given to them; others prefer a wider area of freedom.)

¶ If they are interested in the problem and feel that it is important.

¶ If they understand and identify with the goals of the organization.

¶ If they have the necessary knowledge and experience to deal with the problem.

¶ If they have learned to expect to share in decision making. (Persons who have come to expect strong leadership and are then suddenly confronted with the request to share more fully in decision making are often upset by this new experience. On the other hand, persons who have enjoyed a considerable amount of freedom resent the boss who begins to make all the decisions himself.)

The manager will probably tend to make fuller use of his own authority if the above conditions do *not* exist; at times there may be no realistic alternative to running a "one-man show."

The restrictive effect of many of the forces will, of course, be greatly modified by the general feeling of confidence which subordinates have in the boss. Where they have learned to respect and trust him, he is free to vary his behavior. He will feel certain that he will not be perceived as an authoritarian boss on those occasions when he makes decisions by himself. Similarly, he will not be seen as using staff meetings to avoid his decision-making responsibility. In a climate of mutual confidence and respect, people tend to feel less threatened by deviations from normal practice, which in turn makes possible a higher degree of flexibility in the whole relationship.

*Forces in the Situation*

In addition to the forces which exist in the manager himself and in his subordinates, certain characteristics of the general situation will also affect the manager's behavior. Among the more critical environmental pressures that surround him are those which stem from the organization, the work group, the nature of the problem, and the pressures of time. Let us look briefly at each of these.

*Type of Organization.* Like individuals, organizations have values and traditions which inevitably influence the behavior of the people who work in them. The manager who is a newcomer to a company quickly discovers that certain kinds of behavior are approved while others are not. He also discovers that to deviate radically from what is generally accepted is likely to create problems for him.

These values and traditions are communicated in many ways—through job descriptions, policy pronouncements, and public statements by top executives. Some organizations, for example, hold to the notion that the desirable executive is one who is dynamic, imaginative, decisive, and persuasive. Other organizations put more emphasis upon the importance of the executive's ability to work effectively with people—his human relations skills. The fact that his superiors have a defined concept of what the good executive should be will very likely push the manager toward one end or the other of the behavioral range.

In addition to the above, the amount of employee participation is influenced by such variables as the size of the working units, their geographical distribution, and the degree of inter- and intraorganizational security required to attain company goals. For example, the wide geographical dispersion of an organization may preclude a practical system of participative decision making, even though this would otherwise be desirable. Similarly, the size of the working units or the need for keeping plans confidential may make it necessary for the boss to exercise more control than would otherwise be the case. Factors like these may limit considerably the manager's ability to function flexibly on the continuum (see Chapter 7).

*Group Effectiveness.* Before turning decision-making responsibility over to a subordinate group, the boss should consider how effectively its members work together as a unit.

One of the relevant factors here is the experience the group has had in working together. It can generally be expected that a group which has functioned for some time will have developed habits of cooperation and thus be able to tackle a problem more effectively than a new group. It can also be expected that a group of people with similar backgrounds and interests will work more quickly and easily than people with dissimilar backgrounds, because the communication problems are likely to be less complex.

The degree of confidence that the members have in their ability to solve problems as a group is also a key consideration. Finally, such group variables as cohesiveness, permissiveness, mutual acceptance, and communality of purpose will exert subtle but powerful influence on the group's functioning.

*The Problem Itself.* The nature of the problem may determine what degree of authority should be delegated by the manager to his subordinates. Obviously he will ask himself whether they have the kind of knowledge which is needed. It is possible to do them a real disservice by assigning a problem that their experience does not equip them to handle.

Since the problems faced in large or growing industries increasingly require knowledge of specialists from many different fields, it might be inferred that the more complex a problem, the more anxious a manager will be to get some assistance in solving it. However, this is not always the case. There will be times when the very complexity of the problem calls for one person to work it out. For example, if the manager has most of the background and factual data relevant to a given issue, it may be easier for him to think it through himself than to take the time to fill in his staff on all the pertinent background information.

The key question to ask, of course, is: "Have I heard the ideas of everyone who has the necessary knowledge to make a significant contribution to the solution of this problem?"

*The Pressure of Time.* This is perhaps the most clearly felt pressure on the manager (in spite of the fact that it may sometimes be imagined). The more that he feels the need for an immediate decision, the more difficult it is to involve other people. In organizations which are in a constant state of "crisis" and "crash programming" one is likely to find managers personally using a high degree of authority with relatively little delegation to subordinates. When the time pressure is less intense, however, it becomes much more possible to bring subordinates in on the decision-making process.

These are the principal forces that impinge on the manager in any given instance and that tend to determine his tactical behavior in relation to his subordinates. In each case his behavior ideally will be that which makes possible the most effective attainment of his immediate goal within the limits facing him.

## LONG-RUN STRATEGY

As the manager works with his organization on the problems that come up day by day, his choice of a leadership pattern is usually limited. He must take account of the forces just described and, within the restrictions they impose on him, do the best that he can. But as he looks ahead months or even years, he can shift his thinking from tactics to large-scale strategy. No longer need he be fettered by all of the forces mentioned, for he can view many of them as variables over which he has some control. He can, for example, gain new insights or skills for himself, supply training for individual subordinates, and provide participative experiences for his employee group.

In trying to bring about a change in these variables, however, he is faced with a challenging question: "At which point along the continuum *should* one act?"

*Attaining Objectives*

The answer depends largely on what he wants to accomplish. Let us suppose that he is interested in the same objectives that most modern managers seek to attain when they can shift their attention from the pressure of immediate assignments:

1. To raise the level of employee motivation
2. To increase the readiness of subordinates to accept change
3. To improve the quality of all managerial decisions
4. To develop teamwork and morale
5. To further the individual development of employees

In recent years the manager has been deluged with a flow of advice on how best to achieve these longer-run objectives. It is little wonder that he is often both bewildered and annoyed. However, there are some guidelines which he can usefully follow in making a decision.

Most research and much of the experience of recent years give a strong factual basis to the theory that a fairly high degree of subordinate-centered behavior is associated with the accomplishment of the five purposes mentioned.[4] This does not mean that a manager should always leave all decisions to his assistants. To provide the individual or the group with greater freedom than they are ready for at any given time may very well tend to generate anxieties and therefore inhibit rather than facilitate the attainment of desired objectives. But this should not keep the manager from making a continuing effort to confront his subordinates with the challenge of freedom.

CONCLUSION

In summary, there are two implications in the basic thesis that we have been developing. The first is that the successful leader is one who

---

[4] For example, see Warren H. Schmidt and Paul C. Buchanan, *Techniques that Produce Teamwork* (New London, Conn.: Arthur C. Croft Publications, 1954), and Morris S. Viteles, *Motivation and Morale in Industry* (New York: W. W. Norton & Company, Inc., 1953).

is keenly aware of those forces which are most relevant to his behavior at any given time. He accurately understands himself, the individuals and group he is dealing with, and the company and broader social environment in which he operates. And certainly he is able to assess the present readiness for growth of his subordinates.

But this sensitivity or understanding is not enough, which brings us to the second implication. The successful leader is one who is able to behave appropriately in the light of these perceptions. If direction is in order, he is able to direct; if considerable participative freedom is called for, he is able to provide such freedom.

Thus, the successful manager of men can be primarily characterized neither as a strong leader nor as a permissive one. Rather, he is one who maintains a high batting average in accurately assessing the forces that determine what his most appropriate behavior at any given time should be and in actually being able to behave accordingly. Being both insightful and flexible, he is less likely to see the problems of leadership as a dilemma.

CHAPTER 6

## The Introduction of Change
## in Organizations*

Today, every manager is concerned with the many technological and structural changes that affect his current operations. In addition to these changes, he is conscious of another factor that very strongly characterizes modern organizations—their rapid growth. Many units that started as very small concerns have, in recent years, emerged as medium- or large-sized entities.

Often, these changes bring a great deal of pressure to bear on the individuals and work units that must adapt to them. Employees may experience considerable stress because they can no longer do their work in the way they formerly did. They may have to face uncertainties that are upsetting to them; thus they may react negatively to change— either individually or as members of groups.

### RESISTANCE AND ITS SYMPTOMS

The most characteristic individual and group reaction to change is called *resistance*.[1] There are a number of signs of resistance—but this doesn't mean that these symptoms *always* indicate resistance. Sometimes they may be indicators of other difficulties in the organization.

* This chapter is based upon the following publications by Robert Tannenbaum: "The Introduction of Change in Industrial Organizations," American Management Association's General Management Series no. 186 (*Improving Managerial Performance*), 1957, and "When It's Time for a Change," *Supervisory Management*, July, 1956.

[1] For an analysis of the nature of resistance and its causes and prevention, see Alvin Zander, "Resistance to Change—Its Analysis and Prevention," *Advanced Management*, January, 1950, pp. 9–11.

When we look at the individual *as* an individual, we sometimes find considerable hostility or aggression. The hostility may only be expressed verbally, in the way the individual strikes out at the boss, a fellow worker, or even a subordinate; but hostility and aggression can also take physical forms where the striking out is of a more intense character.

Sometimes we find apathy. The individual loses interest. He tries to escape the situation in which he finds himself. He is not highly motivated. Sometimes we find careless effort; the individual is spoiling material or is not performing up to the standards expected of him.

Absenteeism and tardiness are often signs of resistance. Perhaps these are forms of apathy or attempts on the part of the individual to escape his work environment. Separation, for example, may be an extreme illustration of this attempt to escape.

The development of anxiety and tension in the individual is often a sign that resistance exists. An individual may be edgy and shaky; he may not be able to relax and give himself completely to the job. Often discouragement sets in, and he just gives up.

Individuals organized as a work group may exhibit additional signs of resistance. Slowdowns and strikes are possible indicators of group resistance. Another response that has often occurred and that has been studied in considerable detail is the reaction of groups of workers called "restriction of output." Often great care is exercised in timing operations, setting standards, and otherwise working out the details of a wage-incentive system; and yet at least part of the work group forms into an informal group, under a leader of its own choice. This group decides what a fair day's work is and develops methods of keeping the nonconformist in line. The individual who starts to respond to the incentive is held in check by sanctions which the informal group is able to bring to bear against him. This restriction-of-output device has also been used in dealing with other types of change that management has tried to introduce.

These are some of the manifestations of resistance—some of the ways in which individuals and groups behave when their work environment is subject to change. But these manifestations are merely symptoms.

## THE CAUSES OF RESISTANCE

What is much more important from the manager's point of view is to try to understand more fully the *underlying causes* of resistance. Often, when the introduction of change has been discussed, administrators have felt that people are primarily concerned with the technological or structural change itself. But this really isn't the case. Instead, they are concerned about the potential impact of the change on them as individuals or as members of work groups. Essentially, what individuals or groups ask themselves are the questions: "What is the change going to mean to me? Will it be important to me and to my group?"

Each individual and each group develops for itself a kind of island of security. This island of security is defined by everything that is important to the individual or to the group. The individual, for example, gets real security in knowing that he can do his job and in knowing where he stands in his relations with other people. However, when a change comes about, his sense of security is disrupted. The individual is no longer free from anxiety, and he is faced with the necessity of taking another look at his island. The same thing is certainly true of the group. Work groups establish values, beliefs, ways of doing things, and relationships that provide considerable comfort to their members. The implication of a technological or structural change to the group is that all these security factors in its life are now threatened.

In a sense, the individual and the group are like turtles whose shells represent the security available to them in their present situation. They can always crawl into their shells for protection, and they become very concerned about coming out of them to explore a new environment that is threatening.

Of course, the security of an individual is not always threatened by potential change. Certainly there are instances where individuals or groups see change not as a threat but as something that is beneficial to them.

In those instances where the change is seen as beneficial, there will be no resistance. However, in this connection, there is a very important warning. In changing situations, we too often look only at the surface manifestations. Individuals and groups may *seem* to be adapting to change, but this appearance may be rather misleading.

How can we explain the current statistics on heart disease, ulcers, nervous breakdowns, and psychosomatic manifestations that increasingly plague management as well as the rank and file? There seems to be increasing evidence that the very rapid change which characterizes our modern industrial life is one of the key factors underlying these psychosomatic conditions. Often, at the surface level, individuals and groups are adapting to change, but perhaps this adaptation is being made at a terrific price to the people involved.

The nature of the factors underlying resistance can be well illustrated with reference to the typical growing concern. Here resistance is felt at all levels and in all units of the company. Subordinates are certainly faced with uncertainty. They are aware that many changes are occurring which involve the company's organization, product line, and so on. But they don't know quite how these changes will affect them personally, and this uncertainty generates a lot of tension within them.

More specifically, a subordinate becomes concerned about the obsolescence of his present know-how. Because he can perform a job in a particular way, he receives a pay check that is important to him. Then he learns, often via the grapevine, that the company is planning to purchase new equipment or that it is going to reorganize, and he begins to ask himself: "Am I going to be able to do the job I know how to perform in this new setup?"

Another thing that bothers the individual in a growing concern is the movement away from personally meaningful informal relations. One of the advantages of a small firm is the close, face-to-face relations that exist within the organization. Very often, the employees know the boss and each other by first names. But as the firm begins to grow in size, a gradual introduction of physical and psychological barriers between individuals will result. People become separated from each other.

As the company's organizational units grow, it becomes increasingly necessary to use rules and regulations and to introduce many new formalities. Certainly, a change in the individual's existing social relationships may occur. New people come into work groups, and individuals are moved from one group to another.

Work groups in a growing concern may often sense that their status within the organization is being changed. Perhaps a given work group has had considerable importance in the firm; then an organizational change is made, and other units gain more prestige. Very often, this change in status will affect the group's goals and values and may even interfere with the group's customary work patterns.

The impact of potential change in the growing concern also affects the top management level and, particularly, the top executive of the firm. Often the pressures that accompany growth have made it difficult for the top executive to adapt to the change in his own firm.

One of the questions that the top executive frequently asks himself is: "Can I personally keep up with the growth of my firm?" When his organization was small, he was able to keep on top of his responsibilities; but when it grows beyond a certain point, he suddenly senses that things are getting out of hand. He wonders whether he will be able to cope with the new responsibilities he must assume.

He is increasingly worried about the fact that he loses touch with his employees. He, too, has valued the close association with his subordinates. As his firm grows, he no longer sees the people he used to see every day—perhaps he only sees them once a month—and this troubles him.

Another trend that troubles him is that he has been forced to change from a "doer" to an "organizer." Perhaps he was formerly a production man, and that is his key interest. When the firm was small, he was able to spend all his time on production activities. Now he has to devote more and more attention to organization and other purely managerial functions. He is concerned about this, because he had previously felt secure in his ability to handle all phases of the production end of his business. Now he has to "think" much more and "work" much less.

Also, he must delegate much of the work he formerly did himself. Often, because of the pressure of growth, he must assign this work to people who, in his opinion, will not handle the job as competently as he could. Thus, he is caught in the dilemma of either trying to do everything himself or delegating to others jobs he feels better able to do himself.

Finally, as a coordinator of all the activities of the business, he is increasingly faced with financial, marketing, personnel, and other problems with respect to which he often feels little competence.

The examples we have cited describe only a few of the pressures that are faced by individuals from the very bottom of the organization up to the top. The anxiety and fear that these pressures cause represent the real problem in trying to introduce change in the industrial organization. How, then, can we deal with the problem of resistance as it exists today?

## APPROACHES FOR INTRODUCING CHANGE

Of over-all importance is the human atmosphere that exists between the person trying to introduce the change and the individuals and groups who are subject to the change. If mutual confidence is not present, the strength of the resistance will be greatly increased. When we have a real sense of trust and confidence in another person, we are much more likely to go along with what the other person is trying to do.

For individuals and groups to accept new ideas or methods, probably three different things have to occur. *First, it is important that they understand the reasons for the change.* They have to get some insight into why a change is going to be made. Very often, supervisors will simply announce the change and say, "Here it is, boys; from now on we behave in this way." There is no explanation, no indication to the people involved as to why the change has to be made. Understanding of the need for the change is important if people are not to resist.

*Second, individuals and groups have to see that the change is going to be good for them.* This point relates back to the question: "What does this mean to me?" If it is not going to involve something better for the individual or group—or at least something as good—the change is apt to be resisted. People are going to want assurance that there will not be any reductions in need satisfaction, and that the change will at least leave them no worse off than they are right now—or, even better, that it may improve their present situation.

Finally, after the individuals or groups understand the reasons for the change and have seen what the change is going to mean to them, generally *some new behavior will be called for on their part.* They may have to learn some new skills; they may have to develop some new attitudes; they may even have to change their whole frame of reference in order to deal with the new situation.

In bringing about change in the industrial organization, it is essential to be sensitive to the potential threats and anxieties that are inherent in the change. It is important to see what the change is going to mean to the individuals and work groups involved.

Although managers have used somewhat different approaches in dealing with individuals on the one hand and with groups on the other, these approaches are psychologically quite similar. First, they are characterized by the fact that they attempt to build security for the individual and the group rather than to generate anxieties within them. Second, they are similar in that they try to make it possible for the individual or the group to have some self-direction or control over the impact of the change rather than to have it imposed by an outside individual or group over whom the employees have no control.[2]

Finally, the two approaches are characterized by the fact that they are oriented toward the frames of reference of the individuals and the groups involved rather than primarily toward the frame of reference of the individual who is imposing the change. In other words, management is concerned about the ways the individual or the group looks at the change in addition to the way the imposer of the change looks at it.

In introducing change at the individual level, it is extremely important that management establish an atmosphere of "permissiveness," which suggests mutual respect as well as confidence in and concern for the individual. Second, there must be a real desire on the part of management to understand the individual's ideas and feelings from his point of view.

Finally, management must attempt to be nonevaluative or nonjudgmental in its approach to the individual. This suggests an absence of

[2] Cf. D. Cartwright, "Achieving Change in People: Some Applications of Group Dynamics Theory," *Human Relations*, vol. 4, no. 4, pp. 381–392, 1951; Lester Coch and John R. P. French, Jr., "Overcoming Resistance to Change," *Human Relations*, vol. 1, no. 4, pp. 512–532, 1948; Paul R. Lawrence, "How to Deal with Resistance to Change," *Harvard Business Review*, vol. 32, no. 3, pp. 49–57, May-June, 1954; and Leo B. Moore, "Too Much Management, Too Little Change," *Harvard Business Review*, vol. 34, no. 1, pp. 41–48, January-February, 1956.

critical appraisal of the individual, so that he does not immediately feel the need to defend himself. He must be able to look at the situation more or less constructively and to adapt to it in a way that is meaningful to him.

From the group point of view, the approach has somewhat the same psychological significance, but the technique is different. In this case, the newer techniques are *participative* in nature. Rather than approaching a group and disrupting it by moving people around or forcing some other change on the group for which it is not prepared, the group is given an opportunity to suggest ways in which the change might be made, to receive answers to the questions which concern the group members, and to adjust to the change in ways that are meaningful to the group itself.

This participative approach reduces the threat that a potential change may pose to the group, since it allows the group to have considerable control over the change which it faces (see Chapter 7).

## MANAGERS, TOO, MUST CHANGE

These approaches to the individual and to the group which attempt to reduce threat and anxiety may present the manager personally with some real areas of internal conflict, for they involve behavior that is, in fact, inconsistent with the traditional way in which managers operate.

At the level of the individual, the permissive, understanding, and nonevaluative approaches mentioned above seem to be in conflict with many traditional managerial practices.

First, there is the boss's customary way of exercising authority. His feeling is: "I am boss, and my decisions are right." After all, he has typically come up through the ranks; he has more experience than the others; he has more knowledge available to him; he sees the problem in the only correct way; therefore, his view of this problem and the way it should be introduced is the only important one. He finds it difficult to see the problem from anyone else's point of view.

Second, managers traditionally feel it important to generate competition between individuals. Such competition leads people to be concerned about their own status relative to the status of other persons. However, it is certainly not a means of threat reduction.

Third, the suggested approaches for introducing change are also inconsistent with many of the standard employee-rating methods, which involve an evaluation of the individual—including an enumeration of his weaknesses and inadequacies—from management's vantage point. Certainly, evaluation has its place in an industrial organization. But the evaluation of an individual creates a situation where it becomes necessary for him to build a protective layer around himself to hide his inadequacies and his feelings of discomfort from the boss. He feels that if he discloses these feelings, he will be hurt as a result of them.

Finally, traditional methods of management bring pressures on the individual for conformity. Traditional management finds it very difficult to accept differences in individuals and to make it possible for them to be what they want to be.

Thus, all these traditional modes of management are inconsistent with a method of dealing with individuals that reduces threat and anxiety.

Likewise, at the level of the work group, the participative methods for introducing change also seem to conflict with the traditional management methods. The traditional boss who is used to running the business by himself is not the kind of individual who can effectively use the participative method. He cannot comfortably sit with his staff and work out an effective method for dealing with a change, nor does he really feel that they have anything to contribute to the solution of the problem. Some traditional managers do attempt to use what they consider to be the participative approach. Too often, however, the boss makes the final decision before going to the group and then subtly manipulates it toward the conclusion at which he has already arrived. Further, many traditional managers strongly feel that the responsibility to decide and to act is theirs and no one else's.

This conflict between the methods suggested above for introducing change and the traditional management methods poses a real challenge to managers. The effective implementation of these new approaches requires changed behavior on the part of the managers themselves. They must divest themselves of some of the traditional ways of managing and develop newer means of dealing with individuals and groups. Such personal change is not easy. It is not the kind of change that can be brought about by an individual's deciding: "I am going to manage in a new way tomorrow." The traditional methods of managing are very much a product of the personalities of each manager; thus they represent the manager's own island of security. A new type of behavior poses a threat to the manager because it means that he, too, will have to change.

Thus, modern management is faced with a dilemma. To be successful, it must skillfully facilitate the introduction of change; but to do so, it must often give up many of its traditional ways of managing. This dilemma suggests that it may be the resistance of the managers themselves to the adoption of new methods of management which currently represents one of the most serious barriers to the introduction of change in organizations.

# CHAPTER 7

# Participation by Subordinates*

## INTRODUCTION

The role of "participation" by individuals or groups in American culture in general and in industrial organizations specifically has been treated by many writers. Its implications for political theory as well as for a theory of human relations in formal organizations are numerous. However, in spite of this academic and extra-academic interest, a clearcut, operational definition of the concept, or a precise set of hypotheses regarding its dynamics, has not been developed. While to do so will be the object of this paper, the treatment will not be completely operational.

A review of the literature indicates that three major approaches have been taken in dealing with "participation":

### The Experiential Approach

This approach is exemplified by writers who in the course of their experience in enterprise work have obtained a "feel" for the role of participation in the decision-making process and have put down their experiences in article or book form.[1] Writings such as these provide a set of insights and hunches whose verification in any systematic fashion

---

* This chapter is a slightly modified version of "Participation by Subordinates in the Managerial Decision-making Process," by Robert Tannenbaum and Fred Massarik, *The Canadian Journal of Economics and Political Science*, pp. 408–418, August, 1950.

[1] For example, H. H. Carey, "Consultative Supervision and Management," *Personnel*, vol. 18, no. 5, pp. 286–295, March, 1942; Alexander R. Heron, *Why Men Work* (Stanford, Calif.: Stanford University Press, 1948); Eric A. Nicol, "Management through Consultative Supervision," *Personnel Journal*, vol. 27, no. 6, pp. 207–217, November, 1948; James C. Worthy, "Changing Concepts of the Personnel Function," *Personnel*, vol. 25, no. 3, pp. 166–175, November, 1948.

has not been attempted. The actual referants from which these formulations are derived often are single sets of observations in a single or in a few enterprises—observations generally made in an uncontrolled fashion.

The experiential approach, operating outside the bounds of scientific method, nonetheless adds to scientific knowledge indirectly by providing the raw material from which hypotheses may be moulded. The precise structure of these hypotheses is not stated neatly by the experiential writers, but rather remains to be formulated.

## The Conceptual, Nonexperimental Approach

This approach characterizes the writings of authors who are essentially academicians with strong theoretical backgrounds. It is typified by writings that deal with "conditions," "functions," and other abstractions, generally of a sociopsychological nature, that attempt to explain the dynamics of participation.[2] The conceptual, nonexperimental approach at its best is the process of hypothesis or theory formulation. Ideally it lays the groundwork for actual testing and experimental work, but much of this type of technical literature so far published on participation lacks the clarity of conceptual definition necessary to make it useful as a basis for experimental work.

## The Experimental Approach

This approach is found in the writings of authors who have seen fit to apply experimental techniques either in especially constructed social situations involving participation, or in natural settings in which participational activities prevail.[3] With adequate controls and with a meaningful theoretical structure within which individual findings may be placed, this approach is doubtless the most fruitful. Ideally it indicates what will happen under specified sets of conditions and with what degree of probability. Unfortunately, up to now experimental work on the dynamics of participation in the decision-making process has been sporadic.[4]

---

[2] For example, Douglas McGregor, "Conditions for Effective Leadership in the Industrial Situation," *Journal of Consulting Psychology*, vol. 8, pp. 55–63, March–April, 1944; Gordon W. Allport, "The Psychology of Participation," *Psychological Review*, vol. 52, pp. 117–132, May, 1945.

[3] For the concept of the "natural experiment," see F. Stuart Chapin, *Experimental Designs in Sociological Research* (New York: Harper & Brothers, 1947), and Ernest Greenwood, *Experimental Sociology, A Study in Method* (New York: King's Crown Press, 1945).

[4] For a good summary of relevant experimental work, see Ronald Lippitt, "A Program of Experimentation on Group Functioning and Productivity," in Wayne Dennis et al., *Current Trends in Social Psychology* (Pittsburgh: University of Pittsburgh Press, 1948).

The present chapter is of the conceptual, nonexperimental type. Participation in the decision-making process is conceived here as an instrument that may be used by the formal leadership of an enterprise in the pursuit of its goals. No attempt will be made to examine it from an ethical standpoint or in terms of its consistency within the frame of a democratic society, although it is by no means assumed that such considerations are less important than those set forward here.

## DEFINITION OF PARTICIPATION

It is essential, in dealing with participation, to make clear the meaning which is to be attached to the concept. One must specify both who the participators are and in what they are participating. Too frequently in the available literature on the subject the reader must determine these matters for himself because no explicit statements bearing on them are made by the writers.

As already indicated, this chapter is primarily concerned with participation as a managerial device. Attention is therefore focused on the subordinates of managers in enterprises as the participators. It is important to note that these subordinates may be either nonmanagers or managers.[5] If they are managers, they are subordinates of superior managers in the formal organization of the enterprise, in addition to having subordinates who are responsible to them.

Because of space limitations, consideration of the participation of individuals as union members in specific activities of an enterprise is excluded from the scope of this paper. Suffice it to say here that in those cases where the participation of union members is direct and personal, the benefits to be derived by the enterprise are similar to those derived from participation within the superior-subordinate relationship. However, in those cases (which are the greatest in number) where the participation of the union member is indirect and impersonal, it is doubtful whether such is the result. It is our conclusion that most of the statements which follow are relevant to the former cases.[6]

What then is the meaning of participation, and with what type of participation by subordinates are we here concerned? An individual participates in something when he takes a part or share in that thing. Since taking a part or sharing is always involved, participation takes place in a social context. Managerial subordinates in formal enterprises

---

[5] For definitions of these terms as used here, see Chap. 15.

[6] In connection with this discussion, it should be noted that when participation takes place within the superior-subordinate relationship, managers have primary control over the nature of the activity; when it takes place as part of the manager-union relationship, they may or may not, depending upon the relative power of the two parties.

are responsible to their superiors for the performance of designated tasks. In such performance, they are participating in the production of the good or service of the enterprise. They also participate (share), through the receipt of wages or salaries, in the distribution of the total revenue received by the enterprise. These types of participation are common to all enterprises. But there is another type of participation which is much less frequently encountered, although its use as a managerial device has, of recent years, grown rapidly in importance. This type involves participation by subordinates with their superiors in the managerial decision-making process.

Decisions are made by managers in order to organize, direct, or control responsible subordinates to the end that all service contributions be coordinated in the attainment of an enterprise purpose.[7] Since managers are those who accomplish results through subordinates, the latter are always directly and intimately affected by managerial decisions and therefore may have a considerable interest in them. Because of this possible interest, subordinates may have a strong desire, particularly in a nation with deeply ingrained democratic traditions, to participate in the determination of matters affecting them. It is of importance, therefore, to consider the form which such participation might assume.

Decision making involves a conscious choice or selection of one behavior alternative from among a group of two or more behavior alternatives.[8] Three steps are involved in the decision-making process. First, an individual must become aware of as many as possible of those behavior alternatives which are relevant to the decision to be made. Secondly, he must define each of these alternatives, a definition which involves a determination of as many as possible of the consequences related to each alternative under consideration. Thirdly, the individual must exercise a choice between the alternatives, that is, make a decision.

In enterprises, managerial subordinates, as subordinates, can participate in the first two steps of the managerial decision-making process. They cannot participate in the third step. The actual choice between relevant alternatives must be made or accepted by the manager who is responsible to his superior for the decision.[9] However, subordinates can

[7] See Chap. 15.
[8] This discussion of the decision-making process is based upon that presented in Chap. 16.
[9] In a democratic group, the choice can be made through a vote participated in by the rank and file. But in such a case, the leader is organizationally responsible to the rank and file, and the members of the rank and file are not properly, so far as the decision is concerned, subordinates of the leader.
Members of a democratic group, making the final choice in matters directly affecting them, may be more highly motivated as a result thereof than managerial subordinates who are granted the right to participate only in the first two steps of

provide and discuss with their manager information with respect both to relevant alternatives and to the consequences attendant upon specific alternatives. In so doing they are participating in the managerial decision-making process.[10]

The participation with which we are here concerned may take place in two different ways. First, it may involve interaction solely between a subordinate and his manager.[11] This would be the case where a worker originates a suggestion, which he transmits to his boss. Secondly, it may involve interaction between a group of subordinates and their manager. This would be the case where a manager calls his subordinates together to discuss a common problem or to formulate a recommendation.[12]

## POSSIBLE ADVANTAGES OF PARTICIPATION AS A MANAGERIAL DEVICE

It becomes useful to inquire why managers might find it advantageous to use this device. In other words, what are the possible

---

the managerial decision-making process. For evidence of the motivational effects of group decision, see Kurt Lewin, "Group Decision and Social Change," in T. M. Newcomb and E. L. Hartley (eds.), *Readings in Social Psychology* (1st ed.; New York: Henry Holt & Company, Inc., 1947).

[10] It is this type of participation that most writers who deal with human relations in enterprises have in mind when they use the concept. The following examples illustrate this contention: "One of the most important conditions of the subordinate's growth and development centers around his opportunities to express his ideas and to contribute his suggestions before his superiors take action on matters which involve him. Through participation of this kind he becomes more and more aware of his superiors' problems, and he obtains genuine satisfaction in knowing that his opinions and ideas are given consideration in the search for solutions," McGregor, *op. cit.*, p. 60; "I am not suggesting that we take over intact the apparatus of the democratic state. Business cannot be run by the ballot box. . . . We must develop other inventions, adapted to the special circumstances of business, which will give employees at all levels of our organizations a greater sense of personal participation and 'belonging,'" Worthy, *op. cit.*, p. 175; "Action initiated by the responsible head to bring his subordinates into the picture on matters of mutual concern is not a sharing of prerogatives of authority. Rather, it is an extension of the opportunity of participation in the development of points of view and the assembly of facts upon which decisions are made," Carey, *op. cit.*, p. 288.

[11] The concept of interaction as used here is not restricted to direct person-to-person, two-way communication (as in the process of superior-subordinate discussion) but encompasses more indirect forms (such as, for example, written communication) as well.

[12] It may be observed that participation in the latter way, where there is communication between participators and where the act of participation is carried out through the medium of the group (as in cases of "group decision"), may often yield the more useful results. The level of derivable benefits may be higher than if participation had proceeded through channels in which there had been no inter-participator communication. Some factors important in this context are the following: (1) the feeling of "group belongingness" obtained by means of "action together" and (2) the role of norms, set as a result of group discussion, toward which behavior will tend to gravitate.

benefits which might accrue to an enterprise whose managers made it possible for subordinates to participate in the decision-making process? In providing an answer to this question, it is first necessary to indicate the criterion which would guide the managerial choice relating to the use of participation.

A manager of an enterprise (profit or nonprofit) who behaves rationally will attempt to make a selection from among alternatives related to any problem which will maximize results (the degree of attainment of a given end) at a given cost or which will attain given results at the lowest cost.[13] This is the criterion of rationality. Guided by this criterion, rational managers will find it advantageous to use participation whenever such use will lead to increased results at a given cost or to the attainment of given results at a lower cost.

There are many advantages which *may* stem from the use of participation as a managerial device. The following are the principal ones:

1. A higher rate of output and increased quality of product (including reduced spoilage and wastage) as a result of greater personal effort and attention on the part of subordinates.[14]

2. A reduction in turnover, absenteeism, and tardiness.

3. A reduction in the number of grievances and more peaceful manager-subordinate and manager-union relations.

4. A greater readiness to accept change.[15] When changes are arbitrarily introduced from above without explanation, subordinates tend to feel insecure and to take countermeasures aimed at sabotage of the innovations. But when they have participated in the process leading to the decision, they have had an opportunity to be heard. They know what to expect and why, and they may desire the change. Blind resistance tends to become intelligent adaptation as insecurity is replaced by security (see Chapter 6).

5. Greater ease in the management of subordinates.[16] Fewer man-

[13] The term *cost* is here used in its highly precise form to refer to whatever must be given or sacrificed to attain an end. See "Price," *Webster's Dictionary of Synonyms* (Springfield, Mass.: G & C Merriam Company, 1942). The term *end* is broadly conceived to embrace whatever factors (monetary or nonmonetary) the managers themselves define as the formal ends of the enterprise.

[14] For examples, see Lippitt, *op. cit.;* John R. P. French, Jr., Arthur Kornhauser, and Alfred Marrow, "Conflict and Cooperation in Industry," *Journal of Social Issues,* vol. 2, no. 1, February, 1946 (entire issue); *Productivity, Supervision and Morale* (Survey Research Center Study no. 6, Ann Arbor, Mich., 1948).

[15] See, for example, Alex Bavelas, "Some Problems of Organizational Change," *Journal of Social Issues,* vol. 4, no. 3, pp. 48–52, Summer, 1948; Elliott Jacques, "Interpretive Group Discussion as a Method of Facilitating Social Change," *Human Relations,* vol. 1, no. 4, pp. 533–549, 1948; Lewin, *op. cit.*

[16] See, for example, L. P. Bradford and R. Lippitt, "Building a Democratic Work Group," *Personnel,* vol. 22, no. 3, pp. 142–151, November, 1945; O. H. Mowrer, "Authoritarianism vs. 'Self-Government' in the Management of Children's Aggressive (Anti-social) Reactions as a Preparation for Citizenship in a Democracy," *Journal of Social Psychology,* vol. 10, pp. 121–126, February, 1939.

agers may be necessary, the need for close supervision may be reduced, and less disciplinary action may be called for. Subordinates who have participated in the process leading toward a determination of matters directly affecting them may have a greater sense of responsibility with respect to the performance of their assigned tasks and may be more willing to accept the authority of their superiors. All managers possess a given amount of formal authority delegated to them by their superiors. But formal authority is not necessarily the equivalent of effective authority. The real source of the authority possessed by an individual lies in the acceptance of its exercise by those who are subject to it. It is the subordinates of an individual who determine the authority which he may wield. Formal authority is, in effect, nominal authority. It becomes real only when it is accepted. Thus, to be effective, formal authority must coincide with authority determined by its acceptance. The latter defines the useful limits of the former.[17] The use of participation as a managerial device may result in a widening of these limits, reducing the amount of resistance to the exercise of formal authority and increasing the positive responses of subordinates to managerial directives.

6. *The improved quality of managerial decisions.* It is seldom if ever possible for managers to have knowledge of *all* alternatives and *all* consequences related to the decisions which they must make. Because of the existence of barriers to the upward flow of information in most enterprises, much valuable information possessed by subordinates never reaches their managers. Participation tends to break down the barriers, making the information available to managers. To the extent that such information alters the decisions which managers make, the quality of their decisions may thereby be improved.

These, then, are the principal advantages which *may* stem from the use of participation as a managerial device.[18] The conditions under which it *will* accomplish them—under which participation will lead to motivation—are the concern of the section which follows.

## THE PSYCHOLOGICAL CONDITIONS OF EFFECTIVE PARTICIPATION

All managers of an enterprise are faced with the problem of eliciting service contributions from their subordinates at a high level of quality and intensity. These service contributions are essential if the formal goals of the enterprise are to be attained. What induces subordinates to contribute their services? What motivates them?

---

[17] This concept of effective authority is expanded in Chap. 16.
[18] These advantages will henceforth be referred to as "enterprise advantages."

A motivated individual is one who is striving to achieve a goal; his activity is goal-oriented.[19] But it should be stressed that motivation is only *potential* motion towards a goal. Whether or not the goal is reached depends not only upon the strength of the force in the direction of the goal, but also upon all other forces (both driving and restraining) in the given situation.[20] To illustrate, a person may be motivated to produce 200 units of an item per day, but the restraining force in the form of machine failure or a quarrel with the foreman may lead him to attain an output of only 150 units.

In enterprises, the goals toward which individuals strive may be of two kinds. They may be the formal goals of the enterprise, or they may be other goals which are complementary to the formal goals. The latter is the typical case. Individuals may strive for monetary reward, prestige, power, security, and the like; or they may strive for certain psychological gratifications through the very act of doing the job (that is, they work because they like their work). The primary reason why they contribute their services is to attain these latter goals. In attaining these desired goals, they make possible the attainment of the formal goals of the enterprise which to them are simply means to their own ends. In this sense, the desired goals and the formal goals are complementary.

In the former case, the goals desired by the individual and the formal goals are the same. The individual contributes his services primarily because such contribution makes possible the attainment of the formal goals of the enterprise which coincide with his own personal goals. To the extent that this coincidence of goals exists, the necessity for managers to provide complementary goals for subordinates is thereby lessened, and related costs are reduced. It is suggested that participation tends to bring about a coincidence of formal and personal goals.[21] It may be that through participation, the subordinate, who formerly was

[19] A goal is defined as a result which, when achieved, has the power to reduce the tension of the organism that has caused the organism to seek it.

[20] Thus, motion in the direction of goals may be achieved not only by adding forces in the goal direction, but also by reducing forces impeding such motion. See K. Lewin, "Frontiers in Group Dynamics," *Human Relations,* vol. 1, no. 1, pp. 26–27, 1947.

[21] It must be noted that participation as used in this context is only one device which may lead to additional motivation by bringing about a coincidence of formal and personal goals. For example, some other devices that under certain conditions may result in motivational increases and their derivative benefits to the enterprise are permitting personal discretion to the person to be motivated and stimulation of a sense of pride of workmanship. In the former context, managers in all enterprises must always decide the amount of discretion to permit to subordinates. Many considerations naturally underlie this decision. For present purposes, it is important to emphasize that in many circumstances, the granting of considerable discretion may lead to substantial increases in motivation. Several devices may be used concurrently, and the dynamics of the devices themselves are interrelated. For example, use of discretion may bring about an enhanced pride-of-workmanship feeling.

moved to contribute his services only because he sought, for example, security and financial rewards, now comes to be moved additionally because he recognizes that the success of the enterprise in turn will enhance his own ability to satisfy his needs.[22]

Whether one conceives of participation as involving separate subordinates with their superiors or subordinates in groups with their superiors, in the final analysis one must not lose sight of the fact that the subordinate is a unique human being with a given personality. This implies that whether or not participation will bring forth the restructuring of his goal pattern (incorporating the formal goals within the scope of the personal goals) will depend upon a set of dynamic psychological conditions, the primary ones of which are outlined below.

1. The subordinate must be capable of becoming psychologically involved in the participational activities. He must be free from "blockages" which may prevent him from rearranging his particular goal pattern in the light of new experience. He must possess some minimum amount of intelligence so that he may grasp the meaning and implications of the thing being considered. He must be in touch with reality. If he responds to a dream world, any "real" developments, such as opportunities to take part in certain decision-making processes, may not penetrate without gross distortion and as a result miss their point.

2. The subordinate must favor participational activity. In other words, the person who believes that "the boss knows best" and that the decision-making process is none of his business is not likely to become strongly motivated if given an opportunity to participate. It is apparent that for personality types shaped intensely by an authoritarian system, opportunities for participation may be regarded as signs of weakness and leadership incompetence and on that basis may be rejected unequivocally.[23]

3. The subordinate must see the relevance to his personal life pattern of the thing being considered. When he realizes that through participation he may affect the course of his future in such a fashion as to increase its positive goal elements and to diminish the negative ones, he will become motivated. For example, a person who can see the relationship between "putting his two bits" into a discussion of a new way of using a stitching machine and the fact that this may mean greater job security and increased pay for himself may be motivated.

4. The subordinate must be able to express himself to his own satisfaction with respect to the thing being considered. He must be psycho-

---

[22] It must be recognized that typically goal configurations, rather than single goals, act as motivating agents.

[23] For example, see A. H. Maslow, "The Authoritarian Character Structure," in P. L. Harriman (ed.), *Twentieth Century Psychology* (New York: The Philosophical Library, Inc., 1946). For more detailed treatments see the major works of Erich Fromm and Abram Kardiner.

logically able to communicate; and, further, he must feel that he is making some sort of contribution. Of course, if he cannot communicate (owing to mental blocks, fear of being conspicuous, etc.), by definition he is not participating. If he does not feel that he is contributing, he may, instead of becoming motivated, come to feel inadequate and frustrated. This presupposes not only that he is articulate, but that he has a certain fund of knowledge on which to draw. Participation may fail if it involves considering matters that are quite outside the scope of experience of the participators.

All the above conditions must be satisfied to some minimum extent. Beyond this requirement, however, the conditions may be mutually compensating, and a relatively low degree of one (although necessarily above the minimum) may be offset somewhat by an extremely high degree of another. For example, if a subordinate is unusually anxious to take part in participational activity (perhaps for reasons of prestige desires), he may come to be quite involved in the process of restructuring his goal pattern so that it will include some of the formal goals, even though he is not always certain whether or not he is really contributing anything worthwhile. Further, the relationships specified by the conditions are essentially dynamic. Opportunities for participation, reluctantly used at first, ultimately may lead to a change of mind and to their enthusiastic acceptance.[24]

It is apparent that individual differences are highly important in considering the effectiveness of participation as a motivational device; however, the "amount of participation opportunities" made possible by the managers is also a variable quantity. Thus, it is necessary to inquire what the limits to opportunities to participate are in terms of maximum results.

Common-sense experience indicates that when some subordinates are given too many opportunities for participation, or too much leeway in participating, they may tend to flounder; they may find themselves unable to assimilate effectively the range of "thinking opportunities" with which they are faced.[25] On the other hand, if they are given little or no opportunity to take part in the decision-making process, by definition they will not come to be motivated by participational activity. For each

[24] It should be stressed that "life spaces" of individuals (that is, their conceptions of themselves in relation to the totality of a physical and psychological environment) and their readiness for action in the light of these conceptions are never static. Constant change and "restructuring" take place, making for an essentially dynamic patterning of behavior. For alternative definitions of the concept "life space," see Robert W. Leeper, *Lewin's Topological and Vector Psychology* (Eugene, Ore.: University of Oregon Press, 1943), p. 210.

[25] For the belief that "thinking" as a solution for the industrial problem of motivation is usable more effectively on the supervisory level, but is less applicable on the "lower levels" of the organizational hierarchy, see Willard Tomlison, "Review of A. R. Heron, *Why Men Work,*" *Personnel Journal,* July-August, 1948, p. 122.

individual, an amount of participation opportunities lying somewhere between these two extremes will result in a maximum amount of motivation. A hypothesis stemming from this formulation is that for effective operation of participation as a motivational device in a group situation, the members of the group must respond similarly to given amounts of participation, for wide divergences of response may bring forth social tensions and lack of team work within the group.

Of course, many factors act together to motivate an individual. Therefore, the usefulness of the conceptualization advanced depends upon the possibility of breaking down the total of motivational forces into those owing to participation and those owing to other factors. Experimental control methods, matching of cases, and similar devices may have to be utilized to make such an analysis possible. Whether or not the increment of motivation owing to participation is worthwhile depends to an important extent upon the level of intensity of motivation that prevailed previous to introduction of the device of participation. No doubt, there are upper limits to intensity of motivation, and, if motivation has been strong all along, the effect of participation may not be very great.

## EXTRAPARTICIPATIONAL CONDITIONS FOR EFFECTIVE PARTICIPATION

Beyond the factors governing the relationship between participation and possible resultant motivation, certain conditions outside the individual must be considered by the managers in deciding whether or not this particular device is applicable.[26] It would be possible to distinguish a great number of such outside conditions that may determine whether or not the use of participation is feasible in a given situation. Those here indicated are suggestive rather than fully definitive. All are viewed with this question in mind: "Granting that participation may have certain beneficial effects, is it useful in a given instance if the ends of the enterprise are to be achieved?"

To answer this question affirmatively, the following conditions must be met:

### Time Availability

The final decision must not be of a too urgent nature.[27] If it is necessary to arrive at some sort of emergency decision rapidly, it is obvious

---

[26] For analytical purposes, this article differentiates between conditions regarding the dynamics of participation as a psychological process and all conditions outside this psychological participation-to-motivation link. The latter category of conditions is treated under the present heading.

[27] See Chester I. Barnard, *Organization and Management* (Cambridge, Mass.: Harvard University Press, 1948), p. 48.

that even though participation in the decision-making process may have a beneficial effect in some areas, slowness of decision may result in thwarting other goals of the enterprise or may even threaten the existence of the enterprise. Military decisions frequently are of this type.

## Rational Economics

The cost of participation in the decision-making process must not be so high that it will outweigh any positive values directly brought about by it. If it should require outlays which could be used more fruitfully in alternative activities (for example, buying more productive though expensive equipment), then investment in it would be ill-advised.

## Intraplant Strategy

*Subordinate Security.* Giving the subordinates an opportunity to participate in the decision-making process must not bring with it any awareness on their part of unavoidable catastrophic events. For example, a subordinate who is made aware in the participation process that he will lose his job *regardless* of any decisions to which he might contribute may experience a drop in motivation. Furthermore, to make it possible for the subordinate to be willing to participate, he must be given the feeling that no matter what he says or thinks his status or role in the plant setting will not be affected adversely. This point has been made effectively in the available literature.[28]

*Manager-Subordinate Stability.* Giving subordinates an opportunity to participate in the decision-making process must not threaten seriously to undermine the formal authority of the managers of the enterprise. For example, in some cases managers may have good reasons to assume that participation may lead nonmanagers to doubt the competence of the formal leadership, or that serious crises would result were it to develop that the subordinates were right, while the final managerial decision turned out to be in disagreement with them and incorrect.

## Interplant Strategy

Providing opportunities for participation must not open channels of communication to competing enterprises. "Leaks" of information to a competitor from subordinates who have participated in a given decision-making process must be avoided if participation is to be applicable.

## Provision for Communication Channels

For participation to be effective, channels must be provided through which the employee may take part in the decision-making process. These

[28] See McGregor, *op. cit., passim.*

channels must be available continuously, and their use must be convenient and practical.[29]

*Education for Participation*

For participation to be effective, efforts must be made to educate subordinates regarding its function and purpose in the over-all functioning of
the enterprise.[30]

It must be stressed that the conditions stipulated in this section are
dynamic in their own right and may be affected by the very process of
participation as well as by other factors.

## EFFECTS OF PARTICIPATION AS A FUNCTION OF TIME

An area of research that still remains relatively unexplored is that
relating to the variation of the effects of participation with time. Some
experimental studies have examined these effects in terms of increased
productivity over a period of several weeks or months and found no
appreciable reductions in productivity with time; other evidence indicates that in some cases participation may have a sort of "shock" effect,
leading to a surge of interest and increased motivation, with a subsequent decline.[31] Inadequate attention seems to have been given to this
rather crucial question, and we know of no studies that have traced
the effects of participation (or other motivational devices) over periods
as long as a year. However, on a priori grounds, and on the basis of
experiential evidence, it would seem that, after an initial spurt, a
plateau of beneficial effects will be attained, which finally will dissolve
into a decline, unless additional managerial devices are skillfully
employed.

[29] For a rigorous mathematical treatment of channels of communication within
groups, see Alex Bavelas, "A Mathematical Model for Group Structures," *Applied
Anthropology,* vol. 7, no. 3, pp. 16 ff., Summer, 1948.

[30] See John R. P. French, Jr., Arthur Kornhauser, and Alfred Marrow, "Conflict
and Cooperation in Industry," *Journal of Social Issues,* vol. 2, no. 1, February, 1946,
p. 30.

[31] For evidence of no decline in the motivational effect of certain participational
procedures in an industrial retraining situation after a relatively brief time period
subsequent to initiation of participation had elapsed, see, for example, L. Coch and
J. R. P. French, "Overcoming Resistance to Change," *Human Relations,* vol. 1, no.
4, pp. 512–532, 1948. For the hypothesis that under certain conditions decline may
occur with time, see Heron, *op. cit.,* p. 180.

CHAPTER 8

*The Management of Differences**

INTRODUCTION

The manager often experiences his most uncomfortable moments
when he has to deal with differences among people. Because of these
differences, he must often face disagreements, arguments, and even open
conflict. To add to his discomfort, he frequently finds himself torn by
two opposing desires. On the one hand, he wants to unleash the individuality of his subordinates in order to tap their full potential and to
achieve novel and creative approaches to problems. On the other hand,
he is eager to develop a harmonious, smooth-working team to carry out
his organization's objectives. The manager's lot is further troubled by
the fact that when differences occur, strong feelings are frequently
aroused, objectivity flies out of the window, egos are threatened, and
personal relationships are placed in jeopardy.

Because the presence of differences can complicate the manager's job
in so many ways, it is of utmost importance that he understand them
fully and that he learn to handle them effectively. It is the purpose of
this chapter to assist the manager in increasing his understanding of
differences and in improving his approaches to dealing with them, so
that he will be better able to manage effectively.[1]

A large part of what follows will focus, for simplicity of exposition,
on the differences which occur among a manager's individual subordinates. However, we would like to suggest that the principles, concepts,

* This chapter is a slightly modified version of an article under the same title by
Warren H. Schmidt and Robert Tannenbaum, appearing in the *Harvard Business
Review*, vol. 38, no. 6, pp. 107–115, November-December, 1960.
[1] This chapter was originally planned to deal with the problem of conflict. However, as our work progressed, it became clear that conflict is only one way in which
differences express themselves, and that there is real gain to the manager in viewing
differences in the broader, more realistic context which this chapter attempts to
present.

101

methods, and dynamics which we discuss throughout much of the chapter apply to intergroup, interorganizational, and international differences as well.

Our basic thesis is that a manager's ability to deal effectively with differences depends upon the following:[2]

1. His ability to diagnose and understand differences
2. His awareness of, and ability to select appropriately from, a variety of behaviors
3. His awareness of, and ability to deal with, his own feelings—particularly those which might reduce his social sensitivity (diagnostic insight) and his action flexibility (ability to act appropriately)[3]

Underlying our approach to this problem are two basic assumptions:

1. *Differences among people should not be regarded as inherently "good" or "bad."*

Sometimes differences result in important benefits to the organization; sometimes they are disruptive; sometimes they reduce the over-all effectiveness of individuals and organizations.

2. *There is no single "right" way to deal with differences.*

Under varying circumstances, it may be most beneficial to avoid differences, to repress them, to sharpen them into clearly defined conflict, or to utilize them for enriched problem solving. The manager who consistently "pours oil on troubled waters" may not be the most effective manager. Neither is the manager who emphasizes individuality and differences so strongly that cooperation and teamwork are simply afterthoughts. We feel, rather, that the effective manager is the one who is able to use a *variety* of approaches to differences and who chooses any specific approach on the basis of an insightful diagnosis and understanding of the factors with which he is faced at any given time.

## DIAGNOSING AND UNDERSTANDING DIFFERENCES

When a manager's subordinates become involved in a heated disagreement, they tend not to proceed in a systematic manner to resolve their difference. The issues often remain unclear to them, and they talk past each other. If a manager is to be helpful in such a situation, he may consider asking three important diagnostic questions:

---

[2] For insightful treatments of the causes, consequences, and alternative means of dealing with conflict—as well as other expressions of difference—see Lewis A. Coser, *The Function of Social Conflict* (London: Routledge & Kegan Paul, Ltd., 1956), and Raymond W. Mack and Richard C. Snyder, "The Analysis of Social Conflict—Toward an Overview and Synthesis," *Conflict Resolution*, vol. I, no. 2, pp. 212–248, June, 1957.

[3] For definitions and discussions of social sensitivity and action flexibility, see Chaps. 2, 3, and 4.

¶ What is the nature of the difference among the persons?

¶ What factors may underlie this difference?

¶ To what stage has the interpersonal difference evolved when the manager enters the picture?

### What Is the Nature of the Difference?

People may disagree on any one or more of these four kinds of issues: facts, goals, methods, and values.

Sometimes a disagreement occurs because individuals have different definitions of the problem, are aware of different pieces of relevant information, accept or reject different information as factual, or have differing impressions of their respective power and authority. Such differences may be termed *differences over facts*.

Sometimes the disagreement is about what should be accomplished— the desirable objectives of a department, division, section, or specific position within the organization. Such differences are *differences over goals*.

Sometimes individuals differ about the procedures, strategies, or tactics which would most likely achieve a mutually desired goal. These are *differences over methods*.

Disagreements sometimes are over ethics—the way power should be exercised, moral considerations, assumptions about justice, fairness, etc. Such differences—which may affect the choice of either goals or methods —are *differences over values*.

Arguments are prolonged and confusion is increased when the contending parties are not clear on the nature of the issue over which they are in disagreement. By determining where the source of the disagreement lies, the manager will be in a better position to determine how he can utilize and direct the dispute for both the short- and the long-range good of the organization. As will be indicated later in the chapter, there are certain steps which are appropriate when the differences are about facts; other steps are appropriate when differences are over goals; and still others when differences are over methods or values.

Having determined the basic nature of the disagreement, the manager will do well to identify the relevant factors which are influencing the differing parties. This would lead him to the second diagnostic question.

### What Factors May Underlie the Differences over Facts, Goals, Methods, or Values?

When people are faced with a difference, it is not enough that their manager be concerned with what the difference is about (facts, goals, methods, or values). He must also be concerned with *why* the difference exists. In trying to discover useful answers to this *why*, three related questions may be helpful:

¶ Have the disputants had access to the same information?

¶ Do the disputants perceive commonly available information differently?

¶ Is each disputant significantly influenced by his role in the organization?

These questions involve informational, perceptual, and role factors.

*Informational factors* exert their impact when the differing individuals have not been exposed to the same information. Their points of view are developed on the basis of different sets of facts. The ancient parable of the blind men and the elephant dramatizes this point as vividly as any modern illustration. Because each of the men had contact with a different part of the elephant, they disagreed violently about the nature of the animal. In the same way, because two persons receive limited information about a complex problem, they may well disagree as to the nature of that problem when they come together to solve it.

*Perceptual factors* exert their impact when the differing persons have different images of the same stimulus. Each will select from the available information certain items which he deems important. Each will interpret the information in a somewhat different manner. Each brings to the data a different set of life experiences which cause him to view the information through a highly personal kind of filter. The picture which he gets is, therefore, unique to him. Thus, it is not surprising that the same basic facts may produce distinctive perceptual pictures in the minds of different individuals.

*Role factors* exert their impact when each of the differing individuals occupies a certain position and status in society or in the organizational context within which he works. The very fact that he occupies such a position or status may put certain constraints upon him if the discussion is in any way related to his role.

For example, a representative of management may be expected to take a different stand on some issues than a representative of labor. When a manager discusses the problem of production level with a union steward, he may be expected to take a stand favoring higher production. He is aware of this expectation on the part of his superiors. He is aware of many personal and organizational consequences if he "gives in" to the representative of labor. By the same token, the union steward is expected by those whom he represents to support a certain stand which is in opposition to that of management. The individual's freedom to negotiate and to shift his stand in a dispute may, therefore, be limited severely by the role which he occupies.

NATURE OF THE DIFFERENCE

|  | Over facts | Over methods | Over goals | Over values |
|---|---|---|---|---|
| Office-methods expert | "Automation will save the company money." | "The new system should be installed fully and at once." | "We want a system that gives us accurate data rapidly—whenever we want it." | "We must be modern and efficient." |
| Head of accounting department | "The new system will be more expensive to install and operate." | "Let us move slower—one step at a time." | "We need most an accounting system that is flexible to meet our changing needs—managed by accountants who can solve unexpected and complex problems." | "We must consider the welfare of the workers who have served the company so loyally for many years." |

REASONS FOR THE DIFFERENCE

|  | The methods expert takes his position because | The head accountant takes his position because |
|---|---|---|
| Informational (exposure to different information) | He has studied articles about companies (which he considers comparable) describing the savings brought about by automation. Representatives of machine companies have presented him with estimates of savings over a 10-year period. | He has heard about the "hidden costs" in automation. He has priced the kind of equipment he believes will be necessary and has estimated its depreciation. This estimated cost is much higher than the salaries of possible replaced workers. |
| Perceptual (different interpretation of the same data because of differing backgrounds, experience, etc.) | He regards the representatives of the machine company as being alert, businesslike and knowledgeable about the best accounting procedures. He feels that their analysis of company needs is dependable and to be trusted. | He sees the representatives of the machine company as salesmen. Their goal is to sell machines, and their report and analysis must be read with great caution and suspicion. |
| Role (received pressure to take a certain stand because of one's position) | He believes that the company looks to him as the expert responsible for keeping its systems up to date and maximally efficient. | He feels responsible for the morale and security of his team in the accounting office. He must defend their loyalty and efficiency if it is ever doubted. |

To illustrate the concepts we have been discussing, let us take a hypothetical situation in which there is a disagreement over whether a company should introduce automatic record keeping to replace its present manual system. The company's expert on office methods favors immediate introduction of such a system. The head of the accounting department is opposed to it. Some bases of disagreement and the possible reasons for these disagreements are represented in the chart shown on page 105.

In summary, before deciding how to handle a given dispute, the manager will want to ask himself: "To what extent is this dispute (over facts, goals, methods, or values) being sustained because of informational factors, perceptual factors, or role factors?" Both the amount of influence he may exert and the optimal way of exerting that influence will be affected by the accuracy with which he analyzes these factors. To further assess his position and plan his strategy, the manager will want to add the third diagnostic question.

## To What Stage Has the Interpersonal Difference Evolved as I Enter the Picture?

Important conflicts among people do not ordinarily erupt suddenly. They pass through various stages, and the way in which the energy of the disputing parties can be effectively directed by the manager depends to some extent on the stage of the dispute when he enters the picture.

One way of looking at a dispute is to consider the following five stages in its development:

*Stage 1. The Phase of Anticipation.*

EXAMPLE. The manager learns that the company is about to install new automatic equipment which will reduce the number and change the nature of jobs in a given department. He can anticipate that when this information is released, there will be differences of opinion as to the desirability of this change, the way in which it should be introduced, and the way in which the consequences of its introduction should be handled.

*Stage 2. The Phase of Conscious but Unexpressed Difference.*

EXAMPLE. Word leaks out about the proposed new equipment. Small clusters of people who trust one another begin discussing it. They have no definite basis for the information, but tensions begin to build up within the organization. There is a feeling of impending dispute and trouble.

*Stage 3. The Phase of Discussion.*

EXAMPLE. Information is presented about the plans to install new equipment. Questions are asked to secure more information, to inquire about the intentions of management, to test the firmness of the decision which has been made. During the discussion, the differing opinions of individuals begin to emerge openly. They are implied by the questions which are asked and by the language which is used.

*Stage 4. The Phase of Open Dispute.*

EXAMPLE. The union steward meets with the foreman to present arguments for a change in plans. The foreman counters these arguments by presenting the reasons which led management to decide to install the equipment. The differences which have heretofore been expressed only indirectly and tentatively now sharpen into more clearly defined points of view.

*Stage 5. The Phase of Open Conflict.*

EXAMPLE. Individuals have firmly committed themselves to a particular position on the issue. The dispute has become clearly defined; the outcome can only be described in terms of win, lose, or compromise. Each disputant attempts not only to increase the effectiveness of his argument and his power in the situation, but also to seek ways to undermine the influence of those who oppose him.

The power of the manager to intervene successfully in a dispute will differ in each of these stages. He is likely to have the most influence if he enters the picture at stage 1; he is likely to have least influence if he enters at stage 5. The range of behaviors available to him changes as the difference passes through the various stages. For this reason, it is important for the manager to assess not only the nature of the given dispute and the forces affecting the individuals involved, but also the stage to which the dispute has evolved.

## SELECTING AN APPROACH TO DIFFERENCES

After the manager has diagnosed a given dispute (or a potential one) between subordinates, he is next confronted by two additional questions:

1. What actions are available to me?

2. What must I keep in mind in selecting the best course of action from among the available alternatives?

Assuming, first, a situation in which the manager has time to anticipate and plan for an impending dispute, we suggest that there are four general approaches typically available to him: avoidance, repression, sharpening into conflict, and transformation into problem solving. In deciding which approach to use, the manager's primary concern should be in selecting the alternative which will contribute optimum benefits to the organization.

### Differences Can Be Avoided

It is possible for a manager to avoid the occurrence of many differences among his subordinates. He can, for example, staff his organization with people who are in substantial agreement. Some organizations select and promote individuals whose experiences are similar, who have had similar training, and who come from a similar level of society. Because of such common background, these individuals tend to see things similarly, to have common interests and objectives, and to approach problems in much the same way. A staff thus developed tends to be a very secure one, in which the reactions of one's fellows are both readily predictable and congenial to one's own way of thinking about and doing things.

The manager may also avoid differences among his subordinates by controlling certain of their interpersonal contacts. He can, for example, assign two potentially explosive individuals to different groups or physical locations, or he can choose not to raise a particularly divisive issue because it is "too hot to handle."

*When Is This Approach Appropriate?* Some organizations depend heavily on certain kinds of conformity and agreement among their employees in order to get the task performed. Political parties and religious denominational groups are perhaps an extreme example of this. If an individual holds a different point of view on a rather fundamental issue, he may become a destructive force within the organization. This approach of avoiding the occurrence of differences may also be important if one is dealing with somewhat fragile and insecure individuals. Some persons are so threatened by conflict that their ability to function effectively suffers when they operate in a climate of differences. Such persons work most effectively when they feel safe and secure in an atmosphere of agreement and conformity.

*Difficulties and Dangers in This Approach.* The manager who uses this approach consistently runs the risk of reducing the total creativity of his staff. Someone has said that "when everyone in the room thinks the same thing, no one is thinking very much." In an atmosphere where differences are avoided, not only do new ideas appear less frequently, but old ideas are likely to go unexamined and untested. There is genuine danger of the organization slipping unknowingly into a rut of "organization-man" complacency.

### Differences Can Be Repressed

Sometimes a manager is aware that certain differences exist among members of his staff, but he feels that the open expression of these differences would create unproductive dissension and reduce the total creativity and productivity of the group. He may, therefore, decide to keep these differences under cover. He may do this by continually emphasizing loyalty, cooperation, teamwork, and other similar values within the group. In such a climate of "positive thinking" and "sweetness and light," it is none too likely that subordinates will express disagreements and risk conflict. The manager may also try to make sure that the potentially conflicting parties come together only under circumstances which are highly controlled—circumstances in which open discussion of latent differences is clearly inappropriate. Or he may develop an atmosphere of repression by consistently rewarding agreement and cooperation and by punishing (in one way or another) those who disrupt the harmony of the organization by expressing nonconformist ideas.

*When Is This Approach Appropriate?* It is most useful when the latent differences are not relevant to the organization's task. It is to be expected that individuals will differ on many things—religion, politics, their loyalty to cities or states, baseball teams, etc. There may be no need to reach agreement on some of these differences in order to work together effectively on the job. It may also be appropriate to repress conflict when adequate time will not be available to resolve the potential differences among the individuals involved. This would be particularly true if the manager's concern is to achieve a short-run objective and the potential disagreement is over a long-run issue. The wounds of disagreement should not be opened up if there is insufficient time to bind them.

*Difficulties and Dangers in This Approach.* Repression almost always costs something. If the differences are indeed important to the persons involved, their feelings may come to be expressed indirectly, in ways that could reduce productivity. Every manager has witnessed situations in which ideas are resisted, not on the basis of their merit, but on the basis of who advocated the ideas; or he has seen strong criticism occurring over mistakes made by a particularly disliked individual.

Much has been said and written about "hidden agenda." People may discuss one subject, but the way they discuss it and the positions they take with respect to it may actually be determined by factors lying beneath the surface of the discussion. Hidden agenda are likely to abound in an atmosphere of repression.

When strong feelings are attached to unexpressed differences, the blocking of these feelings creates frustration and hostility which may be misdirected toward "safe" targets. Differences and the feelings generated by them do not ordinarily disappear by being ignored. They fester beneath the surface and emerge at inopportune moments to create problems for the manager and his organization.

## Differences Can Be Sharpened into Conflict

When this approach is used, the manager not only recognizes the fact that differences exist, but attempts to create an arena in which the conflicting parties can "fight it out." Like the promoter of an athletic contest, however, he will want to be sure that the differing persons understand the issue over which they differ, the rules and procedures by which they can discuss their differences, and the kinds of roles and responsibilities which each is expected to bear in mind during the struggle.

*When Is This Approach Appropriate?* A simple answer is when it is clarifying and educative. An individual may be forced to clarify his thinking and to mobilize his evidence when strongly challenged. Many an individual will not pause to examine the assumptions he holds or the positions he advocates until he is called upon to clarify and support them by someone who holds contrary views. In the same way, the power realities within an organization can come into sharper focus and be more commonly recognized through conflict.

For example, the manager of production and the manager of engineering may develop quite different impressions of how the board of directors feels about the relative importance of their respective units. Each is sure that the board is most impressed with the caliber of the staff, output, and operational efficiency of his department. When a dispute arises over which group is to get priority space in a new building, the top management may permit both departments to exert all the influence they can on the board. During the struggle, the two managers may gain a more realistic assessment of, and respect for, the power of the other.

Another thing which individuals learn during the course of a conflict is the cost of conflict itself. Almost invariably at the end of a long dispute, there is a strong resolve that "this shall not happen again," as the individuals involved reflect on the financial costs, tensions, embarrassments, uneasiness, and wasted time and energy it caused.

*Difficulties and Dangers in This Approach.* Conflict can be very costly. It not only saps the energy of those involved in the conflict, but it may irreparably destroy their future effectiveness. In the heat of conflict, words are sometimes spoken which leave lifelong scars on people or forever cloud their relationship.

Because the risks involved in conflict are so great and the potential costs so high, the manager will want to consider carefully the following questions before he uses this approach:

1. What do I hope to accomplish?
2. What are the possible outcomes of conflict?
3. What steps should be taken to keep the conflict within organizational bounds and in perspective?
4. What can be done after the conflict to strengthen the bonds between the potential conflicting parties, so that the conflict will be of minimum destructiveness to them and to their ongoing relationship?

*Differences Can Be Utilized in Problem Solving*

"Two heads are better than one" because the two heads often represent a richer set of experiences and because they can bring to bear on the problem a greater variety of insights. If the differences are seen as enriching rather than in opposition to each other, the "two heads" will indeed be likely to come up with a better solution than either would have arrived at alone. For example, had the six blind men who came into contact with different parts of the same elephant pooled their information, they would have come up with a more accurate description of the animal than any single one could give on the basis of his limited experience. In the same way, many problems can be seen clearly, wholly, and in perspective only if the individuals who see different aspects can come together and pool their information.

When it comes to searching for alternate courses of action to deal with a given problem, the differences among the individuals in an organization can help to increase the range and variety of alternatives suggested.

The channeling of differences into a problem-solving context may also help to deal with some of the feelings which often accompany disagreement—frustration, resentment, and hostility. By providing an open and accepting approach, the manager helps to prevent the development of undercurrents of feelings which could break out at inopportune moments. He also helps to channel the energy which feelings generate into creative rather than destructive activities. Whereas conflict tends to cause individuals to seek ways of weakening and undermining those who differ with them, the problem-solving approach leads individuals to welcome differences as being potentially enriching to one's own goals, ideas, and methods.

*Difficulties and Dangers in This Approach.* To utilize differences requires time. Often it is easier for a single individual (rather than two or more persons) to make a decision. Also, when a rapid decision is required, it may be easier and more practical to ignore one side of an argument in order to move into action. Finally, unless a problem-solving situation is planned with some care, there is always the risk of generating conflict which will be frustrating to all parties concerned.

### TRANSFORMING CONFLICT INTO ENRICHED
### PROBLEM SOLVING

Assuming now that the manager enters the picture when his sub-ordinates are already involved in conflict, what are the things he can do if he wishes to transform this conflict into a problem-solving situation?

*He can welcome the existence of differences within the organization.* The manager can indicate that from the discussion of differences can come a greater variety of solutions to problems and a more adequate testing of proposed methods. By making clear his view that all parties are making contributions to the solution of problems by sharing their differences, he reduces the implication that there will be an ultimate "winner" and "loser."

*He can listen with understanding rather than evaluation.* There is abundant evidence that conflicts tend to be prolonged and to become increasingly frustrating because the conflicting parties do not really listen to one another. Each attempts to impose his own views on the other and to "tune out" or distort what the other person has to say.

The manager may expect that, when he enters the picture, the individuals will try to persuade him to take a stand on the issue involved. While each adversary is presenting his "case" to the manager, he will be watching for cues which indicate where the manager stands on the issue. It is therefore important that the manager make every effort to understand both positions as fully as possible, recognizing and supporting the seriousness of purpose of each where appropriate, and withholding judgment until all available facts are in.

In the process of listening for understanding, the manager will also set a good example for the conflicting parties. By adopting such a listening-understanding attitude himself, and by helping the disputants to understand each other more fully, he can make a most useful contribution to transforming potential conflict into creative problem solving.

*He can clarify the nature of the conflict.* In the heat of an argument, each participant may primarily focus on specific facts, methods, goals, or values. Frustration and anger can occur because one individual may be talking about facts, while another is eager to discuss methods. The manager, having carefully listened to the discussion, can clarify the nature of the issues so that the discussion can become more productive.

*He can recognize and accept the feelings of the individuals involved.* Irrational feelings are generated in the midst of a controversy, even though the participants do not always recognize this fact. Each wants to believe that he is examining the problem objectively. The manager, recognizing and accepting feelings such as fear, jealousy, anger, or anxiety, may make it possible for the participants to face more squarely what truly motivates them. The manager does not take a critical attitude toward the existence of these feelings by in effect saying, "You have no right to feel angry!" Rather, he tries sincerely to communicate that "I think I can understand how you feel."

We do not ordinarily help people by aiding them in repressing their real feelings or by criticizing them for experiencing fear, anger, etc. Such criticism—whether implied or expressed openly—may block the search for new ways out of the controversy. There is considerable evidence that, when a person feels threatened or under attack, he tends to become more rigid and therefore more defensive of positions to which he has committed himself.

*He can clarify who will make the decision being discussed.* Sometimes heated disputes go on with respect to issues over which one or more of the persons involved have no control. When people have differing notions about the formal authority available to each with respect to the matter at issue, a clarification by the manager of the authority relationships can go far toward placing the discussion in clearer perspective.

*He can suggest procedures and ground rules for resolving the differences.*

*If the disagreement is over facts,* the manager may assist the disputants in validating existing data and in seeking additional data which will more clearly illuminate the issues under dispute.

*If the disagreement is over methods,* the manager may first want to help the parties see that they have common objectives in mind; that their disagreement is over means rather than ends. He may suggest that before examining in detail each of their proposed methods for achieving the goals, they might together establish a set of criteria to be used to evaluate whatever procedures are proposed. He may also want to suggest that some time be spent trying to generate additional alternatives reflecting new approaches. After these alternatives have been developed, he may encourage the parties to evaluate them with the aid of the criteria which these persons have developed together.

*If the difference is over goals or goal priorities,* he may suggest that time be taken by the parties for the purpose of describing as clearly as possible the conflicting goals which are being sought. Sometimes arguments persist simply because the parties have not taken the trouble to clarify for themselves and for each other exactly what they do desire. Once these goals are clearly stated, the issues involving them can be dealt with more realistically.

*If the difference is over values,* the manager may suggest that these values be described in operational terms. Discussions over abstractions often tend to be fruitless because the same words and concepts mean different things to different people. To help the individuals become more fully aware of the limitations to which their actions are subject, the manager can ask the question: "What do you think you can do about this situation?" This usually leads to a more productive discussion than the question: "What do you believe in?" Because value systems are so closely related to a person's self concept, the manager may want to give particular attention to protecting the egos involved. He may make clear that an individual's entire ethical system is not being scrutinized, but only those values which are pertinent to a particular instance.

*He can give primary attention to maintaining the relationships between the disputing parties.* Sometimes during the course of a heated dispute, so much attention is paid to the issue under discussion that nothing is done to maintain and strengthen the relationship between the disputing parties. It is not surprising therefore that disputes tend to disrupt ongoing relationships. Through oversight or deliberate action, important functions are neglected which sustain or further build human relationships—for example, the functions of encouraging, supporting, reducing tension, and expressing common feelings. If a conflict is to be transformed into a problem-solving situation, these functions need to be performed by someone—either by the manager or, through his continuing encouragement, by the parties themselves.

*He can create appropriate vehicles for communication among the disputing parties.* One of the ways to bring differences into a problem-solving context is to ensure that it is easy for the persons who hold differing views to come together. If they can discuss their differences *before* they become committed to crystallized positions, the chances of their learning from each other and arriving at mutually agreeable positions are increased. Having easy access to one another is also a way of reducing the likelihood that each will develop unreal stereotypes of the other.

Misunderstanding mounts as communication becomes more difficult. One of the values of regular staff meetings, therefore, is that such meetings, when properly conducted, can provide a continuing opportunity for persons to exchange ideas and feelings. When frequent opportunities for communication exist, it is unlikely that people will be faced suddenly with interpersonal problems of crisis proportions.

If the manager wishes his subordinates to deal with their differences in a problem-solving framework, he will want to ask himself: "In what kind of setting will the parties to this dispute be best able to discuss their differences with a minimum of interference and threat?" He will exclude from such a setting any individuals whose presence will embarrass the disputants if the latter "back down" from previously held points of view. It will be a setting which reflects as much informality and psychological comfort as possible.

It might be emphasized again that one of the most helpful factors is a listening-learning attitude on the part of the people involved. Here the manager's own behavior can set an example. If he is one who listens easily and seems to enjoy learning from the people around him, he will help to generate a climate in which many differences can be reduced in intensity and in which significant disagreements can be understood better and dealt with more objectively.

*He can suggest procedures which facilitate problem solving.* One of the key needs in a dispute is to separate an idea from the person who first proposed it. This increases the chance to examine the idea critically and objectively without at the same time implying criticism of the person. Techniques like brainstorming, for example, are designed to free people from the necessity to defend their ideas during an exploration period. Another facilitating action involves the outlining of an orderly set of procedures (e.g., examining objectives, obtaining relevant data) for the disputants to follow as they seek a constructive resolution of their difference.

RECOGNIZING AND DEALING WITH ONE'S OWN FEELINGS

Thus far we have tended to make the unrealistic assumption that somehow the manager has been able to maintain his own objectivity in the face of a difference among his subordinates. Obviously, this does not easily happen, because the manager's feelings also tend to become involved. It is, in fact, not unusual for people to react to differences more from the basis of their own feelings than from the basis of some rational approach to the problem at hand.

A manager may be deeply concerned about the disruptive effects of a disagreement. He may be troubled about how the persistence of a dispute will affect him personally or his position in the organization. He may worry about the danger of coming under personal attack, or of incurring the anger and hostility of important subordinates or a superior. He may become anxious as another expresses deep feelings, without really understanding why.

Sometimes personal feelings of this kind are at the conscious level; frequently they are unrecognized by the manager himself because they lie in the area of the unconscious. This, then, highlights the importance of the manager's own self-awareness—a point which has been made before in this book.[4] While we do not intend to deal at any length with this important topic here, it might be well to note some "alerting signals" to which the manager might pay attention when he confronts a difference.

[4] See particularly Chaps. 2 and 4—and later, Chaps. 9 and 10.

The following kinds of behavior may indicate that the manager's handling of differences is strongly influenced by his personal needs and feelings rather than by objective interests of the organization:

1. A persistent tendency to surround himself with "yes men"

2. Emphasizing loyalty and cooperation in a way that makes disagreement seem equivalent to disloyalty and rebellion

3. A persistent tendency to "pour oil on troubled waters" whenever differences arise

4. Glossing over serious differences in order to maintain an appearance of harmony and teamwork

5. Accepting ambiguous resolutions of differences which permit conflicting parties to arrive at dissimilar interpretations

6. Exploiting differences to strengthen his personal position of influence through the weakening of the position of others

Any of these behaviors could, as we have already suggested, be appropriate in certain situations and actually serve the general interest of the organization. If, however, they represent rather consistent patterns on the part of the manager, it may be worth his while to examine more closely the reasons for his actions.

There are times in the lives of most of us when our personal needs are the strongest determinants of our behavior. Fortunately, most organizations can tolerate a limited amount of such self-oriented behavior on the part of their managers. The danger occurs when an individual believes that his actions are solely motivated by the "good of the organization," when, in fact, he is operating on the basis of other kinds of personal motivation without being aware of it.

The summary of this section might well be the old phrase "know thyself." The manager who is more fully alert to his own feelings and inclinations is in a better position to diagnose a situation accurately and to choose more rationally the kind of behavior which is in the best interests of the organization.

## DEALING WITH DIFFERENCES AT OTHER LEVELS

Although our major emphasis has been on diagnosing and dealing with differences occurring among individuals, the same ideas might well be applied, as we suggested earlier, to differences which occur among other entities—among groups, organizations, nations, and cultures.

By way of example, let us apply these categories and principles to the arguments which tend to occur in many labor disputes. In a labor dispute, there is essentially a difference between two organizations—one called a union and another, represented by managers, the company. In such a situation, any or all of the following may occur:

*Differences over Facts.* The union and the company may disagree as to the size of the profits made by the company in the previous year. They may have different figures to quote as to the financial soundness and stability of the company. Their charts relating previous wage raises to inflation might have a different base. Management may cite statistics which clearly "prove" that a previous wage increase contributed significantly to higher prices. The union has other figures which "prove" just as conclusively that any increase in price was due to an increase in profits. The possible threat of competition from foreign products and countless other factors may become centers of dispute.

*Differences over Methods.* Both company and union may agree on the desirable goal of employing a steady, responsible, productive work force. However, they may disagree as to the best way to achieve this goal. The union may argue that productive labor is more likely to come from well-paid, satisfied workers, while the company may argue that stricter discipline and the restoration of "management's right to manage" may be needed in order to secure productive work.

*Differences over Goals.* Which should take priority—a company which is strong financially and more competitive or a company which has a reputation for being considered fair in its dealings with its work force? The company and the union may agree that both of these goals are desirable, but which is to assume greater importance?

*Differences over Values.* Frequently these differences are oversimplified in terms of "property rights" versus "human rights." Implicit in many disputes between managements and unions is a question of whether the investor or the worker is entitled to a greater reward for his contribution to the total product. In some cases this dispute may involve the extent to which an employer has the right to control the lives of those whom he employs.

Behind these differences often lie the three reasons that have been dealt with earlier in this chapter. The union members, as a group, may have been exposed to different information than the representatives of management. Union newspapers frequently carry information which is quite at variance with information carried in company papers. As a result, the judgments of the two groups on the issues and concerning the rightness and wrongness of the varying positions are rooted in substantially different bases of fact.

Even the interpretation of a single fact which is recognized by both groups may vary between them. For example, the increased production rate of the workers during a given period of time may indicate to the union that the worker is contributing more toward the company's profits, while the company may attribute this increase to the costly and efficient machinery which has been placed at the workers' disposal. From the company's point of view, therefore, the fruits of the increased production should logically go to those who paid for the new equipment, whereas the union would feel that wages or other benefits for the worker should be increased.

Role differences also play a part when two groups such as a union and a company are in disagreement. Union members tend to develop an image of the company which emphasizes an obsession with profits and a determination to use workers as cheaply as possible. Managers sometimes are seen, not as unique human beings, but as symbols of authority and the power of money. The union may see itself as representing average, decent, hard-working people who have generally had to fight for every bit of recognition which they have succeeded in wresting from the unconcerned rich. This sense of being identified with the democratic forces and "the little man" in society lends great emotional support to the positions taken by union leaders and helps to crystallize these positions. On the other hand, the management team as a group may regard itself as representing honest, responsible, efficient, and civilized behavior in a free society. It may see the union as selfish, immature, and irresponsible—interested only in less management control and more money and unwilling to contribute its fair share to the total company effort. As a result, the management team sees itself highly justified in using all the authority and power at its disposal to press the work group to fulfill its legitimate responsibilities and to prevent the workers from using their group power to secure unwarranted benefits. Thus, the public behavior of managers and of union leaders is often determined by the necessity to be consistent with the expectations of others—expectations rooted in role definitions of the types just described.

Many of the approaches to differences presented earlier in this chapter are also useful (with some appropriate adaptation) in dealing with intergroup, international, or intercultural disputes. The insightful and skillful labor arbitrator, international diplomat and race relations consultant —as well as the artful organizational manager—reflect much in common as they proceed to manage differences in their respective areas of *expertise*.

This chapter began with the assumption that many managers are uncertain and uneasy when differences arise. Because their own emotions and the feelings of others become quickly involved, they often deal with differences in a haphazard or inappropriate manner. We have attempted to suggest some more systematic ways to view differences and deal with them. We believe that if a manager can approach a difference with less fear and with greater awareness of the potential richness which lies in disagreement, he will better understand the basic nature and causes of the difference. Having done this, he will be in a better position to discover and implement more realistic alternatives for dealing with it.

# PART TWO

# Sensitivity Training: A Personal Approach
# to the Development of Leaders

Effective leadership requires people who can correctly assess the personal and situational variables with which they are confronted and who have the behavioral repertory necessary to act appropriately and efficiently in their efforts to influence others.

There is no doubt that people vary in their social sensitivity and their behavioral flexibility. Some perceive and accurately assess the relevant facts which make sound judgments possible, while others see not, hear not, and feel not; some can change their personal behaviors to meet the needs of circumstances as they arise, while others are rigidly fixed in the kinds of responses they make under varying conditions.

*Sensitivity training* is the designation we have used since 1954 for one approach for facilitating the development of human relations understanding and skills. It aims, first, to increase a person's sensitivity to and knowledge about personal and interpersonal factors and their influence on thought and action and, second, to help him in his efforts to behave more effectively in different and changing interpersonal relationships.

Our experience with sensitivity training tends to confirm the old maxim that "knowledge makes men free." As participants appear to gain in understanding of themselves, others, and social pressures to conform, they tend to become more aware of their own individual strengths, to distinguish between real and imaginary pressures, and increasingly to speak and act as free, strong, and considerate individuals. To the extent that they attain these growth objectives, we believe, they are able to function more creatively, productively, and comfortably as individuals and in group situations.

119

The core of the sensitivity training experience is provided in small group meetings, where a high level of individual participation and involvement becomes possible. Related general sessions, theory presentations, film forums, and the like give additional meaning to the small-group discussions. All are intended to establish free and open communication as a basis for productive learning.

The ethical values of sensitivity training can be inferred from the following underlying assumptions upon which it is based: first, the essential direction and resources for personal improvement lie within the trainees themselves; second, the function of the trainer is primarily to help create the conditions under which most effective growth and development can take place; third, no attempt is made to tell the participants whether to change or how to change. They are helped to see themselves more objectively; then if they are dissatisfied with certain aspects of their attitudes or behaviors, the decision to change and the direction of change are matters for their own choice.

Sensitivity training appears to provide a participant with opportunities to learn more about himself and his impact on others, to understand his own feelings and how they affect his behavior toward others, to become more sensitive to the ways people communicate with each other, to learn "active listening"—for meanings and for feelings, to learn how people affect groups and how groups affect people, to behave more realistically in face-to-face situations with another and in groups, and to learn how to help groups function more effectively.

In recent years, sensitivity training has been conducted with a wide variety of groups. Business, industry, government, education, and community organizations have participated in a great many programs, all of which shared the same over-all objective of making the participants more effective in their interpersonal relations. Perhaps the most interesting development of late has been the recognition that members of the professions—doctors, dentists, lawyers, architects, ministers, and others engaged primarily in the client type of counseling relationships—can profit from the applied insights of the behavioral sciences. Programs directed particularly at the professions emphasize the important notion that all deal first and foremost with people whose problems are, after all, genuinely human.

The part of the book which deals with sensitivity training and its applications is divided into six chapters. Some of the chapters that follow (in contrast with most of those in Parts 1 and 3) are based on articles that have been rather drastically edited and rearranged from the way in which they were initially published. This has been done in order to integrate the presentation of sensitivity training into a more unified and meaningful whole, and to avoid the unnecessary overlap and duplication which would have resulted from use of the original articles.

An introduction to sensitivity training is provided in Chapter 9, where goals, the manner of training, the role of the trainer, and expressions of resistance are discussed. Chapter 10 is designed to provide glimpses of a sensitivity training group in action. It tries to describe in broad and selective etchings the reactions of the trainer, of his group members, and of a clinical observer as they committed themselves to the stream of a single training group experience. Communication difficulties and their resolution are highlighted. We are grateful to be able to base this chapter on a skilled adaptation by Prof. Paul Pigors, of the Massachusetts Institute of Technology, and by Mrs. Faith Pigors, of our original, more lengthy monograph *Inside a Sensitivity Training Group*.

Using the device of a fictional story, Chapter 11 deals with the introduction by a management consultant of a vertically structured sensitivity training program for the executive team of an industrial manufacturing concern. In Chapter 12, the special difficulties inherent in the trainer role and their relation to the trainer's personality are covered by means of a case study which is here presented for the first time in published form. Chapter 13, also an original contribution, traces in empirical fashion the systematic stages of group development which were characteristic of at least three groups under investigation and which suggest similar patterns for other groups engaged in related training activities. Finally, Chapter 14 concerns the problems inherent in the evaluation of human relations training in general and sensitivity training in particular. The setting of objectives, the nature of the training process, and the variables entering into the evaluation process are covered in detail. The chapter closes with a brief description of current evaluation research and makes recommendations for further studies.

CHAPTER 9

# Looking at Ourselves: A New Focus
# in Management Training\*

It happened at the fifth meeting. For four weeks, thirty executives had been coming to the campus of the university to attend a workshop in supervision. At each meeting they had sought to clarify their aims, and they had continually tried to get the "professors" to lay down a set of rules. "You're the experts here," they said, "you tell us what we can do to become more effective!"

At the fifth meeting, the group's feeling about its own progress became the initial focus of discussion. The "talkers" participated as usual, conversation shifting rapidly from one point to another. Dissatisfaction was mounting, expressed through loud, snide remarks by some and through apathy by others.

George Franklin appeared particularly disturbed. Finally, pounding the table, he exclaimed, "I don't know what is going on here! I should be paid for listening to this drivel. I'm getting just a bit sick of wasting my time around here. If the 'profs' don't put out—I quit!" George was pleased. He was angry, and he had said so. As he sat back in his chair, he felt he had the group behind him. He felt he'd had the guts to say what most of the others were thinking! Some members of the group applauded loudly, but others showed obvious disapproval. They wondered why George was excited over so insignificant an issue; why he hadn't done something constructive rather than just sounding off, as usual. Why, they wondered, did he say their comments were "drivel"?

\* This chapter is based on the following publications: "A New Focus in Executive Training," by Irving R. Weschler, Marvin A. Klemes, and Clovis Shepherd, *Advanced Management*, vol. 20, no. 5, pp. 17–22, May, 1955; "Training Managers for Leadership," by Robert Tannenbaum, Verne Kallejian, and Irving R. Weschler, *Personnel*, vol. 30, no. 4, pp. 254–260, January, 1954; and "Yardsticks for Human Relations Training," by Irving R. Weschler, Robert Tannenbaum, and John H. Zenger, *Adult Education*, vol. 7, no. 3, pp. 152–168, Spring, 1957 (the latter reprinted with bibliography as Adult Education Monograph no. 2, Adult Education Association, 1957).

George Franklin became the focus of discussion. "What do you mean, George, by saying this is nonsense?" "What do you expect—a neat set of rules to meet all of your problems?" George was getting uncomfortable. These were questions difficult for him to answer. Gradually, he began to realize that a large part of the group disagreed with him; then he began to wonder why. He was learning something about people he hadn't known before. New questions were raised—some relating to the job. "How does it feel, George, to have people disagree with you when you thought you had them behind you?" "Is it important for you to know who is really with you and who isn't?" "How does this apply to the plant?" "What can we do to find out how our employees really feel about us?"

Bob White was first annoyed with George and now with the discussion. He was getting tense, a bit shaky perhaps. Bob didn't like anybody to get a raw deal—and he felt that George was getting it. At first, Bob tried to minimize George's outburst, and then he suggested that the group get on to the real issues; but the group continued to focus on George. Finally, Bob said, "Why don't you leave George alone and stop picking on him? We're not getting anywhere this way."

With the help of the leaders, the group focused on Bob. "What do you mean, 'picking' on him?" "Why, Bob, have you tried to change the discussion?" "Why are you so protective of George?" Bob began to realize that the group *wanted* to focus on George; he also saw that George didn't think that he was being picked on, but felt that he was learning something about himself and about how others reacted to him. "Why do I always get upset," Bob began to wonder, "when people start to look at each other? Why do I feel sort of sick when people get angry at each other? Why don't my people ever talk back to me—do I let them get it off their chests, or do I cut them off?" Now Bob was learning something about how people saw him, while gaining some insight into his own behavior. Not much yet, but just enough to work on—perhaps. Some other time he would feel free to explore this a bit further.

## THE GOALS OF SENSITIVITY TRAINING

Sensitivity training is an approach to human relations training which is aimed at getting people to *feel* and *behave* differently—and not merely to *think* differently—with reference to the day-to-day handling of human problems.

Many people can talk the "human relations language," but fewer are able to practice what they preach. They would be surprised to discover that they don't truly hear as well as they think they do; that they don't really listen; that they interrupt; that they are aggressive and arrogant in imposing their ideas on others; that they are insensitive; that they don't understand what other people think and feel.

Countless examples could be given to illustrate how people fail to see themselves and others realistically; how they fail to understand their own feelings and prejudices; and how they prove to be insensitive to the ways people relate to each other. Seeing ourselves as others see us is not easy, as Robert Burns lamented so long ago.

Sensitivity training is based on the following premises:

1. Much work is done through personal contacts with others, either as individuals or as members of groups.

2. Effectiveness in dealing with others is often handicapped by lack of specific kinds of interpersonal *understanding* and *skills*.

3. People who have such understanding and skills seem more effective in their interpersonal relations.

4. There is evidence that people can learn to improve their interpersonal understanding and skills.

The kind of understanding that is important here is called "social sensitivity" (or "empathy"), the ability accurately to sense what others think and feel. This does not mean "putting yourself in their shoes" and projecting how you would feel, but rather understanding how others think and feel from *their* own point of view.

Dealing with people requires more than *just* understanding. We must also have "behavioral flexibility" (or, synonymously, "action flexibility"), the ability to behave appropriately, in light of our understanding (see Chapters 2 and 5). This requires us to select from our repertory of alternative behaviors those which are most appropriate in any given instance as indicated by our understanding.

Broadly speaking, sensitivity training aims to develop both social sensitivity and behavioral flexibility. This means that this training method seeks to produce both attitudinal and behavioral changes. These changes are not to be made in a specific direction pointed out by the trainer; instead, each trainee is encouraged to get a better look at himself and to experiment with new, perhaps personally more appropriate behaviors.

In the process of developing social sensitivity and behavioral flexibility, a number of more specific goals must be considered.

## Greater Self-understanding

Deficiencies in social sensitivity and behavioral flexibility are often related to unresolved personality conflicts within us. The existence of these internal conflicts often blurs our understanding of others and impedes our effectiveness in behaving appropriately. As we probe beneath the surface of our personality makeup, we may succeed in eliminating some of these conflicts. We may come to make allowances for the unique mode of functioning of our personalities. Thus, we may prepare the way for greater social sensitivity and behavioral flexibility.

Therefore, the starting point of sensitivity training is to help the trainee gain better insight into himself.

People are often unaware of their impact on working associates, friends, or even family. The training situation enables trainees to receive "feedback" on their behavior—the kinds of information about self rarely obtainable in other settings.

At an early meeting in a recent workshop, one executive got up and announced heatedly, "We are getting nowhere! I move we appoint a committee to set up an agenda and report back its recommendations. Maybe this way we'll get something done! Are there any objections?" No one said anything. "All right, then, who would like to be part of this committee?" There were four volunteers, and five left the room.

It soon became apparent that most of those who had remained in the room were very annoyed with the "committee." When asked why they had made no objections, they said there was no point in "getting killed by a steam roller."

Upon their return, the secessionists prepared to make their report, obviously confident that everyone was eagerly waiting for what they would have to say. When the trainer asked for a show of hands, they were stunned to discover that no one was the least bit interested.

The rest of the session was spent in helping the five see what had happened. Much was said about authoritarian attitudes, "talking down," lack of respect for the integrity of the group, and aggressive, irritating mannerisms. A rude shock was followed by a slow awakening.

One aspect of understanding ourselves is learning to recognize defenses we use to ward off real or imagined threats to our personal security. For instance, many people find that they are unable to accept criticism. At the first hint of a remark critical of their statements or actions, they start justifying them. Often the justification reverts back to the one who did the criticizing. "He's just jealous." "He never has liked me." Often, the person criticized does not stop talking long enough to "hear" the criticism; or if he does, he seldom gives it the thought needed to evaluate its worth. During the later stages of the training process, the trainees become quite adept at recognizing these blind spots in themselves. And in finding ways to compensate for them, they discover that they can function more effectively.

"After our last meeting," Rick reported to the group, "I had a helluva time falling asleep. I just couldn't help thinking about what we had been talking about. You know—it really hit me! I think I am beginning to see why I get so mad at Chuck every time he says something, and want to hurry him along. I guess I too have had trouble coming to the point!"

"It's funny you should mention this, Rick," another member continued. "I find Chuck's slow delivery real stimulating. My greatest trouble is in understanding Bill. He always sits there grinning like a Cheshire cat. I get the impression he is laughing at us, and it makes me feel damned uncomfortable."

Bill was startled. He was concerned that someone could so misinterpret his actions, as he saw them. He had no intention of belittling anyone, and yet he wondered, "What's the matter with Fred? How come he gets all bothered by my smile? Isn't he the one who is always trying so hard to be funny?"

## Understanding Others

Until we understand ourselves, it is not fully possible to reach the second goal—that of *understanding others*.

Focusing on "the other" is not new. For centuries, numerous attempts have been made to develop ways of understanding people. The phrenologists thought that they could discern character by outward bumps on a man's head. Physiognomy taught that a man's face was the reflection of his inner character. How many of us recognize the "honest face," the "shifty eyes," or the "evil look"? The astrologers thought that man's characteristics could be discovered by studying the orbits of the heavenly bodies. Somatotypists attempt to link body shapes to personality characteristics: fat people, some say, are jolly, outgoing; thin people are reserved, introverts.

The inaccuracy of most of these systems is now well known. Getting at the inner man is too complicated a process. Progress will probably come not merely from studying physical characteristics or other external forces, but from giving people the opportunity to expose their thoughts, feelings, and actions to the scrutiny of their fellow men.

In many ways, this is what sensitivity training attempts to do. A climate is created in which people are able to observe, study, and react to each other. As the participants check the accuracy of their perceptions as to what other people are like, they tend to discover those stereotypes which, if strong, may drastically color their perceptions. They learn to recognize individual differences, to accept them for what they are, and to understand better how their own needs and desires distort their views of the world around them.

In order to relate to each other, people seem to have a need to pigeonhole each other into typologies that help them make sense of the social vacuum in which they find themselves. First impressions are usually based almost entirely on these mental short cuts which form the foundation for the existence of stereotypes—those beliefs which ascribe to an individual the seeming personality characteristics of a larger group, nationality, or race.

A recent training group spent an unusual amount of time sorting out the prejudices of its members, thereby permitting corrections to be made for frequently wrong perceptions. We talked about "big people" and "little people"; the "strong" and the "weak"; "loudmouthed New Yorkers" and "big-shot Texans"; "spoiled children"; "smart kids" and "old wise men"; "bullies" and "cowards"; "chatterboxes" and "living organisms who don't even chatter"; "attractive girls" and "dogs"; "frat rats" and "bookworms"; those who "are sharp" and those who "haven't got it"; "papal representatives" and "pushy Jews"; "in-groups," "out-groups," and "those who are so far out they are in"; the "Corvette crowd" and the "Vespa hot rods"; "soloists" and "choristers"; "pillars of strength" and "crumbling stones"; "leaders" and "followers"; "gods" and "sinners."

Countless specific incidents could be cited to illustrate the unfolding of stereotypes in action. For example, in one group, both Chuck, a rather good-looking boy of Scotch descent, and Jake, a fairly insecure stocky Jewish immigrant, were habitually late for meetings. Chuck's entrance was mostly ignored, while Jake's caused considerable annoyance. When the difference in reactions was examined, someone mused loud enough for everyone to hear: "Would we feel the same way about what Jake is doing if he were blond and blue-eyed?" The answer to many in the group was obvious—and so was its irrational component!

### Insight into Group Process

The participants are helped to become more aware of group process: those forces unique to a group which ultimately may result in its success or failure. As they develop their sensitivities, they tend to recognize functional and blocking member roles; they become aware of, and learn to deal with, "hidden agenda," those personal or situational pressures which simmer underneath a surface of good manners and friendly interchange. They become acquainted with the procedural skills which allow a group to get its work done in the most expeditious manner.

Many people are unaware of what "really" goes on in group meetings. Side remarks, facial expressions, apathy, dominance, formation of cliques, active blocking, barbs of hostility, acts of snobbery—all these, plus many more, constitute important cues to the diagnostician of *group process*. These cues—some subtle and elusive, others more clear-cut and obvious—can indicate how well the group is functioning. Certain people are able to feel the pulse of the group; of others, it may be said that "eyes they have and see not—ears they have and hear not."

"I'll tell you what's wrong with us," one executive said to another in an in-plant training session. "We have just been pussyfooting with each other all evening. It seems to me there are just too many of us who are afraid of something. Why do we have to talk about the Dodgers and Giants? Let's talk about us!"

"How do you mean—afraid, Jack?"

"Well, I don't know—I mean, take a look at this for example. Every time John (the executive vice-president) gives his viewpoint, we seem to give up.

Are we afraid of John's status? Or is he doing something that keeps us from showing him how we really feel about some of these issues?"

Many times the group fails to utilize its talents. By the use of pressure tactics and aggressive, dominating behaviors, some of the "stronger" members frighten others into apathy and submission.

During a discussion on why people fail to participate, Len, one of the more able members, was asked why he appeared as an "eight-cylinder man operating on four cylinders." In response, Len turned toward one of the strong men in the group, saying: "Remember, Mike, some time ago you asked me a question and I couldn't answer. I felt you really didn't care to hear what I would have to say. I felt like a puppet, with you pulling the strings. But now, I think you fellows want to know how I feel and that makes it easy for me to tell you. You see, throughout these years, I have developed some sort of defense—it's like going down, digging a foxhole, letting the shells come over me; every once in a while, I'll stick my head up to see how the weather is. If it's clear, I'll be ready to come out. I really want to be on the team, and I'll work my heart out if given a chance. When my boss lets me show him how much I can do, I get rid of these weights that pull me down and do a man-sized job. People *do* participate if they have the feeling they can produce something worthwhile. But if you are made to feel, well—what's the use, if you have to fight to get a word in edgewise, I for one would just as soon watch the scrimmage from the side lines."

## Recognizing the Culture

Every club, class, church, and corporation has its own "personality." Sears Roebuck differs from Montgomery Ward in more ways than the merchandise they carry. Personnel policies, leadership styles, organizational values, and countless other variables create the organization's total personality: the "culture" in which the organization's members operate. The influence of the culture on interpersonal relations is often underestimated.

Some writers have described in colorful detail the folkways of our industrial society. Among the most cogent observers is William F. Whyte, who has analyzed the impact of technical and physical factors upon the social system of many industrial and business organizations.

Take, for instance, the restaurant industry: Whyte describes the "caste system" in vivid detail. The social structure of one kitchen revolved around the large range upon which all food was cooked. The closer the worker was to this range, the greater his status. Greatest in prestige were the chefs, further distinguished by tall hats. Other workers, in no way marked by dress, gained status by subtle means. It was obvious that salad workers had far greater status than the meat and chicken workers. They, in turn, had more prestige than those who prepared vegetables. Even here, those working with "decorative" vegetables—chives, parsley, or mint—had far more status than those working with potatoes and onions. When all workers were concentrating on the preparation of one vegetable, the low-prestige workers performed early preparation tasks while the high-prestige workers did the finishing work. Worst off were the fish preparers—and it was only when their title was changed to "sea-food-station attendants" that people seemed willing to stick with this job.

Others who have demonstrated the importance of the work environment include Zaleznik, Christenson, and Roethlisberger, who have successfully predicted the structure of leadership and informal organization in departments in which the technology, layout of work, placement of workers at specific stations, pay system, and worker characteristics were known. Recently, Leonard Sayles similarly has shown that understanding of the cultural and environmental forces in an industrial organization permits meaningful predictions of work group behavior.[1]

To the casual observer, the intricacy of the social structure may be meaningless; to the practicing executive, it is a matter of vital importance. Through sensitivity training, the trainees may develop an awareness of the character of their respective organizations and of the forces which facilitate or prevent their use of new behaviors on the job.

## Developing Specific Behavioral Skills

Last, but not least, sensitivity training is designed to enable the trainee to behave appropriately in light of both his retained old and his newly developed understandings. Insights without the behavioral skills to implement them are not too useful.

As the participants put into practice their understanding of themselves and others, they learn how to communicate effectively—how to listen and interview, how to inform and evaluate, how to praise and discipline. These specific communication skills usually cannot be acquired until self-understanding, understanding others, insight into group process, and an awareness of the culture have been attained sufficiently.

All interpersonal relations involve communications. In sensitivity training, listening, or "receiving," skills are initially stressed. Members gradually become aware that they do not always listen effectively in the typical conversation or discussion. Some hear only the rushing sound of words; some filter out what they don't want to hear; some are

[1] See William F. Whyte, *Human Relations in the Restaurant Industry* (New York: McGraw-Hill Book Company, Inc., 1948), pp. 33–46; also A. Zaleznik, C. R. Christenson, and F. Roethlisberger, *The Motivation, Productivity and Satisfaction of Workers: A Prediction Study* (Boston: Harvard Graduate School of Business Administration, 1958); and L. Sayles, *The Behavior of Industrial Work Groups* (New York: John Wiley and Sons, Inc., 1958).

busily thinking of their next retort; some are too bored to pick up anything. Next, emphasis is placed on "sending" properly. Though "receiving" is the more difficult task for most of us, we frequently have trouble in adequately conveying our ideas or feelings. Even with the necessary skills, lack of confidence or other emotional barriers may get in the way.

"Frank, there's something that has irritated me about you since our first meeting. I never know how you really feel about our discussions. I see you getting red under the collar, but you sit there like a sphinx. You may not know it, but it really bothers the hell out of me!" Others in the group agreed. Frank thought he was politely listening, but many were concerned about where he stood. One member caught the spirit of this frustration by quoting the old actor's remark: "Throw tomatoes, money, or clap your hands, but dammit, don't just sit there!"

Sometimes we communicate unintentionally. The unconscious frown, staring into space, droopy eyes, side conversations, slumped posture— all these may convey a feeling of disapproval or boredom that really was not intended to be transmitted.

When we attempt to combine the "sending" and "receiving" aspects of communication, the difficulties are compounded. For example, we have a strong tendency to stop listening while we are talking.

In one workshop, a trainee was nominated to serve as moderator. Behaving as he thought all good moderators should, he firmly took the meeting under his wing, frequently injecting his own ideas. As he droned on, a rebellion mushroomed of which he was totally unaware. Many became restless, some openly aggressive. A replay of the tape proved the point that, even while talking, the successful conference leader had better listen to the group about him.

## THE NATURE OF SENSITIVITY TRAINING

Historically, the sensitivity training approach has grown from some of the work of the applied group dynamicists,[2] from the method exemplified by the National Training Laboratory in Group Development,[3]

[2] D. Cartwright and A. Zander (eds.), *Group Dynamics: Research and Theory* (2d ed.; Evanston, Ill.: Row, Peterson & Company, 1960). Also see P. Hare, E. F. Borgatta, and R. F. Bales, *Small Groups* (New York: Alfred A. Knopf, Inc., 1955).
[3] National Training Laboratory in Group Development, *Explorations in Human Relations Training: An Assessment of Experience, 1947-1953* (Washington, D.C.: National Education Association, 1953). Also see Herbert A. Thelen, *Dynamics of Groups at Work* (Chicago: The University of Chicago Press, 1954), and L. P. Bradford (ed.), *Theory of T-Group Training* (in preparation).

and from the approach of some schools of group psychotherapy and nondirective counseling.[4]

While the characteristics of the sensitivity training process vary somewhat, the educational method used is primarily trainee-centered. Trainees are permitted a maximum amount of leeway of action, and their interactions subsequently provide the subject for discussion and analysis. During the training experience, it is the *process* (the "how") rather than the *content* (the "what") that receives most attention. Trainees are encouraged to deal with their feelings about themselves and about others and to explore the impact they have upon each other. Thus, they examine feelings, expressions, gestures, and subtle behaviors which in everyday life often are taken for granted.

Sensitivity training is still experimental. As carried out in university workshops, group development laboratories, and plant settings, no formula or "cookbook" for conducting this type of training has been nor is it likely to be developed. In general, however, certain essential elements have emerged.

First, this training is primarily "process-oriented" rather than "content-oriented." We believe that, so far as new attitudes and behaviors are concerned, people learn as a result of new experiences. One learns by doing and feeling. Reading material may be provided at each training session and occasional "theory" presentations are made—both ideally following and growing out of related experience. However, the principal emphasis is on emotional, as contrasted with conceptual, learning.

At one workshop, Paul, a sales manager of a large firm, had been singled out for his seemingly boastful remarks. In this group, where no one had revealed his occupation, he consistently made comments like "as division head," "as sales manager," or "at our last convention." He further implied that salesmen had a natural gift for understanding people. Several in the group strongly disagreed. After much discussion, one thoughtful member of the group observed: "I have done a great deal of thinking about Paul. Contrary to what others have said, I don't think he alludes to himself to impress us as a person of supreme self-confidence. I feel he needs to reassure himself to remain comfortable in this group. I no longer resent all these references to himself and his position. I bet Paul doesn't have a college degree; he probably came up the hard way and really made good. Now he has to show his title to himself to see that it's for real." Paul, after a moment of silence concurred.

Second, the training design is partly unstructured. Opportunities are provided for the trainees to decide what they want to talk about, what

---

[4] C. Rogers, *Client-centered Therapy* (Boston: Houghton Mifflin Company, 1951); George Bach, *Intensive Group Psychotherapy* (New York: The Ronald Press Company, 1954).

kinds of problems they desire to deal with, and what means they want to use in reaching their goals. As the trainees concern themselves with these problems, they begin to act in characteristic ways—some participate freely, some remain silent, some dominate the discussion, and some become angry. These and other modes of dealing with problems become "grist for the mill"—they provide jumping-off points for discussion and analysis.

"It seems to me," one young girl wrote in her diary after an early session, "that this afternoon we were each intent on getting over our own ideas and having the group accept them. I now know that I wasn't listening closely to what others were saying, for I was busy formulating my answers to what I thought they were saying. . . . I am sure this is progress. . . . If the other members were doing the same, no wonder we couldn't reach any conclusions!"

Third, a certain amount of frustration appears to be essential to the success of the training. Each person attempts to keep his concept of himself intact, and little training impact can be expected unless the trainee is motivated to examine his self concept, to reevaluate it, and to instigate those changes which he feels would benefit him.

Sensitivity training usually does not satisfy the initial expectations of the trainees because of the lack of structure and the inherent ambiguity this causes. Yet, unless we are jarred out of complacency, we seem to see no reason to change our ways with which we have become so comfortable throughout the years.

"Today," Bob confided in his diary, "I was on the 'hot seat.' I felt quite tense and uncomfortable when the group started to talk about me, and I was glad when we later shifted to someone else. . . . Still, I knew they were on the right track. They were getting at the truth. . . . I was told that I am 'judgmental,' that I don't accept people for what they are, . . . that I try to have them jump according to my tune. . . . This 'nugget of wisdom' is deeply disturbing, and I have, as they say, learned it at the 'gut level.' . . . Accepting others as they are (including acceptance of myself as I am), without judgment, is fundamental I guess to effective interaction."

Fourth, the heart of sensitivity training is found in small groups, allowing a high level of participation, involvement, and free communication. Auxiliary training devices and techniques may be used to facilitate the interaction process; these include films, TV kinescopes, case studies, role-playing exercises, sociometric tests, and the like.

One training technique that is especially effective in making clear to the trainees how little they actually hear—particularly during a heated discussion —requires each person to stop before he gets onto his own point and repeat what was said and felt by the person who spoke just before him. "For the first time in my life I find that I am *really* listening to what others say" is a comment frequently made by trainees who are asked to evaluate their experience.

Fifth, the maintenance of a permissive atmosphere is attempted. When people know that their attitudes are respected and their feelings accepted, full participation is facilitated. Since the expression of attitudes and feelings is essential to the training process, even when people feel they might appear unkind, impolite, or perhaps ridiculous, the group atmosphere must remain friendly enough so that these sentiments can be elicited.

A permissive atmosphere is not easy to describe. We know it does not exist when the discussion leader insists on imposing his own goals, ideas, and methods. We must not be fooled by the "let's-all-join-in-the-fun" appeal of some service organizations, the "let's-be-a-happy-family" flavor of some industrial concerns or college campuses, or the phony "hi-Joe!" variety of "hearty atmosphere." It is only when discussions are characterized by a lack of moralistic or judgmental attitudes toward almost anything that might be said, when people feel free to speak frankly and to listen with understanding, that true "permissiveness" can be said to exist. When the atmosphere is free, a member who has been typically withdrawn can express himself.

"Dick, there is something I want to tell you. Your superior attitude bothers me. You seem to think you know everything. Frankly, you don't know so much more than any of the rest of us!" George by this time does not fear reprisal. Dick appears quite calm. Instead of boiling up in anger or withdrawing completely, he is pleased that George feels free to say something to the effect, "I react to you in a certain way, and I thought you should know." Dick also realizes that this is just one person's opinion, and it may not be widely shared. More important, feelings are facts, and there is no use in playing ostrich and pretending they don't exist.

And indeed, silence—as well as verbal participation—comes to be accepted.

## THE ROLE OF THE TRAINER

The amount and nature of direction which the trainer should provide to foster the most meaningful learning experience is highly controversial. Some trainers feel that they can be most helpful to their trainees by confronting them with at least some problems, some challenging ideas, or how-to-do-it techniques. Others believe that in human relations real learning can best be fostered if the trainees have mostly to shift for themselves in order to experience at the "gut level" the kinds of feelings which will later make them ready to accept and internalize whatever insights and skills they have gained.[5]

Thus, in sensitivity training, the functions of the trainer vary considerably, depending upon his competence, his theoretical orientation, the nature of his group, and his perception of the demands of each situation. Nevertheless, it is possible to classify these functions into five main categories.

## 1. *Creating Situations Conducive to Learning*

The trainer plays a vital role in helping to structure some of the situations in which the trainees interact. His very presence as initial authority figure provides a meaningful problem which the group must face. If, in addition, situations are skillfully set up, the relations between trainees are certain to provide numerous focal points for useful learning. For example, the cautious use of brief sociometric questions (indications of liking, desirability as work partner, recognition of leadership skills, etc.) involving the members of the group in a given training session typically yields data on the way in which each group member is perceived by his fellows. Each trainee is provided with potentially useful insights, which in turn can be strengthened by interpretive group discussion.

## 2. *Establishing a Model of Behavior*

The trainer provides a model for behavior by his activity in the group, his acceptance of criticism, his nonevaluative comments, his willingness to deviate from planned programs, and his ability to raise questions and to express his own feelings. By his own behavior he helps to establish an atmosphere of acceptance and freedom of expression in which the group can discuss interpersonal problems that otherwise might be circumvented or avoided.

## 3. *Introducing New Values*

The trainer, by his behavior, implicitly or explicitly introduces new values into the group. The way he reflects feelings, clarifies comments, and actively behaves focuses attention on those problems which he feels the group should eventually become aware of and deal with. For example, his willingness to relinquish a position of authority and leadership carries with it a host of implications for the group.

## 4. *Facilitating the Flow of Communication*

The trainer helps to identify barriers to the flow of communication between individuals. By raising questions, clarifying issues, and en-

[5] See Chap. 12, "Observations on the Trainer Role," for a fuller treatment of this dilemma.

couraging full participation of all members of the group he facilitates the development of mutual understanding and agreement. Frequently when sources of difficulty are below the level of awareness, the trainer, who is less personally involved with these difficulties than the group, is better able to identify the problems and help bring about their recognition and potential solution.

## 5. *Participating as an "Expert"*

At times the trainer is called upon to introduce knowledge derived from his experience or from research findings, which the group may want in order to proceed with the solution of a given problem. However, he is likely to minimize his "expert" role and wish to share it with the group members.

There is a tendency for groups, particularly at their initial stages, to push responsibility for their progress onto the trainers. There are attendant costs to the trainees in doing this. By putting the trainers in a position of answering questions, of making decisions for the group, of establishing goals and setting group values, the trainees' involvement in the training process is reduced. Therefore, the trainers try to keep maximum responsibility for determinations affecting the group itself with the trainees.

## EXPRESSIONS OF RESISTANCE TO THE TRAINING PROCESS

Most people resist change. When something happens to call into question their present self concept, they typically feel personally threatened and react in a way to protect the notion of self with which they are most secure. To bring about change, the trainees must be helped comfortably to abandon old views and habit patterns in exchange for newer, more realistic insights.

One member became upset because his suggestions rarely seemed to get accepted. After bringing attention to himself, he defended himself against every comment. Tom felt he could be helpful at this point: "Bruce, for some time now, many of us have been trying to tell you what you do, but you don't seem to want to hear us. . . . Let me try it again. I just don't think you have the patience to hear a man out. You don't give the other guy a chance. You always seem to have the answer . . . This is what gets me— it's not what you say. Does that make sense to you?"

The trainer aids in this process by making it possible for people like Bruce to come out of their shell in order to get another view of themselves. "I wonder, Bruce," he reflected, "if you would care to hear from some others before replying to Tom?"

Bruce nodded. Now it was Frank's turn. "Remember, Bruce, what happened to the suggestion you made to fill out the 'buddy-rating forms' on how we see each other? You just didn't give us a chance to respond. Shortly after that, George made a similar suggestion, and the whole group bought it. What do you think?"

Bruce began to "hear." "This really concerns me—what you fellows have been saying. I really would like to know what I *do* that makes you annoyed with me."

Paradoxically, many of those who really want to profit from the training process find themselves blocked by feelings, fears, and anxieties from experiencing the deeper impact of the training process. These defenses keep them from making the kind of progress which they so earnestly desire.

Every one of us utilizes defenses, usually those with which we feel most comfortable. We use different ones at different times and in various combinations and proportions, some more effectively and appropriately than others. Each person's particular pattern of defenses largely characterizes his personality.

It is rather easy to see some of the more familiar defenses in others, but very difficult to recognize them in ourselves: the "sour-grapes" attitude ("we didn't want this contract, anyhow"); the displacement of hostility upon an inappropriate person (arguing with one's wife when really feeling angry at the boss); the blaming of equipment for poor personal performance; the flight into fantasy ("when I am in charge of this department, things will be different!"). Some of us are great rationalizers; some of us take our troubles out on our subordinates; some of us see no faults in ourselves, but only in others; some of us develop bodily symptoms which have no organic basis. In any event, it is important to realize that we are not always conscious of the true motivation of our actions; too often, we are blissfully ignorant of the needs and fears which make us act as we do.

The training process focuses in part on the identification of those defenses that interfere with effective personal functioning. While some participants are able to achieve insight into how they act and react, others markedly resist this process and rigidly adhere to their original views of themselves and the world around them.

In the course of our experience, we have learned to identify some expressions which we think reflect typical resistances to this type of training.[6] Although any or all of these feelings may have some rational basis, the participants commonly fail to examine their validity and

---

[6] Jack R. Gibb, who some years ago conducted leadership training programs at the University of Colorado, first described a similar set of expressions which served his trainees as defenses against real or imagined threats to their self concepts. See J. R. Gibb and Lorraine M. Gibb, *Applied Group Dynamics: A Laboratory Manual for Group Training in Human Relations Skills*, 1953. Mimeographed.

prefer to hold to their notions of what they are and how they are seen by others. Among the common phrases through which these feelings of resistance are expressed are the following:

"You can't change human nature." This assumes that our personalities are fixed, that we are born to be stubborn, talkative, honest, treacherous, late for work, or leaders of men. If we believe this, then training can accomplish nothing. There is no point in getting involved in something which is bound to have little, if any, impact.

"I know myself better than anyone else ever will!" This person cannot accept the idea that hidden or unconscious drives and motives do exist. His best defenses for dealing with his unknown self—his proved tactics for avoiding possible exposure—are denial and rationalization.

"If there is one thing I know, it's how to deal with people." This person may readily admit lack of knowledge about the technical aspects of his job, but his self picture does not permit weakness in the human relations department. He may believe strongly in himself and come to the training to be approved "as is." He often claims knowledge of how to handle a situation and doesn't hesitate to tell someone else what to do. Prevented from getting evidence which might be contradictory to his expressed feelings of adequacy, he avoids testing the reality of whatever fears he has with reference to his abilities to relate to people.

"We are here to learn about human relations. You are the expert—so give us the answers." Behind this attitude lies the more customary school experience which utilizes lectures, case materials, tests, and the like. Most people have learned to expect this type of activity whenever they take a course; moreover, experience with books and newspaper columns has taught them to look for specific answers and for rules and gimmicks to solve their human relations problems. Thus, they wish to submit to the trainer's authority, and yet at the same time refuse to accept his caution that they will find answers only by participating in a dynamic group process.

"Let's stop getting personal—let's be mature and look at the facts!" The person who holds this belief does not like to deal with emotions, feelings, and perceptions. He thinks it unnecessary, if not outright dangerous. To him, every situation calls for a rational principle—the problem is to find the principle that applies. Demanding "the facts" in each instance, he refuses to accept emotions, feelings, and perceptions as facts.

"What do you expect us to do—psychoanalyze everybody?" This question reflects major misunderstandings about the training process as well as about psychoanalysis. Implied is the notion that amateurs are here engaged in a process of "cheap psychotherapy," of treating the maladjusted, for which they are suited neither by calling nor by training. The fact is that sensitivity training is designed to help basically healthy people to "see and hear better" so that they can react more effectively to the demands of their interpersonal contacts. Since people relate to each other so much on the basis of feelings, it is important to know the sources of their existence and the nature of their impact. The intensive "open-thyself" explorations of the training process, however, do require a special setting and skilled supervision and are not designed to be transferred into the day-by-day operations of normal living.

"I think this is great—I'm learning a lot by sitting back and watching all the others." This individual is convinced that there is something to the training process, but he does not wish to get involved. By not participating, he avoids exposing himself. Thus he decreases his potential learning experience.

"We run a business, not a nursery school." This attitude implies that the training encourages impractical, time-consuming, and unrealistic supervisory practices. The trainee assumes that knowing the technical and administrative features of a job is sufficient; he believes that the way to solve problems in human relations is either to avoid them or to discipline those with whom he has difficulties. He fails to admit the possibility that his poor record in interpersonal relations may have its roots in his own behavior and is likely to cite the ample supply of labor as his main reason for not fooling with "employees who won't do their jobs."

"I don't know what you are doing to us, but I don't like it." Behind this expression is a fear that the person's individuality will be lost, that his initiative will disappear, that his abilities will be attacked and his weaknesses magnified. He thinks that sensitivity training is an attempt at indoctrination over which he has no control. He does not realize that the training process is largely of the group's own making—that what is done is mainly a function of what the group wants to do and how it wants to do it. The possibility that individuality is encouraged and enhanced by this type of experience through increasing realistic understanding is not admitted.

## A QUESTION OF ETHICS

Most training by nature involves doing things to other people. There is great temptation for us to be manipulative, to create situations in which we mold people in directions that we, playing God, consider appropriate. Yet what right do we have to play with people's "psyches"?

As far as sensitivity training is concerned, we try to be guided by the belief that each individual is probably his own best judge of the direction in which his growth and development should proceed. As has already been stated, no attempt is made to tell participants whether to change or how to change. They are helped to see themselves more objectively; if *they* are dissatisfied with certain aspects of their behavior, the decision to change and the direction of change is up to them. Given insight into what they are and how they relate to others both inside and outside of their organization, most trainees will be able to undertake those personal corrective steps which, as they see them, should make them more useful to themselves and to the organizations which they serve.

One more question deserves the fullest consideration. Can people be psychologically damaged by the frustrations inherent in the training process? Can people be hurt by shaking their defenses, which seemingly protect them against the pressures of real or imagined threats?

The trainers should be competent to sense when a trainee has been pushed to his limits and be able to help reduce the pressure by providing acceptance and support for the harassed member. Fortunately, the group's inherent drive to protect its own and the individual's ability quickly to modify his defenses help in these protective efforts. In our experience, we know of no "nervous breakdown" which can be traced to the training experience. We do know of many people who after training have entered psychotherapy in order to deal more fully with the personal problems of which they have become aware.

# CHAPTER 10

# A Sensitivity Training Group in Action*

Sensitivity training has been a subject of practice, experimentation, and research by the UCLA Human Relations Research Group for a number of years. Seminars and workshops in sensitivity training for top executives, managers, and members of the professions are being conducted on a continuing basis. Industry, government, the military, and community organizations have participated in sensitivity training and in numerous similar training activities. In addition, sensitivity training is part of the School of Business Administration curriculum through a course entitled "Leadership Principles and Practice," which currently is offered both on campus and in university extension.

As most people who have participated in it will no doubt be willing to verify, sensitivity training produces a deeply personal experience. Perhaps more than any other form of human relations training, it stirs and prods people into taking a good, close look at themselves and at their relations with others. Throughout a full-length training experience, spasmodic peaks of excitement, even exhilaration, seem inevitably followed by long periods of apathy and frustration, characterized by expressions of futility, disgust, and anger.

Until recently, very little was known about the individual, personal reactions of the trainees as—for better or for worse—they committed themselves to the uncertainties, the trials, and the tribulations of the typical sensitivity training experience.

* This chapter is based on an abbreviated adaptation by Paul and Faith Pigors of a draft edition of *Inside a Sensitivity Training Group*, by Irving R. Weschler and Jerome Reisel. A version of this shorter case study will be published in *Case Method in Human Relations: The Incident Process*, McGraw-Hill Book Company, Inc., 1961. The final edition of the Weschler-Reisel study appeared as Industrial Relations Monograph no. 4, Institute of Industrial Relations, University of California, Los Angeles, 1959.

As part of the research program on the nature and impact of sensitivity training, one UCLA class in "Leadership Principles and Practice," consisting of twenty-four students (college seniors and graduates: eighteen men and six women), was intensively studied. This group, which met during the spring of 1956 for a period of thirty meetings of two hours each, had experiences which in some ways were similar to those of many groups that had preceded it and of many that followed it. Yet in time, place, and composition, this group was also truly distinctive, with a "group mix" of personalities the like of which will never be together again. With outstandingly different "characters" to bring on more than its share of "critical events," this group's life cycle seemed particularly worth describing.

This chapter provides a series of glimpses into one sensitivity training group—as seen through the eyes of its participants, of its trainer, and of a clinical observer. *Trainee diaries* are the key raw material upon which this report is based. The participants were requested to record fully in their diaries, after each session, their true feelings, opinions, and reactions as to anything that might have affected them during that period. In addition, the *trainer's comments* indicate how the progress of the group looked from his point of view. The trainer (I. R. Weschler, often referred to by members of the group—at their option—as Irv) faced numerous problem situations, and, as is invariably the case, the nature of his interventions had great bearing on the way in which the group finally emerged from its experience. The *clinical observer* (J. Reisel) attended all meetings, tape-recorded everything, and intensively interviewed the trainer at the close of each session. His observations are designed to add insights and depth.

The diaries accomplished a number of objectives. Most important, they helped the trainees to reflect upon and evaluate their own experiences as they went along. They also provided continuous feedback on feelings and reactions about which so far very little had been known. Since by their very nature their content was largely determined by the trainees themselves, they dealt with experiences and relationships that often had intense personal meaning. Furthermore, since the training process proceeded for thirty meetings over a period of four months, they constituted a series of successive subjective impressions (samples), each large enough to provide information and insights on individual development and group growth.

The choice of the specific diary excerpts which are quoted is of course, somewhat arbitrary. They reflect a desire to cite those quotations which best described the feelings, doubts, insights, and inner struggles of the trainees as they found themselves "inside a sensitivity training group."

The reader is encouraged to read the original monograph on which the following report is based and to utilize it to bring his own ideas into play. In this regard there are countless foci of investigation which permit useful follow-up. The interaction between the trainer and his trainees, identification of the power structure, description of roles, the development of phases of individual and group growth, changes in stereotyped thinking, the evolution of facilitative or inhibiting behavior patterns, the discovery of individual differences in personality, the relationship between men and women, the nature of participation, the utilization of private or "hidden" agenda, the expression of feelings, attitudes and assumptions, the nature of leadership—all these aspects of group life and many more can be elicited from the original data, which are subject to a wide variety of interpretations.

The objectives of this particular adaptation are as follows:

1. To draw attention to certain habits and skills of language, as a form of social behavior. For that purpose, passages were selected to illustrate communication difficulties (within or between members of this sensitivity training group).

2. To highlight (*a*) what the members of this group noticed about each other, (*b*) their interpretations of what they perceived, and (*c*) what they seem to have learned about, and from, each other.

## FOURTH MEETING: THE FIRST "CRITICAL EVENT"

TRAINER: . . . . The history of every sensitivity training group is highlighted by some "critical events" which eventually give it its unique character and history. . . . The first of these "critical events" took place when Beverly succeeded in cutting off further discussion on the moderator subject by asking for volunteers to serve as recorder, observer, and moderator. Al volunteered to be recorder, while Lew offered to observe the group. The decision was forced quickly, and all three were immediately accused of "railroading." Beverly was only too ready to admit the impact that she had helped create.

BEVERLY: My impatience is going to be my ruination. I react so strongly to the things that are being said. . . . Why do I react so violently???? I often felt complete shame and guilt because I got so heated up. . . . I am sure I had no business "railroading" the observer and recorder issue through. It was probably very unorthodox and domineering, but unfortunately, I would do the same thing again, should the situation arise.

## SIXTH MEETING: DUKE LEADS A WALKOUT

TRAINER: . . . . Beverly created the greatest controversy with her suggestion that the group try for complete consensus. For the first time, the notion of a "tyranny of the majority" (control by the many) versus the "tyranny of the minority" (blocking by the few) appeared.

BOB: As soon as Beverly had expressed her desire for consensus, a number of people started throwing questions at her. . . . No one waited for recognition from the moderator. . . . Many appeared overtly fed up with what was going on.

TRAINER: . . . . In the midst of the floundering, another "critical event" took place. Under the active leadership of Duke, seven members walked out. . . .

HANK: . . . We spent two whole hours arguing—not discussing— . . . how to decide an issue. . . . When Beverly, "the railroader," raised the point of consensus, she was talked down, mostly by me. . . . Duke, Ben, and I finally pulled the walkout because we were disgusted and ready for a break. . . . Later, various members tried to rebuke us for leaving, but since Irv (the trainer) had said it was O.K., I don't care what they think. I wish we could get more concrete problems to work on, but I guess this is not the purpose of the class. . . .

## SEVENTH MEETING: ORGANIZING THE SMALL-GROUP PROJECTS

TRAINER: The initial phase of the group's development was rapidly coming to an end. During the first hour, everyone took the *California Psychological Inventory*, part of the test battery designed to assess the impact of sensitivity training. . . . During the second hour, we proceeded to organize the small-group projects. I listed four acceptable topic areas, all very broadly defined. . . . The students could form their own groups as they saw fit—as long as each group contained either four or five members.

BOB: Mr. Weschler made a diagram on the blackboard, designating where people interested in a given topic could meet. He then asked whether we thought that we should allocate ourselves first by a show of hands on each project to keep the groups equal, or whether we should just go to the designated topic area. It was interesting to see that the consensus compromise was 100 per cent for just going to the area.

LEW: I must say that there was, and still is, some confusion in my mind as to just what Dr. Weschler wants us to accomplish in our group projects. I guess this will all clear up as we go along.

## EIGHTH MEETING: WHY DOESN'T BEN SAY ANYTHING?

TRAINER: . . . Lew . . . asked Ben why he never saw fit to say anything in class.

LEW: Ben stated that he did not feel motivated. . . .

HANK: Some of these guys such as Lew and Al turn my stomach. They all jumped on Ben for not talking. They were reading all kinds of things into his nonparticipation in class. . . . I feel just like Ben; most of the time the discussions haven't been worth taking part in. . . . I would have laughed if some of these wise guys had hopped on me. . . . I wonder if they are just talking to appear to Irv as though they were working. Most of their remarks are just rehash of what someone else has already said. . . . I don't think we should ever get so personal again, because before too long there are liable to be some pretty nasty remarks flying around.

## NINTH MEETING: "TO HELL WITH IRV"

DUKE: . . . . My buddy, Ben, rated[1] the highest. Immediately the pseudo-psychiatrists in the class jumped into the act and began studying him. It seems to me you can't even breathe without some idiot investigating why you do it. I am rapidly developing a temper restraint in this group lest I smash a few people in an emotional outburst.

TRAINER: . . . . After the experiment, which to many may well have been personally too threatening, the group floundered at length.

BEVERLY: I'm afraid my reaction is despair bordering on disgust. . . . At this stage I question the value of letting the class flounder to the point of frustration, which I think we are reaching. . . .

FRANCES: I wish the instructor would step in, clarify what has been going on, and give the group some leads as to why, how and where we are being blocked. . . .

TRAINER: At one point, while the discussion dealt with "feedback," Don asked me to define the meaning of the term. Before a reply was possible, Red burst out with the comment, "To hell with Irv"—followed first by a stunned silence, then by uproarious laughter. . . .

CLINICAL OBSERVER: This meeting featured the "ritual slaying of the father". . . .

## TENTH MEETING: TO SPEAK OR NOT TO SPEAK

TRAINER: . . . . The plight of some of the nonparticipants was clearly brought out in the discussion. . . . The highlight of the session was a long and animated exchange between Red and Beverly on the subject of "attacking."

ART: I want to participate, and I am interested. Usually I talk a great deal, but not here. . . . Why didn't I speak up. . . .

LARRY: I don't feel I have enough confidence within myself or the class in me so that what I say will be looked upon as important. . . .

BEVERLY: . . . . How can I decide when to talk and when to keep quiet?

LEW: I am trying not to talk so much. . . . But it seems that once one starts speaking in the group it is just as hard to stop as it is to start.

---

[1] That rating was on a test which consisted in guessing how Beverly, who had been selected by vote as "understood best," had answered a questionnaire.

ELEVENTH MEETING: DUKE TAKES THE LEAD

Trainer: Another slow starting period. . . . Those who wanted to talk about the trainer role couldn't seem to find the right opening. . . . Out of a "clear blue sky," Duke suddenly demanded that the group do something "more practical." Outside of class he had prepared a set of role-evaluation sheets, which he was now passing out to the group. This inventory was based on Benne's and Sheats' role analysis,[2] and required the members to list names for each of the roles that were described. . . . Before the group could act, a few members objected to the procedure.

Duke: Red immediately took on his "mightier-than-thou" role and questioned my motives. It took all the restraint I had to keep from hitting that Alf Landon in the chops.

Maurice: I was completely amazed to find someone going out of his way to do something for us. . . .

Dick: . . . . Everyone seemed greatly relieved when Duke passed his forms out. . . .

Trainer: Nondirective counseling was one of the skills that some experimented with during the discussion.

Lew: Today I was trying to encourage a person who does not often participate. I tried indirect counseling. . . . It was extremely interesting to see that these methods that Irv talked about actually do work.

Clinical Observer: . . . . In opposing the resolution of the trainer problem, Duke in turn becomes a problem, not only to the group and to himself, but to the trainer as well. . . . He is extremely influential, in the sense that he keeps the group on primitive levels. . . .

TWELFTH MEETING: ROLES BY THE NUMBER

Duke: Well, I just about walked out. Irv's role again. Some people just have sawdust for brains. I don't know what Irv is trying to do, but from appearances I think he tends to be a self-centered egotist! . . . . We finally got off the trainer-role bender. . . . Through "railroad tactics" some of the role-sheet supporters got the group to use them and tabulate the results. . . . Some people thanked me (for preparing the role sheets), while others, which I overheard, were condemning it. Of course, they stopped talking about me when I appeared . . . . the two-faced bastards!

Max: Of twenty-five possible roles listed I made almost half—an even dozen to be exact. . . . When I think of these roles, I have to ask myself, am I really that negative? . . . . I am unable to arrive at an unbiased answer, but I have decided to try an experiment during the next two meetings. I am going to try not to "toe-step." It will be tough, but I'll try.

Lew: I noticed that many people put me down as "blocker," "irritant," and "aggressor" . . . . Some people saw me as "idea innovator," "supporter," or "acceptor". . . . I do believe that I have contributed somewhat to the

[2] "Spotlight on Member Roles," *Adult Leadership*, vol. 1, no. 8, January, 1953 (entire issue).

group process. . . . [But] I do wish I knew how to shut up. Well, at least I am motivated.

BEVERLY: No one was singled out as being the cause of the group's ills, as I was afraid might happen. . . .

CLINICAL OBSERVER: . . . . Now the group is mad at Duke, and so they turn on the trainer. . . .

## THIRTEENTH MEETING: THE MOST SIGNIFICANT "CRITICAL EVENT"

TRAINER: This was to become the group's most satisfying meeting to date. It started, in a low key, with a somewhat academic discussion . . . of leadership. . . . During the discussion there was obviously better communication —we were carefully listening to each other, and the attacks on persons and the display of negative attitudes were conspicuously missing.

MAX: I went into class today with one aim—to prove what type of person I really am. I had come to the conclusion that a change was needed. . . . So this was a new Max who walked into the room. . . .

TRAINER: After the break, I assumed what many saw as a "forceful and dynamic" role in trying to sum up where I felt we stood as a group. . . . One of my comments produced what, in my opinion, was to turn out to be the most significant "critical event" in this group's history. I pointed out that one of our problems was a "bloc within a bloc," composed of Duke, Hank, and Ben, who either through active or passive resistance seemed to be preventing the group from making genuine progress. I tried to be as noncritical as possible, wishing merely to point out a key problem so that the group could deal with it. . . . Right or wrong, the observation caused a tremendous storm. . . . The reactions of the three "blockers" were startling. . . . [3]

DUKE: When Irv suddenly had Hank, Ben, and me placed in a category of "a bloc within a bloc," I was amazed. . . . Hank gave very blunt answers to the class which made me very happy. . . . Ben screwed up the works by hemming and hawing about something. I wish he would get some self-confidence. . . . The general idea is that we present a problem. I didn't know we even fitted into some people's narrow thoughts but discovered that people notice our seating habits. Now at last the group has something controversial to chew up, and I hope they continue their attacks so I, too, can get in a few licks.

HANK: During the break Irv asked me what it would take to get me into the class. I told him I could see no point in the discussion and therefore didn't have enough interest to do much participating. . . . After the hour started, Irv forcefully brought out the idea of "hidden agenda" again. Before I knew it I was telling the class how I felt about it. . . . Soon I was being questioned from all sides. I really enjoyed this hour. . . . There was at last something real and concrete to get my teeth into. . . . I didn't

[3] Note the unfortunate similarity between "bloc" (a subgroup) and "blocking" (resisting).

realize that our little group had such an impact on the class but I will
admit that maybe we do owe it to the group to bring out how we feel.
. . . Maybe something can be done about it still to rectify either the class
or else my attitudes toward the class. I will have to try to do something
more, but I can't enter into a discussion if there is no point to it. . . .

BEN: When Irv mentioned that Duke, Hank, and I were sitting together,
forming a bloc which had influence on the class, it was something I had
not known or been aware of before. Hank . . . said he had no use for the
class, that nothing was being done or accomplished. This really started
something. He was asked if the same applied for Duke and myself. We
answered with a loud "yes". . . . I am glad this was finally brought into
the open for everyone to see. . . . I believe from now on there will be
more understanding among the group members, and I hope we won't swing
back into the same rut again. . . . I'll try to do my part to see that we
don't.

MARIE: I was so against it all that I couldn't enter into the discussion. I was
afraid there could be no other result than to increase the hostility of the
fellows and to make matters worse. . . .

TRAINER: By labeling the three "blockers" as a clique, I may have made it
more difficult for them to act as individuals at future meetings.

BOB: I personally don't feel the three are a bloc because they don't participate; they probably have not as yet found enough stimulation to enter the
group. . . . All three impressed the fact upon the group that they were
speaking for themselves. I believe . . . they definitely want to be thought
of as individuals.

MAURICE: . . . We again continued in our Mr. District Attorney role of
making Ben, Duke, and Hank more a part of the class. . . . Why not try
to understand them instead of directly attacking them?

CLINICAL OBSERVER: . . . It became apparent about this time that despite
his conscious efforts to be nondirective, the trainer had in fact been just
the opposite. . . . To complicate the situation further, a hostile, competitive situation had developed between the trainer and Duke. This, too,
could not be bypassed. . . . Having decided upon action of some sort,
the trainer managed a startling coup. In one motion he became both directive and supportive, and at the same time showed his strength by taking on
not only Duke, but two additional members of the group, whom he identified as a "bloc within a bloc". . . . The group is both awe-struck and
satisfied! . . . . Members for the most part are relieved to find that the
trainer has a point of view and is willing to stand up for it. . . .

## FOURTEENTH MEETING: CHRISTMAS IN MARCH

TRAINER: Christmas in March, good will toward men, friendliness toward all!
In a genuine climate of permissiveness, almost everyone who wanted to talk
seemed able to get in. . . . Some who hadn't been heard from for many a
meeting took part today. . . .

DUKE: Well, today we really had a surprise. The girls brought coffee and doughnuts for the group. This proved to be a boon for mixing. It gave me faith in the group again.

BEVERLY: We are really coming as a group. . . . I think I'm helping the atmosphere to become better. I have become a real listener. . . . The Rogerian (nondirective) technique is working, though every time I see it, I am just as amazed and impressed as I was the first time around.

PETE: Today Dick and Bob opened the door for me to have a say . . . . this made me want to hear everything everyone else had to say. . . .

RED: It's strange to experience the "camaraderie"—this sort of "oh, well, we're all in this together" feeling. It has resulted in my being able to accept more readily other points of view and ideas, even though they may be antagonistic to my own. . . .

LARRY: Today I finally expressed my true feelings—how I felt with regard to my position in the class. I guess Pete provided the stimulus for me. It really wasn't easy. . . . I hope I shall find the security I am looking for, the feeling that what I have to say is of importance and will be accepted by the rest of the group.

LEW: . . . The only point that seemed to stymie us was getting the Hank bloc of nonspeakers into the group. . . .

ART: When I asked Hank . . . what he would like to see done, his reply was, "something concrete—something you can get your teeth into and not this dribble which has been going on." He mentioned a discussion of fraternities. . . . To me the exposition of fraternities was utterly wasteful and definitely away from the purpose of our discussion. When I commented on this, Red became annoyed and snapped at me. . . . What shall we do? Right now my attitude is to hell with them. This I realize is bad, but I dislike being jumped at, when I am trying to solve a group problem.

HANK: . . . These nebulous questions . . . do not raise any interest in me. . . . I am sure I am missing the purpose of the class somehow or other, but I don't think it's because I have a closed mind in the subject. . . . I wonder what Irv's idea is in aligning the "unholy three" against the rest of the group. Are we really a problem to him, or are we just something that the class can talk about?

DON: . . . We are picking on Ben, Hank, and Duke. To a point we have made it almost impossible for them to enter our group effectively.

FRED: Putting these three fellows on the spot is not the way to get them into the group. We are merely severing them further. . . .

TRAINER: My original reference to "the bloc within a bloc" has created stereotypic thinking which now has become difficult to break down. The label sticks, and Ben especially has trouble getting out from under its corrosive cover.

BEN: It seems that every time Hank gives his negative views, the class thinks he is talking for Duke and myself, but it isn't true.

TRAINER: Toward the end of the meeting, the discussion became even more hostile. During one rapid fire exchange, one of the girls was thrown off balance by a forceful, unfriendly line of questioning. . . .

ROBIN: I was so totally unprepared for all this being directed at me. . . . I am not sorry it happened, but usually I acquit myself with more agility than today. . . . It took a jolt to make me realize that I am as vulnerable to attack as anyone else.

CLINICAL OBSERVER: . . . Paradoxically, the directive behavior of the trainer actually opens the way for close interpersonal relationships. . . . Unfortunately, the soothing effect of mother's milk is only temporary. . . . If coffee and doughnuts could make a lasting peace, the Gray Ladies long since would have displaced the diplomats at the conference tables of the world.


SIXTEENTH MEETING: "WHAT ARE WE GOING TO DO
    WITH RED?"

TRAINER: At the beginning of the period, I returned the results of the quiz. Beverly and Ben, a member of the "bloc within a bloc," received the highest grades.

BEVERLY: There goes Ben—highest grade in the test. Once again his abilities and insight come to the fore. I think it's just too bad we can't help him to express himself. . . .

RED: Was I shook today! That test! I have to admit I was figuring on being top dog, but to be beaten by a woman—that was too much!

DUKE: We got the quiz back today—and it looks like any other. He who parrots best gets the highest grade. . . . What phoniness!

TRAINER: This was the day on which we started work on the big *grading problem.* [The students had been asked] . . . to arrive at criteria as well as weights for the various components making up the final grade. . . . A total of four hours, to be spread over a number of meetings, was allotted to this task. . . . The initial discussion fell flat on its face. . . .

BILL: Today many of us were operating very poorly. There were definite cliques operating, with people joining one clique or the other in order to satisfy their own selfish goals.

DICK: What are we going to do with Red? And others like him? . . . . Why should the group become bogged down because of one person? Here is one individual whose opinions are contrary to those of twenty-three others. Is his feeling that important? . . . . I feel strongly that when there is only one member on the "other side of the fence" it is up to him to try to make the move. If he doesn't, then he stands as the single blocker—he hinders progress!

TRAINER: Should the group prove unable to reach a workable consensus, the grading problem was to revert back to me for final decision. . . . Before the end of the meeting, a number of attempts were made to get the group to evaluate its progress. I offered some of my own observations. . . . Once again I more or less inadvertently focused on the "big three" by pointing out that their sitting together and whispering to each other might be disturbing to the group. . . .

DUKE: After much of nothing, Irv closed the meeting with some of his "sage" advice. I am sick of it!!!

MARIE: When Irv accused me after class of sitting there and not helping the group, I knew he was right. . . .

RED: I don't know if Irv was aiming his comments at any particular people, but they certainly hit home with me. For example, when he talked about people letting the class down because of delusions of grandeur, I felt he was referring directly to me.

FRED: I personally never noticed Duke, Ben, and Hank sitting in a group until Irv mentioned it. . . . I honestly believe that a person is looked at with a double eye if he is pointed out by Irv in this class. . . . Their presence may have had some negative influence on us, but I feel the problem was doubled when they were pointed out. They were pressured, labeled, and ridiculed . . . all to make them talk. Maybe this is why they later moved—to find out what the hell was going on.

BOB: I think Irv has brought definite pressure to bear on these three people. . . . The three became rather indignant at . . . being questioned as to why they were sitting together. As Duke stated, "It's none of your damn business."

CLINICAL OBSERVER: . . . The "grading problem" set before the group was a big order. The time limits and consensus proviso insisted on by the trainer caused an immediate build-up of tension. . . . In the course of this session the issue of the clique arose once more. It was to come up again and again. . . .

## SEVENTEENTH MEETING: "D DAY"

DUKE: Today was D-Day—meaning—disperse. We split up to see if the "preachers" in the class would be happy. I asked if it made any difference to them. . . . They got onto Hank again, and he came through with flying colors. . . . He said he would not conform. I agree with him 100 per cent. If we are going to be mentioned as a bloc (of blockers), I wish they would leave Ben out. . . . He doesn't say anything, just sits and gets embarrassed. Irv helped our strength with some more remarks at the end of the class. Tyranny of the minority!! Ha! Ha!

TRAINER: As the gulf between the "big three" and the majority of the class widened, prospects for reaching full consensus on the grading problem became dimmer and dimmer. Duke especially had begun to taste the power which his nonconforming behavior wielded over the group, and he relished the attention which was focused on him and his cohorts. . . .

DICK: I think the blame for this mess rests with the group. If we hadn't made such a fuss about Ben, Hank, and Duke, things would not be as they are now. . . . The "silent three" were put under pressure and resented it. They rebelled. A simple problem in the early stages of our group development has turned out to be quite a large problem by now.

PETE: Beverly said she was scared to death of the "big three". . . . She especially didn't appreciate their talking among themselves while she was trying to get a point across to the group. It's funny, but to me these three offer no threat. . . . In fact Beverly and several of the other high-powered talkers give me more fear. . . . When they (Duke, Hank, and Ben) split around the room, they first monopolized the group by cross-conversations strictly between themselves. . . .

ART: Perhaps the best thing that happened today was the separation of Hank, Ben, and Duke. This to me represents a definite improvement in our group. All of them, but especially Duke, entered into our conversation. . . . I was very pleased with their action. . . .

LARRY: Frankly, I am getting fed up with the entire situation. . . . For weeks everyone sat around and asked why certain individuals weren't participating. . . . Frankly, I don't care one bit whether Ben, Hank, and Duke sit at all, and neither do they, I think. It seems we have put sufficient time on them. What about us—myself, Pete, and Art—don't we count? . . . .

TRAINER: . . . During a discussion of some of the "hidden agenda," I . . . indicated that I felt some of our people who had eight cylinders were operating on only two or four. . . . The analogy was readily picked up; Mike was especially singled out as one individual who had been sitting back too much. . . .

FRANCES: I felt the accusations against Mike were unjust. . . . If silence alone is an indication of nonfunctioning, I could name at least half a dozen others, myself included, who were possibly less active verbally and mentally than Mike. . . .

MAX: When it was said that we are all using defenses, it hit right home with me. . . . It is so much easier to see someone else than yourself. . . . When I walked out of class today, I said to myself—who do you think you are— Jack Benny? It seems that every time I get the opportunity, I try to make them laugh.

CLINICAL OBSERVER: . . . It was noticed that the "clique" members were now sitting separate from one another. Duke could hardly wait to bring this to the attention of the group. It was obviously a peace offering to the group and to the trainer. . . . Unaware of the real implications of the clique's split, Duke announces that it was preplanned. This affords the group an opportunity to descend en masse. The clique is perceived as physically split up but psychologically still intact.

The new attacks goad the clique into a morose unanimity. They now have a central value about which to rally—nonconformity. . . . They voice their contempt of the group and the training process by labeling it phony, weak, and unreal. They claim to remain in the group only because it is too late to get out. Besides, they need the grade. . . .

## EIGHTEENTH MEETING: TIME IS REALLY RUNNING OUT

TRAINER: . . . . The full two hours were spent on criteria for grading and the percentages to be assigned to each performance to be graded.

BEVERLY: None of us knew what to do with Duke, so we bogged down. I wonder if he really is a tyrant or if I am seeing him this way because I want it to be that way. Poor old Duke. . . . I really feel for him! . . . I think of the understanding it will take to help him get settled in a job and I worry about the strife this kid is going to have. . . .

DUKE: These people are *all* afraid to try something new—just as I told them. . . . We will undoubtedly end up with a parrot final, but not if I have anything to do about it. It seems I am becoming a real blocker. I don't think so. The weak ones said they would compromise, which made my opinion all the firmer. I'll "block" them to the very end!

HANK: Well, time is really running out on us. . . . As far as I can see, this group will never have 100 per cent consensus on anything—not even the time of day.

BEN: Today, one hour and fifty minutes were spent haggling. . . . We only have one more hour left for discussion. From the way things have been going I know the whole thing will be a big flop and wind up in Irv's hands.

## NINETEENTH MEETING: RED "BLEW HIS CORK"

DICK: If we had tackled the grading problem today, we would not have made it. . . .

TRAINER: After sidetracking the grading problem, we again focused on the "hidden agenda," on fears and defenses which we use to protect ourselves—sometimes against the impact of training.

DOROTHY: . . . . I enjoyed our discussion of "fear" and was surprised—no, that was not the right word—disappointed that more of us weren't interested or did not feel involved.

DICK: I was of the opinion that it was not the responsibility of the group to draw in these nonparticipants. . . . After seeing what happened today I am not sure that this is true.

RED: At first, when this class started, I thought I would put out a good deal of effort and be satisfied with any grade. . . . As of now, I feel the hell with it!

TRAINER: When Red could stand it no longer, he literally "blew his cork." He attacked the class as a "bunch of hypocrites," and accused members of not saying what they meant when they put their inner thoughts in their diaries.

BOB: I knew this was going to happen because our small-project group discussed withholding personal feelings with Irv when we met with him last Tuesday afternoon. . . .

HANK: Red finally took off this morning, telling us . . . that the class stunk. I thought to myself—here was a fellow who finally was saying what he felt—this could lead to some good! . . .

BEVERLY: Today we had a real good session. Many things were brought into the open which needed to be said, *and* we accepted them and worked with them. . . .

LEW: This was the most disgusting meeting we ever had! . . . We have in our midst a few with very negative attitudes. . . . I personally am so disgusted that I don't know what to do. . . .

CLINICAL OBSERVER: . . . Red's blow-up emphasized the feeling of schism in the group. Underneath it all is the perpetual and crucial problem that members of all groups must face: Is membership in the group inhibiting the aims of the individual? . . . .

## TWENTIETH MEETING: HEADING FOR DERAILMENT

TRAINER: For a number of sessions the storm had been brewing. . . . Numerous unresolved issues were affecting the group, whether people wanted to admit it or not . . . At the beginning of the meeting I used a tape recorder to play back a portion of the last session and tried to summarize the complaints made by group members, as I heard them. . . .

BEN: The usual feeble attempts to try to come to grips with these problems met with no success. . . . Very little enthusiasm was shown, and only a few participated.

RED: We are really suffering these days. Throughout practically the whole meeting, my feelings, opinions, etc., were all negative. . . . I couldn't see any particular point in participating, and I didn't. . . . Something in the way of realization is beginning to creep up on me. . . . I thought a person could shut himself off from the rest of the class, after having been fairly active, much as I was. . . . Obviously I was wrong. . . . Apparently the only real way to get something out of this is to get involved to the extent that you work up a set of ulcers. . . . Then what happens to your other classes?

ART: Today I formed some reactions. If I listed my gripes about certain members of this group, I would fill volumes. . . . [4]

TRAINER: . . . Robin suggested that the group have a party at her house, sometime in the near future. This suggestion was received with mixed emotions. . . . The party discussion was followed by the "long break"—twenty-two minutes, as someone timed it. . . . When we finally reassembled, we nostalgically observed how nice it was to get together in little groups and just talk. This was kicked around for a while, but really not much else was happening.

Once again I felt the urge to "insert the needle". . . . I subconsciously didn't rely on [my belief] that a group is strong enough to work out its own destiny. . . . I hinted darkly that unless some of the blockers were dealt with, this "train would surely head for derailment". . . . Max, then Duke and Lew, demanded to know whom I had in mind as "blockers". . . .

HANK: Today we asked Irv to back up some of the vague statements he keeps making about mysterious problems we are evading and elusive persons who are "blockers." He refused to answer. . . . I really felt boiling about this, although I think it is a waste of time to get worked up. . . .

[4] He then gripes about five people, none of whom is a member of "the bloc within a bloc."

DUKE: My sentiment for the whole day is crap! . . . Irv . . . mentioned "blockers" again, and I got the feeling it was us, Hank and I, whom he was talking about. . . . By now I am almost positive Irv is down on Hank and me.

BEVERLY: What we did to Irv today shouldn't happen to the grubbiest worm. I think it was good that he didn't show how strongly he really felt about things. . . . Duke did not want to know for any constructive reason if he was a "blocker". . . .

CLINICAL OBSERVER: This session had a retrogressive quality. Tension-provoking issues, which had lain dormant, burst to the surface again. . . . The situation is extremely difficult. . . .

## TWENTY-FIRST MEETING: AT LAST—NAMING NAMES

TRAINER: General nervousness and restlessness characterized the opening minutes. No one wanted to "face the music." The silence appeared so embarrassing that Robin felt the need to break in with "Well, good morning, everybody," and Maurice tried to relieve the tension by offering "to sell tickets to the party."

MARIE: I felt pretty scared, too, but was determined to see if we could get back where we left off last meeting. I asked the group if they would like Irv to play back the tape of the end of our last session. . . . Again silence reigned. . . . Then Beverly gathered her courage, leaped in, and launched us on a discussion of how others affected us.

LEW: . . . We finally got down to naming names. . . . I wonder why it took so long. . . . Believe we will rapidly progress in our last few meetings—but there are so few meetings left now.

LARRY: Today was *the* crowning day. I finally made my contribution, which is something I've been waiting to do for eleven weeks. . . . I really feel most of the credit goes to Beverly, who gave me the support I needed. . . .

DICK: For the first time I noticed Pete today. When he spoke he had something valuable to say, and the class seemed to be very interested. . . . His remarks impressed the group so much that now—when he is going to speak —the group will surely take notice. The same thing happened to Larry and Hank. Maybe this will come to some good. I think it will.

MARIE: We talk about permissiveness and acceptance. . . . I have read about it, have heard of it, have believed in it; but it is an entirely different story when you personally experience it. . . . It was wonderful. . . . I felt I was more effective than at any other time. . . .

TRAINER: . . . It was impressive to see how many members of the group were truly aware of each other and sensed the processes going on in the group as a whole. Beverly was largely responsible for providing support and directing the group. . . . Her efforts appeared primarily group-oriented. What a difference between her behavior now and that during the "railroading" episode, many a meeting ago!

BEVERLY: If we clocked the minutes I talked today in relation to my mathematical share, I should go into a shell for two weeks!!! . . . . I thought

I controlled the group for almost the entire two hours, but I don't think it was too bad, or they wouldn't have kept on the track for so long. . . . I was really pleased with my participation. . . .

MARIE: I think Irv did a terrific job today. . . . I'm sure that his comment, "I listened to the tape in my office and must say I'm not very pleased with what I said or the way I used the term 'blockers,'" had a very good effect on many people. We were again able to see Irv as a human being, with feelings, and to realize that he has more interest in the group than just being the instructor.

LEW: Irv finally came through—as if he knew what he was doing! His comments and encouragements were spontaneous (for the first time this semester). . . .

BEVERLY: . . . Today [Irv] entered the group and really helped us. I think the kids accepted him better for it.

TRAINER: For the first time in weeks, the group carried through without taking a break. As usual, our concern focused on the "big three."

MARIE: Our situation with Hank and Duke is more serious than I was able to comprehend before today's meeting. . . . Duke said after class, "We can do anything we want to this group, and you can't do a thing about it". . . . At the end, Lew asked Hank if he felt he had made progress, and Hank answered "No." Then he laughed and turned to Duke. I wondered why he laughed and asked him. Before he could speak Duke answered for him, "Can't you see—he can't say anything else—if he did, your whole world would collapse!" I think what Duke meant to say was that Hank's whole world would collapse—including Duke's. . . . Mike seemed to be aware of this when he told Hank, "Whatever you do—don't lose the protection of your castle."

TRAINER: By now, both Duke and Hank seemed trapped, partly by their own machinations, and partly by the role which the group had assigned to them. . . .

DUKE: I am getting frustrated more and more. . . . I find I have several roles to play. I want to help the class, but I also feel I have to defend my friends when they are attacked. Things aren't helped when Hank blurts out his disgust with the group. I guess I will have to stick by Hank and give up on the group. . . . In my opinion, Irv doesn't foster people who are individualists. . . . I think we, Hank and I, have the group where we want them. . . . Everybody bitched about long breaks, so today we didn't have one. . . . I bet if Hank and I had gotten up, the class would have followed. What a bunch of sheep!

HANK: Today I told the class what I really thought of them. . . . Irv was very astute in his observation of me. I do like to be in the limelight. . . . There are many things going on that I believe to be worthwhile and interesting. I have, however, assumed the role of the disinterested, disgruntled student, and I will be stuck with it for the rest of the semester. I shall have to tell the class the things that they have come to expect to hear from me. . . . I would like to know if Irv feels I am a blocker or if he is aware that I am overplaying the role I have taken up. At first, the role was not a conscious one, but of late I am working at appearing disinterested. If I didn't like the class somewhat, I would miss many more sessions than I have.

BEN: Today Marie told us how uneasy she feels when Duke makes side remarks to either Hank or me while she is speaking. She thinks that we are talking about her. Hank gave out with his usual negative attitude of utter disgust. . . . It was brought out that this might be his way of attracting attention to himself, but I don't go along with this. . . . I noticed we didn't take a break today, and no one called for one. What does this mean?

CLINICAL OBSERVER: By this time, it was apparent that this was not to be a "happy-ending" group. . . . The divergence of private interests would not permit smooth and satisfying resolutions. . . .

Despite waves of dissatisfaction that tended to overrun the group, honesty and integrity were nonetheless visible as individual members tried to face up to the sources of the conflict. The fact that the group did not take a break reflects the intensity of their need to cope with one another. . . .

Like many of the recent sessions, this meeting had moments both of warmth and of anger. At this stage, the members were much like a large scrappy family, often engaged in violent civil war, but quick to unite in the face of any threat from the outside. . . .

The clique became a symptom of the group's differences rather than their cause. As far as the "big three" were concerned, the fires of hell couldn't rend them asunder. Visibly upset and disgruntled, this subgroup had a unique individuality which gained it a great deal of gratifying attention. Were it not for Duke, the remaining members of the clique might have suffered the fate of anonymity. Now their union gave them notoriety.

## TWENTY-SECOND MEETING: HANK'S PEACE OFFERING

TRAINER: What an amazing surprise! Hank, perhaps the group's most negative member, passed out cigars and candy after becoming the father of a baby boy. A greater peace offering seemed hardly possible.

BOB: For the first time, Hank really thought of our group. . . . When people offered him their sincere congratulations, I believe he felt the group had a personal interest in him rather than in "Hank, the blocker," as I believe he had been classified.

BEVERLY: Hank came through today—as he has not all semester. . . . Duke, too, was a good influence today. He had a point, and he made it well. . . .

TRAINER: The discussion continued . . . with a searching analysis of feelings. Duke noted that by labeling certain people we fixed them deeper into their role. . . .

MAX: As I sat and listened, I thought to myself what fools some of these people are! I mean, why do they continue to put people into pigeonholes?

If I tell a person that he is a "blocker," even if he isn't, after a while he will begin to believe it and assume the role which has been created for him.

MARIE: Today Hank felt free to say that he had enjoyed and gained a lot from our last meetings. This is surely an important step for him. . . . He really thinks more of the group than he lets on. After all, he passed out the cigars and candy in our class rather than in another of his classes. . . .

LEW: Yes! Hank *does* care about the class. I am beginning to see Duke's point now. He said that Hank acts like he does because people expect it of him. . . . Today Irv died in the first hour. . . . In the second period, Irv gave it the old college try, and he was fairly effective.

ART: Today we had a permissive atmosphere in our group, but . . . I am not motivated to join in; maybe it's working with intangibles all the time. . . . I am interested, but I don't know quite what to say, where to go, or what to do. . . . This in particular is a new experience for me, as I have always been an active member in every other group I have ever belonged to.

RED: This class has the damnedest capacity to put me in a bad mood. . . . I just don't feel like putting any effort into it any more. . . . Actually, the reason I am having much trouble may be because I would be admitting my own shortcomings in not being able to help. . . .

LEW: It was most interesting to hear Red say he didn't like Beverly to get the upper hand in class. I believe what he means is that he wouldn't like anyone to get ahead of him in the struggle for leadership. . . .

BEVERLY: Red said he hated to work under a woman. He also mentioned that I controlled the class. . . . Red tried to soften his comments, but I believe his choice of the word "control" was significant. . . .

CLINICAL OBSERVER: Hank's distribution of cigars and Red's statement of his feelings about women were the key events of this session. These occurrences were interrelated.

Hank's gesture was telling because it forced a reorganization of the way in which Hank was perceived by the members of the group. . . . The collapsing of the Hank stereotype was loud enough to be heard. . . .

Red, however, was rubbed the wrong way. . . . Turning on the women, he created a new clique, and vigorously attacked them. In doing so, he broached still another area of conflict within the group.


## TWENTY-THIRD MEETING: TACKLING "CITY HALL"

BILL: Today we had a regular joke fest! Boy, was the atmosphere relaxed! We spent the first forty-five minutes laughing, and some very sharp wits were displayed. Much of the laughing was done at the expense of others. Many of the "chops" were out-of-place sarcasm. Once we were going, it became impossible for anyone to gain attention to start a serious discussion. Eventually most of us were afraid to try to get in.

TRAINER: . . . Toward the end of the first period, Don indicated that he "had had enough" and "preached" to the group about their misguided behavior. . . .

DICK: When Don finally got desperate and brought the group to order, I felt greatly relieved.

BEN: Don tried to make us feel like bums. . . . After his outburst, the atmosphere got so thick you could cut it with a knife.

DUKE: . . . I told the group about Irv. I point out his power. But I can't fight "city hall" by myself. . . . Right now, I might be killing my grade, but I will keep speaking until someone shuts me up.

ART: Irv has a role in this class. To some people he is a force which they can't fight. Although he doesn't act wrong, his very presence is bad for some members.

BEN: When Duke brought up his very good point about Irv's authority and power, Maurice tried to tell us that he wasn't aware of it, that it really didn't bother him. . . . I believe anyone who can say this about Irv's power, or that of any instructor for that matter, is a liar!

DON: Duke had a field day in trying to make himself look important. He made some good statements. . . . One was that he did his blocking as a jest. . . . I doubt that he will get by with it again. Red called him a "nasty so-and-so," and I was in full concurrence.

HANK: I wish the class knew how much I like the group at times. . . . I think Irv can see how I feel. . . .

## TWENTY-FIFTH MEETING: WILL DUKE BE SATISFIED?

TRAINER: . . . The first hour was taken up with an examination, while during the second hour we spent some time on the grading problem and some time looking at process.

BEVERLY: . . . Irv softened his ways, first by allowing us to choose our questions and second, by having us code our papers. Life is pretty tough when one has to go to such lengths to prove (attempt to prove) one has honorable intentions. Still, I think it helped.

DON: Duke is afraid that Irv will grade him down. But on this exam there were no names, and perhaps Duke was satisfied.

DUKE: This was one of the best tests I have ever taken. . . . Still, I didn't like the phony bit of assigning numbers to the papers because I think Irv will still be able to tell who wrote them.

RED: Whew—I must confess something! I had absolutely no motivation for studying for the test. My morale is shot. I couldn't see going through the work that would be necessary just to get a lousy "B". . . . I was actually considering dropping this course in order to concentrate on other courses where I stand a much better chance. I was within a whisker of dropping, to tell the truth. . . . It's a crime I'm so worried about grades.

CLINICAL OBSERVER: The major feature of the twenty-fifth session was the trainer's effort to prove that he was a person of good will. . . .

TWENTY-SIXTH MEETING: IN THE WAKE OF
  THE STEAM ROLLER

TRAINER: Returning the examination papers, I indicated considerable satisfaction with the results and mentioned that if we could put into practice
what we seemed to know intellectually we would have a most exceptional
group. There were three "A" papers—Beverly, Red, and Maurice.

JEAN: I wonder if Irv is not contributing to antagonism toward Beverly by
publicly announcing that she again made an "A". . . . I would like to
know her better, but I feel that many members in the group are strongly
against her.

DUKE: We got our quiz back today and I got a "C." What disillusionment!
Irv asked our opinion, and we got graded down for it. Am I really mixed
up? Ben and Hank got high grades. I am now resigned to a "C" in the
class and will just have to forget law school. Such injustice!

TRAINER: . . . There were thirty minutes left [for the group to reach a decision on the "grading problem"]. To most people's surprise, Max walked up
to the board, and with the help of a few confederates, literally propelled
the group toward a solution.

ART: To me it was evident that if we were to get things done, we would
have to "steam-roller" the whole thing through. . . . For me it would
have meant complete defeat if the problem had to go back to Irv. . . . I
am glad it was Max who got up because he is strong. . . . Two people
[Bill and Red] walked out, although I think it was for show only. . . . In
the end Max naturally got condemned, but anyone would have been who
had been up there. . . .

MAX: Assuming the role of authoritarian today, I was instrumental in getting
the grading problem solved in twenty-nine minutes. . . . With the help
and support of Mike, Duke, and Art, we pushed through the following
standards. . . .

LEW: Today Max pushed the grading problem through. I supported him
throughout by voicing agreement. Many, including Irv, did not like the
way we reached consensus, but to me at least, it was important to get the
job done. . . . I say to hell with anybody who gets in the way. I know
this is not what the course teaches, but if you are going to succeed in
business, you must produce! . . . .

BEN: At certain times it seemed as if everyone was trying to get his ideas
through at the same time. Bill was cut down at least three different times
when he tried to speak. So was Maurice. After a while there were only a
few who really tried to get the thing done, with the others sitting back
and not caring. . . . If there were any negative attitudes, the members
were either too scared to say anything or just didn't give a damn. . . .
For Red, everything is "hurrah for me" and "the hell with you." What a
phony!

TRAINER: During the discussion, as more and more objections were bypassed
and people got almost physically suppressed, Bill and Red got up and left
the room. . . .

DON: Why these guys walked out was not obvious at the time. True—they did appear dissatisfied with something, but what it was I didn't know. For a while they disturbed me greatly by talking to each other; they thus failed to contribute to the general good of the group.

AL: I felt somewhat guilty when Bill and Red left the room because I hadn't opened my mouth throughout the whole meeting. . . . I rather hoped the group would fail and that grading would revert back to Irv.

DOROTHY: . . . My first reaction to the walkers was "How infantile can you get?"

FRED: Bill and Red probably walked out because they felt they had no influence. Red's influence has slipped, and he gets peeved when he sees someone (girl or boy) take the spotlight away from him.

JEAN: After Bill and Red walked out, I was most uncomfortable for the rest of the hour. Bill is a member of my small [project] group, and Red had lunched with some of us following class. I felt I knew both of them well enough to comprehend their feelings. . . . I felt so utterly inept to handle the situation.

HANK: We finally got the grading problem solved just as I had predicted— by jamming it down the throats of a number of people. . . . Those people should have stood up and fought. . . . I got a kick running over some of these people—if they let it be done, then to hell with them.

DUKE: Today I just heckled. Beverly called me on it, and this just got me madder . . . I showed this by abstaining from discussion. I really feel my ideas don't count any more.

TRAINER: . . . We again had a long break, with many small groups carrying on animated and sometimes hostile discussions. Upon reconvening, we tried to discuss the process by which the grading problem was finally solved. . . . People yelled at each other, not in an accepting, friendly way, but rather with considerable anger and hostility.

HANK: I finally told Red what I thought of him. He is a phony, a real fake, a big jerk!!! . . . . I would have liked to tell Red a few more things, but Mike sensibly put a stop to the name-calling. This is one of the few times I have really got worked up in this damn class. I hope it's the last time.

BEN: After the break, Max point-blank asked Red and Bill what the hell was wrong with them. In turn Red told Max he resented his trying to be "the big man". . . . Max was accused of "railroading". . . .

MAX: I believe Beverly will be the first woman president of the United States. . . . I really respect her for her knowledge, but somehow she rubs me the wrong way. As for Red and Bill I am just fed up with them. . . .

MAURICE: My resentment toward Red subsided when I told him what I thought of him . . . I appreciate he really needs the grade in here to get into grad. school. . . . At present, he is in a poor position with the group, but no longer with me. . . .

BEN: I did nothing today to help the discussion. There were already enough people talking—those who needed a chance to blow off. . . . Still, why don't I speak up and support those whose views are similar to mine? It might be due to a combination of reasons . . . retaliation [against] a person . . . who I feel doesn't accept me. . . . Also, to a person who doesn't accept me, my support would not mean much. . . . On the other hand, maybe I am not accepted because I don't let people know where I stand. . . . I also don't want to be classed as a "yes man" or part of a clique who always support some people and not others. . . . I guess I hate to make enemies, want to remain neutral, and would prefer to be anonymous rather than the target of unfavorable attacks.

## TWENTY-SEVENTH MEETING: A CURVE AND A HIT

TRAINER: . . . The first oral presentation by a small [project] group was scheduled for the second hour . . . and the opening period merely served as a warm-up.

LEW: To me the course is now dying . . . as it has been for the last few meetings. . . . The power strugglers were struggling. A few comments were made. But not much more.

FRED: There was a lot of disinterest. Maybe the group is just plain tired of talking about certain things they don't find problems any more. . . .

TRAINER: When a spokesman for the first small-project group requested an extra ten minutes, Hank objected. . . .

HANK: . . . I enjoyed using the tyranny of the minority [toward Red and his boys]. . . . Now, I am afraid I'll watch them give us the shaft when our project comes up. I bet we'll get straight "Cs" from them.

FRANCES: I was honestly ashamed and disgusted that we didn't give the project group the five extra minutes of time which they requested. What difference would it have made? . . . .

LARRY (a member of the first project group to report): My faith in human nature is again beginning to dwindle as a result of this incident. . . . I fear people will judge our group by their reactions to one particular member in the group.

BEVERLY: When Pete made his comments, I wanted to hit him hard enough to blacken both his eyes. . . . On second thought, I wanted to take him by the hand and lead the poor, warped soul to safety. . . . (Is he warped because he doesn't believe as I do—interesting thought, isn't it?)

TRAINER: . . . Although the presentation was well organized and moved right along, the content was fairly routine and the progress report somewhat tedious. Still, in view of the personalities of the group, its achievement must be considered rather impressive.

RED: By God, no matter what the class thinks, *we had the best group project!* Furthermore, I am willing to bet that we got far more out of analyzing our own group process than did the others. In short—it took us a long time to work up respect, trust, and admiration for each other, but when it came, *it stuck!*

LEW: When I think back on our project, I must say I gained respect for every member in our group. I know our presentation was superior (and I am not one to brag much). As for our written report, I am sure we . . . will set the standard for the rest of the class. I feel our group could now manage any problem.

LARRY: Today I left the session feeling really good. . . . Our project was so successful. . . . I was really pleased the way it worked out, not only because we presented a good project, but because we had the experience of working with four other fellows with whom we had little in common.

BEVERLY: I don't think we are nearly as hostile and unobjective as we let on. . . . I bet most of us gave those kids in group I the benefit of the doubt.

FRANCES: After our own small-group meeting last night, my mood was horrible today. . . . Still, I hope I didn't let my personal preoccupation or mood influence me too greatly when I graded them.

HANK: I sure thought their project was rather boring, but I gave them a "B+" anyway. We go on next Tuesday. I hope we won't get graded down too far.


## TWENTY-EIGHTH MEETING: THE "BIG THREE" PERFORM

TRAINER: During the first period, the "big three," augmented by Fred and Maurice, presented their project. . . . The topic was not particularly original, nor was the presentation especially creative. But again, a lot of work had obviously gone into the project, and much had been accomplished.

BEN: Today was our day. . . . Once the project got started, it went along very well. I felt we really gave a fine report, especially comparing it to the first group, which left me cold.

DUKE: Today did it! I am finished! All last night I didn't get any sleep. . . . It was only after much fooling around that we finally got started. All in all, things turned out pretty good. . . . After we were through, we began fighting among ourselves, amid some congratulations.

MAURICE: . . . I was sorry I was late. . . . It made for a poor initial impression which hurt our group. . . . Duke and Hank's speeches sounded like mumbo jumbo. . . . Fred got up and talked, talked, and talked! . . . It really burned me up, especially since Duke had sent him a note to summarize. . . . When I finally got on, I had only five minutes left. . . . I roared over my main topics at high speed. . . . When we had finished, I knew that we had done poorly in comparison to our potential. . . . We needed the rehearsal which we didn't have. . . .

TRAINER: . . . The group received a "B—" for its efforts. Not bad, considering the quality of both the content and the presentation, and more important, the past reputation which the members of this small group had acquired in the class.

MAURICE: I was quite satisfied with our "B—," but Duke, Hank, and Ben were boiling at it. . . . I see they are really worried about their grades. . . . Surprisingly, Fred also joined in their chorus of yelps. . . . I just cannot see how those fellows whom I admired and respected can act so contrary to the standard that I expected from them. . . .

DUKE: When I saw our grade during the break, I sank to despair. Irv . . . added insult to injury by stating how good our project was. . . . I felt like slugging him. . . . What really got me was the way the class judged our group. I don't know on what basis we got two "Cs" and an "E"—but we did. . . . I felt a personal setback because I went to all the trouble to prepare the visual aids and most of the information which we provided. Such injustice has never been dished out before. Irv was basking in his "see, I told you so" look. What a sneaky, low-down way to get back at people you don't like!

HANK: As I predicted, we were given the shaft today by our fair-minded friends who took out their resentment against us. . . . What else can you expect from this bunch of knot-heads?

BEN: I know Duke, Hank, and I wouldn't win a personality contest, but I believe these feelings should have been kept out of it. I know no matter how much I dislike anyone, I try not to let it show in my grading.

TRAINER: The topic [presented by the third group] was not particularly interesting, but the presentation clicked and was interspersed with considerable humor.

MAURICE: Even though this presentation was weak on theory, I was tremendously interested in the report. . . . Max was just great. . . . I wonder if he knows his potential as a speaker? . . . .

BEN: I really got burned up—the third group got a "B+" for a talk that came from nowhere. . . . Max cracked a few jokes.

HANK: . . . this group got a "B+" for doing nothing. Max got his laughter, but so what! He is a "frat rat," so they got a "B+." Some justice.


## TWENTY-NINTH MEETING: CLOWNS OR TOPS?

TRAINER: Two more project reports. . . . Both groups took considerable risks by using spontaneous teaching techniques. The city-council project utilized the total class in a giant role-playing demonstration, whereas the Alcoholics-Anonymous project regaled the class with a very sensitively portrayed and carefully etched sketch of the problems of a typical alcoholic.

HANK: It is now clear that if we had acted as class clowns, sang, joked, and polished the old apple, we too would have gotten a better grade. . . . Still, I must say I enjoyed some of the presentations. What did it prove? Nothing!

MAX: The A.A. project . . . . ranked tops with me. They deserved the "A" they received. Once again, there were a few "Cs" thrown into the grading, which almost seems unbelievable to me.


## THIRTIETH MEETING: THE END AS BEGINNING— "WHAT HAVE WE LEARNED?"

TRAINER: Well, here it was—the final meeting. Most everyone was in a good mood. . . . On one occasion, the discussion again became rather heated, with a few people talking right past each other. . . . In evaluating the course [in diary entries] the reactions ranged from Red's "Oh, the hell with it!!" to Max's "without reservations—the best course I ever had at UCLA!!!"

FRANCES: This meeting was just a final get-together. . . . Any serious discussion seemed . . . . sort of a meaningless gesture. . . . We couldn't hope to iron out all the difficulties. . . . At the end, our discussions were loaded with just as much confusion, misunderstanding, frustration, and conflict as they were at the beginning. A good many individuals left the class with essentially the same attitudes and ways of thinking with which they had entered. . . . People who didn't show immediate, outward improvement in behavior may have gained some inner benefits. . . . I think the course stimulated some real thinking and perhaps laid the basis for some for a positive future. . . . As for myself—I got no immediate help . . . but I think I was made to realize that there are just as many insecure, frustrated individuals among the vocal, seemingly confident members as there are among us quiet, inhibited ones . . . that, in general, people are more concerned with what they have to say . . . than in listening to others; that they remember more distinctly what concerns them personally than what primarily involves someone else; and that all people have a pretty basic need to belong, to be accepted, to be well thought of, liked, and encouraged.

DICK: At times today, we carried on in our usual manner. . . . If an outsider had come in to observe us and had been told we had been meeting for the last fifteen weeks to learn about group dynamics, I'm afraid he would have said we hadn't learned a thing. And he would almost be right! . . . .

DUKE: During the break, I finally got up to see Irv and talk over various problems. He still rates as a good individual, but his teaching abilities need to be expanded. . . . In retrospect, I think I really learned something —in spite of myself. Maybe thanks to Irv.

MAX: I'm sorry it's all over—for many a reason. For one, I have learned more about myself and others than through any other single experience in my twenty-two years. . . . I have learned something that isn't written in the books—about myself, my fears, my actions, needs, and drives. Irv . . . is the best instructor I have had. . . . He made me think for myself.

HANK: At last the class is over! I won't forget it for some time. . . . I'm glad it's over with and finished! The last class ran true to form—a lot of talk and not too much accomplished. . . . There is no class where I am going to polish the apple to get a grade. . . . And here I'm not going to do anything that will make people think I am knuckling under. . . . Maybe sometime in the future I can look back and say "By God, I did get something out of this damn class." Only time will tell!

MAURICE: How anyone can walk out of this class and not feel a sense of accomplishment and deep impression is beyond me. . . . I am happy because over the last few weeks people have listened to what I've had to say. This is what I have tried to accomplish. Almost everyone left, whether they knew it or not, with a more permissive attitude.

LARRY: When I think of the uneasiness that existed at the beginning of the class, I realize what a great change has taken place. We have a great bunch of people—many of whom I would like to have as friends. . . . The class has done a lot for me. . . . Some of it I have already put to use. . . .

ROBIN: I still do not see how I was trained to be a leader. I can deal no more effectively with people now than I could before. Perhaps unknown benefits have accrued to me, but then perhaps, too, there may have been some disadvantages. Let's just chalk it up to experience, although I'm glad I took this course.

MIKE: It's hard to say what one gets out of a course like this—in the short run. I know I tried to apply some of the techniques in class and haven't been successful too often. Still, I've learned to become aware of the personal feelings and problems of individuals. After this awareness comes knowledge, and then perhaps action. I wish I could take the same course over again with the same group—perhaps some things would be different.

ART: For me, it has been both fun and beneficial. . . . I now know how I would have acted if we had to do it all over again. . . .

BEN: Looking back there are some sessions which I enjoyed and from which I probably learned more than my actions show. . . . I have often been very bored, but still something seemed to soak in. . . . Most people have remained the same to me as before I knew them. Only a few such as Max, Red, and Don have changed their stripes. I cut myself out of a good grade by my negative participation and by what has been said—but what the hell, it won't count ten years from now. It's been quite an experience, I must say!

BEVERLY: . . . Irv, . . . I hope you know how very much I gained from this class and how much I enjoyed it. . . . Congratulations to your dedication and most of all to your personal security and perspective which enabled you to take the jabs without ever feeling the need to fight back. . . . I realize it's your work. I also realize what strength it takes. . . .

CLINICAL OBSERVER: The ending proved to be an exercise in euphemism. As a group, there was literally no place to go. . . .

They had been through much together. They were a "group"—whether they knew it or not, whether they liked it or not. In one way or another, they all had changed. . . .

. . . The encouraging thing taking place in the meeting was its look toward the future. . . . The group seemed to be saying—and for once with the kind of consensus unknown to it during its lifetime—that the end was only apparent; more than likely it was really a beginning.

# CHAPTER 11

# Sensitivity Training
# for the Management Team*

Getting the management team to work together smoothly and effectively is sometimes a more complex and difficult problem than setting up production procedures or a control structure. One way to tackle the job is to institute a sensitivity training program for a management hierarchy within the organization.

The development of vertically structured, sensitivity-oriented leadership training groups reflects a growing recognition that interpersonal problems which arise on the job cannot be ignored. Even though these problems are frequently due to factors which are below the level of acute awareness, they should be tackled if an organization is to function at the highest level of effectiveness.

A large majority of on-the-job interpersonal problems stem from misunderstandings, from attributing one's faults to others, and from distortions due to lack of a free flow of interpersonal communication. These can be suitably handled by this kind of training and often resolved with a minimum of serious tension or conflict.

## THE NATURE OF TRAINING PROGRAMS

### Conventional Training Programs

Conventional training programs often have some serious limitations:
1. The trainee is removed from the social setting in which he cus-

---

* This chapter is based on the following publications: "Training Managers for Leadership," by Robert Tannenbaum, Verne J. Kallejian, and Irving R. Weschler, *Personnel*, vol. 30, no. 4, pp. 254–260, January, 1954, and "Managers in Transition," by Verne J. Kallejian, Irving R. Weschler, and Robert Tannenbaum, with the writing collaboration of Chandler Harris, *Harvard Business Review*, vol. 33, no. 4, pp. 55–64, July–August, 1955.

tomarily performs. With relatively few exceptions, each manager in performing his job must get on well with his subordinates, equals, and superiors. Training him in human relations apart from the humans to whom he must relate is like training an albacore fisherman in a trout stream.

2. Programs designed merely to impart human relations information may have little or no effect in inducing desirable changes in behavior. A prerequisite for the successful outcome of leadership training is the motivation to learn about oneself, others, and group process. Unless the trainee feels a need for human relations information, he is not going to "hear" it. Even if he is able to "hear" it—i.e., to accept the information—he will not necessarily be able to apply it on the job. If the new information conflicts with other of his needs, attitudes, and feelings, it will be difficult—if not impossible—for him to behave appropriately.

3. There may be little transfer of learning from the training situation to the work situation. We are not at all sure that insights and skills which are gained in the conventional training session can readily be utilized in the actual work situation. There, the social pressures on the individual to maintain his customary modes of behavior are often so strong that any attempt on his part to change is likely to fail; such change may very well conflict with the larger organizational "ways of doing things," so that he may be forced either to maintain his old behaviors or to resign.

Training vertically structured groups in sensitivity, on the other hand, is likely to yield several desirable outcomes:

1. Changes in interpersonal behavior developed through the training sessions can be carried over to work relations. As new ideas and feelings are discussed, understood, and accepted by the group in the training sessions, there is a good possibility that their impact will be reflected in the daily work contacts of the trainees.

2. The emphasis of this kind of training program is primarily oriented toward awareness of self, of others, and of interpersonal relations rather than toward the acquisition of book knowledge. When awareness occurs at the "gut level" (emotional) as well as the "head level" (intellectual), changes in behavior are more likely to occur.

3. Experience indicates that working together on mutual problems of interpersonal relations produces a more cohesive work team. In the long run, the values and techniques introduced in training may become an important part of day-to-day working procedures, so the point is reached where the group can function at a new level of efficiency. Thus, at regular staff meetings and in other work contacts where serious interpersonal problems may well arise, the members themselves are in a position to deal adequately with these problems which previously remained unrecognized or ignored.

In the vertically structured training group, it may soon become clear that the "executive neurosis" works all the way up and down the line in such a way that each individual in the group protects his status, power, and security.[1] Until the participants learn how to accept and deal with the reality of status, not much progress can be expected. Since the adverse effects of status are largely fostered by the behavior of the "top wheel," it may be necessary for the trainer to deal privately, in advance of the training, with the top individual's own relevant fears. He must be made to realize, for example, that unless he is able to accept criticism, little interchange of opinion is possible. Other private interviews with individuals who are threatened by the training process might also be necessary, before the training program can progress. In some cases, it has been found useful to have the trainer or some other professional act as a personal counselor to those individuals who feel the need to work through, outside the group sessions, personal anxieties which may be generated by the training.

As the participants with the support of the trainer and other members of the group learn to discuss and to understand such problems, they attempt to develop greater skill in dealing with them. As issues become clarified and understood, each trainee is helped to appraise his own behavior with respect to them. In time the training group becomes more secure in its ability to deal with material of this nature, and more complex problems are raised for discussion. This serves to further understanding and acceptance among members and to promote a more cohesive management team.

## Sensitivity Training Programs

The training meetings of the group are likely to differ from other work-oriented meetings (such as staff meetings) in several important ways:

*The Relative Lack of a Planned Agenda.* Though considerable planning on the part of the trainer is involved in setting up and carrying through the training program, the actual content of the program is highly flexible. External time pressures ("to get things done") are kept to a minimum.

*Participation in Leadership.* Work-oriented meetings are usually chaired by the high-status person in the group; in the training sessions the leadership may pass to the group trainer, to any other person in the group, or they may be conducted as "leaderless" discussions.

*Motivation of the Participants.* In the training sessions, the partici-

[1] The "executive neurosis" has been described by Robert N. McMurry in a stimulating article which appeared in the *Harvard Business Review*, vol. 30, no. 6, pp. 33–47, November–December, 1952.

pants are prepared to deal with problems which are rarely, if ever, introduced in conventional work-oriented meetings. Discussion tends to focus on the clarification of interpersonal perceptions, as contrasted with technical job issues which often dominate conventional meetings.

The description of sensitivity training in conventional ways sometimes loses much of the flavor of the training process. Therefore, what such a program involves and how it progresses can at times be best described and made meaningful through the device of a narrative.

In this fictional account of "managers in transition" based on a composite of our consulting experiences with many organizations, we learn what happens at Comet Television in Central City when Marv Ingham, management training consultant, is called in to survey the relationships among the members of the plant management team and to make his recommendations for improving life in the "executive suite."

## MANAGERS IN TRANSITION

Michael J. Hunter, plant superintendent of the Comet Television Company, hung his hat in the closet and tossed his brief case onto his desk with a gesture of annoyance. He always felt a little worn after conferences at the home office; besides he hadn't slept very well on the plane. He pressed the button on the intercom, and said, "Betty, get hold of Bill Simpson and Art West and ask them to come in for a few minutes. And send in some coffee, will you?"

Leaning back in his chair, he lit a cigarette. He'd been handed a tough problem, but he was sure he'd made the right decision. It was an opportunity, really, if everybody pitched right in, Mike told himself.

After all, things had gone pretty well since he'd been transferred to Comet's Central City plant a year ago to "put new life into the organization." The president had shown a lot of faith in him, and he had worked hard to do a good job. He thought he *had* done pretty well, too. He liked the spot and, generally speaking, was feeling better than he had for years. Also, he was able to spend more time with his family, and he'd started playing golf again. Certainly he had every right to feel confident of his own abilities. He'd already demonstrated that he had the courage to make decisions and the drive to carry these decisions through.

### The Problem

He took a final drag on the cigarette and crushed it out in the ash tray as his secretary opened the door to admit his two division chiefs, Bill Simpson, head of design and engineering, and Art West, head of production. When they were settled with their coffee, Mike told them,

"Well, we're off again. The 14-inch color set hasn't been moving as well as they hoped it would. The old man has bought the rights on the new Bergstrom process for the 21-inch color tube. He told me he'd give this plant the first crack at it if we wanted to convert from the 14-inchers. I told him we could handle it. I was counting on you, of course, but . . . do you think we can do it?"

"We'll sure try," said Art amiably. "Of course, it's going to cost something to switch from the 14-inch lines, but we should be able to change over without too much trouble."

Bill couldn't keep a little tone of exasperation out of his voice. "Mike, I don't mean to say I told you so, but remember last February I told you I'd seen Bergstrom's first reports in the journals? That they looked so good I didn't see how we were going to avoid winding up with a multiple prism system? After all, you get a much better balance in color values, and there's a lot less halo, and besides you can handle a larger screen. I even made up a little abstract of his paper for you, remember? But when I didn't hear anything more about it from you, well, I didn't go into it any further. Now we'll have to start absolutely from scratch. It'll take us at least a month, and . . . ."

"O.K., O.K.," Mike cut in, "That's all water over the dam, now, and there's no point in fretting about it. We're just going to have to buckle down and get going on it. Put your boys on overtime if you need to. Couldn't you have something for Art to start on in three weeks?"

When his division heads had left the office, Mike fished another cigarette out of the pack and studied it intently. What was eating Bill, anyhow? A brilliant guy, but sometimes so touchy. Certainly not much like Art, who was really *too* easygoing, especially when it came to handling subordinates. Soft, almost. Sometimes he wondered why people worked as well for Art as they did. Still, Art was easy to talk to, except when he came up with one of those bumbling compliments of his, which embarrassed you so much that you had to change the subject.

*Outside Viewpoint*

Everyone, Mike reflected, had his peculiarities, and that didn't keep both Bill and Art from turning out good work when the chips were down. At the same time, he was rather glad he'd decided to call in that consultant earlier, even though he wasn't quite sure why he had. To his wife, to the home office, and to his staff members, Mike had said that Marv Ingham, the consultant, was just interviewing the managerial personnel to see if anything could be done to improve plant operation, good as it was. Might be something to it, too. Mike remembered his own days as a cog in a big machine, and he knew a stranger could find out more in a few days than the boss could discover in years through the usual channels.

Mike reached for his brief case and pulled out the report that Marv had submitted. Marv had been interviewing for five days; he had seen everyone in the plant down through the first level of supervision; he also had talked to a few employees on the line and in the shops—not many, but enough to get a feel of things.

The tone of the report was different from any Mike had ever read. Not much about production problems, working conditions, or general plant operation. Instead, there was a lot about seeing things differently, failures in communication, some disturbing "interpersonal problems" among the management group. There was also a suggestion that Mike should look into these problems in the not-too-distant future. Mike believed in action; if a thing was worth looking into, it was worth looking into now. He decided to ask Marv for more details.

*New Ideas.* Two hours later, Marv sat down with him to explain what he had in mind. Actually, he wasn't much more specific than the report; and Mike, at first, was not too pleased with what he was getting. Marv said something about not being able to violate confidences, and besides he had few facts, only feelings and often contradictory perceptions on which to base his judgments. No statistics, no specific findings —just something about the atmosphere being charged—just some tenuous impressions about people not working well together.

Marv remembered his interview with Bill in engineering. Bill had talked a lot, but said little. He seemed cautious—perhaps too cautious; when asked about Mike, he parried, "Mike is all right—I guess. We get along fine." Marv got the impression that Bill had hostile feelings about Mike that embarrassed him.

Marv hadn't got much further with Art in production. Art seemed more spontaneous than Bill, especially when talking about his own division, but became noncommittal when asked about his relationship to people in the management group.

Some of the others Marv had talked to tried hard to make everything look good, while a few sounded like prophets of impending doom. Some seemed jumpy and talked about trivial issues with more emotion than seemed warranted.

Also, there was a definite lack of communication between management levels. Most of the first-line supervisors often described a common gripe, while the next higher level of management didn't seem to be aware that the complaint existed. Altogether, Marv's impressions of his forty interviews added up to a definite pattern—"all was not well at Comet Television in Central City!"

*Mike Resists.* Mike felt a certain resistance to these ideas. "I just don't think we have any particular personnel problems," he said. "Don't these things happen in every plant?"

"Yes, they do, but sooner or later they backfire in one way or another. Trouble develops in ways that are hard to deal with—like increased turnover, breakage, delays, breakdowns in communication, secretiveness, and lowered morale and productivity."

Mike frowned. "Are you sure you aren't just oversensitive to these so-called interpersonal relationships?"

"Maybe so. That's my job. But I think the possibility is worth exploring. Do you mind if I ask *you* a few questions?"

Mike leaned back in his chair. "Not at all. Fire away."

Marv's few questions seemed more like a hundred:

"How about your staff meetings? Who talks?"

"How are decisions made? Who makes them?"

"What effect do you think you have on your subordinates? What do you do that they like? What do you do that they don't like? Why not?"

"What kind of a person is Bill? Art? What kind of a relationship do they have to each other?"

"Do you do anything special to help communication between members of the divisions?"

And so on and on.

Mike felt a bit resentful of the questions—they were disturbing, and he didn't have really good answers to them. What finally set him off, though, was Marv's looking squarely at him and asking, "Are you concerned about how your people feel?" Mike barely suppressed a surge of violent anger. He knew it showed in his face. He didn't know why he was so mad; but he was. Obviously Marv didn't understand the cold realities of the business world—he wanted to make a tea party out of a well-ordered business.

"I want to think about these things a little more," he told Marv. "Right now we've had a big production problem tossed in our lap, and it may tie us up for days. I'll get in touch with you later."

Mike discovered that he couldn't put Marv's questions out of his mind. One thing that returned to disturb him was his own angry reaction to Marv's probing. He wondered if there was some connection between his own feelings and the reactions of his men after he had bombarded them with penetrating questions.

At lunch, as he looked across the table at Art and Bill, he wondered if he had more than a superficial understanding of the key men with whom he worked. Maybe he didn't, and maybe that was why he was always so concerned about them. Still, he told himself, there was no use in attempting a curbstone psychoanalysis of everybody in the plant and then trying to adjust himself to their idiosyncrasies. It wasn't his fault if some people couldn't adjust themselves to his way of doing business. He had enough to do without worrying about how other people felt about him. After all, they were paid to do a job.

## The Men under Mike

Marv, for his part, welcomed the opportunity of a day or two away from the plant. He wanted time to rearrange the enormous jigsaw puzzle with which he had been struggling, especially now that the talk with Mike had provided some of the missing pieces. He went back to his office and revised his notes. If Mike wanted to go ahead, he would be ready with some suggestions.

Marv was primarily concerned with seven key people. Mike stood at the top of the management pyramid. Directly under him were Bill and

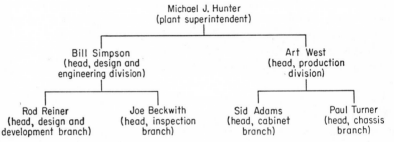

FIGURE 11-1. The top executive group of Central City Plant, Comet Television Corporation.

Art, each of whom had two branch heads. Bill, in design and engineering, was assisted by Rod Reiner, his chief of design and development, and Joe Beckwith, his chief of inspection. Over in production, Art's top aides were Sid Adams, in charge of cabinet production, and Paul Turner, in charge of chassis production.

What was it that made it difficult for these people to work together effectively? And which courses of action were most likely to bring about improvements? From the copious notes he had made after each interview, Marv had gathered together the material necessary to understand better each of these six men under Mike and their relationships to each other and to the boss.

## What about Bill?

First, there was Bill. He had an engineering degree from a leading university. He was brilliant and able, and he knew his job. He also was competitive, and he liked power. Bill wanted recognition from the boss and worked hard to get it. Often, when Mike had a suggestion, Bill went to great lengths to indicate that he had thought about the possibility before. These little lectures were always tinged with overtones of annoyance and aggression.

In the face of them, Mike was emotionally immobilized. He worked so hard to suppress any aggressive feelings of his own that he found it difficult to deal with aggression in Bill. Moreover, it never occurred to Mike that Bill was eager for him to show some approval and support of his efforts. And even if this had occurred to Mike, he wouldn't have known what to do about it. Mike appeared to regard Bill as a self-contained machine.

It would be a waste of time, Marv reflected, to suggest to Bill that he represented a constant threat to his boss. Bill was so concerned with himself that he was not very observant of the inner feelings of others. If he had spoken frankly about Mike, Bill would probably have said that Mike was always stubborn. Yet, he would have sensed no connection between Mike's stubbornness and his own behavior.

*Bill's Assistants.* Turning to Bill's assistants, Marv noted that their situation was colored by Bill's relationship to Mike. Since Mike was incapable of dealing with Bill's drives, these drives were turned toward Rod and Joe.

During the war, Rod had been in the Navy and had learned some engineering tricks which left Bill baffled. Rod had no degree, but he had ingenuity and initiative. His designs were clean, his ideas good. His work was always out on time, and he liked to work on several projects at once. To say that Bill was jealous would be doing Bill an injustice; he knew that Rod was capable. But Bill just wasn't able to accept the contributions of other people easily. Although it would have been impossible to isolate any single clear-cut instance to support his conclusion, Rod felt that his efforts were minimized and resented. He was puzzled, but he didn't question. He had too much regard for Bill's competence.

On the page headed by Joe's name, Marv had little to write. Joe had refused to talk with him. Obviously, Joe was scared. He was also plenty mad. Marv knew this much, but he didn't know why. If he had been in Joe's office a few days earlier, he'd have understood. Joe's wife had called him on the phone again complaining about the kids, the house, Joe's working late. Joe was also in financial trouble. He was mad at somebody, and he didn't know who. Working for Bill made Joe's troubles twice as unbearable. Joe was a tough, unreasonable inspector, and when Bill got tough, Joe got tougher. When Bill manipulated Joe, Joe manipulated twenty people. If Bill set Rod up for a little ridicule, Joe would dish out twice as much. And so it went, in an endless, cumulative circle.

*Art Was Different*

In the production division, things were different because Art was different. Art had been with the plant a long time. He had started out making jigs and fixtures; later he had set up production lines. After long years of experience, he'd finally been promoted to head of production. Art was slow, tolerant, patient. He was liked by most of his own people, who depended on him heavily.

Art solved his personal problems by himself. He never got mad. He always gave the appearance of a man who took things easy. He said frankly that he knew when to keep his mouth shut. Art performed best when he was comfortable and secure. In staff meetings with Bill, he said little. He harbored his annoyances. When Bill interfered with his production schedule, he would consider it carefully—and then do nothing. When Mike made decisions that Art should have made, he didn't say a word.

From Bill's point of view, Art was something like Mike. But since Art was an equal, Bill considered him weak and ineffective. At times Bill would become so exasperated with him that he wouldn't talk to him for days except on the most urgent plant business.

Strangely enough, Mike had somewhat the same feeling about Art. He considered Art soft and couldn't understand why he appeared to have such good morale in his unit. When Art talked somewhat affectionately about his people in the plant, Mike and Bill often united in annoyance. At times, Mike would admit to himself a bit of jealousy at Art's way with people. Art was a man in whom people confided easily; Mike himself would be more likely to talk over a fishing trip with him than with anyone else.

For Art's part, he liked Mike. He admired his abilities and education, something he never had or would have. He also learned from Mike. Art found it difficult to express his appreciation; whenever he tried, something strange happened to Mike. Instead of accepting Art's feelings, Mike felt compelled to go into a long discussion on some unrelated topic. In spite of Mike's front of adequacy, he appeared to feel uncomfortable when reminded of his achievements.

*Art's Assistants.* With Sid, his cabinet man, and Paul, his chassis man, Art had an unspoken understanding: if one was loyal to Art, and Art alone, nothing outside the division could interfere with the work. Art ran interference on everything, and Sid and Paul answered only to him.

Sid didn't make a move without consulting Art. Marv smiled as he recalled Sid saying that Art gave a lecture at least once a week about everyone's having the responsibility of his own unit—adding that Art would be hurt if decisions were made without his prior approval. Sid liked this relationship because it relieved him of all responsibility, but Art spent a considerable portion of his time doing the work of his branch head.

In some respects, Paul seemed a misfit in this group. Paul was middle-aged, a self-taught man who knew his limitations. In the process of growing up, Paul had learned to respect himself. He liked people and was well liked in the plant. He got along well with his superiors. If Art wanted to take over an operation, Paul didn't complain. In a sense, Paul complemented Art as Rod complemented Bill. While Bill needed someone meek and vulnerable, Art needed someone understanding who was personally secure. Art felt comfortable with Paul, and sometimes he'd have long talks with him. These talks left Art feeling better than he had in days, and Paul would sense some inner satisfaction that he'd have found difficult to put into words.

## Looking for Improvement

Considering the alignments and the tensions among these seven top men, some observers might have thought it surprising that anything came out right at Comet at all. It didn't surprise Marv, though. He'd seen business teams function even when every issue became a sparring ground for status. He'd seen staffs in which "sheer logic" became an intellectual exercise by which each person attempted to outsmart the other, bringing up facts which were irrelevant and withholding really pertinent information. No, it was not surprising that considerable work was getting done at Comet in the midst of certain conflicts. But that didn't mean that there wasn't plenty of room for improvement.

As to how that improvement could be accomplished, Marv considered the possibilities. He could suggest that he and Mike have a series of talks. There was the possibility of sending individuals to management-training seminars. That procedure had the advantage of putting the minimum strain on the organization. But sometimes, when the individuals returned to the job, they were caught up in the same patterns of activity as before. In the seminars they found out what they should do; however, circumstances on the job just didn't seem to permit change, and some people found it difficult to apply the new skills which they had learned. Sure, if the boss had got this training, it might be different, but after all—he hadn't!

Training the management team right in the plant itself was another possibility. In a way, Marv found this idea the most acceptable. Certainly such a program had many risks, but it also had the greatest potential. *The key person was Mike.* If Mike proved willing to embark on such a program, in full awareness of all the implications, it had a good chance of success. He decided to recommend it if the opportunity arose.

## DEVELOPING A PROGRAM

Later that week he received a call from Mike, asking him to come in. When he entered the office, Marv found that Mike's coolness of the last meeting had vanished. Mike was affable and ready to listen to suggestions. Marv outlined a program in which the key men of the plant would meet together once a week for a two-hour session.

"You mean there'd be lectures?" asked Mike.

"No, very few lectures, plenty of discussion. The meetings would be very informal; there would be no specified objective except to explore problems of common interest."

Mike seemed a bit doubtful. "Sounds like an awfully indirect approach. You really think anything would be accomplished?"

"I think there's a good chance. The real objective, of course, would be to develop better understanding between the members of your group and to work on skills which will improve their effectiveness."

Mike's mind was busy with silent questions:

¶ Would people talk about him?

¶ Were there some problems between Bill and Art which might get into the open?

¶ Would Marv be able to straighten things out?

¶ What if Bill and his outfit opposed it?

¶ Isn't this playing with fire? What if somebody blew up?

¶ What would people at the home office say once they heard about the program?

¶ Wouldn't they think he'd gone off the deep end?

He had some spoken questions, too. Wouldn't some other alternative be better? Mightn't things get worse instead of better? Had Marv ever tried this before? How did it work out?

Marv answered as accurately as he could. He wasn't trying to oversell the idea—the program could never be any better than Mike's willingness to make it work. "If you like, think about it for a few days and let me know," he told Mike. "You know where to reach me."

### Mike Decides

At noon, Mike had his lunch sent in and ate alone, as he often did when he was threshing out some problem. Afterwards, he leaned back in his chair, put his feet up on the low window ledge, and smoked his cigarette. This thing reminded him of the time he set up a profit-sharing committee. They all said he was radical, undermining the spirit of free enterprise. He grinned at the thought that many of his critics had since followed the pattern he'd helped develop. Still, pioneering had its risks, and he had considerable misgivings about Marv's proposal.

He wondered what other Comet people would think. All you really needed to be a good supervisor was a firm grasp of the business and a little common sense. Still, if there were hidden difficulties. . . . But no one would wonder about calling in an accountant or an engineer to straighten out a particularly tough problem. Was this essentially any different?

One other thought caused a little frown on Mike's forehead. How would the sessions affect his own relationship with the other men? He'd once read that people who go out of their way to be nice to everyone are merely trying to cover up other feelings of hate and anger. Seemed a bit farfetched, but sometimes he wondered about his own ability to tolerate people who didn't work at the same pace or in the same spirit that he did. There were a lot of other angles, too. When he found himself thinking about time and cost, he knew that he had made up his mind.

The following morning he called in his group, outlined the program as he saw it, and asked what they thought about it. All the men had already met Marv in individual interviews, and that helped. There were no serious objections. Bill was the only one who had much to say, and he was not too critical. Partly to avoid open disagreement with Mike, partly because they saw an opportunity to get some things off their mind, and partly because there was something about the idea that awakened some sparks of real hope, the group acquiesced. A few days later it embarked on its initial training venture.

*First Meetings*

The first meeting was stiff, perhaps somewhat tense. Marv carried the ball during most of the session. Toward the end of the meeting he asked the group what problems they'd like to take up at subsequent sessions. Rod suggested a discussion on office memos. "Why do we have to put everything in writing; besides, whatever happens to all the suggestions in those memos?" Sid and Paul seemed more concerned with techniques for getting people to tackle a job they were supposed to be doing.

Bill thought they ought to talk about lines of authority in the plant and in relation to the home office. "Why does so much stuff have to be referred to New York? By the time I get permission to hire a hot engineer, somebody else has him." Art suggested they consider methods of improving staff meetings. Joe had nothing to say at all.

Even though nearly everyone had made a suggestion, there was little comment on the ideas from anyone else in the group. When the meeting was over, there was a general feeling of apathy. Most of the men seemed to feel they'd gotten nowhere. There was considerable antagonism toward Marv, who was expected to offer sound advice on each problem raised.

During the second meeting, the group became concerned about getting started. Marv suggested that they appoint an observer each time to help keep track of what happened in the meeting and, as a result, he became the object of some ill-disguised anger.

Afterwards, Marv listened to the recordings of the first two sessions to check his general hunches about how the group was going. Mike and Bill dominated most of the discussion. Very few ideas were picked up by anyone besides the man who offered them; once in a while Rod and Joe followed Bill's suggestions, while Paul and Sid supported Art. Every decision was made by Mike. Marv sensed some strong mixed feelings toward himself. It was apparent that the group was not yet ready to look at the real problems.

By the end of the third meeting almost everyone agreed that the discussion of theoretical topics was impossible. At the end of the fourth meeting, Bill said he didn't think that the meetings were getting anywhere. No one dissented. Marv suggested that it might be worthwhile to look at some of the reasons why this was true. The suggestion was passed by—unnoticed.

*Change of Pattern*

At the fifth meeting the pattern began to change. A few cautious remarks were made to Mike about his attitude in the meetings. Mike expressed surprise and asked for clarification. The talk was a little more open, and a few seemed to want to talk at the same time. Bill's cynical smile disappeared occasionally as he became immersed in the discussion. Joe was still quiet, but several times he'd have spoken if he'd been given a chance. The fifth meeting ran twenty minutes over the usual two hours.

Marv, always sensitive to any change in atmosphere, began to feel that the group was getting on its way. To check his impressions, he spent an afternoon in the plant. Mike told him, "I can't understand why anybody should feel he can't talk freely to me. People shouldn't be so sensitive!"

"If you can't understand it, why not ask a few questions about it in the next meeting?" Marv hoped his suggestion would take root.

When he dropped in on Bill, Marv found him friendly but, as usual, vaguely superior. Bill said he thought the sessions were wasting two hours a week for nothing. "Not that I'm not getting *something* out of them. Undoubtedly I've learned a few things, but nothing that you couldn't read in a book. Tell you what, though. We'd probably get along a lot faster if you could keep people like Paul from talking so much."

Art welcomed Marv into his office. Something was happening to Art, Marv reflected. Each person takes something different away from each session, and Art apparently was on the verge of certain insights. Art recounted an incident in his office in which he had used the listening technique they'd discussed in training; he was obviously pleased at the way it had worked out.

Incidents like this had long ago convinced Marv that what he said in a group was frequently lost, but what he *did* left strong impressions. Long after a training session, people would draw on these techniques for handling similar situations. Talking later with Paul and Sid, Marv was convinced that Art was getting the point.

## THE TURNING POINT

There was nothing unusual about the beginning of the sixth meeting. Marv opened the session by asking the members of the group to bring up whatever they felt like discussing. Mike announced that Joe had told him he'd have to miss this session—a rush order was in the process of being inspected.

During the first fifteen minutes there was the usual sparring as to what to talk about. Bill pointed out that they still hadn't come to grips with problems of overlapping authority. Paul thought that plant operations might be improved by a better system of communication. Both of these ideas were allowed to curl up and die.

### First Open Discussion

Throughout the preliminary discussion, Mike seemed a bit preoccupied and slightly on edge. At last, during a slight pause, he took the plunge. "You know, after the last meeting I was rather concerned about the feeling you fellows had that you couldn't say what you wanted to me. I've been thinking about it. . . . I can't help it, but it seems to me you're all wet. What I'd like to have are some good, concrete examples. How about it?"

There was a long and slightly uncomfortable silence. Rod picked up a pencil and began drawing fancy doodles on a scratch pad. Paul knocked the ashes out of his pipe and began searching his pockets for his tobacco pouch. "Well, Mike," he said, "I've sometimes had the feeling that you cut Bill and Art off before they'd really finished what they had to say. It's sort of difficult to put your finger on any particular incident; I don't know if I could think of one right now or not."

"I'll give you an example, Mike," said Bill. "Remember a few weeks ago when we were discussing the Bergstrom tube? You cut me off just when I was telling you that we could have got the jump on most of the industry if we'd only followed my hunch that Bergstrom was on the right track. You know, the top engineers in most of these outfits don't really follow the scientific journals closely; they take a look at a couple of the engineering trades and figure they've covered the field. When I saw Bergstrom's report in *Science* a year ago, I knew he had the answer to color. If we'd moved then. . . . "

"Bill, I know all that," Mike interjected, "but, as I told you when we were talking about it, it's water over the dam now. I'd just like to hear some concrete examples of any time that I haven't been willing to listen to any ideas you fellows have. Don't I ask for a report from each of you at staff meetings?"

Art nodded his head. "Yes. Yes, that's right," he said. "I don't think I'd say that you reject what other people have to say. In fact, I can think of times when I've made suggestions and you've shown me how to change them around a little bit so that they worked out even better than I thought they would."

### Growing Awareness

Mike stared down at the table and squirmed a bit in his chair. "Uh . . . well, I don't know," he said. Frowning a bit, he turned to Marv. "I'd like to get your ideas on this, Marv. Do you think from what you've seen around here that I make it hard for people to talk to me?"

Marv thought for a moment and said, "Well, that's hard to say, Mike. You may want to look more closely at what has been going on here in this last interchange between you and Bill or between you and Art. After all, this is a problem in communication, and you may want to ask Art or Bill how they felt. Do you think there is anything to this?"

Mike looked surprised. "No, I don't see how. They both had a chance to speak, didn't they?" A long silence followed.

Later, while reviewing the recorded tapes of this meeting in the privacy of his office, Marv became convinced that things were beginning to happen. As he saw it, Mike was gradually becoming aware that he was having a negative impact on his staff, and that some people felt that he did not give them a chance to express their feelings.

But while intellectually willing to look at this, Mike wasn't really prepared to accept it emotionally. His opening question immediately forestalled the kind of response which might have been helpful to him. By challenging the group to provide specific instances of his behavior, he tried to defend his own position that his "door was always open."

The interchange with Bill showed he was quite insensitive to Bill's need for recognition and his own role in not letting Bill express himself fully.

In his interchange with Art, Mike handled his embarrassment at receiving praise from Art by ignoring his comments. As a result, he reinforced Art's basic belief that Mike made it difficult for him to express some of his real feelings to him.

Mike's response to Marv's suggestion rather clearly indicated that he was not yet prepared to lower his defenses and look at the impact he was having on others. This incident seemed to Marv to have inherent in it some key to the interpersonal relationship between Mike, Bill, and Art. Similar instances, Marv knew, would inevitably occur in subsequent sessions, but a time might be reached when Mike and the others would be able to look back on these exchanges, and accept fully the implications of their behavior.

The discussion next ranged briefly over a number of topics mostly related to communication problems in the management team. Then Art again expressed dissatisfaction with recent staff meetings. Sid said he had a feeling that the meetings never really came to grips with his own particular problems in coordinating cabinet manufacture with the rest of the plant. Rod suggested that the meetings were too cut and dried—just a series of reports without much discussion on anything except the set agenda. Bill said he didn't see anything wrong with that— you had to have some kind of set program for the meetings or you'd just wind up chasing your tail. Paul thought Rod had a point, though; sometimes things came up at the last minute that ought to be discussed even if unscheduled.

"Well, of course, our meetings may not be perfect," Mike admitted, "but I've always felt they were letting everyone know what the others are doing. You haven't said anything, Art; what do you think?"

"Oh, sometimes the meetings seem helpful, and then again some of them don't seem to be getting anywhere. I think it's sort of a matter of your point of view."

## The Flare-up

Rod looked as if he were about to explode. "Art, you really get me sometimes! What *is* your point of view? I'd like to know for once— how you *do* feel about our staff meetings."

Art's bland expression underwent no change. "I think I feel a lot like you guys do. You've just about covered the water front; there isn't much more that I could add."

"Damn it, Art, that's just what I mean! Right here is one of the key difficulties in our meetings—we never know where you stand on anything! When an issue comes up, we have to guess what your position is. I never know whether you think your guys can handle a new set of designs or not."

Art's eyebrows went up. "Gosh, Rod, I didn't mean to get you upset. What I just said is how I really *do* feel about our staff meetings."

"I'm not talking just about staff meetings, Art," Rod persisted. "It seems as if you always keep us in the dark. I'll bet some of the other guys have had similar experiences."

"I don't mind saying that *I* have!" said Bill. "I can think of half a dozen times, Art, when you've clammed up and left me stranded up the river. Remember a couple of weeks ago, when we were talking about a new suppressor circuit for 6218A? You complained that the first designs had a bug in them, but when I suggested that maybe your boys hadn't quite followed specifications, you were noncommittal. I couldn't decide whether the thing ought to be reworked or not!"

"Well, Bill, you'll have to admit that's a heck of a thing to say about the production side unless you really had something to go on," Paul said. "What Art probably wanted to tell you was to take your specifications and go jump in the lake. But he's a peace-loving guy, so he bit his tongue instead."

"O.K., so he bit his tongue. Where did that leave me?" asked Bill.

"Up the creek, probably. I'll admit, Art, there are times when you do a pretty good imitation of the Sphinx," said Paul. "I suppose you could lay it on the line and let the chips fall where they may."

Art looked just the least bit hurt. "Well, a lot of these questions have two sides to them, and some have even more. I think I do the best I can to tell you what I think."

"Only it doesn't work that way in practice," said Bill, resuming his complaint. "I'll give you another example. Remember when Rod came up with an idea for a cove-type picture frame? You didn't want to put an off-white finish on it; you said it might pick up too much light. I told you I thought you were crazy and asked you to talk it over with Rod. After that I never could get you to say much about it, and neither could Rod."

"That's the kind of thing I mean, Art," Rod added; "usually you're easy to work with, but sometimes it just seems as if you won't take a firm position on anything."

"I think you guys are being a little bit unfair," said Sid. "You make it sound as if Art didn't have the courage of his convictions, and you know that isn't true. Sure . . . sometimes he puts off saying just what he thinks. But Bill, if Art takes a position you don't like, you jump all over him. He's just trying to do his job."

"Well, it would be a lot easier for everybody if we knew just where he stood," said Bill.

The thoughtful look on Mike's face had darkened into the suggestion of a frown. Glancing at him, Marv sensed that it made him uneasy to have Art on the hot seat. "Now, wait a minute, fellows," Mike broke in. "I wonder if we're really accomplishing anything all piling on one man. What do you think, Marv?"

### Developing Insight

Marv was pleased. He saw real progress in the making—feelings stirred up, important insights developing. Mike wouldn't understand about that—certainly not after what happened before. "I guess it all depends. Art, how do you feel about it? Do you understand what the others are saying to you?"

Art's smile was wry. "I guess so, more or less. It looks as if most of you wish I'd be a little more outspoken. Bill thinks I clam up if I don't agree with him, and even Paul and Sid seem to feel that I don't let them know how I feel."

"And do you think these comments are justified?" asked Marv.

"Well, I suppose they are if everybody feels the same way about it—though to tell you the honest truth, I never noticed it myself. In some cases I figured that, once I'd had my say, I wasn't going to keep belaboring the point; and other times I just couldn't see any advantage in getting into a big hassle which wasn't going to solve anything anyhow. I just don't know."

Marv turned to Mike. "Just a moment ago you asked me what I thought, Mike. Since you haven't made any comment, how do you look at all of this?"

"I don't think Art has much to worry about, myself," Mike replied. "I've always found him easy to talk to. The only question I've had in my mind, Art, is that I only seem to be able to get the good news from you. . . . When things aren't going well in your division, I don't hear a peep out of you. And, well, one other thing. I'm sure that you must not approve of every decision I make, and yet if you don't approve, you never say so. In a way that's very complimentary, and in another way it isn't."

Rod leaned forward and caught Art's eye. "Art, there's just one other thing I'd like to say. I certainly didn't mean to imply that *I* think you're hard to work with, because I don't. What I meant was that when you sort of put me off, I don't know how to proceed. I couldn't decide whether to go ahead on that cove framing or throw it on the junk heap."

"Well, I see what you mean," said Art. "Maybe I just naturally avoid saying so if I think something you do is not so hot. I've always figured that a lot of these things will just work themselves out if you give them enough time. But I can see it makes it hard not to know where you stand."

Marv was pleased with the insight that Art seemed to be gaining. The progress of the group was slow, but undeniable. The recorded tape showed it. Though Paul and Sid had supported Art in the discussion, as they usually did, even they had indicated that Art's failure to communicate had bothered them at times. Bill, characteristically, had used the occasion to become aggressive toward Art, and Art had given him his typical reply—which was none at all. Mike had been disturbed at so much criticism of Art, and yet he too was able to voice some of his real feelings about Art.

Art in turn was able to achieve some intellectual and perhaps even some emotional understanding of what had been said. Perhaps he hadn't found a way of dealing with this problem, but the chances were that he would be much more alert to similar actions on his part in the future. Altogether, it seemed to Marv that Art was making considerable progress. Undoubtedly the others would, too, as the sessions continued.

As the meeting drew to a close, Marv noticed that the atmosphere was more relaxed than it had been before. After a lengthy and not very conclusive discussion of how staff meetings might be improved, Mike glanced at his watch and said, "Well, I guess that's about all for today, fellows—we had to cut the session because of the holiday tomorrow. I'm sure we all have a lot to think about from this meeting—I know that I have some real thinking to do."

## TAKING STOCK

Marv wondered if Mike really had learned something from Art's experience, or, perhaps, even from his own. Did these experiences have direct relevance to him as a person? Could he be searching his own behavior for things that antagonized others? Some of the others may also have taken a new look at themselves. Certainly Art had. These things take time. Time—and again more time. Sometimes it seems like rambling —not getting any place, not showing any concrete accomplishments. But, then, some people do see the light; they do change, and everyone seems the better for it.

Marv again thought of the sixth meeting as a whole. It may well have been the turning point. The barriers were falling. The men were learning to listen and talk to each other—not about things out in space, but about themselves, their aspirations, and their fears of and feelings for each other. They were learning to be sensitive—to their own needs, and to those of others. They were seeing each other differently. They were working on their own blind spots—getting a better perspective on what life in the "executive suite" at Central City was really like. They were beginning to accept each other, not for what they would have liked each other to be, but for what they in fact were—with all their strengths and shortcomings.

What was the future to be like? Marv wondered about that too—and so did all the rest. There was a different spirit emerging—nothing radically different, but perhaps embracing just a little bit more cooperation, a little less competition. Some problems would still be dealt with for what they were—technical difficulties, breakdowns in scheduling, and the like. Others, however, would be recognized as stemming from the men themselves, their likes and dislikes for each other, their frustrations and ambitions. These would be recognized and dealt with—not as before by hidden aggressions or displacements, but by handling them openly and in a mature and forthright manner.

Managers in transition. That's one way of describing what was happening at Central City. Transition takes time. Marv knew this. But at least time was on his side. The top management of Comet was on its way to becoming a team.

# CHAPTER 12

# Observations on the Trainer Role: A Case Study*

Seeing different trainers at work can be most revealing. Each has his own personality, his theories of training, and different skills in varying degrees of competence. Some act as catalysts; others as sources of wisdom; others as counselors; still others as teachers. Some respond to the overt, conscious needs of their trainees; others to what appear to them as more significant unconscious wants and drives. Some actually do what they think they do; others give lip service to one mode of operation while actually performing in another. Some are blocked by their own personality difficulties from helping their trainees face up to similar problems within themselves; others appear reasonably well adjusted in the interpersonal arena and are not bothered by undue tensions in the efficient execution of their jobs.

Direct appraisal of the trainer role in human relations training programs has generally been neglected, despite the fact that both leadership theory and leadership method have received considerable attention in the literature devoted to group behavior. For the most part, research on group processes has tended to recognize the trainer implicitly, but to ignore his explicit behavior. This has sometimes led to the erroneous impression that events occurring in a training group are only indirectly affected by the trainer's activities.

## STUDY PURPOSE

We aim here to present a way of looking at the trainer role, to identify and describe problems which are most likely to be encountered par-

* This chapter is based on a paper, "The Trainer Role in Human Relations Training," by Jerome Reisel, delivered before a meeting of the Western Psychological Association, San Diego, Calif., April, 1959.

ticularly by those who undertake a sensitivity training assignment, and to demonstrate the basic premise that the trainer is a potent factor in the total interaction of his group. His influence, it appears to us, must be given serious consideration if full-scale understanding of the training process is to be achieved.

In order for sensitivity training to be effective, conditions must be set up which allow for an integration of emotional and cognitive learning. From the trainer's point of view, his task is primarily one of creating an atmosphere conducive to learning. He also must assess how much can be learned by the group with which he works. For every group encountered, the trainer is apt to vary his objectives in some degree. If his training function is to be well carried out, his efforts must be based on an accurate assessment of group potentials. This is his core problem, and it is by no means a simple one. This view of the training role stresses trainer sensitivity in the selection of appropriate goals as a factor of key importance in increasing the likelihood of his doing an effective job.

In his work, the trainer cannot avoid involvement in the flow and counterflow of activity of his group. It is only in this fashion that he picks up the cues that should enable him to provide the kind of assistance that will help the group to work out conflicts that arise. His capacity for discovering cues and his ability to determine an appropriate course of action on the basis of these findings are, we believe, direct functions of his personality.

This case study focuses on the trainer, so far as his role is defined by what he perceives and how he acts on these perceptions. A clinical frame of reference is used. Viewing training behavior in its psychodynamic aspects immediately admits trainer personality as a fundamental variable in the process of human relations training. The clinical approach also challenges the validity of the notion that all the structural and functional properties of such groups can be studied meaningfully apart from the trainer.

Two key hypotheses underlie the clinical point of view. First, the trainer is a constant source of motivational stimuli for the group; second, the stimuli put forth by the trainer are a direct function of his total personality organization.

The assertion that the trainer is a constant source of motivational stimuli for the group implies that the trainer is always a force for encouragement, facilitation, hindrance, or inhibition to the group. By tracing the source of these motivational stimuli to the personality organization of the trainer, one is able to assess his behavior as a function of his needs, beliefs, values, and attitudes. Thus, his training role is the result of a constellation of such factors as the degree and kind of intelligence he possesses; his imaginative capacity; his direct responsiveness to the environment; his outlook toward past, present, and future; the presence and amount of anxiety within him; his range of emotional reactions; and his general pattern of character traits.

It should be added that the hypothesis of a close functional relationship between trainer and group should not lead to the inference of a one-to-one relationship. If it did, a "great-man" theory would provide the necessary and sufficient conditions for comprehending all group phenomena—which it does not!

## SUBJECTS AND METHOD

The subjects of this investigation were two trainers, both of whom are men of established reputation in the field of human relations training. They have contributed substantially to the literature on group behavior and are currently active as trainers in various training programs. They are frequently engaged as speakers by organizations or groups representing business, labor, education, government, etc. Neither of them is a clinician, and their knowledge of dynamic psychology and its methods comes mainly from academic study, with training experience providing a second source of information. Both were aware of the nature of this study, but they have not dictated or influenced its form or content in any way.

The study was carried out by a clinical research psychologist who observed the subjects as they worked with two sensitivity training groups in an academic setting. These particular training groups consisted of seniors and graduate students who were planning to enter such fields as labor relations, personnel management, administrative nursing, business management, public service, and teaching.

Each training group consisted of twenty-four persons. In both groups the men outnumbered the women by about three to one. Each group was organized in a manner that allowed for free and spontaneous interaction during the meetings. Formal course material was in the form of prescribed readings on which the group members were examined at specified times during the sixteen-week semester. Lectures were not given. Each training group had thirty two-hour sessions.

During the semester, there was a subdivision of the members within each group into smaller groups for the purpose of working out a project related to the course content. This work was accomplished in out-of-class time. The small groups were organized on the basis of mutual interest in a topic. The kinds of problems chosen had to do with such matters as the introduction of change, the nature of effective leadership, or the relation between morale and productivity. In each case, the small group had to decide upon a substantive content to illustrate the topic (e.g., one small group concerned with effective leadership studied the activities of two well-known athletic coaches; another dealt with the use of interpersonal influence on the top-management team of a medium-sized company; a third studied the sources of resistance to the introduction of a highly efficient modern appliance).

The psychologist attended all sessions for both training groups, a total of 120 hours in all. He was introduced to each group as a research person, and they were advised that questions could be asked of him at the end of the semester if the group members so wished. The psychologist observed the group and trainer from a point outside the circle of the group. The content of all sessions was recorded on tape so that a complete group history would be available.

After each of the group sessions, each trainer met individually with the psychologist for about thirty to forty-five minutes. These interviews were taped. The meetings with the psychologist were essentially a series of depth interviews, and although these often had a frankly therapeutic quality, no attempt was made to use them for psychotherapy. A total of sixty interviews took place, thirty with each trainer.

The data of this study are essentially qualitative. The use of a clinician who acted as observer and interviewer led to the accumulation of information dealing with the experiences of the trainers as they carried out their jobs.

## THE PERSONALITY OF THE TRAINERS

So far as this study is concerned with a description of the training role in terms of the problems attendant on it, the following personality sketches tend to emphasize sources and manifestations of trainer anxiety. This leads to the kind of presentation which focuses on weaknesses and deficiencies rather than on strengths and skills. A one-sided view such as this has the advantage of highlighting the relationship between trainer personality and the problems associated with the training role. It has the disadvantage of making the trainers appear inefficient.

The trainers under observation are not generally anxious individuals. They are, however, subject to anxieties in much the same fashion as many another person. Their anxieties stem in part from an intense need to improve their already substantial skills rather than from a lack of training ability. It is also quite likely that being subject to observation and interview helped to build tensions in them.

In working with the trainers, care was taken to avoid the assumption that successful trainers had to have the same personal characteristics or, for that matter, any special set of qualities. Furthermore, it was not assumed that the personality structure of the successful trainer reflected some form of optimal emotional adjustment.

The interviews with these two trainers served the purpose of helping them to evaluate their training behavior in terms of its conscious and unconscious determinants. The context for these evaluations was always in terms of trainer efforts to provide an experience designed to enable the group members to learn about the effect of interpersonal factors as these were manifested in their group activity. The extent to which the members were able to learn how their actions affected each other could serve as a yardstick for trainer effectiveness.

In this phase of the study, the clinician's task was to help the trainers identify some of their resistances to facing how they really felt about what transpired in the groups. The role of unconscious needs in the trainers, their connection with what the trainers saw themselves as doing, the influence of these needs on the group—all these factors proved interesting and worthy of detailed exploration.[1]

*Trainer I*

Perhaps the most striking characteristic of this trainer was his self-effacing attitude toward himself and toward his work. He was constantly surprised by his successes and looked upon them as some sort of profound luck. Though exceedingly skillful in handling his group, he had difficulty in accepting himself as skilled, as if to do such a thing would be to commit the sin of pride. A warm and friendly person, he played the role of a benevolent, kindly father figure for his group. He was highly sensitive and alert to the needs of the group members, and he could communicate this with facility.

As it turned out, these character traits served to mask considerable underlying anxiety over the expression of hostility. As will be seen, many of his problems arose as a consequence of an intense need to be liked and a fear that lack of affection is tantamount to rejection. His role of trainer was carried out without full awareness of the fact that it brought him the attention and respect that gratified his powerful need for affection. His behavior was of a kind that unconsciously averted any direction of hostility toward him. He could deal with expressions of resentment and anger if he was sure that these feelings were not directed at him, or if he deliberately engendered them.

Consciously, he was aware of a hampering passivity within him that led him to deal with heavily emotion-laden situations by exercising

---

[1] Prior to and during the four-month period when the research was being carried out, contact with the trainers was limited to the clinician-trainer relationship. Every effort was made to maintain an attitude of clinical objectivity.

excessive caution. He had a tendency to blame himself for this and to react to it with some anxiety and lowered mood. It was almost as if his expectation of failure was so great that it led to a fear of success.

In a sense, his effectiveness as a trainer was due to the fact that he provided a protected environment where the trainee's basic needs were satisfied. Most people have conflicts over the expression of hostility, and in such an environment there is little impetus for anger. This trainer's group achieved success almost as a present to the trainer for his kindness in helping them to avoid any unpleasantness.

The trainer's basic consideration must be whether or not the group members learn enough to enhance their abilities in interpersonal relations. Any other concerns must be viewed as superfluous and therefore a distortion of reality stemming from the trainer's intrapsychic conflicts. In this instance, clinical observation makes it appear that this trainer's doubts were unfounded—he was effective; the group was helped to work within its limits, and it reached its training goals with a sense of cohesiveness and integrity.

## Trainer II

This trainer was characterized by a powerful need to produce. He could not mask this, and in his desire for the trainees to gain the kind of insights he felt they should, he seemed driven by almost voyeuristic impulse to see results. Intense, serious, highly responsive emotionally, in his role as trainer he showed a kind of ambivalence that rendered him indecisive at one moment, fully in command at the next. In discussing his activities in the group, he seemed to encounter blind spots with which he tried to deal by intellectualization and projection. Much as trainer I seemed to come upon success as if by accident, trainer II chased it as one would a will-o'-the-wisp.

Urged on by powerful drives to be seen as successful both by himself and by others, this trainer frequently tried to overextend himself. For example, it was not enough for him that he was highly intelligent; his intelligence had to scintillate. He seemed engaged in a constant competition for some goal that would gain him recognition. One might say that he used training techniques with the efficiency of a surgeon and took it for granted that his patient must survive if the technique was correct. He approached his work with a zealous sincerity and an intense faith. To the observer it seemed that, in trying too hard, he was creating problems where there might be none.

The façade of flourishing activity in this trainer indicated some concerns about his adequacy and his ability. Prone to feelings of insecurity and upsurges of anxiety, he found in the training role a way of dealing with strong conflicts over authority. By identifying with the authority role and then consciously trying to avoid being authoritarian, he attempted to prevent the anxiety consequent to being forced to compete for recognition. He enjoyed the power of his position but tended to deny the existence of this power by not using it.

Although apt to experience somewhat excessive tensions, these were periodic and he managed to complete his training task with good results. His purity of motive and his intensity of purpose communicated themselves to the majority of the group members. His behavior in the group encouraged the members to fight him, to block him, to reject him; but they seemed unable to hate him. He provoked their hostility unconsciously despite his difficulty in handling resentment, and then neutralized its adverse effects by accepting such expression. In his group this behavior took the form of living dangerously by attacking resistances and rousing affects. At the same time, however, he was perspicacious enough to protect those who had low anxiety tolerances.

Most of the learning in this trainer's group took place on an unconscious level, thus frustrating his need to see results. As he explored this need, he gradually came to accept the notion that productive ends can come about as a result of nonverbal insights as well as by means of the usual "aha!" experiences. In one sense, most of his problems as a trainer were traceable to his diffuse anxieties inducing, perhaps, too many critical incidents in his group, thereby giving the impression of too much going on rather than too little.

## SOME KEY TRAINING PROBLEMS

The foregoing descriptions of the trainers make it evident that they differed markedly. The kind of impact each had on his trainees could be attributed to personality differences—to different ways of handling the anxieties which the training situation caused for them. Still, the problems they encountered were largely the same. This should not be surprising, inasmuch as both were in a situation where the general objectives and training methodology were largely the same. What seems to be a contradiction of the notion that trainer problems are a function of trainer personality (i.e., if trainers differ in personality, then problems should differ) is only apparent. Actually, it is the manner of handling the problem that differs. It is on this level that personality enters; and individual variations in dealing with problems—problems that were the same for both—are what produced differences in impact.

In observing these two trainers in action, five major common problems were uncovered. Each can be viewed as a potential source (or a consequent) of trainer anxiety and difficulties: the first is *time limitation;* the second is *group composition;* the third, *exposure and vulner-*

*ability;* the fourth, *reconciling behavior and theory about group functions;* and finally, the fifth, *content versus process orientation.*

This list is by no means exhaustive, but it represents the major problems confronting the trainers under consideration here. These problems will be encountered by all trainers in varying degree. Certainly every trainer is faced with the necessity of achieving his objectives within a specific period with a particular group. Every trainer must also decide how much to give of himself, that is, how deeply personally to get involved. He must face the fact that what he wants to do and what he actually does may not coincide; finally, he has to take a stand on how much structure to provide for his group and at what level of depth he will help it to operate.

## Time Limitation

Every trainer is somehow concerned with whether his training goals will be achieved in the time allotted. The time variable is a real one, and it cannot be avoided by the trainer. It can be a source of trainer anxiety if he is driven by powerful needs to achieve. Temporal reality then becomes a threat because its implacability signifies a constant possibility of failure.

The time dimension, if it is a source of trainer anxiety, can account for numerous critical incidents occurring in the group. This proved to be the case with trainer II, but not with trainer I. The decisive factor was the way in which the trainers organized the didactic aspect of the group experience.

Trainer I organized his course so that none of the meetings was devoted necessarily to outright discussion of training materials. This meant that the group members were held responsible for completing their readings and their small group projects by certain specified dates. There were examinations to cover the readings, and these took place at a designated time. Reports on small group projects were to be completed no later than the date for the final examination. The members of the group tried to make an issue of these requirements, but the trainer stood fast and they did not press their point. As a consequence, the group meetings were free to take any direction desired by the members (including discussion of course content if they wished), and a tense and urgent need to meet deadlines was avoided. Trainer I treated the trainees as adults who were presumed to have a sense of responsibility and an ability to meet it. He also prevented the arousal of anxiety within himself by identifying with the realistic elements of the teacher role, thus enabling him to act with authority and deflect any challenges that might lead to a stirring up of his passive conflicts.

Trainer II was in constant fear that he would fail to help the group have a positive learning experience; this created difficulties, because it was communicated to the group in terms of expressed impatience with them and a frequent resort to training gadgetry in order to speed them along. For this trainer, the limitation of time was an important source of anxiety. His need for achievement had to be realized in terms of objectively discernible goals. In the process of achieving these goals, the trainer perceived the group as hindering and blocking itself in the decision-making process. This seemed a direct affront to him. He could not blame the group *in toto* for this recalcitrance, because this would mean his shouldering too much guilt. So he declaimed against the strictures of a reality that inhibited his freedom. The academic pressures were seen allied with time against him. The developmental tendencies in the group were pushed rather than allowed to emerge in a natural fashion. The latitude of experimentation in the group was narrowed, and the cohesive atmosphere so desired by the trainer seemed missing.

*Group Composition*

Group composition is also a factor with which the trainer must deal and to which he must adjust himself. Meeting with a newly organized group for the first time, a trainer is generally curious to see "what he has." He is then confronted with the delicate task of using his perceptive skills to determine what his expectations ought to be. Further, he must be ready to accept the idea that so many unknowns enter into the phenomenon of group composition that he can never know precisely how a given set of events manages to occur. The trainer is limited, in his task, by the nature of the materials with which he has to deal. Within this limitation, he must set his goals in terms of what can be achieved rather than what ought to be achieved.

Trainer I was very sensitive to the needs of his group members. He had a good capacity for empathizing with them and helping them to see the manner in which their reactions affected themselves and others. He represented a form of reality that was acceptable to the group because it was not perceived as threatening. As a consequence, the group generated little in the way of organized resistance to the trainer's efforts to exert influence. His characteristic methods of averting anxiety in himself were generally so effective that few of his needs were projected onto the group, and he could seem calm, self-assured, and helpful. He kept his distance from the group by being assiduously protective. By mobilizing very little of the anxiety potential of the group, few crises were precipitated; the trainer knew where he stood, ambiguity was averted, and no disruptive tendencies emerged in strength.

The group that trainer II had to work with seemed, for the most part, less mature and more demanding than that of trainer I. If trainer II was the spark, the group was the fuel; needless to say, this led to pyrotechnics. Whereas group I was characterized by sobriety, control, and warmth, group II was characterized by excitement, frequent aimlessness, and heat. The members tried to avert the arousal of anxiety and resisted the trainer's efforts to help them toward insight into what they were doing. This may have represented rejection to the trainer and seemed to rouse his anxieties above threshold level; thus he created renewed anxiety in the group, and a vicious cycle was instituted. Although this condition can be attributed partly to the trainer's personality, it cannot wholly be laid at his feet. Without benefit of any evaluations of group composition, it is felt that most observers would agree (if afforded the opportunity to compare both training groups) that the source of the trainer's difficulties with this group lay in his stars, as well as in himself. If he could have accepted the fact that the group, by dint of its own make-up, was going to be limited in its attainment of goals, he might have avoided many other conflicts in the course of working with it.

## Exposure and Vulnerability

The training role, if it is to reach its objectives, generally involves the arousal of affects; this is in order that the emotional elements in the learning process be made conscious. The rousing of affects is equivalent to grabbing a tiger by the tail. Pressures to deal with feelings are generally experienced as something painful by most people, since their development has proceeded largely by a process of successive repressions. The trainer thus becomes a noxious influence for most and a delight to some. The net effect is that he is subject to a host of displaced attitudes and projections from the group members—the target of a wide variety of feelings, many of them negative and hostile, some protective, some loving, others even seductive.

The trainer, by his very position as the original center of authority in the group, cannot avoid being the target of a certain amount of hostility. In both groups, the members could be described in three different ways with reference to their relationship with the trainer: those who were hostile to authority, those who were submissive, and those who seemed to have no major conflicts regarding their relationship with authority.

Both trainers had considerable conflict over the expression of hostility, especially when it was directed toward them.

Trainer I showed his fear of hostility by openly encouraging it ("you can call me an SOB if you feel like it"), thereby serving to inhibit its expression. By this procedure, trainer I also enabled himself to justify the appearance of hostility so that it would not be sudden and un-accepted if it occurred. Trainer II handled hostility either by ingratiat-ing himself with the group ("See, I'm really not a bad guy") or by backing down under pressure ("if the group doesn't want a final exam, there won't be any"). Both trainers resorted to meetings with certain group members outside of class, partly in order to lessen the growing hostility in these persons. Trainer II also used the rationalizing device of imputing most group manifestations of hostility to irrational elements within the hostile members.

Trainer I, despite his adequate surface handling of hostility, seemed to have a much deeper conflict with such expressions. In his group, he did not avoid dealing with hostility when it arose, but he was decidedly uncomfortable with it. In interviews, he recognized this difficulty and made a strong effort to probe its sources in himself. As has been sug-gested, he skillfully avoided tying in the authority-dependence prob-lem to that of hostility and for the most part led the group to bypass the usual struggle for leadership among its members. To be sure, there was much discussion of leadership, but it was always on a fairly in-tellectual level. This trainer was bothered by one or two group mem-bers who tried to take control of the group once they perceived the existence of a power vacuum created by him. He acted protective toward these people even though he did not really feel that way. This neutralized their ability to be angry with him, and when they turned on someone else in the group, the trainer handled the situation more effectively.

Trainer II stirred up hostility, often without being aware that he was doing so. It was difficult for him to see himself as authoritarian, and he projected such tactics onto other group members. Nevertheless, his overt behavior was frequently dictatorial in a subtle way. He would write lists of things on the board with the conscious purpose of helping the members to be sensitive to their resistance techniques. If they then ignored what he wrote or paid lip service to his list, he would point out this behavior and wonder what it could mean. Another device used by him was to give a summary of his observations at the very end of the hour. He thus preserved the last word for himself and averted any possibility of rebuttal. Until given an opportunity to deal with these patterns, this trainer was unaware of their unconscious sources and saw them merely as a part of his usual training practices.

The trainer is confronted with the task of ascertaining whether or not certain of the group members are apt to be greatly threatened or unduly aroused by the emphasis he places on interpersonal factors in trying to attain his training goals. If certain group members become disturbed by what happens to them in the group, they are apt to seek out the trainer for advice, support, and reassurance. The trainer is forced to deal with the fact that a member is looking to him for help. He must have some basis for assessing the degree of upset in the member and then act in a manner designed to be most helpful. He thereupon engages in supportive therapy, much in the manner that a personal counselor, doctor, priest, or other person in a similar role is frequently called upon to do. Part of his responsibility is to know enough about psychodynamics to sense that something is wrong and to suggest referral to an individual or agency if additional help is needed.

Both trainers were constantly faced with the fact that their roles had heavy therapeutic connotations. They were exposed to a great variety of projections, but at times they could not deal with them as intensively as they would have liked. In this vulnerable position, they were forced to carry these projected feelings without any freedom to ascertain the degree to which they were motivated by irrational sources. Both trainers were thus compelled to strengthen their own defenses in order, paradoxically enough, to avoid being defensive in their activities with the group. This was a great burden for them to bear and created considerable feelings of frustration and ambivalence in both men. Trainer I, for example, discussed his tendency to avoid heavily emotion-laden situations and berated himself for being fearful of plunging in and doing something to clarify the atmosphere that seemed to be smothering group progress. He took the blame upon himself and felt as if he were failing in some serious way. He was prone to socialize and "buddy up" to the group members during breaks in the meetings and made it clear, rather more often than necessary, that he would be available, should "any problems come up" which the group members might wish to talk over with him individually. On the one hand, he could not deal as effectively as he desired with the fact that his position necessitated some arousal of anxiety, because his conception of his role limited the degree to which he could engage in this activity. And if he did arouse anxiety, he wanted it understood, in effect, that he had to, but was willing to make this up to the group members by taking a personal interest in them. It was demonstration of a set of circumstances in which a combination of position as trainer and trainer dynamics united to intensify a sense of vulnerability and hamper efficiency.

*Trainer Functioning: Theory versus Behavior*

In undertaking the task of training a group in the principles and practices of human relations, the trainer has certain formalized conceptions about individual and group behavior. He has, in effect, a set of coordinated hypotheses which help him both to understand and to predict what may happen in the group during the course of its development. To the degree that his expectancies are realized, there is confirmation of his hypotheses—he feels confident and assured, there is little extraneous conflict, and anxiety is minimal. Should the patterns of group interaction veer off, however, then the trainer is apt to experience uncertainty and, if he is so predisposed, become anxious.

Both trainers in this study employed the same theoretical approaches. Without going into any detailed discussion of theory, their formal approach may be described as falling under the rubric of perceptual approaches to group behavior. This means that they utilized hypotheses derived from Lewinian field theory and Rogerian personality theory as the major basis for conceptualizing both their activity and that of the group. They tended to play their roles in terms of the permissive, accepting, nondirective leader who, by the very nature of his activity, would provide an atmosphere conducive to the effective realization of the integrative potentials inherent in the group. Essentially, each perceived his role as one of climate production and control. In its broadest sense, they were providing the living experience of democracy in action, and their problems arose when it became apparent that neither they nor many of the group members were prepared fully to accept the implications of such an atmosphere.

Trainer I managed to fulfill the requirements of nondirective leadership rather well; yet he was bothered by a tendency to take a more active and interpretive role. This reflected a desire to overcome the passive trends in his personality. If he could only be aggressive without becoming anxious in the process! He ruminated over his tendency to avoid risking involvement in touchy matters brought up by the group. He was aware that he afforded the group protection without demanding the right to control it in return. He was disturbed if the activity of the group seemed lifeless, inert, or aimless. If he was ignored by the group, he blamed himself for being insensitive or for having defective timing. Despite an accurate understanding of his training techniques and the theoretical implications of these methods, he was disquieted by a persistence of dictatorial attitudes and behaviors in many of the group members. His expectations led him to believe that the light of heaven would eventually be perceived by all. In reality, he recognized that this was not the case, nor would it ever be; yet in good conscience he was unable to challenge the conceptualizations he had incorporated into his own way of perceiving. For him, the nondirective technique was consonant with his personal needs to avoid anxiety by remaining passive and on the side lines.

Trainer II had a tendency to use most of the techniques that were at his command. He often felt saddled by a theory that was somewhat inimicable to his personality. He had to defend it as vigorously as possible in order to free himself to attack it later in the course of the training sequence. He would resort to terms such as "hidden agenda," "consensus," and "group responsibility," especially at those times when his group was failing to act in accordance with expectations induced by theoretical constructs. For example, one of the well-established hypotheses about group behavior is that in the early phases of a group's existence there always occurs a struggle for power. Cohesiveness cannot come about until this struggle is resolved in some manner. This trainer was on the lookout for signs of cohesiveness because this would mean that he was effective in his role. He was unaware that his own behavior was preventing this state of affairs from coming into being. He needed to see his expectations confirmed, and this need was so strong that it led him to punish the group for failing to come through. In this instance, it was not a case of theory failing the trainer, but rather one of the trainer imposing his own needs on the theory. Group theory was a highly valued vehicle for him; yet if the facts as he perceived them didn't seem to fit, it was the fault of the theory and not his own.

It is interesting to note that as the trainers became aware of the interrelationships between their personal needs and their theoretical expectancies, both chose to act along lines more consistent with opposite sides of their personalities. Trainer I could take more directive actions in his group without becoming anxious. Trainer II became less needful of being in charge.

*Introducing an Orientation toward Group Process*

A sensitization procedure is essentially a method for evoking responses to previously neutral stimuli. In human relations training, these responses take the form of new perceptive patterns. Increased social perceptiveness implies a shift in the way one looks at things so that more effective behavior can occur. In the training groups, this shift is manifested by attention to the *way* things are done rather than by a focus on *what* is done. This is commonly denoted as the problem of *process* versus *content* orientation. It is the trainer's task to facilitate this perceptual shift within the group.

Ordinarily, a group tends first to concern itself mainly with content, because this is consistent with its notions of logical procedure. To engage in a discussion on a given topic provides one with a sense of continuity and focus; one knows where one is and where one is going. The members do not as yet know each other, nor are they clear on how their goals are to be achieved. It is a period of acclimatization and/or organization.

Typical of the content phase are discussions of group organization.

How shall the group get started? What is the agenda? Will there be a chairman? Will somebody act as observer? Should these people volunteer or be elected? How can human relations theories be tested in the group? Questions like these are raised and worked over, and the group members have an opportunity to size each other up. The trainer also uses this period in order to see "what he has" (the group-composition problem) and to determine how he can introduce a change from structural concerns (content) to emphasis on the forces at play within individuals and the group (process).

In this respect the trainer's task is analogous to that of the psychotherapist. Both are involved with the question of dealing with either content or process. Generally, there is little emphasis placed upon content after the initial phases of either group experience or therapy. If the experience is successful, group members as well as therapy patients gradually come to perceive the implications hidden behind the manifest content of their behavior. Insight occurs not on the basis of analyzing content per se but rather from the *way in which* it is presented and utilized. Sensitization in human relations training is comparable to insight in therapy; that is, new behavioral patterns emerge as a result of awareness of stimuli that had had little or no evocative power previously.

The shift from a content to a process orientation in the training group is illustrated by two brief interchanges that took place in one of the groups.

### Early in Training.

BILL: Don't you think—after the way we have been floundering—that . . . maybe we ought to have a chairman?

MARY: I agree—maybe a chairman can put some order into what's going on here.

JACK: Quite so—we've got to have some organization to get things done around here.

### Later in Training.

BILL: Earlier I suggested that we have a chairman and well . . . some of you agreed that it was a good idea. But . . . we never got around to doing it. Now—I'm suggesting it again.

MARY: I think, Bill, I was one of those that agreed with you then, but now I get a feeling that *you* are uncomfortable if things aren't done in a highly organized way . . . I mean, just for the sake of organization.

JACK: Bill, I feel Mary really has a point here. Besides—the way you've acted on other things gives me the impression that you're annoyed if people don't pick up your suggestions. Maybe you want a chairman so that it's easier for you to get your own way. What do you think?

The first example represents a concern with the content of what was said. Bill, Mary, and Jack combined to work out some structural organization in the group. The second example shows how there is an emergent concern with the way Bill does things, and there is some effort to recognize his needs and motives for wanting a chairman. The latter reflects a process orientation.

Both trainers had the problem of educating the group members in the nature of group process and providing them with an impetus to deal with the transactions of the group in terms of the forces at work.

Trainer I limited his contributions to a clarification of content in the early phases of the training and, as soon as possible, shifted to remarks designed to reflect feelings and ignore content. He deliberately avoided responding to cues designed to trap him into being the orthodox professor, thereby maintaining a certain amount of ambiguity about his role as trainer. He was expected to be concerned with content because the expectations of the group were those of students relating to a teacher. When the group could not identify him with its stereotyped conceptions of what he would be like, it became easy for him to make the shift toward the process aspects of group behavior.

As has already been stated, trainer II was intensely concerned with the development of "insight into process." For him, such insight was the significant indicator of a successful training experience. At the same time, he could consider himself effective if such insights occurred. He saw insightful behavior among the group members as so necessary that he became anxious when the group seemingly was deliberate in resisting such valuable knowledge. There were times when the group was accused by him of "being blind," "having it laid in their laps and not seeing it," etc. The intensity of his overreactions to resistant and fractious behavior of the trainees gradually came to be seen by the trainer as a projective defense against the anxiety he might experience if he failed to achieve his training goals. He became aware of the fact that the greater the tendency on his part to impose his needs on the group, the greater would be its resistance to any change-producing insights. His need to see results was analogous to that of the therapist who must cure all his patients; in both instances the likelihood of an unfavorable result is increased.

Actually, the creation of frustration and the mobilization of some anxiety are necessary for change. Trainer II apparently tended to create excessive anxiety in his trainees so that many of them became fearful and hid behind the façade of a content orientation. Those of his trainees who had good capacity to withstand frustration reacted positively to the training experience. Trainer II saw these persons as "effective," and in fact they were. Such trainees took the load off the trainer and helped the group to attain a process orientation by their activity during the meetings. Seeing some of his trainees "successful," from his point of view, helped to reduce his tensions, and he could thus become more effective by becoming less of a threat to the group.

CONCLUSIONS

The key conclusions of this study are, first, that the five training problems which have been identified and described may well be encountered by all who do human relations training in general and sensitivity training in particular; and second, that these problems arise from the situational context of the training.

The first conclusion is essentially to hypothesize that having problems is a requisite for the trainer. It implies that every trainer is going to have the problem of attaining his training objectives in a given period of time, and that his objectives will be conditioned by the nature of the group membership. His position requires some skill in dealing with hostile expression in its wide variety of forms. His trainer-leader role invites the trainees to displace attitudes and project feelings onto him. His conceptual grasp of the trainer role may lead him to expect certain outcomes, and if these are not forthcoming, there may be frustration and anxiety. The teaching of others to perceive behavior in terms of motives and dynamics rather than in terms of manifest content is always difficult and sometimes impossible.

The second conclusion is that if these five problems are invariably associated with the conditions of training, then they are aspects of reality existing prior to, and independent of, the trainer. On the surface this might appear as an easy opportunity for the trainer to disclaim any responsibility for his failures, inasmuch as the matter would seem to be out of his hands; by the same token, he could not accept any credit for the achievement of his objectives. Actually, what is implied is that the realities of the training situation include certain general difficulties which the trainer must confront. His personality accounts for the *intensity* with which a problem is manifested. It does not account for the presence of the problem.

From a case-study standpoint, this report has many interesting facets. Persons who serve as sensitivity trainers have a vital interest in developing and utilizing their ability to exercise influence (leadership) in order to help people be more sensitive and skillful in the handling of interpersonal relations. These are not the ordinary goals of leadership activity. There are strong overtones of social responsibility in this kind of teaching-leadership function.

A descriptive study of this kind raises many more questions than it answers. This is probably as it should be. The questions are not limited to sensitivity training alone, but should be applicable to other areas of interest with regard to the phenomena of interpersonal relations.

At this point little is known about the common qualities of trainer personality that are requisite for success. Certainly selection of trainers is apt to be more refined if there is some recognition of the personality correlates necessary for efficient dealing with problems associated with the training role.

Much has been said and written about those who have been subjected to influence, either on an individual basis or as members of groups. One need only consider the abundance of research on educational methods, group dynamics, and psychotherapy. Perhaps the shift of focus away from those who are influenced and onto those who attempt to influence may provide fresh insights on a problem that, for all its obviousness, has no lack of complexity and subtleness.

CHAPTER 13

*Phases of Group Development* *

BACKGROUND

The goal of the research to be treated in this chapter was to seek out and describe systematic patterns of development, or *phasic behavior,* in sensitivity training groups.

At the outset there was no way of knowing whether such patterns existed at all in this type of human relations training. It was therefore important initially to determine the presence or absence of orderly effects.

From a theoretical point of view, there is a considerable body of literature devoted to the phenomenon of phasic behavior in groups. Beginning with the seminal work of the psychoanalyst Bion (1948–1951), there has emerged a series of conceptualizations of group behavior in terms of sequential patterns of activity. Others who have used the psychoanalytic frame of reference for building theories of "group development" include Thelen and Stock (1954), Bennis and Shepard (1956), and Schutz (1958). Miles (1957) has used a learning-theory approach; Bales (1950) and Weiner (1954) have approached the problem in terms of interaction processes.[1] All these formulations lend sup-

---

* This chapter is based on a portion of an unpublished doctoral dissertation in psychology, "A Search for Behavior Patterns in Sensitivity Training Groups," by Jerome Reisel, University of California, Los Angeles, 1959.

[1] The reader interested in a detailed presentation of these theories should find the following references helpful: W. R. Bion, "Experiences in Groups: I–VII," *Human Relations,* vol. 1–4, 1948–1951; H. A. Thelen, Dorothy Stock, et al., *Methods for Studying Work and Emotionality in Group Operation,* Human Dynamics Laboratory Monographs, University of Chicago, 1954; W. Bennis and H. A. Shepard, "A Theory of Group Development," *Human Relations,* vol. 9, pp. 415–437, 1956; William C. Schutz, *FIRO: A Three-dimensional Theory of Interpersonal Behavior* (New York: Rinehart & Company, Inc., 1958); M. Miles, "Personal Change through Human Relations Training," a working paper, 1957 (mimeographed); R. F. Bales, "Some

port to the idea that training groups vary in their activity systematically rather than aimlessly.

Our research problem was not so much one of testing the validity of any particular theory as it was to check the fundamental common assertion of these viewpoints, namely, that *groups with a relatively constant structure in terms of membership, guidance, and duration proceed in identifiable ways.*

Matters of definition forced some early decisions. Most approaches to phasic behavior in groups use the term *development* to describe the patterning of activity. This term may be defined in a number of ways. For our purposes it was sufficient to differentiate two meanings of the term. The first meaning could be understood as implying something *normative*, i.e., movement toward a designated goal. Within the context of this definition, "development" either does or does not take place. For example, retrogression would indicate a group that does not *develop;* it moves in a direction differing from a stated objective. The objective is usually some acquisition of understanding and skills meeting criteria for mature behavior in a variety of situations. The second meaning of the term "development" is a *descriptive* one, i.e., referring to an identifiable sequence of behavior through time. This sequence of behavior need not have any stated objective in order to justify its presence. All that is necessary is evidence of nonrandom elaboration of activity through time.

It can be seen that "development" may be viewed as a set of conditions which *ought* to take place (normative), or it can be viewed as a phenomenon that *is* taking place (descriptive). Our decision was to use a descriptive approach. Henceforth, when the term "group development" is employed, it means simply identifiable sequences of behavior.

Having set up the terminological convention, the next task was to clarify our method of approach. We wished to investigate the problem of phases of group development at a number of levels. First there was the question of training impact, irrespective of considerations such as group composition or differences in trainers. Did the impact of training induce orderly patterns of behavior? A number of groups were to be studied. If the data provided by these groups were pooled and analyzed as if *from a single population,* the foregoing question could be an-

---

Uniformities of Behavior in Small Social Systems," in G. E. Swanson, T. M. Newcomb, and E. L. Hartley (eds.), *Readings in Social Psychology* (New York: Henry Holt and Company, Inc., 1952); M. G. Weiner, *Observations on the Growth of Information-processing Centers* (Santa Monica, Calif.: The RAND Corporation, 1954). A summary and critical evaluation of these theories is to be found in Reisel, *op. cit.*

swered. This was to be called level I analysis. Second, there was the problem of determining the existence of patterns, if any, *within groups*. Here the part played by group composition and trainer factors comes into play. Did groups, taken individually, tend to have patterns? This was to be labeled level II analysis. Finally we wished to *compare groups* in order to elaborate further on questions of similarity and differences between groups due, possibly, to group membership and trainer factors. This was to be called level III analysis.

## SOURCE OF DATA, PROCEDURE, AND METHOD

The subjects were seniors and graduate students in three sensitivity training groups at the University of California, Los Angeles. The membership of the three groups numbered twenty-two, twenty-three, and twenty-four persons, respectively, a total population of sixty-nine persons. Each group engaged in thirty training sessions. Meetings were held twice a week for a period of two hours each. A different trainer was assigned to each group.

The raw data of the study were diaries kept on a daily basis by the group members. The participants were requested to record fully in their diaries, after each session, their feelings, opinions, and reactions to anything that had happened during that session. They could write as much or as little as they desired. In terms of the course procedure, however, they were required to turn in their diaries at the end of the semester.[2]

Since by its very nature diary content was largely determined by the trainees themselves, the diaries chronicled experiences and relationships that often had intense personal meaning. Thus, the diaries constitute a series of successive subjective impressions (samples), potentially revealing of individual and group development.

*Content analysis* was used to transform the qualitative diary materials into a form susceptible of statistical treatment.

*Thought units,* defined as a series of consecutive words expressing a single thought or idea, were utilized as the units of measurement.

Treatment of the diary entries with regard to unit determination was followed by a concern with the *emotional tone* of the trainees' reactions. We were interested not only in what was said, but also in how the respondents felt about what they wrote. Judgments concerning emotional tone fell into four possible classifications: positive feelings

[2] See Irving R. Weschler and Jerome Reisel, *Inside A Sensitivity Training Group,* Institute of Industrial Relations, University of California, Los Angeles, Monograph Series, no. 4, 1959. See also Chap. 10.

(+), negative feelings (—), ambivalent feelings (±), and descriptive or neutral reactions (De). Thus, each entry was coded with regard to how much was said (as specified by the number of thought units) and how the writer felt about it.

From these raw data, indices of involvement (volume), emotionality (EI), and satisfaction (SI) were developed. These indices were subjected to time-series study for patterning, and the significant findings were partitioned on the above-mentioned three levels of analysis: as a total population (level I), by groups (level II), and between groups (level III).[3]

## THE INDICES OF INVOLVEMENT, EMOTIONALITY, AND SATISFACTION

In the present study, the initial problem was that of finding if regularities existed in training groups progressing through time and to describe the similarities that might be found.

The next step was to isolate some components of the training process which could serve as suitable dimensions for describing phases in training-group behavior. Involvement, degree of emotionality, and satisfaction were selected as the most logical dimensions.

The final step was to combine the diary data in such a way as to produce appropriate indices, in this instance indices of involvement, emotionality, and satisfaction. These in turn could be subjected to the kind of analysis that would permit statements about the presence or absence of systematic patterning in the groups under study.

The notion of *involvement* is derived from the work of Miles wherein he suggests that group development is directly related to the degree to which members become engaged in the training process. *Emotionality* is a dimension with which almost all theorists have been concerned, perhaps most emphatically Thelen and Stock, and Bennis and Shepard. Finally, the concept of *satisfaction* has its roots in Bion's writings in which he implies that feelings aroused in groups differ qualitatively for each participant at varying points in time.

Involvement was defined as the total volume of response in diary entries as it varied from meeting to meeting through time. Volume is essentially a quantitative measure of trainee group reactions irrespective of diary subject matter, or degree and kind of emotionality associated with such reactions.

Emotionality was defined as the ratio of affectively toned thought

[3] A detailed technical statement of the procedures used in this study will be found in Reisel, *op. cit.*

units to those which were neutral. This became the emotionality index (EI).

$$EI = \frac{\text{positive, negative, and ambivalent responses}}{\text{descriptive responses}}$$

The higher the EI value, the greater the emotionality being expressed. Satisfaction indicated the direction of emotional reaction. This was measured by the satisfaction index (SI):

$$SI = \frac{\text{number of positive responses}}{\text{number of negative responses}}$$

As with the EI, higher values indicate greater satisfaction.

RESULTS AND DISCUSSION

*Level I Analysis*

By pooling the data of all three groups, we engage in a search for sequence in macroscopic terms. This permits an analysis of the common experience of trainees regardless of differences in group membership or trainers.

The curves for involvement (volume), emotionality (EI), and satisfaction (SI) in Figure 13-1 were subjected to statistical tests for nonrandomness and cyclical nature.[4] Inspection of these curves reveals, first, that involvement and satisfaction patterns are cyclical. Second, involvement and emotionality are closely related to one another (rho $= +0.566$; $p < 0.001$). Finally, as emotionality increases, satisfaction tends to decrease, and vice versa (rho $= -0.333$; $p < 0.10$).

These findings permit two reasonably firm conclusions, and a third

[4] The procedure was, first, to test all the curves for nonrandomness. For this purpose the Runs Test was employed (S. Siegel, *Nonparametric Statistics* [New York: McGraw-Hill Book Company, Inc., 1956] p.r.). The results of this test indicated whether the pattern was one that could have occurred by chance alone. It was also necessary to determine whether a nonrandom pattern was cyclical (i.e., oscillated in a systematic manner). To this end, a second test was employed, the Phase Test for a Cycle (W. A. Wallis and G. Moore, "A Significance Test for Time Series Analysis," *Journal of the American Statistical Association*, vol. 36, pp. 401–409, 1941). In order that the usage can be made clear for the reader, the following conventions are employed: A sequence is defined as the nonrandom elaboration of events through time. A cycle is a pattern of systematic oscillation within a sequence. The establishment of a sequence is prerequisite for seeking the presence of a cycle. Sequences may or may not be cyclical. In general, cyclical behavior suggests stronger patterning in the index studied.

It should also be noted here that all the curves are presented as a plot of a three-period moving average. This method was adopted because breaks in training due to holidays and examinations tended to alter momentum artificially. The short three-period moving average neither causes excessive damping of values nor distorts the contour of the curves.

that is rather tentative: (1) the general impact of training produces systematic patterns of reaction in its participants; (2) the greater the trainee involvement, the greater the emotional reaction; (3) there is a strong suggestion that the greater the emotional reaction, the more the trainees experience dissatisfaction.

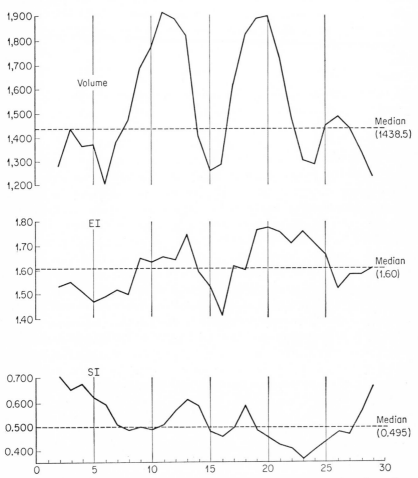

FIGURE 13-1. Volume, EI, and SI for $N = 69$ (absolute values, plotted as three-period moving average).

Ideally, we would hope that a fourth conclusion could be drawn from the data; namely, that the greater the involvement, the more the trainee feels either satisfied or dissatisfied. Unfortunately, there is no relationship between involvement and satisfaction patterns (rho $= +0.038$), a finding which raises some thorny problems. One speculation is that the impact of training produces differential kinds of effects; so that while the emotions aroused can be positive, negative, or mixed, in some cases no emotion is aroused at all. This, of course, would be reflected in the indices.

Within the context of this study, results on this level of analysis also make it quite clear that sensitivity training involves the trainee emotionally, that it is an experience that rouses affect in the trainee. This finding tends to strengthen the view that, if learning is occurring in sensitivity training, it is likely to be emotional as well as cognitive in kind.

Another finding with respect to level I analysis is that emotionality and satisfaction have a negative relationship to one another. Increases in emotional reaction seem to be accompanied by decreased satisfaction. This relationship only approaches statistical significance and should be viewed with caution. It does suggest that training mobilizes tensions perceived as unpleasant by trainees. This is not surprising in the light of frustrations induced by the training procedure. That satisfaction tends to remain persistently low may be a function of the specific population under study, but if replications of this work produce the same findings, it could serve as an indirect confirmation of group development theories that postulate some phasic behavior as traceable to specific kinds of anxiety.

The emotionality-satisfaction results also raise the question whether "happy groups are good groups." It would be interesting to know if groups which are regarded as effective either by self-evaluation or by more objective criteria are, in fact, blissfully happy or characterized by struggles to overcome conflict and feelings of frustration. It is surmised that groups which experience conflict and work through the tensions stemming from this provide a favorable setting in which individuals can acquire the kind of learning that will increase their understanding of both themselves and others. Whether or not the final segment of training would reflect a sense of emotional satisfaction in such groups is a matter for further study.

Viewing the level I findings in perspective there is sufficient evidence to justify a general conclusion that sensitivity training produces specific and identifiable patterns of behavior in the individuals participating in the present study.[5] Precisely what causes these patterns cannot be determined from the data on this level of analysis. Indications

---

[5] It should be pointed out that the mid-training trough in the curves is due to the introduction of an examination. Although the depth of the trough is artifactual, tests have shown that there is no effect on the essential bimodality of the curves and the statistical findings would not be altered in any significant fashion. More than likely under more stringent experimental conditions we would find that breathing spells do occur consequent to peaks in the sequence of group activity.

of what is happening, however, have been provided by a more detailed study of the diary content, in which it was found that early peaks of activity center about problems having to do with the role of the self and trainer as well as the general behavior of the group as a whole, whereas the later peaks of involvement are produced by more personal concern for the relationships among members.[6] Emotionality, likewise, tends to focus around issues concerning self, trainer, and total group early in training and around relationships among members later. Finally, it would seem that whenever members became really "caught up" in the training experience, their reactions appear to be felt as some sort of unpleasant crisis.

In some ways, additional research suggests a developmental pattern in which the earlier peaks focus on the problem of authority and identity, thus providing some support for views that dependence problems serve as a basis for initial activity in groups of this kind.[7] The later peaks seem to signalize a shift in the direction of interpersonal concerns where conflicts and problems among specific members become highlighted. The fact that the peaks are followed by clear-cut drops suggests sequences in which climactic activity is followed by periods of quiescence. This may indicate any number of things—working through issues, allowing new problems to come into focus, and, under certain circumstances, a manifestation of resistance to the training process.

*Level II Analysis*

The reaction to training within each of the three groups is examined in the level II analysis. This involves essentially a process of pulling the level I curves apart in order to ascertain the degree to which patterning factors may be generated by group composition and trainer influences.

Analysis of the curves in Figure 13-2 reveals that only the satisfaction pattern (SI) in group III is random, while all other curves meet criteria for nonrandomness. In addition, the curves in group I also are shown to be cyclical. In the case of group I, this would mean that reaction was not only ordered, but that it ebbed and flowed in a periodic fashion. The jaggedness of the satisfaction (SI) curve for group III provides a good example of what a random pattern might look like.

The major findings on this level of analysis are as follows: (1) group I shows cyclical behavior on all dimensions; (2) group II has well-

[6] This is based on additional research into the specific content of the diary material, some of which is reflected in the monograph by Weschler and Reisel, *op. cit.* A fuller report on this material is to be found in Reisel, *op. cit.*

[7] See Bennis and Shepard, *op. cit.*, p. 417, and Schutz, *op. cit.*, especially chap. 9.

defined patterns (nonrandom sequences) including one cyclical pattern; (3) group III reveals the greatest diversity of behavior, having sequences along the involvement and emotionality dimensions, but demonstrating a random flow for satisfaction. Table 13-1 provides a descriptive sum-

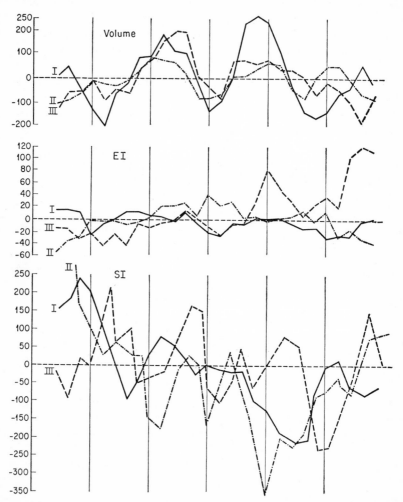

FIGURE 13-2. Comparative relationships for groups I, II, and III (three-period moving average plotted in deviation units from the median).

mary of the statistical results; Figure 13-2 permits visual inspection of the identical data.

These results give rise to a variety of speculations. Why is it that the patterns in group I tend to move cyclically, whereas this appears not to be the case in the remaining two groups?

TABLE 13-1. SUMMARY OF RESULTS FOR LEVEL II ANALYSIS

| Group | Involvement (vol.) | Emotionality (EI) | Satisfaction (SI) |
|-------|--------------------|-------------------|-------------------|
| I | Cyclical | Cyclical | Cyclical |
| II | Cyclical | Sequence | Sequence |
| III | Sequence | Sequence | Random |

A first possibility has to do with the method of testing for a cycle. This test, developed by Wallis and Moore (1941)[8], is rather crude and thus may not pick up the presence of smaller oscillatory movement in the curves for the other groups. If more sensitive tests for cycles were available, the results might indicate that group I had the strongest cyclical component, but that the others also partake of cyclical movement to a certain degree.

A second surmise has to do with group composition. It could be that members of group I constituted a rather unique conglomerate of individuals who responded to the training process in a particular oscillatory fashion. Oddly enough, comparisons of groups in terms of age, marital status, male-female distribution, etc., show no striking differences. Perhaps some other dimensions such as tension, need levels, frustration tolerance are involved. But data on this are unavailable.

Another speculation about the cyclical behavior in group I is related to trainer influence. In a study involving group I (see Chapter 12), it was found that the trainer of this group (trainer I) tended to be a particularly permissive kind of person who acted in a way to limit the build-up of disruptive tensions. As a consequence, irregular outbursts of activity alternating with periods of quiescence were not evident. Behavior tended to flow in one direction more smoothly, reaching the peaks and lows in a definite way. This might have contributed to the more clear-cut oscillatory patterns of behavior in group I.

The lack of any definitive explanation for the uniquely cyclical behavior in group I should not obscure the larger picture which supports the general contention that groups of this kind do develop identifiable patterns of behavior. Thus groups II and III have their own significant patterns, even if these are not as precisely differentiated as those in group I.

This specificity or uniqueness is probably a function of many factors, not the least of which is the complex of personalities interacting with one another for a stated period of time, guided by a specific trainer, in an atmosphere probably quite unlike that which any member has experienced before. It is surprising enough in itself, therefore, that these

[8] Wallis and Moore, *op. cit.*

conditions should provide uniform effects within any given group. To expect that the effects should also be the same for all participants irrespective of the groups to which they belong is to presume a one-to-one relationship between the stimulus source and respondent. As much group development theory goes no further than postulating some measure of orderliness within a context of fluctuation, analysis in terms of individual groups would again tend to confirm these formulations.

Table 13-2 presents a summary of level II statistical findings from a more descriptive point of view. One finds that the involvement (vol-

TABLE 13-2. COMPARISON OF PATTERNS: LEVEL II ANALYSIS

| Group | Involvement (vol.)-emotionality (EI) | Involvement (vol.)-satisfaction (SI) | Emotionality (EI)-satisfaction (SI) |
|---|---|---|---|
| I | Similar | N.R.* | N.R.* |
| II | N.R.* | Dissimilar | Dissimilar |
| III | N.R.* | N.R.* | N.R.* |

\* No relationship.

ume) and emotionality (EI) cycles in group I tend to be similar. There are apparently six phases, three downward and three upward, each of the order of roughly six sessions in length (see Figure 13-2). As in the case of the pooled data, group I seems to reflect a cycle of both low activity and low emotionality at the outset, followed by a wavelike pattern until the end of training is approached, when there is a fall-off in activity only.

For any particular group, involvement, emotionality, and satisfaction do not follow similar patterns. Involvement (volume) and emotionality (EI) are quite similar in group I, but not so for the remaining groups. In group II, involvement (volume)–satisfaction (SI) and emotionality (EI)–satisfaction (SI) are strongly related in a negative, dissimilar fashion (see Figure 13-2). It would thus seem that, whenever the group became involved, it experienced dissatisfaction; and whenever it became more quiescent, it experienced more positive feelings. Also, whenever group II tended to become emotional, it experienced dysphoric reactions. This situation seems unique for group II; it may be that trainees saw emotional expression as something difficult to cope with and reacted with displeasure when such behavior was exhibited. The satisfaction (SI) sequence in group II, more than in any other group, seems to indicate a rather high optimism at the outset, followed by an experience somewhat akin to disillusionment which remained fairly constant throughout the remainder of training (see Figure 13-2).

Group III shows no significant relationship along any of the dimensions studied. Involvement and emotionality, despite evidence of sequence, are quite unrelated. This group seems to be the most variant in its behavior of the groups studied. It could be active and unemotional, and quiescent while seething underneath. Its satisfaction (SI) pattern is a jagged, erratic curve; up one day, down the next. Unpredictability seems to be a characteristic of major importance for this group. Its lability is highly reminiscent of the mood variations found in hysterical behavior. There seems to be little ability for self-containment in group III. Its pattern gives the impression of building from one crisis to another, with no inkling as to whether or not the resolution of one impasse will lead to greater or lesser emotionality, to an increase or decrease in satisfaction.

It would appear from level II results that each group develops an individualized personality, patterning, or identity, coupled with generally meaningful regularities of development.

## Level III Analysis

A further question concerns the existence of possible common qualities among groups. Level III analysis asks: "Along what, if any, of the patterned dimensions do the groups show similarity?"

Evidence from level I analysis suggests that, when all individual members are studied as a unit ($N = 69$), convincing similarities emerge. The effect of training thus is supposedly inclined to be uniform in its effects through time. When the groups are studied as separate entities (level II analysis), considerable variation is noted. This suggests that perhaps group composition and trainer behavior have an impact on the individual independent of the general effect of training.

Level III provides a check on this latter supposition, for it allows a comparison among all and between pairs of groups in a search for possible similarities or differences. Figure 13-2 shows comparative relationships among the groups, and Table 13-3 provides a descriptive summary of the statistical findings.

TABLE 13-3. COMPARING GROUP PATTERNS: LEVEL III ANALYSIS

| Groups | Involvement (vol.) | Emotionality (EI) | Satisfaction (SI) |
|--------|-------------------|-------------------|-------------------|
| I–II–III | Similar | N.R.* | Similar |
| I–II | Similar | N.R.* | Similar |
| I–III | Similar | N.R.* | N.R.* |
| II–III | Similar | N.R.* | N.R.* |

* No relationship.

The results from level III analysis indicate that the three groups tend to have generally similar sequences in degree of involvement and, in part, in feelings of satisfaction, but the sequences of emotionality follow independent courses within any given group.

*Concordance measures,*[9] which are tests for pattern congruence, reveal that the major area of difference lies in the sphere of emotionality (EI). All groups seem to maintain the six-session pattern of involvement, despite the fact that only group I shows this significantly. To less degree, satisfaction patterns tend to be the same: relatively high at the outset, swinging downward as training progresses, and showing similar fluctuations for all groups. This finding with regard to satisfaction (SI) is a bit surprising in view of the fact that group III had a random pattern for this variable. Evidently its fluctuations were not so far from statistical significance that it was devoid of some similarity in contour to the other groups.

On the basis of the similarity measures between groups, it would be expected that involvement patterns would show the most powerful relationships when groups are compared with one another. This would be followed by closer approximations of similarity on the satisfaction (SI) dimension, but emotionality (EI) measures would show no significant association.[10]

Explanation of these findings poses a rather severe dilemma, and the most feasible method seems to be recapitulation of the findings to this point in order to determine whether any resolution is possible.

The level I analysis indicated that training evidently had a systematic effect upon the participants irrespective of group affiliations. For all dimensions there was evidence of sequence. This, of course, included the emotionality measure. Level II showed that emotionality (EI) for each group taken individually also followed a sequential pattern. The composition of each of the groups as well as the influence exerted by the various trainers provided a basis for assuming that interrelationships among involvement (volume), emotionality (EI), and satisfaction (SI) within each group might be unique for that group. It is now discovered that, despite the apparently uniform effect of training on individuals, and despite the unique behavior within specific groups, the only major area of divergence is in the emotionality patterns. How does it happen that effects making for orderliness within a total population and within subpopulations show deviation when a comparison is made between groups?

---

[9] See Siegel, *op. cit.*, p. 231.
[10] This expectation is based on statistical findings which show high levels of confidence as to the nonrandomness of involvement (volume) patterns and lower levels of significance as we proceed into satisfaction (SI) configurations.

One possibility lies in a reexamination of the emotionality index itself. This has been defined as the ratio of affectively toned responses (positive, negative, and ambivalent) to nonaffective responses (descriptive). In effect, the emotionality index was derived in order to include some measure of that phenomenon which all theorists feel to be crucial to the behavior of human relations groups, namely, the affective component. If the absolute levels of affectivity are studied, it is found that in all cases the range of emotionality (EI) scores through the training period is greater than unity (see Figure 13-1). Emotionality, therefore, is a predominant response to training. It follows a systematic order for all groups and for the population as a whole. Yet closer analysis reveals that this order is unique for each group.

The dilemma raises the question of why an ordering common to all members should be different when the members are grouped. It may be that we find here a special instance of a time-lag phenomenon. In some way, the total population tended to pool emotionality in such a fashion that the ebb and flow of responses conglomerated at roughly the same points in time. This permitted similarity to appear in the total population. Within each group it is likely that events were taking place which were anticipated by enough members to be reflected sufficiently in the pooled data. Yet for each group there was disparity sufficient to create a relatively unique pattern of emotionality. It is a most curious situation, and one which demands additional study in order to ascertain whether this deduction is valid.

## REVIEW AND SUMMARY

The results of this study can be interpreted broadly or narrowly depending on the investigator's proneness to make the "big" generalization. Certainly, the evidence is highly suggestive and tends to support a general hypothesis that the training experience progresses in specific rather than haphazard fashion.

On the negative side there are a number of factors which demand appraisal. These factors are chiefly methodological and are concerned with the general question of whether the study could have been carried out in a more powerful or precise manner. A frank limitation of the study resided in the analytical techniques available for dealing with time series. Psychological research, in general, has not focused on highly segmentalized approaches to behavior but has been content, for the most part, to work in the gross temporal partition known as "before-after" studies. What happens in between has usually been inferred from a set of initial propositions. A typical example of this is the learning experience in which a subject is tested before and after being exposed to a given set of conditions. The supposed impact of the experimental condition is usually deduced from some formal theory and the results either confirm or deny the accuracy of the deduction. The detailed sequence of response generally is of secondary interest.

The present research differs from these "classical" designs, as its focus is upon the unfolding process, the *in situ* elaboration of response to a given experience. An investigation of this kind had little to fall back upon by way of previous work; so, in a sense, it had to borrow techniques from fields such as business (stock-market research) and economics (trend analysis). An indirect result of the study, therefore, was to highlight the need for more precise analytical tools.

One further qualification must be noted. The use of the particular three groups considered herein does not presume that they are representative of all human relations training groups, or for that matter, of the universe of sensitivity training groups.

Assuming that the reader is now sufficiently cautious, it is permissible to look at the findings from their positive standpoint. First, we may consider the results in relation to research and theory. Other research has been suggestive of phasic behavior in training groups.[11] While the methodology and populations studied were quite different from those employed in the present investigation, it can be said that the present work is consistent with other research in yielding data supporting the hypothesis of patterned behavior in groups.

Generally, it seems that trainees, regardless of particular group affiliations, differences in trainer, or other parameters (age, intelligence, etc.) become involved in the training process and display behavior that seemingly fluctuates in similar ways. The reason for this is suggested by additional analysis of the data by specific content categories. This analysis discloses that the bimodal pattern seems to contain two specific kinds of trainee concern.[12] The first peak, occurring near the first third of training, indicates that trainees are concerned with general questions of their role, the trainer's role, and relations to the group in general; the second peak, occurring at the beginning of the last third of training, shows a different focus of interest, namely, a particular concern with interpersonal reactions among members. This is quite consistent with the ideas of Bennis and Shepard, and Schutz, among others, who postulate a sequence of dependence-power problems followed by interdependence-personal considerations.

This study reveals that emotional response to sensitivity training is quite high, and often is experienced as disturbing in some way. This is

[11] Dorothy Stock, in L. Bradford (ed.), *Theory of T-group Training*, National Training Laboratories, Washington, D.C., 1957. Mimeographed manuscripts.
[12] Reisel, *op. cit.*

not surprising, in view of the fact that training deliberately sets out to provide learning in emotional as well as cognitive terms. Emotional learning is invariably resisted because it involves an alteration of the established self concept, the view of one's self to which one tends to adhere rather tenaciously.

A further finding indicates that emotionality, although patterned, tends to elaborate through time in a way unique to each group. It can be said that, while groups get involved in an emotional way, each group has its own particular emotional unfolding. This suggests that wide variations in group emotionality are to be expected, although the temporal ebb and flow of affects are likely to peak and dip in an orderly way during the training procedure. The variation in emotionality from group to group is a rather common observation. Finding that the pattern is systematic for any given group only emphasizes the intermixture of uniqueness and order that characterizes this form of training.

There are other questions, many of them still unanswered. What causes the swings from peaks of activity to troughs of quiescence? What are the particular roles of group composition and trainer personality in the fluctuations of group behavior? What is the effect of time itself on the training process? How can we diagnose the end of one phase and the beginning of another in order to ascertain the degree to which training objectives are being approximated? What about individual patterns in members themselves? These are some of the issues raised by research of this kind, but there are many others (see Chapter 14).

If one takes this study in its entirety, the results provide independent empirical support to theoretical views holding that training-group development is a systematic rather than a haphazard process. Despite the restrictions of interpretation that one must accord our findings, here is a genuine source of encouragement for those who contend that human relations training induces effects that are identifiable by direct quantitative testing rather than by casual, anecdotal armchair speculation.

CHAPTER 14

# Assessing the Training Impact*

Many organizations spend a great deal of time, effort, and money on various forms of human relations training. This training typically is intended to provide experiences which will in appropriate ways modify the trainees' attitudes and behaviors. These expenditures have been made on the assumption that training does effectively change the views and reactions of persons exposed, and that it will make them more skillful in dealing with others. Often a mere judgment of faith is involved. Comparatively little is known of the actual impact that may be ascribed to training.

Those concerned with human relations training have recently had something of a damper placed on their enthusiasm. Several research studies have thrown considerable doubt on the effectiveness of human relations training efforts. One report is particularly distressing, in that it points out that some people who returned from a training experience were actually "worse off" than they had been before.[1] It seems that the

* This chapter is based on the following publications: "Yardsticks for Human Relations Training," by Irving R. Weschler, Robert Tannenbaum, and John H. Zenger, *Adult Education*, vol. 7, no. 3, pp. 152–168, Spring, 1957 (reprinted with bibliography as Adult Education Monograph no. 2, Adult Education Association, 1957), and "Sensitivity Training: Useful Implement in Developing Leaders?" by Robert Tannenbaum, *Research Developments in Personnel Management*, pp. 29–37, Proceedings of the First Conference, held on the campus of the University of California, Los Angeles, June 7–8, 1956, Institute of Industrial Relations, University of California, Los Angeles, 1957.
[1] For a review of some of these studies, see Paul Buchanan, "A System for Evaluating Supervisory Development Programs," *Personnel*, vol. 31, pp. 335–347, January, 1955. See also Edwin A. Fleishman, Edwin F. Harris, and Harold E. Burtt, *Leadership and Supervision in Industry* (Columbus, Ohio: The Ohio State University, 1955). For an interesting discussion of the general problem, see Bernard M. Bass, "Ultimate Criteria of Organizational Worth," *Personnel Psychology*, vol. 5, pp. 157–174, Autumn, 1952. For a treatment which focuses more directly on setting

trainees went back to the culture they had left, bringing new ideals and changed attitudes. Training had the effect of making them more perceptive to human relations practices around them which were different from those taught in the training courses. Lacking the power to change these conditions by themselves, the trainees either returned to their old behaviors or became dissatisfied and left for employment elsewhere. The organization in turn, displeased with the "soft look" on the part of their returning trainees, more often than not helped to make the parting of the ways a mutually desirable experience.

As we have gained increasing experience with sensitivity training, we have increasingly wondered what impact, if any, it has on the trainees. As a result, we have launched a series of studies designed to identify and describe more precisely the essential elements of sensitivity training and to evaluate its effectiveness with reference to clearly established objectives.

This effort has led us, first, to think through the essential elements of any evaluation program; and second, to begin the development and preliminary testing of some devices which we think will get answers to the questions that are troubling us. The presentation which follows, though focusing on sensitivity training, will, we believe, be applicable to the assessment of other human relations training activities as well.

The evaluation problem, as we see it, involves three principal areas of concern. First, we shall consider the *setting of objectives*. Second we shall look at the *training process* itself—at the critical stimuli which can be generated to bring about the changes specified in the objectives. Finally, we shall examine the variables entering into the *evaluation process* as we attempt to assess the impact of the training.

SETTING OBJECTIVES

No training program can be evaluated unless its objectives are clearly identified. The sound formulation of these objectives and measurement of progress toward them represent the core of the evaluation process. Many futile, disappointing training efforts can be traced directly to a failure to spell out what the program was designed to do and whose needs were to be met.

Human relations training is conducted both within organizations and in a variety of other settings, such as universities or leadership training laboratories. The goals of any given program are likely to vary, de-

objectives for human relations training, see Robert L. Katz, "Human Relations Skills Can Be Sharpened," *Harvard Business Review,* vol. 34, pp. 61–72, July–August, 1956.

pending upon who sets it up, who pays for it, who participates in it, who conducts it, and where it is held.

If a program is conducted within an industrial organization and the firm is paying for the training, the formal objectives of the firm and the objectives of the bosses who implement them are most relevant. For those who run programs in industry, these objectives are most compelling.

There are many patterns that executives have in mind when they think about training others. Some like to develop men who can "soft sell" others. Some like to have their junior executives act in the image of the strong man—who gives commands curtly and crisply without fear of contradiction. Some like to see their subordinates emerge as kind father figures who look out for the best interests of their people. Some like to teach the trainees to become facilitators who can help people realize the fullest potential that is within them.

The question can be raised whether the superiors' frame of reference in stating objectives is really the only relevant one? Perhaps the peers' point of view might be pertinent. We talk a lot about teamwork and about collaborative effort between individuals. What would the people who have to collaborate with Joe Smith like to see happen to him? He may behave in a way that makes it extremely difficult for his peers to get along with him, to work with him, to communicate with him. They might have a lot to say as to what changes they think should be brought about in Joe.

Further, perhaps Joe's subordinates, from their point of view, might also have something to contribute about what the objectives of. Joe's training should be. The objectives that superiors define for an individual are likely to be quite different from those defined for him by his subordinates. Very often the superior is thinking of task-oriented goals, of greater immediate productivity, and of keeping the pressure on in order to get the work done, whereas subordinates are thinking of greater understanding, greater acceptance, and better recognition. There are the customers and other outside parties who have relationships with people within the organization who may want to influence the objectives toward which Joe's human relations training should be aimed.

Those of us who serve as trainers often face the problem of differences between the objectives which we, as trainers, would like to see implemented and other kinds which have already been mentioned. We have certain notions as to what end results would be most desirable, and these often conflict with the goals of others. In trying to accomplish things that make sense to us, we find ourselves getting into difficulty with people in the organization who don't understand the relevance of the attainment of our training objectives to organizational purposes.

Oftentimes a training group itself starts defining its own objectives—the ones that are most meaningful to the group as a whole. Difficulties arise when these objectives appear to differ from objectives imposed on the group from the outside.

In a sensitivity training class on campus we often face a problem in the area of grades. From the organizational point of view, we, as instructors, have to give the students grades. Yet the students feel that grades involve evaluation, the setting apart of one student from another, the assessment of differences that are subjective and pretty hard to tap. The feeling is that this evaluation process interferes with training, and many students would like to see it abandoned. Yet the pressures from the outside—from the university administration, from the "system"—in the direction of making some sort of formal evaluation are real and define some of the limits within which the trainers must operate.

Finally, the objectives of the individual trainee himself might become relevant. We are always doing things to other people ("for their own good," of course, as we see it). There is great pressure to be manipulative, to try to create situations in which we mold people in directions that we, as trainers, think are appropriate. Yet, in reality, the trainee himself might as a unique human being in his own right have objectives which do not coincide with at least some others that have been listed. In our training sessions, we often discover that the trainee would like to gain certain things for himself which might not have organizational sanction. Thus there is a conflict generated here, and one that has to be dealt with.

What then are the relevant objectives of sensitivity training?[2] We believe that at some deeper level there is a close interrelationship between objectives from many of these different points of view. We think a strong case can be made that the objectives which we have set for sensitivity training, if attained, would facilitate the attainment of most of the other objectives that have been mentioned. This contention itself, however, needs to be evaluated further.

## The Time Dimension

As objectives are defined, is the concern primarily with short-term or long-term effectiveness? Some programs are designed, it seems, to help people do some specific things better right then and there. A group from the business office, for example, might be trained to deal more effectively with customer complaints; some salesmen can be given hints on the art of closing a sale; or a group of supervisors can be taught some skills in interviewing for hiring. On the other hand, with reference to

[2] See Chap. 9 for a full discussion of the objectives of sensitivity training.

sensitivity training, we are primarily interested in broader, longer-term objectives, which we think are realistic ones if some beginnings are to be made in the direction of personality change.

This point needs to be emphasized rather strongly because it poses some real problems for the trainer. The trainer who is oriented toward longer-run objectives has a difficult task when faced with immediate bread-and-butter considerations within an organization. There is often some feeling that the trainer ought to be able to run the trainees through a ten-session program, for example, to have them emerge "newly adjusted and ready to go!" It is hard to get across the notion that an individual who may now be forty years of age has taken forty years to build into himself what he finally has become. The expectation that individuals can be remade in dramatic ways in ten sessions is rather unrealistic.

As one works in terms of long-run objectives in this human relations training field, it seems that one must accept the fact that no single experience is going to alter an individual radically. Any given training program is just one experience in what probably should be a long series of experiences both within and outside organizations, all designed to help improve a person's relations with other people.

### What Kind of Change?

Let us look more closely at some more specific considerations associated with the setting of objectives. Toward what kinds of personal change are human relations training programs aimed? An objective near the surface for many a training program is the attainment of *greater knowledge.* Some programs aim for this objective exclusively. The individual succeeds if he can answer an examination covering certain specific human relations materials. Unfortunately the acquisition of knowledge alone is not necessarily related to more effective behavior. Trainees often pick up the jargon so, when they go back on the job, they talk a good game of supervising without actually practicing it. They may talk, for example, of permissive, democratic approaches for dealing with subordinates while, in fact, their on-the-job behavior is both rigid and authoritarian.

A somewhat more meaningful objective might involve the adoption of new behavioral skills. The trainee might learn to function more effectively at the *public level,* that is, at the level of his overt behavior, but not change at a deeper, more permanent psychological level.

The trainee might change at the *private level,* a level of which he is consciously aware. He may, for instance, after training be better able to accept certain attributes of his own personality as really being him, and yet not wish to show this new self image to people in his external world. He thus gains insights which he may be unable or unwilling to make public.

Finally, some change might be effectuated at the *unconscious level*. After some of our training sessions, we have been intrigued by individuals who verbally report that something has happened to them, that there has been some kind of change, some kind of growth, perhaps the exact nature of which they are unable to describe.

## THE TRAINING PROCESS

The next area of concern with respect to evaluation is the training process itself. We want to identify and describe the input, that is, those training stimuli which are believed to have an impact on the trainee's total experience. Stated simply, our task is to isolate and define whatever it is that brings about changes in our trainees and to become aware of the consequences of input with regard to output. As practitioners, we need to know with some assurance how to relate variations in the training process to specifically desired training outcomes.

This is admittedly a most complicated assignment. Experimentally, we might succeed if it were possible to vary one aspect of the training process at a time, while holding all other conditions constant. In practice, this end can be achieved only by successive approximations. We therefore must continue to speculate on the sources of variation while getting a feel for the kinds of impact which appear related to them.

### Training Input

What generates a change within the trainee in the direction of the objective or objectives which are specified? It would be wonderful if we could look at our "cookbook" and find perhaps that techniques f, g, and m are the ones that ought to be introduced in the training situation to implement the attainment of our objectives. This would be the trainer's utopia, but we certainly are exceedingly far from its attainment.

With regard to sensitivity training, we have made some tentative decisions concerning the "ingredients" which we feel lead to a successful training experience (see Chapter 9). Admittedly, we are still uncertain, but on the basis of experience, we believe that central to the sensitivity training process is a small group, operating with some frustration in a largely unstructured situation with attention paid primarily to feelings and process and secondarily to ideas or content.

### The Training Group

*Composition of the Group.* Some training groups seem to have much richer experiences than others. They seem somehow to move faster; to be able to absorb more; in general, to be more productive. A training experience can be tremendously enhanced if a group "mix" can be achieved which provides the kinds of roles and pressures that generate productive learning. Whatever happens in sensitivity training, for example, may well be "grist for the mill," but we believe that "the better the wheat, the better the bread."

Every trainee brings with him a unique set of abilities, attitudes, and experiences; one future research task is to determine what kinds of personalities should be brought together for optimum training effectiveness.[3]

We recently had one group composed mostly of nice people with rather bland personalities. No one had strong attitudes or points of view on issues; nearly everyone was rather kind and considerate; few appeared willing to get out on a limb or express feelings of disagreement or hostility. As a result, not too much happened. In contrast, in other groups, different kinds of personalities appear to spark exciting events which lead to meaningful learning.

*Level of Intelligence.* In sensitivity training, there seems to be some minimum reasoning ability needed for people meaningfully to tie together numerous events which on the surface seem unrelated and diverse. As a lot begins to happen in these fluid, unstructured training situations, some persons seem intellectually unable to grasp the significance of the process, even when offered a detailed map in terms of observations and analysis. On the other hand, there are some who appear unconsciously to use their intelligence to ward off the deeper impact of the training experience. By operating primarily at the intellectual level, they seem to miss the opportunity to discover their own role in interpersonal relations. Words have become entities in themselves; they no longer communicate the kinds of feelings necessary for effective learning.

*Expectancies.* As we have acquired more experience with sensitivity training, we have become aware of an interesting phenomenon. In our first few programs, most trainees were frustrated because they did not know how this type of training was conducted. Nowadays, most of our trainees are "shockproof." Some have been told by past trainees not to worry, that lots would be going on at first which they wouldn't understand, but that in the long run things were likely to fall into place. Others may have read our written descriptions of the training process[4] and

[3] William C. Schutz of the University of California at Berkeley is doing some very promising research on the construction of productive groups. For an early report of this work, see *FIRO: A Three-dimensional Theory of Interpersonal Behavior* (New York: Rinehart & Company, Inc., 1958).

[4] See, for example, Irving R. Weschler and Jerome Reisel, *Inside a Sensitivity Training Group,* Institute of Industrial Relations, University of California, Los Angeles, Industrial Relations Monograph no. 4, 1959.

become forewarned about the kinds of feelings and reactions which they were likely to experience. Definite expectancies seem to exist now which undoubtedly help determine the course of events within any given training program.

*Readiness for Training.* Some trainees seem immediately to grasp the objectives of sensitivity training and are able to utilize to the fullest the latitude and freedom of action which this approach permits. Others remain in the dark and, in some instances, never truly understand or appreciate the opportunities. Some actively resist the training; others quickly accept or foster the training aims and methods. It would be useful to know what differences there are in people whose responses to the training vary so widely—whether, for example, those who are least sensitive and flexible have as much chance to profit as those who are already fairly effective in their interpersonal relations, or whether those who get more deeply involved—either pro or con—are able to have a richer, more lasting experience.

## The Trainer

The basic problem here relates to the impact of the trainer's personality on the training outcome. What does the personality of the trainer impart to the training environment and ultimately to the trainee himself (see Chapter 12). Is there a gap between what the trainer sees himself as doing and what he is actually doing? Does the trainer tend to see himself in one way and to be seen in another way by the trainees? Do certain of his personality problems keep him from coming to grips with problems in these same areas in the training situation itself? Does he tend to emphasize (or to avoid) problems that occur in the group that are problems within his own personality? We must find out what kind of personality is most effective with what kinds of groups under what kinds of specific circumstances for what purposes.

## Training Methods and Conditions

The human relations trainer has at his disposal numerous techniques and methods. His repertory ranges from straight lectures to case studies, from incident process exercises to role playing, from film presentations to forum discussions, from structured conferences to free-floating, undirected discussions. Many of these are usefully employed in combination.

What is the differential impact of these different methods on the trainee? What guidelines might be set up to help us in choosing one method over another? Is there something to be gained by variety in approaches, or is it better to stick to one approach throughout any given training experience? Until carefully controlled experimental evidence becomes available, the answers will depend on the views, background, and experiences of each individual trainer.

"Bread-and-butter" problems are by no means less important than some of the more perplexing issues with which we have already dealt. Following are some that loom large with reference to training effectiveness.

*The Size of the Group.* If a group is too small, its members are deprived of the variety of personalities and backgrounds which provide the raw materials of the training experience. A large group (with more than twenty people) makes it most difficult for all trainees to participate effectively; it provides opportunities for "hiding" within the group, when visibility is in fact most desirable. For sensitivity training, a group of about fifteen members appears near the optimum.

*Length of the Program.* The total duration of a program, the interval between meetings, and the length of the individual sessions are the key time variables. Most recently, some of us have experienced considerable success with the three- or four-day human relations workshop. At the university, we are experimenting with a ten-session workshop, meeting once a week during the year and twice weekly during the summer. In organizational settings, programs which are conducted without specific durational limitations appear promising.

*Continuity of Group Membership.* Some trainers believe that rotational group membership enriches the learning potential. They feel that new elements added to the training process provide valuable raw material for discussion. We have some doubts about this with reference to our typical, relatively short sensitivity training programs. Until a group has learned to deal with the many problems created through its own permanent membership, outside influences seem to slow the progress of the group. In a group without specific durational limitations, limited rotational membership might prove of real value.

*Voluntary versus Compulsory Attendance.* People who are sent to training programs seem to behave differently from people who come on their own. This is to be expected. A trainee who wants the experience feels differently about the training than one who has been told by his superiors that he had better get it. It is nevertheless worth mentioning that many of those whose initial attitudes toward sensitivity training are negative seem to find something of value to themselves as the training proceeds.

## The Training Setting

Sensitivity training is carried on in two principal ways. In "horizontally structured" groups, people come together who do not relate with each other on the job. They frequently meet at university workshops, at downtown locations, or in the various group-development laboratories which are now functioning throughout the world. These people come from different organizations; they usually have varying backgrounds and responsibilities. By being removed from their own environment, it is hoped that they will be able to exchange ideas and feelings without worrying about repercussions in their "back-home" situations.

"Functionally structured" and sometimes "vertically structured" groups are usually found within one organization where people who work together train together (see Chapter 11). In sensitivity training on campus or in laboratories much resistance to attitudinal and behavioral change is generated because the trainees are thinking about the difficulties of applying what they are learning "back home."

As the trainee gains insights in the training sessions that suggest to him that perhaps he might become more effective by behaving in a different way, he then asks himself the question: "If I start behaving that way back home, what are they going to think of me?" He's faced squarely with conflicting pulls. On the one hand, his training experience leads him toward one kind of behavior; yet he knows that he is still part of a social organization, that he can't change in ways that will be frowned upon back there.

Although the barriers to training success are likely to be greater for in-plant training—status differences being one of the reasons—it seems that training *in situ* can yield more far-reaching results. Insights and skills (particularly those involving the trainees' relations with each other) are more readily transferable to the work situation because they have emerged from a shared training experience. In addition, the trainees become aware that management is concerned about improving human relations on their jobs and may be bolstered in their efforts to change attitudes and behaviors by both fellow employees and the climate coming out of "mahogany row."

## THE EVALUATION PROCESS

Knowing the objectives and the stimuli which go into the training experience, we are at last ready to assess the training impact.

Proper evaluation demands adequate research designs and valid methods for their implementation. Ideally, we should try to get sensitive measurements for each trainee on a number of relevant criteria— before, during, and after the training experience. These "after" measurements appear especially crucial, since we want to see how much of what has happened to the individual remains with him. Whenever possible, carefully selected control groups should be used, from which identical measurements are taken, but which do not receive the training itself. This procedure may be difficult in practice, but it provides the best way by which whatever results are collected can be meaningfully interpreted.

Any human relations training program must be evaluated in terms of aims, methods, and achievements. Ideally, this process should consist of three phases. First, a potential trainee should be appraised by his superiors, peers, subordinates, and himself prior to training. Second, his performance in training should be assessed by the trainers, the group members, and himself. Finally, he should be evaluated again by his superiors, peers, subordinates, and himself some time after the training is completed.

As has been stated already in our discussion of objectives for sensitivity training, the criteria of evaluation are likely to vary for each evaluator and for each situation. On the job, the trainee's superiors may stress the productivity of his work groups, morale, turnover, and similar factors. His peers may look for cooperation and friendliness. His subordinates may be more interested in understanding, acceptance of their frailties, or involvement in decision making. He himself may be most concerned with his ability to handle day-to-day tasks, to keep production up, to deal with arguments and hurt feelings when they occur, and to avoid being "called down" by his superiors.

In the training situation, the trainers may value greater insights into defenses, more realistic perception of others, understanding of communication processes, or newly found awareness of the forces operating in a group. Fellow participants may stress willingness to understand and listen to others, effectiveness in role playing, recognition of the trainee's impact on a discussion, or his efforts to help the group achieve its goals. The trainee himself may most wish to develop feelings of confidence and security, to improve his ability to handle tough situations, to gain skills in interviewing and listening, and to experience relief from some of the tensions and anxieties with which he feels himself saddled.

After the training, each group is apt to look for changes in the trainee's behavior related to the objectives. The trainee himself, however, is likely to alter some of his criteria in terms of the experiences he has had in the training situation. Experience shows that if participation in the training process has "taken," the first impact will probably occur in the trainee's own perception about himself and others. His new self assessment may lead to more confidence and security and to less anxiety in his day-to-day relations on the job. Next, the repercussions of such insights will probably be felt by those with whom he deals. He may "blow up" less often, turn an attentive rather than a deaf ear to suggestions, or play a more constructive role in staff meetings. As he begins to feel his way, he may discard old attitudes and behaviors and become comfortable in more spontaneous, creative, and mature patterns for productive living.

## Common Evaluation Methods

Few of the currently popular evaluation methods appear worth using. Most get at fairly superficial data and are easily biased by the whims and fancies of human nature and by the frame of reference of the evaluator.

The *testimony of the trainees* is one of these much abused tests of effectiveness. Expressions of satisfaction or dissatisfaction must be accepted with caution. Although most are sincere, many are undoubtedly colored by all kinds of wishful thinking—"after all, we have put a lot of time and effort into our training experience; we must have gotten something out of it!"

The *trainer's reactions* may be no more objective. He, too, has a great need to see himself as doing a useful job; his assessment of the training impact may be biased by his search for evidence of his own competence —evidence which he often strongly needs (see Chapter 12).

*Tests of knowledge* are limited in that they get only at what people can verbalize, but not at what they can actually do.

*Observations* by superiors, peers, subordinates, or anyone else, for that matter, are likely to suffer from many of the pitfalls inherent in the rating process.

*Statistical data* reflecting changes in production, labor turnover, absenteeism, and morale are easily contaminated by countless factors other than those related to interpersonal effectiveness, which cannot directly be traced to the impact of the training process.

What we need are more subtle techniques which are capable of detecting changes throughout the training process both in attitudes and in behavior. We must be able to distinguish between changes in attitudes that can be openly expressed, those that are consciously known but privately held, and those deeper personality reorganizations which operate at the unconscious level. We must find techniques which avoid the built-in biases so prevalent in the usual types of observation.

## Some Current Training-evaluation Research

Recently an intensive program of research on the evaluation of the impact of sensitivity training has been under way at UCLA. This program has had two key objectives:

1. *Contributions to Methodology.* The development of new tools and techniques to measure adequately attitudinal and behavioral changes

that can be traced to the impact of any human relations training program.

2. *Contributions to Better Understanding of the Sensitivity Training Process.* The development and testing of hypotheses concerning the specific impact of sensitivity training experiences.

From 1956 to 1959 a number of classes of the "Leadership Principles and Practice" course at UCLA served as subjects for this research. The study design involved the administration of numerous research instruments, both at the beginning and at the end of the training period, and the assessment of change for various subgroups within these classes from beginning to end. Subgroups examined in detail were students who appeared to be particularly "good" or "bad" with reference to various objectives of sensitivity training. The Interaction Inventory, a sociometric test, was used to determine those who were seen as most effective or ineffective, as well as to identify those who were seen as "isolates" (nonentities, from the group's point of view) and "controversials" (people concerning whose effectiveness the group members were unable to agree). Understanding of other people's feelings (social sensitivity) and behaving appropriately in the group (behavior flexibility) served as the two main criteria which emerged from analysis of the intercorrelations among the twelve measures that composed the entire Interaction Inventory.

Through 1959, the Human Relations Research Group collected and analyzed data to answer the following five major questions:

1. *Along what personality dimensions do the trainees differ?* ("*Before*" *versus* "*after*" *the training experience?* "*Successful*" *versus* "*unsuccessful*" *trainees?*)

The California Psychological Inventory (CPI) was chosen as the research tool because it seemed to cover personality areas which we felt were most amenable to change as a result of a sensitivity training experience. The preliminary results suggest some broad aspects of personality that distinguish "successful" from "unsuccessful" trainees. Differences of "before" versus "after" the training experience were found to be generally slight, although some component scales of the CPI appeared to be more useful than others as predictors of success in training.[5]

2. *What are the attitudes of the trainees with reference to their participation in training* "*before*" *and* "*after*" *the training experience?*

A new test, the Attitudes Toward Group Inventory (ATG) was designed to determine the trainees' intimate feelings toward their role in group action. Preliminary analysis of the data suggests that certain attitudes concerning, for example, dependence on authority or willing-

---

[5] The first completed paper dealing with this work is entitled "The CPI as an Indicator of Personality Changes in Sensitivity Training," by Fred Massarik and Gary Carlson (available from Human Relations Research Group, UCLA).

ness to relate intimately with other group members have direct bearing on how well the trainee will fare in his sensitivity training experience. Currently, it is our hope to develop an instrument which will make it possible to facilitate selection of those individuals for training who show the greatest promise of profiting from it.

3. *How do the trainees react to the training process as it proceeds?*

In the spring of 1956, the trainees in three classes kept *diaries* in which they were encouraged to record, after each session, their true feelings, opinions, and reactions to anything that may have affected them. They were asked to write as much or as little as they desired. These diaries provided us with a rich source of data describing the trainee's world from the "inside out." On the basis of content analysis, we are gaining new insights about such varied processes as the stages of growth in training groups, the phases of involvement through which trainees seem to pass, the establishment and maintenance of the trainer role, and the nature of so-called critical events which give each training group its distinct character.[6]

In the spring of 1959, this work was continued with a somewhat different emphasis. New data were collected from four classes which were intended to permit analysis of trainer interventions leading to successful training experiences and the identification of "critical events" characteristic of the successful or unsuccessful training groups. This time the trainees were requested regularly to turn in *after-meeting reaction forms* on which they were to indicate their subjective feelings with regard to over-all meeting effectiveness, personal insights, communications, group cohesiveness, approval or disapproval of the conduct of other members, atmosphere, personal involvement, and personal satisfaction with the instructor's behavior. In addition, room was provided for the trainees to describe the "critical incidents" in which they felt themselves to be personally involved. The trainer filled out another form after each meeting, indicating how he felt the meeting rated in effectiveness and describing in detail those incidents or occurrences which he felt had important training impact for the group. Inspection of these data shows that they are particularly rich sources of conjectures and hypotheses. Once more, analysis of all kinds of data for the group as a whole, between classes, within classes, and between the trainer and his class is feasible and will be undertaken.

4. *How perceptive do the trainees become as a result of the training process?*

---

[6] The diary study has yielded the monograph *Inside a Sensitivity Training Group,* previously referred to (see footnote 4 and also Chap. 10). It has also resulted in a Ph.D. dissertation, "A Search for Behavior Patterns in Sensitivity Training Groups," by Jerome Reisel, which was concerned with the problem of determining whether or not identifiable sequences of behavior could be determined in sensitivity training groups (see Chap. 13 for a synopsis of this research).

A series of short stories (Projective Sketches) was administered to all trainees in some of these classes at the beginning and end of training. The trainees' skill in assessing the personality dynamics at work in these stories became a measure of their understanding of human relations. Improvement in the direction of greater social sensitivity was ascribed to those people whose test responses after training appeared more fully to take into account the subtler aspects of interpersonal relationships inherent in the stimulus materials. This work, which was continued in the fall of 1959, appears to have yielded an instrument of some clinical potency.

5. *How do the personalities and interventions of the trainer influence the training process?*

Little research attention has thus far been paid to the importance of the trainer role. This has led to the erroneous impression that events occurring in the training group can happen relatively independently of the trainer. *Clinical observation* of two trainers during sensitivity training points clearly to the pervasive influence generated by conscious and unconscious trainer behavior. Detailed description has been provided indicating the manner in which these two trainers acted in differentiable ways in order to energize, channel, and mirror the activities of their respective groups (see Chapter 12).

GATEWAYS TO FUTURE RESEARCH

Our initial work on training evaluation has suggested that every phase of training—from the preliminary statement of objectives to the final evaluation of results—contains countless unanswered but researchable questions. At present, the following problems appear most fruitful for further explorations.

*What types of trainer behavior lead to a successful training experience?*

It would be most helpful to determine both the aims and the characteristics of persons who perform the training task successfully. Variations in performance (*trainer interventions*) in relation to specific training objectives could be studied. Both trainees and trainers, participating in various types of human relations training experiences, could be asked to describe specific instances illustrative of what they feel to be particularly helpful or not helpful with regard to their own personal training objectives. Analysis of these types of data could provide better understanding of the specific interventions made by trainers which in turn lead to objectively defined, successful training experiences.

*What are the "critical events" leading to success or failure in sensitivity training programs?*

Every training experience seems to be characterized by a number of specific events which have crucial impact on what happens to specific individuals and to the group as a whole. These events are often trainer-initiated, although more often than not it is the actions by individual members which change the "course of destiny" of their group.

The development of methods whereby the "critical events" can be recognized, described, and analyzed could prove most helpful. Two approaches to this problem appear promising. First, diaries can provide information concerning the kinds of reactions which influence trainees throughout the training experience. As comments regarding specific events for any given session appear in numerous protocols, or as their impact becomes obvious in later references, a given series of events may stand out as critical. Second, clinically skilled observers may provide clues to the nature of the forces initiated by trainer and trainees that shape the training impact. Interestingly enough, our initial clinical study of the role of the trainer suggests that the significance of some "critical events" does not become conscious for either trainer or trainees until, in some instances, considerable time has elapsed.

*What kinds of people (i.e. what different types of personalities) are needed for an effective training group?*

The pioneering work of William Schutz[7] on personality patterns of people who are able to work together successfully suggests that a similar approach might yield data on the personality patterns of people who are able to train together successfully. Through time we have become aware that certain training groups are characterized by a group "mix" which provides the kinds of roles and pressures that generate productive learning. It would be useful to experiment with a number of new test instruments, such as Schutz's FIRO Scales, and with the ATG in order to predict effective training group composition.

*Can personality and behavioral changes in the trainees be traced to sensitivity training?*

It is conceivable that personality and behavioral changes from "before training" to "after training" are not really due to a training experience at all. One may speculate that such changes might simply result from the fact that the trainees were joined together in a social situation for a certain period of time. One might hold—though it is unlikely—that changes are merely a result of maturation and time. It would therefore seem desirable to proceed with a program of rigorously controlled experimentation stemming from appropriate hypotheses and providing for experimental groups (and their replication) and a variety of control groups.

---

[7] See Schutz, *op. cit.*

*What is the duration of the presumed impact of sensitivity training?*
All relationships considered in most research on training impact are
bounded at either side by the beginning and end of a training experience. It is quite possible, however, that this relatively circumscribed
approach provides only a fragmentary picture at best. After all, sensitivity (and some other human relations) training is intended to modify
the attitudes, feelings, and behaviors of trainees not simply for the
moment. Rather, change is hopefully expected for the long run, in the
maelstrom of the "real-life" situation. Accordingly, it becomes necessary
to trace responses of trainees *through time* after they have returned to
their day-by-day activities. Another research approach would therefore
examine selected hypotheses in terms of long-range considerations.

Samples could be selected from among those persons who apparently
have "profited" by a training experience, from those who did not profit,
as well as from those who were either seen as "controversials" or as
"isolates." The members of these subgroups could then be retested at
intervals after they have returned to their jobs or other post-training
situations. This approach could tell us something about the extent to
which changes, or other relationships, which existed during training are
maintained later when the training experience itself is a thing of the
past. Further, some indication could be obtained as to how the trainee
is seen through the eyes of others. At identical intervals, peers, superiors,
and subordinates of the trainees could be interviewed in detail, tapping
their perceptions of the responses and behaviors of the erstwhile
trainees.

## Theoretical Reexamination, Integration, and Applications

Sensitivity training, as a human relations training technique, has
numerous relatives, such as group psychotherapy, counseling, T-group
training, and didactic teaching about human relations. It now seems desirable to spell out explicitly the common theoretical basis of these
various behavior-changing techniques and to distinguish clearly those
aspects in which sensitivity training differs from other approaches. The
time is ripe for the development of a systematic theoretical model which
we hope will specify the place sensitivity training occupies within the
broad spectrum of behavior-changing techniques.

As our training activities with executives and other groups continue
to expand, the results of our research are, as a matter of course, being
utilized to bring about a fruitful integration between theory and
practice.

# PART THREE

# Studies in Organization

In recent years, a continuing—indeed, a revitalized—interest in organization theory and research has been in evidence. A consistent thread of investigations and conceptual formulations in this area has run throughout the work of the Human Relations Research Group since its inception.

Initial efforts were primarily directed toward abstract theorizing concerning aspects of formal organization. Subsequently, a series of empirical studies in a government research laboratory were conducted. These latter studies focused on concepts such as bureaucracy; the formulation of objectives and evaluation procedures; factionalism; job satisfaction, productivity, and morale. One particular point of interest was the development of a methodological innovation: the Multi-relational Sociometric Survey.

Other issues interpenetrating the group's research in the organization area had to do with the relations between the behavioral scientist and the host organization and relations between the behavioral scientist and his subjects.

The first two chapters of this part (Chapters 15 and 16) deal with closely interrelated formal organizational concepts: the ideas of manager and of managerial decision making. In a sense, these chapters are companion pieces: the first delineates the essential functions of the manager, as a theoretical construct; the second analyzes the process of decision making as exercised by the manager. The approach is formal and perhaps, as judged by current standards, somewhat static. While the notion of "rationality" continues to have its useful place in organization theory, our present viewpoint leans toward more dynamic and limited formulations, akin perhaps to those of the "satisficing man," as contrasted with purely rational man.[1]

[1] See H. A. Simon, *Models of Man, Social and Rational* (New York: John Wiley & Sons, Inc., 1957), especially pp. 252–253.

Chapter 17 reports a study conducted in the government research laboratory that provided the setting for much HRRG field investigation during the early 1950s. The approach of this chapter is primarily anthropological and qualitative. The interaction between formal and informal factors in an organization in action is explored. The gap between the classic concept of bureaucracy and emerging organizational reality once more is documented.

Chapter 18 is taken from the proceedings of a conference of research administrators held at UCLA in 1952. This chapter mainly raises questions concerning the definition of organizational goals in research and concerning approaches to assessing the performance of researchers. It also presents a suggested list of criteria that may provide a systematic basis for evaluation.

Chapter 19 may be regarded as a case example of the response of an organization to changed objectives. It links, by empirical data, some conceptual notions dealing with objectives sketched briefly in the preceding chapter. Chapter 20, dealing with problems of evaluation, further pursues issues raised by Chapter 18. Chapter 20 employs the methods of the clinical psychologist. It concludes that, in an evaluation situation that largely lacks firm criteria of a technical sort, over-all perceptions of subordinates by the superior are crucial determinants of performance rating.

Chapters 21 and 22 turn from the evaluation of performance of individual organization members to the assessment of organizational effectiveness. Chapter 21 studies, largely by social-psychological methods, two divisions of the government research laboratory. These were headed by supervisors displaying contrasting leadership styles, one inclined to be restrictive and the other tending to be permissive. While at the time it did not seem to be the major issue, it now appears that this study—together with others published since its appearance in 1952—casts doubt on the assumptions that permissively led groups necessarily exceed restrictively led groups in job satisfaction, or that high job satisfaction and productivity necessarily go together. The need for a frame recognizing the essential complexity of the relationship between leadership style and organizational effectiveness would seem to loom as large as ever.

Chapter 22 serves a twofold function. First of all, and perhaps most important, it is methodologically oriented. Secondly, it provides empirical data that illustrate the methodology and that relate to the findings of Chapter 21. The Multi-relational Sociometric Survey (MSS) extends sociometric method to encompass a variety of interpersonal activities (e.g., order giving, pointing out mistakes, and socializing). Further, it deals not only with the customary attractions and repulsions among people, but it also considers the patterns of organizational prescription (formal organization) and people's view of the formal organization, as well as the actual relationships as they occur day by day on the job. A number of indices using these several factors are devised. These indices seem to be promising yardsticks of organizational functioning, although our own application of them since 1953 (because of a shift in research interest) has been limited.

Finally, Chapters 23 and 24 consider some problems confronting the behavioral scientist or social researcher in his dealings with the host organization that provides a setting for his investigations and with the individual subjects themselves. Specifically, Chapter 23 considers the public relations and interpretational issues that the researcher needs to be aware of when he seeks to arrange for basic social research in industry. Chapter 24 addresses itself to some matters of ethics underlying the use of data-gathering techniques which pretend to search for a given result when indeed their true purpose is hidden from the subject. Of course, the problems of relationship with host and subject are pervasive and continuing.

Ultimately, the researcher and practitioner make value judgments and take implicit or explicit ethical stands that guide their work. We continue to be much concerned with the nature of these value and ethical positions as we formulate plans for our forthcoming research and as we continually assess the nature of our practice.

# CHAPTER 15

# A Look at Formal Organization:
# The Manager Concept*

## MANAGERS AND THE STRUCTURE OF ENTERPRISES[1]

An enterprise may be viewed as an instrument for the transformation of the services of persons and things into a completed product. Of the personal services contributed to an enterprise, some are managerial in character; others, nonmanagerial. Those who contribute managerial services will be called *managers*, while those who contribute nonmanagerial services (although usually called workers or laborers) will be called *nonmanagers*.

This chapter is primarily concerned with the nature of managerial services. The problem is in clearly differentiating them from nonmanagerial services. Such differentiation can best be accomplished by isolating those functions performed exclusively by managers—a task which will later be undertaken. This will make possible a meaningful and useful definition of the manager concept. But it will first be helpful to examine the structure of enterprises and, in general terms, to delineate the positions occupied by managers in that structure.

### Groups and Complexes

The basic structural unit in an enterprise will be termed a *group*. A group is a combination of two or more individuals jointly contributing

---

* This chapter is a slightly modified version of "The Manager Concept: A Rational Synthesis," by Robert Tannenbaum, *The Journal of Business*, vol. 22, no. 4, pp. 225–241, October, 1949.
[1] The development of many of the ideas in this section was particularly influenced by Chester I. Barnard, *The Functions of the Executive* (Cambridge, Mass.: Harvard University Press, 1938), chaps. 6, 7, and 8.

specialized services which are coordinated for the attainment of an enterprise purpose.[2]

This definition involves three concepts which require amplification: specialization, enterprise purpose, and coordination.

1. *Specialization.* The services which individuals contribute to groups are always specialized services; i.e., they differ one from the other. The bases for this differentiation are the place where work is done, the time at which work is done, the persons with whom work is done, the things upon which work is done, or the method or process by which work is done.[3]

2. *Enterprise Purpose.* The members of a group must accept an enterprise purpose; i.e., they must be contributing their specialized services toward the attainment of an end which is specified for them. The purpose or end of the group is its *raison d'être*. This purpose may change from time to time, but the purpose at any time is always the formal objective of all members of the group. However, this enterprise purpose need not coincide with the ends which induce each individual to contribute his services to the group. A football player may recognize the purpose of his team to be the defeat of an opponent. At the same time, his personal reasons for belonging to the team may have little to do with such defeat. In other words, enterprise purpose and individual purpose may not coincide.

3. *Coordination.* Since specialized services are being contributed by individuals for the attainment of an enterprise purpose, it is essential that the specialized services be coordinated if the purpose is to be attained. "Coordination . . . is the orderly arrangement of group effort, to provide unity of action in the pursuit of a common purpose."[4] The specialized services must be so combined in suitable relation one to the other that harmony and balance will be achieved.

A group is sometimes coextensive with the enterprise, but this is never the case when enterprises are large. As a group grows in size, a point is reached beyond which it is undesirable to add more individuals to the group.[5] At this point a new group will be formed; and in like manner and for the same reasons, other groups will be formed.

[2] The word "group" is here given a distinct meaning which is not to be confused with any of the sociological connotations which surround it. The word "organization" would be a convenient one to use here, but we avoid using the word because of a special meaning to be given to it later in the discussion.

[3] For a detailed discussion of these bases, see Barnard, *op. cit.*, pp. 128–132.

[4] James D. Mooney and Alan C. Reiley, *The Principles of Organization* (New York: Harper & Brothers, 1939), p. 5.

[5] The reasons why this is so are primarily related to certain limitations of managers in effectuating coordination. See Elmore Petersen and E. Grosvenor Plowman, *Business Organization and Management* (rev. ed.; Chicago: Richard D. Irwin, Inc., 1948), chap. 4; see also Barnard, *op. cit.*, pp. 105–110.

It will next become necessary to combine a number of groups into what will be called a *complex*.[6] A complex is a combination of two or more groups jointly contributing specialized services which are coordinated for the attainment of an enterprise purpose.[7] A complex thus differs from a group in two respects. First, the basic units of a complex are groups rather than individuals; second, the specialized services contributed to a complex are the services of member groups and not directly of individuals. It is common to think of the services of a group as being specialized; for example, a group may be specialized for advertising, safety work, or time-and-motion study.

As a business enterprise continues to grow, it will become necessary to combine a number of complexes into a *superior complex*. The basic units of a superior complex will be referred to as *subordinate complexes*. Now it becomes necessary to alter the definition of a complex to say that it is a combination of two or more groups or complexes, etc., and to recognize that the specialized services contributed to this new complex are the services of member subordinate complexes.

Further growth can be accomplished by the continued combination of complexes into larger wholes. The new complex will always be called a superior complex; and its basic units, subordinate complexes. Finally, a superior complex at the peak of the hierarchy which has been discussed will be called the *supreme complex* and is to be understood as being synonymous with enterprise.

Thus it will be seen that an enterprise is the result of the combination of individuals into groups, of groups into complexes, of subordinate complexes into superior complexes and finally into the supreme complex. This process of growth is synthetic in nature; i.e., it is from the bottom up rather than from the top down, as it is so frequently portrayed.[8] In practice, various terms are used to designate the groups and complexes to which reference has been made. As an example, however, they might be called (going from groups to the supreme complex) *units, sections, departments, divisions, plants,* and *enterprise.*

## The Managerial Superstructure

In defining groups and complexes it has been said above that they are combinations of two or more units jointly contributing specialized

[6] The maximum desirable number of groups in a complex is determined by the same factors that determine the maximum desirable number of individuals in a group. See the preceding footnote.

[7] This definition of a complex will be altered somewhat in the discussion which follows.

[8] See William N. Mitchell, *Organization and Management of Production* (New York: McGraw-Hill Book Company, Inc., 1939), p. 70, note 2; and Barnard, *op. cit.*, pp. 104–105.

services *which are coordinated* for the attainment of an enterprise purpose. When specialized services are being contributed toward the attainment of a specified end, coordination is essential. Coordination, as has been said, involves bringing into common action, combining in harmonious action.[9] It is the responsibility of managers to achieve this essential coordination.

Each group and each complex is headed by a manager. These managers are responsible for coordinating the services contributed by the units comprising the groups or complexes which they head. They achieve coordination by performing the functions of managers, to which reference has already been made in general terms.

Now, whom do the managers manage? The managers of groups manage the individuals who constitute the groups. The managers of complexes comprised of groups do not directly manage the individuals constituting the groups but only do so indirectly by managing the managers who head those groups. The same may be said of the managers of all the superior complexes, including the manager of the enterprise. Thus, except for the managers of groups, all managers indirectly manage the individuals constituting the groups (i.e., the nonmanagers) by managing the managers of groups or complexes. Furthermore, each manager is a member of the group or complex which he manages.

It will be helpful to examine further the relationships existing between managers. From the preceding discussion it can be seen that these relationships represent a superstructure overlying the structure of groups and complexes. Now, the managers themselves are combined into managerial groups; thus, the managers of a combination of groups together with the manager of the complex comprising these groups may be referred to as a managerial group. The same may be said for the managers of subordinate complexes and the manager of the superior complex comprising these subordinate complexes. Individuals who are managers are therefore members of two units—the unit which they head and a managerial unit. This fact relates the managerial superstructure to the structure of groups and complexes and makes possible an integral whole.

## AN ANALYSIS OF THE FUNCTIONS OF MANAGERS ACCORDING TO SELECTED WRITERS

*Sources of Weakness in the Formulations of Representative Writers*

Numerous writers, primarily during the last twenty-five years, have analyzed the specialized services contributed to enterprises by man-

[9] See Henry C. Metcalf and L. Urwick (eds.), *Dynamic Administration: The Collected Papers of Mary Parker Follett* (New York: Harper & Brothers, 1940), p. 71.

agers. Some have done this principally in an attempt to isolate the basic functions of managers or those of some specified group of managers. Others have done this as a part of a more extensive study—most typically in connection with a treatment of the theory of business organization.

As a result of these analyses, one would expect fairly general agreement, particularly among the more recent writers, as to what these basic functions of managers are and what they should be called. Such general agreement is not the case. The formulations that have been made are far from satisfactory. The principal reasons for this need to be specified in detail, as follows:

1. A business enterprise is a complex economic and social institution. Scientific studies of various aspects of this institution are of fairly recent origin. Real progress has been made in the technological, methodological, and procedural aspects, but the development of adequate related theory, as one would expect, has involved a slower process. Furthermore, with a few notable exceptions, those in the best position to observe the institution have been too preoccupied or inadequately prepared to theorize on the basis of their vast experience, while those with the time or the preparation have had inadequate experience.

2. Similar concepts are common to the formulations of many writers, but no common terminology has been used to designate these concepts. In addition, certain terms are common to many writers, but these terms have been used to designate different concepts. The concepts are indeed complex, and our language is such that in many cases available words are either inadequate to convey all that is implied by the concept or else they have different meanings, so that one is related to one concept and another to another concept. Only compromises can be made.

3. In their use of words, some writers have been careless. Often a writer defines a term ambiguously; or he uses the term in different contexts, where such usage implies different meanings of the term in each context; or he defines two terms in such a way that their meanings overlap.

4. In some presentations it is often difficult, if not impossible, to determine exactly what a given writer believes the functions of managers to be. In these cases the writer, at one point in his discussion, presents one list of functions and at another point presents another list of functions, usually with some duplication. Only confusion can result from this practice.

5. Many writers present as functions of managers items which in fact are not functions but most frequently techniques or tools of managers. A function is a natural, proper, or characteristic action. A technique is a method or the details of procedure essential to expertness of execution in any field. A tool is an implement or anything which serves as a

means to an end. In any theoretical formulation these distinctions must be made clear.

6. A few writers confuse the functions of managers with the managerial processes. A managerial process involves a series of steps followed by managers in the performance of a function. A function and the course followed in performing that function need to be kept distinct.

7. Some writers present the functions of managers at least partially in subjective, rather than objective, terms. These writers often emphasize the mental processes which a manager uses in the performance of his functions rather than the functions themselves. Such an approach does not provide a satisfactory basis for an empirical study of the work of a manager.

8. In some presentations writers intermix the managerial functions and the operational functions of an enterprise.

These are the principal reasons which explain the weakness of many of the formulations of the functions of managers which have been made. They have been offered, not to deprecate the work of others (for their positive contributions have been many, and the amount of agreement among them is considerable), but to indicate the pitfalls and difficulties to which any writer on management theory is subject. They have also been offered to provide for the reader a frame of reference by which to judge the formulations of a representative group of these writers which follow. Where it will be of particular value in this presentation, comments related to one or more of the eight reasons will be made, either in the text or in footnotes.

### The Formulations of the Selected Writers

After analyzing an example of group activity, Brech, a British writer, presented the following formulation:[10]

(1) Planning, i.e., the broad lines that will direct the operation and prepare the basis and methods by which it is to be carried out.

(2) Co-ordination, i.e., balancing and keeping together the team, by ensuring a suitable allocation of tasks to the various members, and seeing that the tasks are performed with due harmony among the members themselves.

(3) Inspiration, or motivation, or ensuring morale, i.e., getting the members of the team to pull their weight effectively, to give their loyalty to the group, to carry out properly the tasks they have accepted and generally to play an effective part in the job that the group has undertaken; with this general inspiration goes a process of supervision to ensure that they are in fact playing their part properly.

(4) Control, i.e., the process of checking actual performance against the

[10] E. F. L. Brech, *Management: Its Nature and Significance* (New York: Pitman Publishing Corporation, 1948), pp. 30 f.

agreed standards or plans, with a view to ensuring adequate progress or satisfactory performance, and also "recording" such experience as was gained as a contribution to possible future need.

Supervision (called a process by Brech) is included under the function of inspiration or motivation; but it would appear that this "process" overlaps the control function as defined in the quotation. Furthermore, coordination—and particularly the phrase "seeing that the tasks are performed with due harmony among the members themselves"—seems to overlap, in part at least, both the third and fourth functions.

Mary C. H. Niles, in her book dealing with the middle segment of management, observed:[11]

The job of management is to achieve the common objectives with the resources available. This is done through:

1. *Leadership*—inspiring the whole organization and carrying it forward toward the realization of the objectives.
2. *Organization*—developing appropriate form and function for the attainment of the objectives.
3. *Administration*—providing the policies and methods by which objectives can be realized, and marshaling the human and physical resources.
    a. *Policy making*—anticipating the future and planning for it, laying down policies for securing objectives, and modifying objectives and policies for better results.
    b. *Executive action*—carrying out and interpreting the policies and dealing with the present, particularly with the problems and difficulties which arise from day to day.
    c. *Control*—knowing that the execution is proceeding according to plans and policies laid down—with a view to further policy making and planning.
4. *Coordination*—at all times securing harmony of action toward the objectives, through leadership, organization, and administration.

If coordination is achieved through the other three "jobs" of management, the question arises as to how it can be listed as a distinct "job" coordinate with those other three.

It is difficult to determine what Dimock considers the functions of managers to be. A few examples will demonstrate this to be the case:[12]

There are several practical requirements of administrative theory which enter into the doing of a good job. In the first place, the executive must define his objectives as precisely as possible. . . . Next, he must lay out the broad lines of administrative structure and get the key people to develop

[11] Mary Cushing Howard Niles, *Middle Management* (New York: Harper & Brothers, 1941), p. 15.
[12] Marshall Edward Dimock, *The Executive in Action* (New York: Harper & Brothers, 1945), p. 195. This formulation involves both functions and processes.

them. And finally he must assign to his top officials that portion of the load which falls appropriately within their bailiwicks. His problem thereafter is co-ordination, direction, supervision, and control.

And again, by way of summary and introduction:[13]

Despite the difficulties of classification and articulateness, however, certain terms representing steps in the continuous flow of function stand out with some clarity. In preceding chapters we have seen the connections between organization, delegation, co-ordination, and direction. In an earlier chapter also we dealt with units of administrative measurement, the yardsticks by which output and efficiency are objectively judged. We come now to the control function, which is related to all of these and which represents a distinct and important term in the vocabulary of management.

Does "control" represent a distinct term? Dimock defines control as "the analysis of present performance, in the light of fixed goals and standards, *in order to determine the extent to which accomplishment measures up to executive orders and expectations.*"[14] But earlier he has said that direction "consists of the processes and techniques employed in issuing instructions, setting an example on how the work should be done, and *seeing that the operating program is carried forward as planned.*"[15]

The classifications and terminological usages employed by Petersen and Plowman are nothing short of confusing. While only a few examples will be cited here in support of this contention, numerous others could be supplied.

After implying that what is to follow represents a preliminary or tentative statement, these authors say that "business management includes the organization, direction, control, and supervision of the operations of a business unit."[16] Later, it is pointed out that[17]

. . . executive authority in a business organization is the right to perform certain *organic functions of management.* When these *organic functions* are reduced to their essential qualities, the right of executive authority divides itself into six categories or elements. They are the rights to plan, decide, organize, command, enforce, and coordinate.

In a discussion of the classification of executive activities, it is stated:[18]

[13] *Ibid.,* p. 216. This statement involves functions, processes, and tools.
[14] *Ibid.,* p. 217. Italics are ours.
[15] *Ibid.,* p. 195. Italics are ours.
[16] Petersen and Plowman, *op. cit.,* p. 32.
[17] *Ibid.,* p. 66. Italics are ours.
[18] *Ibid.,* p. 145. Note particularly (1) that there are two usages of "supervision,"

Each of these five major fields of management [policy management, executive personnel management, employee personnel management, operating management, and financial management] may be divided into three subgroups. First, there are activities of primary importance to ownership, which tend to be performed in detail by the board of directors or under its immediate supervision. Second, there are management problems peculiarly coordinative in character. Finally, there are executive activities—more or less routine in their nature—which are called "direction and control" if performed by major executives and "supervision" if performed by minor executives.

Definitions of key terms lead only to further confusion. For example: "'Direction and control' is the executive process of issuing orders and then following them up to make sure they are promptly and properly executed."[19] "'Direction' denotes guidance and *coordination* of the activities of subordinates for the purpose of accomplishing desired results."[20] "The terms 'direction' and 'control' are often used to describe the executive activities of department heads. One phase of the activity of direction is planning. . . . "[21] "Control is a function of management that has both positive and negative characteristics. In its positive aspects, it is the purpose of control to secure and maintain acceptable productivity from all the resources of an enterprise. In a negative sense, it is the purpose of control to prevent and reduce inacceptable and incorrect performance."[22] "Supervision is the indispensable complement of direction. 'Supervision' means 'to oversee and to instruct persons in the detailed performance of their work.' Closely associated with supervision is 'inspection,' which involves examination, testing, and appraisal."[23]

Marshall holds that "'control of business activities' includes three things: (1) the establishment of *policies,* (2) the planning and setting up of the *organization* which is to be used in carrying out those policies, and (3) the *operating* or running of the organization."[24] In this formulation it is not clear what is meant by "operating the organization" or in what respects this function differs from the other two.

A part of White's statement is subjective in character. He maintains that management may be divided into two general classes of activities

---

(2) that coordination activities comprise a separate subgroup, and (3) that here "direction and control" and "supervision" are differentiated only in terms of the executives involved.

[19] *Ibid.,* p. 148.
[20] *Ibid.,* p. 171. Italics are ours.
[21] *Ibid.,* p. 353.
[22] *Ibid.,* p. 373.
[23] *Ibid.,* p. 171.
[24] L. C. Marshall, *Business Administration* (Chicago: University of Chicago Press, 1921), p. 2.

—those of organizing and those of control, and he states that "the functions of organizing are to *analyze*, to *initiate*, to *plan*, and to *promote*, while the functions of control are to *direct*, to *coordinate*, to *maintain*, and to *measure*."[25]

Barnard discusses what he refers to as the essential executive functions. These are three in number. The first is to develop and maintain a system of communication which jointly involves a scheme of organization and an executive personnel. The second function is to promote the securing of the personal services that constitute the material of organizations. The third function is to formulate and define the purposes, objectives, ends of the organization.[26] Although these functions have not been given single-word designations, it will be noted that they are closely related to at least some of the functions suggested by other writers.

Sheldon subdivides what we have been referring to as "management" into three aspects—management, administration, and organization—and says:[27]

Management is coming to mean the control of the process of executing a given policy and is to be clearly distinguished, as regards both the activities involved and the abilities required, from the formulation and determination of that policy, which is the task of the process known as administration. The two together constitute the control of the enterprise. In order that they may function a living structure is built by the process of organization, so that what is to be done and the persons to do it are grouped for the most efficient working.

Holden, Fish, and Smith, in examining the top segment of management, recognized three zones or levels of this segment: the board of directors, general management, and divisional management.. The trusteeship function (involving the board of directors) is to represent, safeguard, and further the stockholders' interest, determine the basic policies and the general course of the business, appraise the adequacy of over-all results, and, in general, protect and make the most effective use of the company's assets. The general-management function includes the active planning, direction, coordination, and control of the business as a whole, within the scope of basic policies established and authority delegated by the board. Thus, this function involves the determination of objectives, of operating policies, and of results. Finally, the divi-

---

[25] Percival White, *Business Management* (New York: Henry Holt and Company, Inc., 1926), p. 98.

[26] Barnard, *op. cit.*, chap. 15.

[27] Oliver Sheldon, "Management," in E. R. A. Seligman (ed.), *Encyclopaedia of the Social Sciences*, vol. 10, 1930. See also Sheldon, *The Philosophy of Management* (Englewood Cliffs, N.J.: Prentice-Hall, Inc., 1923), pp. 31–33.

sional-management function involves the active direction and management of the respective parts or divisions of the company, within the scope of operating policies and authority delegated by general management.[28]

Gordon has analyzed what he calls the leadership function, which he defines as "the function of organizing and directing business enterprises, of making the decisions which determine the course of a firm's activities."[29] At another point he says: "In general, then, business leadership in the large firm includes initiation and approval of decisions affecting important economic variables which have a strong impact on the firm's activities (including choice of the men who make these decisions) and co-ordination or the creation and maintenance of organization."[30]

## *A Classification of Functions Based on the Formulations*

In introducing the formulations presented above, it was stated that there is a considerable amount of agreement among the writers in spite of the weaknesses that have appeared in their presentations. A careful examination of the formulations will indicate that this is true.

Taking into account the definitions employed and differing terminological usages, eliminating in most cases terms which represent processes, techniques, or tools, and allowing for ambiguities, it is possible to classify into five groups the various functions discussed by the writers. Each group is characterized by the fact that (*a*) the functions of which it is comprised are the same or similar but are assigned different names or (*b*) that the functions are different but are closely related or (*c*) that they overlap in content.

In the first group are "organization," "lay out the broad lines of administrative structure," and "develop and maintain a system of communication which jointly involves a scheme of organization and an executive personnel." In the second group are "initiation and approval of decisions," "planning," "formulate and define the purposes, objectives, ends, of the organization," "formulation and determination of policy," and "direction." In the third group are the terms "control," "supervision," and "appraisal." In the fourth group are "inspiration," "motivation," "leadership," and "promote the securing of personal services." And in the fifth group are "trusteeship" and "representation."

---

[28] Paul E. Holden, Lounsbury S. Fish, and Hubert L. Smith, *Top-management Organization and Control* (Stanford, Calif.: Stanford University Press, 1941), part B, sec. 1.
[29] Robert Aaron Gordon, *Business Leadership in the Large Corporation* (Washington, D.C.: The Brookings Institution, 1945), p. 5.
[30] *Ibid.*, p. 53.

Finally, it should be noted that "coordination" appears as a function in many of the quotations.

This grouping of the functions of managers as presented by various writers provides a convenient basis for the development of a synthesis of the manager concept, which is attempted in the following section.

## THE FUNCTIONS OF MANAGERS: A SYNTHESIS

### The Functions in General

The functions of managers may now be listed and discussed in detail. No claim to complete originality is made for this presentation. It represents, for the most part, an effort logically to combine selected ideas of many writers into a meaningful and useful functional definition of the manager.

No special brief is held for the terminology chosen or for the particular grouping of activities used. The terms and groupings to be found in the presentation are those which seem to be most appropriate and useful to this study and which, in most instances, closely conform to general usage. Wherever exception is taken to earlier formulations or wherever new ideas or terminology are presented, such exceptions or novelties will be specifically indicated.

In speaking of the functions of managers, it is not intended to imply that each manager in an enterprise performs all the functions. Such is seldom, if ever, the case. Managers, like nonmanagers, are specialists. They typically specialize in specific functions or a specific function. The functions of managers are those performed exclusively by managers as a group.

It is the thesis of the present discussion that all managerial activities are included in three functions: organization, direction, and control. These are derived from the groupings presented at the conclusion of the preceding section and will now be discussed.

### Organization

The term "organization" implies an arrangement in which all units are so related to each other that they may work as a whole, each unit having its proper task to perform; and "to organize" means "to arrange or constitute in interdependent parts, each having a special function, act, office, or relation with respect to the whole."[31] These statements include two basic concepts, namely, units or parts each having its

---

[34] By permission. From *Webster's New International Dictionary, Second Edition,* copyright 1959 by G. & C. Merriam Co., Publishers of the Merriam-Webster Dictionaries.

proper or special task to perform and an arrangement involving an interdependence or relationship between the units or parts. The managerial function of organization involves these two concepts. Managers must determine the degree and type of specialization to be effectuated within the enterprise, and they must determine the relationships that are to exist among the specialized units.[32]

With respect to the degree and type of specialization, it should be recalled that one of the characteristics of the individuals, groups, and complexes that constitute an enterprise is that they each contribute specialized services to the group or complex of which they are a part. The determination of these specializations involves analysis first and then synthesis.

The function of organization begins with the objective of the enterprise, i.e., with the good or service to be produced. It must be determined by analysis what services of individuals will be necessary to produce the good or service in question. This determination entails questions relating to both degree and type. How specialized should be the services to be contributed by each individual occupying a position, and what should be the type of these services? Both these questions must be answered.[33] When they are, the process of synthesis can begin.

[32] Organization as a managerial function has been defined variously by different writers. Some of the definitions include the two concepts presented above. Some include only one, while others include concepts which we would not include as a part of the function of organization. Some examples of these definitions follow: "Organisation: the structure of (1) the responsibilities and duties by means of which the activities of the enterprise are distributed among the (executive and supervisory) personnel employed in its service; (2) the formal inter-relations established among the personnel by virtue of such duties" (Brech, *op. cit.*, p. 41). "The act of defining the responsibilities of the members of an enterprise and the relations between them" [Alvin Brown, *Organization* (New York: Hibbert Printing Co., 1945), p. 269; Brown defines "responsibility" as "the prescribed endeavor of an individual" (*ibid.*, p. 270)]. "Organization . . . may be defined very simply as—'determining what activities are necessary to any purpose (or "plan") and arranging them in groups which may be assigned to individuals'" [L. Urwick, *The Elements of Administration* (New York: Harper & Brothers, 1943), p. 36]. "Organization . . . refers to the means ordinarily employed by management in the analysis of activities involved in operation of the business enterprise and in the synthesis of these into a coordinated whole" (Mitchell, *op. cit.*, p. 70). "It (organization) means the authority relationships between the personnel employed in the enterprise . . ." and "organizing is the process of determining the kind and extent of the specialization to be employed in performing tasks" [Lewis C. Sorrell, *Transportation, Production and Marketing* (Chicago: Traffic Service Corp., reprinted from *Traffic World*, issues of 1930 and 1931), p. 75].

[33] Ideally, these questions should be answered in the abstract, i.e., without reference to specific individuals and the services they are capable of supplying. Practically, it is often impossible to do this, both because no individual may be available capable of contributing the desired services and because adaptations must be made with reference to the services present members of the enterprise are capable of contributing. The important point here is that emphasis should be on the positions in the enterprise structure rather than on specific individuals.

First, the individuals contributing specialized services must be combined into groups. The nature of these groups is similarly determined by the degree and type of group specialization desired. Next, groups are combined into complexes and these into superior complexes, and so on until the supreme complex is achieved; and always the degree and type of specialization are the determinants of the nature of each of these units.[34]

The services contributed by the managers who constitute the managerial superstructure are also specialized, as has previously been indicated; and the determination of the degree and type of the specialization of these services must be made by managers. Certain aspects of this determination lead to a consideration of the second concept involved in the managerial function of organization, namely, the determination of the relationships that are to exist among the specialized units in an enterprise.

The relationships established among the managers of an enterprise determine the relationships among the groups and complexes which they head. So it is upon the former relationships that attention must be focused. The managerial relationships are always expressed in terms of authority and responsibility, and they are established by delegation. Therefore, each of these three concepts must first be defined.

Authority is the right to command or to act. Thus, a person having authority has the right not only to act himself but also to expect action of others. But what is the source of this right? In practice, authority appears to originate at the top of a structural hierarchy—under private enterprise, with the owners—and to flow from owners to their representatives, the managers, and from superior managers to their subordinates. Hereafter in this presentation, authority, when viewed in this customary manner, will be referred to as formal authority.[35]

Responsibility involves being subject to another who may exact redress in case of default. Responsibility is answerability or accountability. One is typically responsible to another for the performance of tasks assigned to him by the latter.

Delegation is the act of investing with formal authority to act for another. "Delegation always means the conferring of authority, and can never mean anything else."[36] A delegation of formal authority must

---

[34] In the literature on organization, the question of the type of group and complex specialization is frequently discussed under the heading of "departmentation." The three most frequently mentioned types of specialization are territorial, commodity, and functional. For example, see Petersen and Plowman, *op. cit.*, chaps. 8 and 9, and Sorrell, *op. cit.*, pp. 74–79.

[35] In the next chapter occasion will be taken to examine adequately the source of the ability to exercise effective authority.

[36] Mooney and Reiley, *op. cit.*, p. 17.

always include a definition of the limits within which that authority may be exercised.

As has been indicated, the fountainhead of all formal authority in a private enterprise is the owners—in a corporation, the stockholders. The latter typically retain some formal authority but delegate most of it to their elected representatives, the board of directors. The board, in turn, becomes responsible to the stockholders for exercising the delegated formal authority within the specified limits.[37] The board retains some formal authority and delegates the balance to the manager who heads the supreme complex. The delegation establishes the specialization for this manager, and he becomes responsible to the board within the limits of the delegation. This process continues downward through the managers of superior and subordinate complexes to the managers of groups. The latter delegate to the individuals constituting their groups formal authority to perform designated tasks, and the individuals become responsible for such performance. *These individuals are never delegated formal authority to command, nor are they able to delegate authority to others.*

A manager who delegates formal authority to subordinates does not thereby escape responsibility to his superior for the exercise of the formal authority which the latter delegated to him. He is able to assume that responsibility by holding his own subordinates responsible for the formal authority which he has delegated to them.

The formal authority which is delegated to subordinates may itself be specialized into the authority to prescribe and the authority to enforce. The former is authority to indicate how designated activities shall be performed; the latter is authority to see that the activities are performed. Some managers exercise both types of authority; others, only one type. Formal authority may also be centralized or decentralized. The more centralized the authority, the more it has been reserved for execution by managers at the higher levels in the managerial superstructure; the more decentralized the authority, the more it has been delegated to the managers at the lower levels in the managerial superstructure.

The process of delegation establishes definite relationships between managers and therefore between the specialized groups and complexes

[37] The relationship indicated between the stockholders and the board is the one imposed by law and generally assumed in theory. But in the modern, large-scale corporation, in which there is often a significant separation between ownership and management (including the board), the relationship is often quite tenuous. See A. A. Berle and G. C. Means, *The Modern Corporation and Private Property* (New York: The Macmillan Company, 1932); Marshall E. Dimock and Howard K. Hyde, *Bureaucracy and Trusteeship in Large Corporations,* Temporary National Economic Committee Monograph no. 11, Washington, D.C., 1940; Gordon, *op. cit.,* chaps. 2 and 3.

which they head. These relationships are those of superior and subordinate. A subordinate is always responsible to a superior for the accomplishment of that for which he has been delegated formal authority. Formal authority is delegated downward through the managerial hierarchy; responsibility extends upward through the same hierarchy. The superior-subordinate interconnections are the channels of formal communication, both downward and upward, within an enterprise; and the managers are themselves the centers of communication.

## Direction

Once managers have determined the degree and type of specialization to be effectuated within the enterprise and the relationships that are to exist among the specialized units, they have provided themselves with a mechanism for the attainment of purpose. They must next employ the mechanism. The first function of managers involving such employment is the function of direction. Direction is the use of formal authority in order to guide subordinates.[38] Direction involves devising the purposes of action and the methods or procedures to be followed in achieving them. The decisions to be made in connection with direction must answer the questions: "What?" "How?" "When?" "Where?"

Devising the purposes of action provides the "what content" of direction. It has already been seen that the individuals constituting groups, the groups constituting complexes, and the subordinate complexes constituting superior complexes must in each case have an enterprise purpose, end, or objective. In addition, each individual, manager and nonmanager, has a purpose to achieve in his own activity. Managers must formulate these purposes for their subordinates and order them put into effect.

Devising purposes begins with the broad purpose or purposes of the enterprise. These are then translated into subpurposes for the superior complexes constituting the supreme complex. The subpurposes are further subdivided for the subordinate complexes, and so on down the structural hierarchy until each individual has his own purpose. These translations or subdivisions are made successively by managers, starting with those at the top of the hierarchy of the managerial superstructure (typically the board of directors) and moving down to those who head groups. As Holden, Fish, and Smith have said:[39]

First, there is the broad general objective for the company as a whole. . . .
It is usually established by the board of directors, through approval of the

[38] No available term is adequate for the proper designation of this function. The term "direction" seems to be the most appropriate, although in usage "to direct" is often synonymous with "to conduct, manage, or control."

[39] *Op. cit.*, pp. 203 f.

objective proposed either by general management or originated by the board itself. . . .

It is not enough to establish the general objective. As a matter of fact, that concerns mostly the first and second zones of management. To be really successful the co-operation of every person in the organization is needed. The general objective must therefore be translated into terms of each and every department. For example, the sales department's objective may be to sell a given volume at a price, and with a certain expense; that of the manufacturing department may be to produce the quantity and quality desired, at a given time and cost. These departmental objectives may in turn be broken down to divisions, locations, and individuals. The final test is to have every single person with his own particular objective, all being co-ordinated to produce successive cumulative results leading to the general objective for the company as a whole.

Devising methods or procedures to be followed in achieving purposes provides the "how," "when," and "where" content of direction. Here, again, the broad and general decisions are made by managers at the top of the managerial hierarchy, and these decisions are made ever more specific by successive subordinates down through that hierarchy.

Directive decisions, once made, serve as a basis for the guidance of action. The vast majority of directive decisions are made to guide subordinates in actions which are repeated frequently. Relatively few such decisions are made to guide actions which are performed but once. In the case of any action frequently repeated, a tremendous burden would be placed on managers if a duplicate decision had to be made each time the action were to be repeated. To avoid this unnecessary duplication in decision making, managers have developed numerous devices or tools to be used in providing guidance for repetitive action.[40] In practice these devices are variously referred to as "budgets," "policies," "procedures," "practices," "methods," "rules," "regulations," "routines," "schedules," "instructions," "specifications," "designs," etc.[41] The importance of these devices to managers cannot be overly stressed. Because they obviate the necessity for redeciding questions, they release for other purposes much valuable time which otherwise would have to be devoted to such redecision. These devices are also used by managers as criteria

---

[40] Some of these devices are also used in providing guidance for nonrepetitive action.

[41] Some of these terms are by no means mutually exclusive from the point of view of definition. Furthermore, in practice they are often used to refer to different things. There is a crying need for standardized terminology here. The term "policy" provides an excellent example of this need. It has been used in so many ways that it is necessary for each user to define the term in order for it to have any precise meaning in the context in which it is used by him. See Chester I. Barnard, "Comments on the Job of an Executive," *Harvard Business Review*, vol. 18, no. 3, p. 296, Spring, 1940.

of action, since each of them implies a standard of performance to be attained. Serving as a guide to action and a criterion of action are simply two aspects of the same thing.

## Control

The second function of managers involving the employment of the mechanism for the attainment of purpose (the organization) is the function of control. Control is the use of formal authority to assure, to the extent possible, the attainment of the purposes of action by the methods or procedures which have been devised. The execution of this function involves the selection and training of individuals, the provision of incentives, and the exercise of supervision.[42]

One aspect of the function of organization previously discussed is the determination by managers of the degree and type of specialization to be effectuated within an enterprise. In part, this determination results in specifications of the types of services which will be required of individuals. Managers must next match these specifications with individuals —managers and nonmanagers—able to contribute the desired types of services. Such individuals may be found either within or without the enterprise. If they are found, they may be selected to fill positions calling for the types of services they are able to contribute. If such individuals are not found, then other individuals, either from within or without the enterprise, with the capacity for contributing the desired services must be selected and then trained until their capacity becomes ability.

The task of matching individuals with specifications is not an easy one. An individual's ability to contribute the desired types of services is often closely related to such intangible personal factors as his character, personality, temperament, and the like; and when individuals work together in cooperative groups, these factors are important determinants of interpersonal compatibility. Since no completely adequate measures of these factors have as yet been devised, the selection of individuals requires the exercise of judgment on the part of the manager making the selection.

Now, each manager is responsible to his superior for the accomplishment of assigned tasks; and since the ability of a manager to meet such responsibility depends in part on the quality of his subordinates, and since the determination of that quality is based to greater or less extent on the exercise of judgment, he must be able to select his own

---

[42] These components of the function of control (selection and training, incentives, and supervision) may appear at first glance to be unrelated activities. They do, to some extent, involve different managerial techniques. However, each is essential to the attainment of purpose by the methods or procedures which have been devised and is therefore logically classified under the function of control as defined.

subordinates. In no other way can he reasonably be held for their performance. The selection of subordinates is particularly crucial from the point of view of control when those subordinates are themselves managers. This is true because the intangible personal factors play such an important role in their work.

By selecting subordinates and training them when necessary, managers try to provide themselves with individuals able to contribute the types of services necessary for the attainment of purpose. Any single manager can reasonably be held responsible for such attainment only if he has been the one whose judgment has determined the ability of his subordinates.

It is not enough that individuals be found who are able (or who can be trained to be able) to contribute desired services to the enterprise. They must also be willing to do so. Ability must be supplemented by strong motivation. Unlike the flow of services from a machine, that from an individual is subject to considerable variation in intensity through time depending upon the motivation of the individual; thus it becomes necessary not only to make individuals willing to contribute desired services but to regulate as far as possible the intensity of the flow of the services. Incentives must be provided for these purposes.

An incentive as here viewed is any device which is offered to induce an individual—manager or nonmanager—to contribute services at a desired intensity to an enterprise. The inducements which may be offered to motivate an individual are numerous. They include various material things; opportunities for distinction, prestige, personal power, and the like; desirable physical conditions of work; pride of workmanship, sense of adequacy; feelings of altruism, loyalty, etc.; social compatibility; customary working conditions and conformity to habitual practices and attitudes; opportunity for the feeling of participation in the course of events; solidarity or satisfaction of the gregarious instinct; and coercion.[43] The proper use of incentives by a manager is a method by which he may secure and regulate the service contributions of subordinates that are so essential to the attainment of the purpose for which he is responsible.

Individuals who are able and adequately motivated to contribute services may still, for many reasons, execute commands imperfectly. It will be recalled that directive decisions are often expressed in terms of criteria of action or standards of performance. The observation of performance, the comparison of it with the predetermined criteria or standards, and the taking of remedial steps where called for are essential if

---

[43] This listing has been adapted from Barnard, *The Functions of the Executive*, chap. 11. This chapter, titled "The Economy of Incentives," contains an excellent discussion of incentives. See also *ibid.*, pp. 83–86 and 227–231.

the purposes of action are to be attained by the methods or procedures which have been devised. These entail the exercise of supervision.[44] Supervision involves overseeing, inspection, the use of accounting and statistical devices, the use of reports, etc., for the purpose of determining the facts of performance; and it involves appraisal or evaluation for the purpose of comparing performance with standards. It is important to recognize that supervision is exercised not only by the managers of groups but by all managers who have subordinates, including the manager of the supreme complex and the board of directors.

## A Comment on the Managerial Technique of Command

Command is a managerial technique used in connection with the execution of all the functions of managers. A command is an order from a superior to a subordinate to do something. Through command organizational, directive, and control decisions can be translated into action. Command, therefore, is (along with decision making) probably one of the most important and pervasive of the managerial techniques.

## Additional "Functions" Considered

In the classification of functions based on the formulations of other writers presented at the end of the preceding section, "trusteeship" and "representation" constituted the fifth group of functions. In our opinion, the so-called "function of representation" is not one of those functions performed exclusively by managers, nor can it serve as a basis for differentiating managers from nonmanagers.

It is often pointed out that managers must represent the enterprise, or some portion thereof, in dealings with such external units as stockholders, consumers, suppliers of goods used by the enterprise, organized labor, competitors (either individually or in trade associations), government units, and the general public. Managers speak and act for the units they manage. They often enter into contracts with an external unit, acting as an agent of the enterprise of which they are a member. All this is true, but it is also true, at times, of nonmanagers as well. The act of representation on the part of a nonmanager is never sufficient in practice to give him the status of a manager.

In this connection, it is important to note that all the services contributed by certain individuals to an enterprise are not necessarily man-

---

[44] Many writers use the word "control" to stand for what is here designated as "supervision." Others follow the practice used above. Still others use the words "appraisal" or "evaluation." Here, as before, no available word is completely satisfactory to connote all that one would desire. The weakness of "supervision" is that it often implies work carried on by those near the bottom of the managerial hierarchy. Regardless of the word used, the ideas behind the words are usually similar.

agerial in character. Managers often reserve to themselves some non-managerial work to perform which they consider too important to delegate to someone else.[45] Much representation work performed by managers is of this character.

It was also noted at the end of the preceding section that many writers consider coordination to be a function of managers. Again we disagree with such a point of view. Coordination and its relationship to management has earlier been discussed, and more will be said of this concept in the section to follow.

## MANAGERS AND NONMANAGERS DIFFERENTIATED

At the outset of this chapter, it was indicated that primary concern would be with differentiating managerial services from nonmanagerial services and that this could best be accomplished by isolating those functions performed exclusively by managers. Such isolation has been attempted. Now the separate threads of this chapter can be drawn together and combined into meaningful conclusions.

*It is our thesis that managers are those who use formal authority to organize, direct, or control responsible subordinates (and therefore, indirectly, the groups or complexes which they may head) in order that all service contributions be coordinated in the attainment of an enterprise purpose.*

Managers always stand in a relationship of formal authority over subordinates who, in turn, are responsible to their superior. Managers use formal authority in order to execute the functions of managers— organization, direction, and control. The objective of the execution of the functions is the coordination of service contributions in the attainment of an enterprise purpose. *An individual is not a manager, does not manage, unless he has and uses formal authority to organize, direct, or control responsible subordinates. Unless he conforms to this specification, he is a nonmanager.*

It has previously been observed that, when specialized services are being contributed toward the attainment of an enterprise purpose, coordination is essential. This coordination is supplied by managers through their execution of the functions of managers. As has been indicated, many writers consider coordination to be a function of managers. Coordination is not properly a function; it is something to be achieved. And it is achieved by adequate organization, direction, and control. *The services of managers (involving organization, direction, and control) are necessary to coordinate the specialized service contributions of the*

---

[45] See Barnard, *The Functions of the Executive*, pp. 6 and 215 f., and Sorrell, *op. cit.*, p. 80.

*units which they head in the attainment of an enterprise purpose. The services of managers are needed for no other reason.*

From what has been said it can be seen that managers can be differentiated from nonmanagers. Managers always have subordinates; nonmanagers never do. Nonmanagers may organize, direct, or control (in a sense) themselves or the material objects with which they work, but they never organize, direct, or control responsible subordinates. Furthermore, it is important to see that managers as well as nonmanagers may be managed. All managers, except the one (or ones) who heads the supreme complex, are managed by their superiors. They, in turn, manage their subordinates. The crucial distinction to be made is between managers and nonmanagers—not between managers and the managed.

One final point needs emphasis. The services of all individuals are essential if the purpose of the enterprise is to be attained. The distinction between managers and nonmanagers is based on differences in the types of specialized services contributed by the two groups and on no other criterion.

# CHAPTER 16

# A Look at Formal Organization:
# Managerial Decision Making*

## THE NATURE OF DECISION MAKING[1]

Human behavior results from either unconscious or conscious processes. When these processes are conscious, decision making is involved.[2] Decisions, when made, affect the behavior of an individual.[3] An individual may make decisions which affect his own behavior, or he may make them to affect the behavior of another or others. In the latter case social processes are involved.

In the preceding chapter it was concluded that managers are those who use formal authority to organize, direct, or control responsible subordinates in order that all service contributions be coordinated in the attainment of an enterprise purpose. One of the most important techniques of managers is that of decision making. This technique pervades the performance of all the functions of managers.[4] In order

* This chapter is a slightly modified version of "Managerial Decision-making," by Robert Tannenbaum, *The Journal of Business,* vol. 23, no. 1, pp. 22–39, January, 1950.

[1] The writing of this section was greatly stimulated by Herbert A. Simon, *Administrative Behavior* (New York: The Macmillan Company, 1947). Many of the ideas presented herein were developed by us before Simon's book came to our attention; but Simon's clear analysis sharpened our thinking with respect to many points.

[2] See Chester I. Barnard, *The Functions of the Executive* (Cambridge, Mass.: Harvard University Press, 1938), p. 185. Cf. also Simon, *op. cit.,* pp. 3 f.

[3] The various ways in which decisions can affect the behavior of an individual will be analyzed below.

[4] Robert Aaron Gordon, in *Business Leadership in the Large Corporation* (Washington, D.C.: The Brookings Institution, 1945), pp. 53–55, has developed the following incomplete, but informative, classification of the more important types of business decisions:

to organize, direct, or control responsible subordinates, managers must make decisions which affect the behavior of those subordinates. The decisions of managers are made to affect not their own behavior but rather that of others. On the other hand, nonmanagers, in performing their work, must also make decisions, but these decisions affect only their own behavior. The decisions of managers have a social import; those of nonmanagers, an individual import. Furthermore, decisions are made by other individuals and groups which affect the behavior of managers. These decisions also have a social import.

In the discussion which follows, primary attention is given to decision making in its social context, since this is the context which is relevant so far as an understanding of the work of managers is concerned. First, the nature of decision making will be analyzed. Then the interindividual and intergroup relationships which make it possible for the decisions of

---

    I. Promotion and initial organization
      A. Determination of main objectives
      B. Setting up initial organization, involving:
         1. Decisions as to size, legal organization, financial structure, internal organization, specific products to be produced and methods of producing and distributing them, and so on
         2. Choice of key personnel
      C. Negotiation for the hire of the factors of production, particularly capital
   II. Existence as a going concern
      A. Maintenance of organization through personal leadership and continuous exercise of authority
      B. Determination of the more important decisions relating to:
         1. Volume of output and control of production
         2. Prices
         3. Marketing (sales organization and methods, advertising, purchasing, and so on)
         4. Wages and other labor problems
         5. Financial problems, such as changes in capital structure, maintenance of working capital, securing new funds, and so on
         6. Changes in the size of the firm (expansion or contraction)
         7. Changes in the location of the firm or of important branches
         8. Changes in internal organization and procedures
         9. Changes in products and in (technical) methods of production
       10. Relations of the firm with outside groups, either with specific groups, such as consumers, bankers, or government, or with the public in general (that is, "public relations")
       11. Distribution of profits
      C. Choice of the men who will make the above decisions and also of those primarily responsible for directing the execution of them
 III. Reorganization or liquidation
      A. Reorganization
         1. Decision to reorganize
         2. Determination, for the transition from the old to the reorganized firm, of the matters listed under I
      B. Liquidation
         1. Decision to liquidate
         2. Deciding the terms for the liquidation, primarily with respect to the distribution of assets

one to affect the behavior of another will be explored. Finally, the conclusions will be related to the work of managers, indicating how managers affect the behavior of their subordinates and how others affect the behavior of managers.

## THE DECISION-MAKING PROCESS

Etymologically, "to decide" means "to cut off." In its present usage it suggests the coming to a conclusion. It "presupposes previous consideration of a matter causing doubt, wavering debate, or controversy and implies the arriving at a more or less logical conclusion that brings doubt, debate, etc., to an end."[5]

Decision making involves a conscious choice or selection of one behavior alternative from among a group of two or more behavior alternatives.[6] In making a decision, an individual must become aware of relevant behavior alternatives, define them, and finally evaluate them as a basis for choice. To understand clearly what is involved in the making of a decision, it will be helpful carefully to examine each of these steps in the decision-making process.

### 1. *Awareness of Behavior Alternatives*

Before making a decision, an individual should become aware of *all* those behavior alternatives which are relevant to the decision to be made. But this is seldom, if ever, possible. To a considerable extent he must depend upon his own limited experience and information. And memory of these is often sketchy and incomplete. He can discover relevant behavior alternatives through investigation, by tapping the experience and knowledge of others. But this process is often excessively time-consuming and does not guarantee complete coverage of all alternatives.

[5] By permission. From *Webster's Dictionary of Synonyms*, copyright 1951 by G. & C. Merriam Co., Publishers of the Merriam-Webster Dictionaries.

[6] Various attempts have been made to define "decision." Examples of these are the following: "The selective determination of an end for action by choice between alternatives" ("Decision," James M. Baldwin [ed.], *Dictionary of Philosophy and Psychology*, vol. 1, 1940); "A preliminary to conscious activity is a decision between alternatives—to do this or to do that, to do or not to do. In the process of decision-making the individual assesses a situation in the light of these alternatives. A choice between values congenial to the larger value-system of the individual is somehow reached" [R. M. MacIver, *Social Causation* (Boston: Ginn & Company, 1942), p. 296]; "At any moment there are a multitude of alternative (physically) possible actions, any one of which a given individual may undertake; by some process these numerous alternatives are narrowed down to that one which is in fact acted out. The words 'choice' and 'decision' will be used interchangeably . . . to refer to this process. Since these terms as ordinarily used carry connotations of self-conscious, deliberate, rational selection, it should be emphasized that as used here they include any process of selection, regardless of whether the above elements are present to any degree" (Simon, *op. cit.*, p. 4).

For these reasons, it is exceedingly doubtful whether most decisions are based upon an awareness of all relevant behavior alternatives.

### 2. *Definition of Behavior Alternatives*

Once the individual has become aware of certain behavior alternatives, he is next faced with the problem of defining each of them. Ideally, this definition involves a determination of *all* the consequences related to each behavior alternative under consideration; but this ideal can never be achieved for the following reasons: *a.* The most significant characteristic of the behavior alternatives is that their consequences lie in the future and therefore must be anticipated. But whenever the future is anticipated, uncertainty is present. This uncertainty is present for two reasons. In the first place, an individual never has the knowledge to make it possible for him accurately to determine the nature of the consequences which will follow upon the choice of a given behavior alternative or their probability of occurring, assuming that all other related elements remain constant. And because he does not have knowledge of the future, he must use imagination in attaching values to the consequences, which values may not obtain when the consequences are actually experienced. In the second place, all other related elements will not remain constant. *b.* It is impossible for an individual to be aware of all the consequences attendant upon any given behavior alternative. *c.* The time involved in discovering consequences and determining their nature is often such that a decision must be made before all the foreseeable relevant possibilities can be explored.

### 3. *Evaluation of Behavior Alternatives*

After an individual has become aware of certain behavior alternatives and has considered many of the consequences attendant upon each of these alternatives, he must next exercise a choice between them, i.e., make a decision. What can be said of the mental processes which culminate in decision?

The decisions which an individual makes are basically of two types. Some (a very small proportion) of his decisions relate to his system of values—they determine his ultimate ends. All other decisions are directly or indirectly related to means for the attainment of these ultimate ends. The adjective "ultimate" is used advisedly. An individual's behavior is guided by innumerable intermediate ends, for each one of which there are related means. The end of one means-end nexus becomes a means to a higher-order end. Decisions relating to ultimate ends cannot be judged as to their efficacy. They have primarily an ethical content. But such is not the case with all other decisions. These are made in terms of related intermediate ends. In choosing between alternatives, a rational individual will attempt to make a selection, within the limits of his knowledge, which will maximize results (the degree of attainment of the relevant end) at a given cost or which will attain given results at the lowest cost.[7] Thus, he has a criterion to guide his choice— the criterion of rationality.

There are definite limits, however, to rational behavior viewed objectively (i.e., from an omniscient point of view). These limits stem from the individual's lack of knowledge with respect to the existence of behavior alternatives and the consequences that will follow from them, from the subjective processes which are necessarily involved in defining alternatives when uncertainty is present, from time limitations, and from the psychological difficulties involved in holding alternatives and their consequences in focus preparatory to making a decision. Because of these factors, it is most difficult to describe the mental processes which culminate in decision.

The necessity for making decisions arises out of the fact that knowledge of relevant existing facts is inadequate and that the future is uncertain—individuals can never have complete knowledge of all factors underlying their choices. If such knowledge were available, decisions would not have to be made. If an individual were aware of *all* the consequences related to each of these behavior alternatives, judgment would not have to be exercised. One alternative would clearly be superior to all others. Individual behavior could be completely rational. In a real sense, that behavior would be determined by the consequences related to the superior alternative rather than by a choice between alternatives. The relationship of uncertainty to decision making has been stated by Frank H. Knight as follows:[8]

> With uncertainty absent, man's energies are devoted altogether to doing things; it is doubtful whether intelligence itself would exist in such a situation; in a world so built that perfect knowledge was theoretically possible, it seems likely that all organic readjustments would become mechanical, all organisms automata. With uncertainty present, doing things, the actual execution of activity, becomes in a real sense a secondary part of life; the primary problem or function is deciding what to do and how to do it. . . .

One further point demands attention in connection with this discussion of the nature of decision making. What initiates the decision-making process? At any given moment of time, there are often many

---

[7] The term "cost" is here used in its highly precise form to refer to whatever must be given or sacrificed to attain an end (see "Price," *Webster's Dictionary of Synonyms*); cf. Simon, *op. cit.*, chaps. 4 and 9.

[8] *Risk, Uncertainty, and Profit,* Series of Reprints of Scarce Tracts in Economics and Political Science, no. 16 (London: London School of Economics and Political Science, 1933), p. 268.

problems which might compete for an individual's attention. What determines the particular problem with which he will deal? Simon points out that decision making is initiated by stimuli, internal or external to the individual, which channel his attention in definite directions. Very often these stimuli, impinging upon the individual, are accidental and arbitrary in character. To the extent that they are, the individual's behavior cannot be rational. Also, since the attention-directing stimuli can be external to the individual, they can be provided by others who desire to affect the individual's behavior.[9]

The preceding discussion of the nature of decision making has, for the most part, dealt with decision making in the abstract. It has indicated the limits to rational behavior on the part of the relatively isolated individual—limits which are greatly reduced when the individual is a member of a group, as will be pointed out later. Decision making actually takes place in an environment which significantly affects the decision-making process. In the two sections which follow, the various aspects of this environment will be explored.

## THE CONCEPTS OF AUTHORITY AND INFLUENCE

At the beginning of the preceding section it was stated that an individual may make decisions which affect his own behavior, or he may make them to affect the behavior of another or others. The latter case, as was pointed out, is the relevant one so far as the work of managers is concerned. This relevancy is present for two reasons. First, in order to organize, direct, and control responsible subordinates, managers must make decisions which affect the behavior of those subordinates. Second, managers themselves are in a subordinate position both with respect to their own superiors and formal subordinates within an enterprise and, often, with respect to others. Thus managers make decisions affecting the behavior of subordinates at the same time that decisions are being made which affect their own behavior. The concern here is with social processes. These processes are those of authority and influence. In this section the discussion will be devoted to an analysis of these two processes.

### The Nature of Authority

A superior is able directly to affect the behavior of a subordinate if he possesses authority with respect to that subordinate.[10] In the preced-

[9] See the excellent discussion of these and related points in Simon, *op. cit.*, pp. 84–96.
[10] For purposes of this discussion a "superior" will be defined as one who has effective authority over another, and a "subordinate" will be defined as one who is subject to the effective authority of another.

ing chapter it was stated that authority is commonly viewed as originating at the top of an organizational hierarchy and flowing downward therein through the process of delegation. When viewed in this way, it was called "formal authority." In reality, effective authority does not originate in this manner.

The real source of the authority possessed by an individual lies in the acceptance of its exercise by those who are subject to it. It is the subordinates of an individual who determine the authority which he may wield. Formal authority is, in effect, nominal authority. It becomes real only when it is accepted. An individual may possess formal authority, but such possession is meaningless unless that authority can be effectively used. And it can be so used only if it is accepted by that individual's subordinates.[11] Thus, to be effective, formal authority must coincide with authority determined by its acceptance. The latter defines the useful limits of the former.

The concept "authority," then, describes an interpersonal relationship in which one individual, the subordinate, accepts a decision made by another individual, the superior, permitting that decision directly to affect his behavior.[12] An individual always has an opportunity, with respect to a decision made by another directly to affect his behavior, to accept or reject that decision. If he accepts it, he thereby grants authority to its formulator and, for this matter, places himself in the position of a subordinate. As a subordinate, the individual permits his behavior directly to be affected by the decisions of his superior. If the

---

[11] The term "accept" is used here, in its various forms, to include acquiescence as well as active assent or approval. The import of this will become clear in the discussion which follows.

[12] Many writers have similarly defined the concept of authority. Some examples of these definitions follow: "Authority can thus be defined as a behavioristic concept describing a relationship between subject and object in which the subject takes an acquiescent attitude to behavior prescribed by the object on the basis of power either possessed by or delegated to the object" [Abram Kardiner, *The Individual and His Society* (New York: Columbia University Press, 1939), p. 40]; " . . . the power which operates in and through an authority relation is always in some measure the joint creation of the bearer and subjects of authority. . . . The power of the bearer of authority grows out of the acceptance of his direction and guidance as bearer of authority by the subjects of his authority, not the other way round" [Kenneth D. Benne, *A Conception of Authority* (New York: Bureau of Publications, Teachers College, Columbia University, 1943), pp. 149 f.]; "Authority is the character of a communication (order) in a formal organization by virtue of which it is accepted by a contributor to or 'member' of the organization as governing the action he contributes; that is, as governing or determining what he does or is not to do so far as the organization is concerned" (Barnard, *op. cit.*, p. 163); " 'Authority' may be defined as the power to make decisions which guide the actions of another. It is a relationship between two individuals, one 'superior,' the other 'subordinate.' The superior frames and transmits decisions with the expectation that they will be accepted by the subordinate. The subordinate expects such decisions, and his conduct is determined by them" (Simon, *op. cit.*, p. 125).

individual rejects the decision, he does not grant authority to its formulator. Thus the sphere of authority possessed by a superior is defined for him by the sphere of acceptance of his subordinates.

If this line of analysis is to be followed it must be recognized that an individual may possess authority in a given situation without having formal authority. In other words, the channels through which effective authority is exercised do not have to follow the lines of formal organization within a given complex. These channels may extend outside the given complex.

### Determinants of the Acceptance of Authority

Since the sphere of authority possessed by a superior is defined for him by the sphere of acceptance of his subordinates, it is important to inquire into the factors which determine this latter sphere. Why do subordinates accept, rather than reject, the authority of their superiors? In answering this question, it must be remembered that the choice between acceptance or rejection involves a decision between two alternatives. This choice is made only after the individual has appraised, to the extent possible, the consequences attendant upon each of these alternatives.

An individual will accept an exercise of authority if the advantages accruing to him from accepting plus the disadvantages accruing to him from not accepting exceed the advantages accruing to him from not accepting plus the disadvantages accruing to him from accepting; conversely, he will not accept an exercise of authority if the latter factors exceed the former. Thus a decision to accept or reject a given exercise of authority results from a relative evaluation of the consequences—both positive and negative—attendant upon the choice of each of the competing behavior alternatives. To understand better the factors underlying a decision to accept or reject, it will be helpful to consider in more detail the nature of the positive and negative consequences—the advantages and disadvantages—related to each behavior alternative.

The possible advantages accruing to an individual from accepting a given exercise of authority are many. While the following listing of types of advantages is by no means complete, it will serve the end of indicating the variety of such advantages. (1) By accepting an exercise of authority, an individual is able thereby to contribute to the attainment of an enterprise purpose which he recognizes as being good.[13] In

[13] See James D. Mooney and Alan C. Reiley, *The Principles of Organization* (New York: Harper & Brothers, 1939), pp. 177 f.; Henry C. Metcalf and L. Urwick (eds.), *Dynamic Administration: The Collected Papers of Mary Parker Follett* (New York: Harper & Brothers, 1940), p. 59; and L. Urwick, *The Elements of Administration* (New York: Harper & Brothers, 1943), pp. 94 f.

the preceding chapter it was pointed out that group activity involves the specialized service contributions of individuals which must be co-ordinated in the attainment of an enterprise purpose. Such coordination can be achieved only through the exercise of authority on the part of the individual who heads the group.[14] An awareness of this necessity leads individuals who recognize the enterprise purpose as being good to accept authority. (2) By accepting an exercise of authority, an individual may thereby attain the approbation of his fellow workers. For most individuals, social acceptance is a strong motivating factor. (3) By accepting an exercise of authority, an individual may thereby obtain rewards from his superior. These rewards might be increased pay, promotion, prestige, opportunity for increased personal power, and the like. (4) By accepting an exercise of authority, an individual may thereby be acting in accordance with his own moral standards. Some individuals believe they ought (that it is right) for them to obey duly constituted authorities. (5) By accepting an exercise of authority, an individual may thereby avoid the necessity of accepting responsibility. Chester I. Barnard has commented upon this point as follows:[15]

. . . if an instruction is disregarded, an executive's risk of being wrong must be accepted, a risk that the individual cannot and usually will not take unless in fact his position is at least as good as that of another with respect to correct appraisal of the relevant situation. Most persons are disposed to grant authority because they dislike the personal responsibility which they otherwise accept, especially when they are not in a good position to accept it. . . .

(6) Finally, by accepting an exercise of authority, an individual may thereby be responding to the qualities which he perceives in his superior. In part, this point overlaps some of the preceding ones, but it also includes a recognition of the fact that some individuals obey others out of respect for their age, superior ability or experience, character, reputation, personality, and the like.

An individual, after considering the advantages to him, may often decide to accept an exercise of authority. Such a choice would be a free one—one not involving compulsion. But he might also decide to accept an exercise of authority even though the advantages attendant thereto, taken alone, would not be sufficient to induce him to accept. In this case his decision would be compelled by another or others; he

[14] " . . . all men engaged in common enterprises, the most mature, rationally autonomous, self-directing persons among others, need commonly accepted rules, norms, or principles of order to guide and direct the processes of their cooperation" (Benne, *op. cit.*, p. 158).

[15] *Op. cit.*, p. 170.

would simply acquiesce to authority because of the disadvantages accruing to him from not accepting. When an individual is forced by another to do something against his will—something he otherwise would not have done—coercion is involved. Horace M. Kallen has defined and elaborated upon the concept of coercion in these terms:[16]

> Coercion as a trait of human behavior may be said to obtain wherever action or thought by one individual or group is compelled or restrained by another. To coerce is to exercise some form of physical or moral compulsion. . . .
> . . . When it [coercion] is direct we call it physical; when indirect, moral. Both compel or restrain conduct by *force majeure*. . . .
> Most social coercion is indirect; it only threatens force. . . . But all coercions involve fear of penalties. Without belief that the coercer can and will impose penalties no indirect coercion can be effective. . . .

There are numerous coercive devices the actual use or fear of which is often effective in obtaining an acquiescence to authority. Some examples of these are social disapprobation, expulsion from a group (ostracism), formal disciplinary action, exertion of economic pressure (monopolistic and monopsonistic power), torture, imprisonment, and taking a life.

In order to understand the full implications of coercion, it will be useful briefly to digress in order to contrast this concept with the concept of *sanctions*. In every social group there are certain modes of behavior which are generally approved and others which are generally disapproved. The reactions of approval and of disapproval represent general formal or informal social consensus. Now in every group there are some individuals who have urges toward nonconformity. Sanctions are devices used to induce these individuals to conform to the group will. Sanctions may be positive or negative in character. Positive sanctions are the social reward of conformity, and negative sanctions are the social consequences of nonconformity.[17] All negative sanctions are coercive in their effect—they are used to impel an individual to conform against his will to group norms of behavior. Heads of groups who impose negative sanctions on recalcitrant individuals have the support of the vast majority of the group in so doing. But heads of groups might also induce conformance to behavior patterns which are not generally approved by the group. Here coercion is involved but not nega-

---

[16] "Coercion," in E. R. A. Seligman (ed.), *Encyclopaedia of the Social Sciences*, vol. 3, 1930.
[17] The discussion of sanctions to this point is based upon R. M. MacIver, *Society: Its Structure and Changes* (Toronto: The Macmillan Company of Canada, Ltd., 1931), pp. 248–257; and A. R. Radcliffe-Brown, "Sanctions, Social," in *Encyclopaedia of the Social Sciences*, vol. 13, 1930.

tive sanctions. Furthermore, one individual with respect to another individual or a group or one group with respect to another group or an individual outside the group might induce conformance to specified behavior patterns through the use of coercion. But here again negative sanctions are not involved. Thus coercion includes more than negative sanctions. The latter term is applicable only when general group consensus is involved. When the head of a group uses coercion not based upon general group consensus, he is acting in an autocratic or arbitrary manner.

In raising the question whether an individual will accept an exercise of authority, only the advantages accruing to him from accepting plus the disadvantages to him from not accepting have thus far been considered. But he will accept only if these factors exceed the advantages accruing to him from not accepting plus the disadvantages accruing to him from accepting, as has previously been pointed out. These latter factors, however, are the same in nature as the former ones. An illustration should suffice to make this clear. An employee may be a member of a group most of whose members are restricting output in opposition to a wage-incentive plan. The implicit or explicit order of the employee's boss is that each employee should produce the maximum output reasonably possible. Should the employee accept this exercise of authority, or should he restrict his output (i.e., accept the authority of the work group)? If he accepts the authority of his boss, he can earn more, he may get a desired promotion, etc. If he does not accept, he may be demoted or fired. On the other hand, if he does not accept, he may receive the approbation of his fellow workers, additional status in the group, etc. If he accepts, he may receive the disapprobation of his fellow workers or be ostracized from the group. His decision to accept or not accept the boss's exercise of authority will be based upon an evaluation of these and similar relevant consequences.

In order to make complete this discussion of the determinants of the acceptance of authority, one further point calls for attention. Authority is often accepted where conscious processes are not involved. Such acceptance does not entail a conscious choice between acceptance and rejection. Rather, it is reflective of unconscious, habitual processes. Authoritative pronouncements which are unconsciously accepted lie within what Barnard has called the "zone of indifference."[18]

---

[18] *Op. cit.*, pp. 167–169. Cf. Simon, *op. cit.*, pp. 12 and 133 f. Simon apparently misinterprets Barnard's concept of a zone of indifference when he holds it to be the equivalent of what he calls the "zone of acceptance." In fact, this latter zone is more inclusive and is equivalent to what has been referred to above as the "sphere of acceptance."

*Authority versus Influence*

The use of authority is one means of affecting the behavior of another. The subordinate who accepts an exercise of authority does not critically evaluate the behavior alternatives underlying the decision of his superior. He accepts the decision and permits it directly to affect his behavior. But there is another means by which one individual can affect the behavior of another. In this case the latter individual is free to make those decisions which directly affect his own behavior. But, since he never has complete knowledge with respect to all relevant behavior alternatives and to all the consequences related thereto and since the ends toward which he directs his behavior are subject to change, it is possible for another individual or for others to provide him with information which can affect his decisions. This additional information simply adds to or changes the relevant factors (means and ends) which he otherwise would take into account in arriving at his decision. It might or might not result in a decision different from the one that would otherwise be made. In any event, the individual, taking the additional information into account, freely arrives at his own decision. Such provision of relevant information by one person to another (who then takes that information into account in arriving at a decision) will be called "influence."[19] The individual who exercises influence may offer advice, make suggestions, enter into discussions, persuade, use propaganda, and the like; but he does not exercise authority.[20] In so doing, he indirectly affects the behavior of another.

Managers make decisions to affect, both directly (through authority) and indirectly (through influence), the behavior of their subordinates. Likewise, others make decisions which affect the behavior of managers.[21] In the two sections to follow the next one, the implications of

[19] No available term is completely satisfactory to connote the meaning here intended. The term used seems most closely to conform to that meaning. However, note that the specialized meaning attached to the term here differs from that given to it in other chapters in this book where "influence" and "the influence process" are referred to.

[20] Cf. Gordon, *op. cit.*, pp. 150 f., and Simon, *op. cit.*, pp. 126–128. It is recognized that the precise dividing line between authority and influence is sometimes difficult to draw.

[21] The social processes here described, involving both authority (including positive inducements and coercion) and influence, are those generally encompassed within the term "social control." See and compare Joseph S. Roucek (ed.), *Social Control* (Princeton, N.J.: D. Van Nostrand Company, Inc., 1947), p. 3; L. L. Bernard, *Social Control* (New York: The Macmillan Company, 1939), p. 11; Paul H. Landis, *Social Control* (Philadelphia: J. B. Lippincott Company, 1939), chap. 1; Frederick E. Lumley, *Means of Social Control* (New York: Appleton-Century-Crofts, Inc., 1925), p. 13; John M. Clark, *Social Control of Business* (2d ed.; New York: McGraw-Hill Book Company, Inc., 1939), pp. 5–7; Helen Everett, "Control, Social," in *Encyclopaedia of the Social Sciences*, vol. 4, 1930.

these decisions for the performance of the functions of managers will be considered in detail. First, some additional factors relevant to decision making will be explored.

## SPHERES OF DISCRETION

### Constraints

With respect to any given problem involving the necessity of coming to a decision, there are typically many desirable behavior alternatives from among which a choice might be made. But, for reasons to be discussed below, the individual who must make the decision is not always free to choose from among all these desirable behavior alternatives. Some of them may be excluded, by one means or another, from his range of choice. It is only from among those alternatives which remain —the available alternatives—that a choice may be made.

In the discussion which follows, it will be said that an individual exercises discretion with respect to available alternatives, since discretion is the power of free decision, of undirected choice. And the available alternatives pertinent to any given decision will be considered as falling within a sphere of discretion. For each problem calling for decision, there is such a sphere. A sphere of discretion has limits within which the exercise of discretion is confined. Those factors which set the limits to spheres of discretion—which restrict, restrain, or limit the exercise of discretion to available alternatives—will be referred to as *constraints*. The types of constraints which thus define spheres of discretion are numerous and call for more detailed attention.

1. *Authoritative Constraints.* A subordinate may have designated for him by his superior certain behavior alternatives which cannot be considered by him in the making of a given decision. Thus a salesman might be told by his superiors that all sales made of a given item must be made at a price falling within a specified range. Within that range the salesman may exercise discretion. Of all the constraints, the authoritative is the only one that is personal in nature—that is imposed by one or more individuals on another.

2. *Biological Constraints.* When a decision is being made which will directly affect the behavior of the individual making the decision or the behavior of another, the sphere of discretion of the decision maker can be constrained by certain biological characteristics of himself or of the other individual, as the case may be. These characteristics may be permanent in nature (a human being cannot fly), or they may be temporary and therefore subject to change (a person may not now know how to operate a lathe, but he may be able to learn to do so).

3. *Physical Constraints.* The constraints of the physical environment

are ever present. They include such factors as geography, climate, physical resources, man-made objects, and the chemical elements, as well as physical and chemical laws. These factors are typically important in defining spheres of discretion.

4. *Technological Constraints.* These constraints are determined by the state of the arts. For example, in determining how to make a given product, the decision maker is limited in his choice to those alternatives which are technologically possible.[22]

5. *Economic Constraints.* In a freely competitive economic system, prices of products and of productive services are impersonally determined through the operation of market forces. To the individual or business enterprise in the system, these prices are "givens." The same is true of consumer wants. These "givens" are constraints with respect to economic decisions relating to maximization. Furthermore, the economic resources available to an individual or an enterprise are often also important economic constraints in decision making.

These types of constraints, where relevant, define spheres of discretion. They determine those behavior alternatives which are not available for choice. It is from among those alternatives which remain—the available alternatives—that a choice is made. Decision making is judgment exercised within constraints.

*Ways in Which the Behavior of One Can Be Directly Affected by the Decisions of Another*

In the preceding section dealing with authority, it was stated that authority is used by a superior directly to affect the behavior of a subordinate. The ways in which a superior can so affect the behavior of a subordinate can now be considered.

1. The superior can impose constraints on a sphere of discretion of a subordinate as discussed above, thereby limiting the subordinate's discretion to the behavior alternatives which remain.

2. The superior can completely eliminate spheres of discretion from the province of a subordinate. In this case the subordinate is permitted no discretion with respect to the given problems, and no behavior is expected of him with respect to them.[23]

3. The superior can impose a decision on the subordinate to the effect that the subordinate act in a particular manner. Here, again, no discretion with respect to the problem is permitted to the subordinate, but specified behavior (including forbearance) is expected of him.

[22] Of course, he may attempt to extend the state of the arts, but such an extension involves a different kind of problem.

[23] This limitation can also be viewed as involving the imposition of constraints. Here the alternatives are the various problems with respect to which an individual may decide to deal. The constraints imposed limi* his range of choice in this respect.

Each of these devices which might be used by a superior stems from a decision made by him and results in some direct effect upon his subordinate's behavior.

## THE MANAGED AND DECISION MAKING

It has previously been pointed out that managers make decisions to affect, both directly (through authority) and indirectly (through influence), the behavior of their subordinates. In this section consideration will be given to the implications of these managerial decisions to the behavior of the subordinates—the managed.

It has been seen that the relatively isolated individual is faced with insurmountable difficulties in his attempt to achieve rational behavior. But when individuals become members of organized groups, it is at least possible for their behavior to achieve a high degree of rationality when viewed in terms of group purposes. The decisions of managers, operating upon the managed through authority and influence, make this possible in ways which will be examined below.

In the discussion which follows, it will be important to remember that the term "managed" includes most managers and all nonmanagers. A manager is such only with respect to his subordinates; he is managed with respect to his superior. Of all the managers in an enterprise, only the head of the supreme complex is a manager who is not at the same time being managed. The concern in this section is with the managed as such, including individuals who are both managers and nonmanagers.

### *The Behavior of the Managed as Affected by Managerial Decisions*

The decisions of managers (made to organize, direct, or control responsible subordinates) operate to increase the rationality of the behavior of subordinates—when viewed in terms of enterprise purposes—in the following ways.[24]

1. Decisions are made by superiors which define enterprise purpose. This purpose is the end for the attainment of which the specialized services of the members of the group are being contributed. It is important that the decisions made by each member of the group be made with reference to the group end and not a differing personal end. Through training it is possible to indoctrinate individuals in the enterprise purpose; through incentives, to induce individuals to accept it; and through supervision, to ensure that the enterprise purpose will guide individual decisions.

---

[24] Much of what Simon has to say in his book is directly related to rationality and the ways of attaining it in group activity (*op. cit., passim,* and particularly the summary, pp. 240–244).

2. Superiors establish the criterion of rationality to guide subordinates in making the choices which they are called upon to make. It will be remembered that this criterion requires that a choice be made between alternatives which will maximize results (the degree of attainment of the relevant end) at a given cost. For a business firm seeking to maximize profits, this cost is a money cost. As in the preceding case, training, incentives, and supervision are the relevant managerial devices to be used in establishing the criterion of rationality as the basis for individual choice.

3. In establishing the degree and type of specialization to be effectuated within an enterprise, superiors thereby define the general kind of activity to be expected of individuals filling particular positions. Such definition significantly reduces the number of spheres of discretion which are relevant to the particular activity to which an individual is assigned. This limitation is an aspect of the managerial function of organization.

4. Another relevant aspect of the function of organization is the determination of lines of formal authority. This determination establishes for the subordinate the individual (or individuals) to whom he is to look for decisions made to affect his behavior.

5. With respect to those spheres of discretion relating to the general kind of activity expected of a subordinate, superiors frequently impose additional constraints, thereby limiting the number of available behavior alternatives from among which the subordinate is expected to choose.

6. Superiors can provide subordinates with relevant information. This information may relate to behavior alternatives about which the subordinate is not aware; or it may relate to the consequences attendant upon specific behavior alternatives. This information may be supplied through training, through the use of reports and memoranda, through conversation, and the like.

7. Superiors may request that particular decisions be made at or by a specified time. Such requests are stimuli which direct the attention of subordinates to designated problems and therefore initiate the decision-making processes at particular moments of time.

8. With respect to given problem areas, superiors may expect specific behavior responses of their subordinates which permit no discretion to them. Here the subordinate is not expected to make a decision to guide his own behavior but simply to act in the manner specified by his superior. The superior may specify the action of the subordinate through an on-the-spot order; or he may use such devices as rules, regulations, routines, standing orders, policies, and standard methods and procedures to accomplish the same purpose. In this connection it should be

noted that the same purpose can also be accomplished by selecting people with desired attributes or by training them. Through selection or training, particular individual modes of response can reasonably be ensured so that the number of direct orders which must be given can be reduced. Thus, if a novice is hired to do clerical work, his superior must specifically tell him what to do, how to do it, etc. But if a trained person is hired or the novice is trained, then such specific orders are no longer necessary.

In summary, the subordinate (the individual managed) is expected to focus his attention on a greatly restricted number of problems calling for decision. With respect to these problems, authoritative constraints are often imposed on the pertinent spheres of discretion which further limit his range of choice. Information is provided which calls the subordinate's attention to behavior alternatives relevant to particular decisions and which adds to his knowledge of the consequences attendant upon those behavior alternatives under consideration. The ends toward which his decisions must be directed are specified for him, as is the criterion of rationality to guide the choices which he must make. Lines of formal authority are specified for him which designate the individual (or individuals) to whom he is to look for decisions to affect his behavior. His superior often determines for him the particular problems calling for his decision to which he should direct his attention at specified moments of time. The superior often expects specific behavior responses of the subordinate which permit no discretion to him. Through incentives and supervision the superior reasonably ensures that all the behavior responses of the subordinate conform to those desired. As a result of these factors which originate with superiors, it is possible for the behavior of the subordinate to achieve a high degree of rationality when viewed in terms of enterprise purposes.

## THE MANAGERS AND DECISION MAKING

The decisions of managers are made to affect the behavior of responsible subordinates in the ways considered in the preceding section. But these decisions are themselves not made in a vacuum. They are subject to all the restrictions which have previously been discussed and to influence. In this section, particular attention will be given to the sources from which stem the authority and influence which can directly and indirectly affect the managerial decision-making process.

### Authority and the Decisions of Managers

In making decisions, managers can be subject to the authority of many individuals and groups. The determination whether they will be subject to such authority, of course, always rests with the managers. They, like others, can either accept or reject any exercise of authority. If they accept the exercise of authority (because of positive inducements or coercion), they thereby assume a role of subordination with respect to the individuals or group possessing the authority. The superior can directly affect the behavior of the subordinate in the ways previously discussed—by imposing constraints on spheres of discretion, by completely eliminating spheres of discretion from the province of the subordinate, and by imposing a decision on the subordinate to the effect that the subordinate act in a particular manner.

There are many individuals and groups who do, at varying times, exercise authority with respect to managers. While no attempt will be made in the discussion which follows to consider all those who might authoritatively impinge upon managers, the principal ones will be given attention.

First, nearly all managers, as managed, are subject to the authority of their managerial superiors. This relationship was probed in the preceding section. At this point it is simply necessary to point out that this exercise of authority directly affects, among other things, the decisions made by the subordinate manager to affect the behavior of his own subordinates.

Second, managers are subject to the authority of individuals who, from the formal point of view, are their own subordinates. At first glance, this may be difficult to visualize, but it is a fact the understanding of which is crucial to the effective performance of the functions of management.

It has previously been stated that the sphere of authority possessed by a superior is defined for him by the sphere of acceptance of his subordinates. It is likewise true that the sphere of nonacceptance of authority of formal subordinates defines the sphere of nonauthority of the formal superior. This limiting effect imposed upon the managerial decision-making process by formal subordinates is indeed real. Barnard has stated the case in these positive terms:[25]

---

[25] *Op. cit.*, p. 167. Donald C. Stone has commented upon this same point as follows: "The executive is often seen as the man sitting at the top of the organization possessed of a dangerous amount of authority, hiring and firing at will, whose every suggestion or order is responded to promptly and completely. This view reflects one of the greater misconceptions about the nature of executive work. The government executive may have a large grant of legal authority, but he will find that in actual fact it must be used in an economical fashion. If he lacks discrimination in the use of his power, he will debase its value and perhaps find himself impotent at the moment of crucial importance" ("Notes on the Governmental Executive: His Role and His Methods," in *New Horizons in Public Administration* [University, Ala.: University of Alabama Press, 1945], pp. 55 f.). See also Marshall E. Dimock, *The Executive in Action* (New York: Harper & Brothers, 1945), pp. 236–240. Charles

There is no principle of executive conduct better established in good organizations than that orders will not be issued that cannot or will not be obeyed. Executives and most persons of experience who have thought about it know that to do so destroys authority, discipline, and morale.

One of the arts of leadership is that of widening the sphere of acceptance of formal subordinates and, therefore, the sphere of authority of the leader.

Third, managers are subject to the authority of individuals and groups who are not members of the formal organization of the enterprise. Among these are the following:

*Governmental Agencies: Local, State, and Federal.* Government agencies impinge upon the decision-making processes of management through the adoption of constitutions or charters, the passage of legislation, the interpretation of legislation by the courts, and the action of administrative bodies. They establish the rules of the game (the institutional framework within which enterprises operate), impose restrictions, demand specific action, settle disputes, and approve certain managerial decisions before these can become effective.

*Parties to Contracts with Management.* When management enters into a contract with another party (an act involving the acceptance of the authority of another), it thereby agrees to meet certain obligations or to accept certain restrictions upon its activities.[26]

*Monopolistic and Monopsonistic Economic Groups.* In those areas of economic activity where conditions of perfect competition do not exist, buyers of the enterprise's products and sellers to the enterprise of productive services are often able, through the use of monopsonistic and monopolistic power, respectively, directly to affect the behavior of managers. Among the monopsonists are consumers' organizations and large private buyers of the products of the enterprise. Among the monopolists are large suppliers of capital funds (banks, bondholders, etc.), raw materials, and labor services (unions).[27]

Because of the growing importance of unions in relation to managers,

---

E. Merriam has analyzed the authority relationship here under discussion primarily with reference to a government and the governed (see his *Political Power* [New York: McGraw-Hill Book Company, Inc., 1934], chap. 6).

[26] Roscoe Pound, the eminent legal scholar, implies this in the following statement: "A contract . . . is a legal transaction in which the declared will takes the form of a promise or set of promises; in which the intent to which the law gives effect is that one of the parties shall be bound to some performance—either by way of action or abstaining from action—which the other may exact, or that each of the parties shall be so bound toward the other" ("Contract," *Encyclopaedia of the Social Sciences,* vol. 4, 1930).

[27] These monopolists and monopsonists are often parties to contracts with management. However, managers also often become subject to their authority where contractual relationships are not involved.

it is desirable to give additional attention to these monopolistic groups. The kinds of restrictions and the demands for particular actions which they impose upon managers are numerous.[28] They often impose these restrictions and demands through the threat or use of coercive economic power. It has previously been stated that managers are subject to the authority of individuals who, from the formal point of view, are their own subordinates. In this case the limitations to the exercise of managerial authority are imposed by isolated individuals and informal groups. These same individuals, by joining together in unions, can impose the limitations much more effectively because of the coercive power available to strong, formal groups. Finally, in this connection, it should be pointed out that, although coercion is an important device of the union in obtaining managerial acceptance of its exercise of authority, positive inducements are also used. For example, a union may offer something of value to managers in return for an accepted limitation of managerial authority.

*Arbitrators.* When managers accept arbitration as a means for the settlement of a dispute (labor or otherwise) to which the enterprise is a party, they thereby assume a subordinate role with respect to the arbitrator.[29]

*Cartels, Trade Associations, and Other Business Associations.* Enterprises often are members of one or more such business associations. Decisions are frequently made in these associations which are accepted as being authoritative by the managers of the member enterprises.

*The General Social Order.* The decisions of managers are always subject to the general social order. Custom, tradition, convention, mores, and the like are the relevant authoritative principles; and sanctions (both positive and negative) are the factors which determine managerial acceptance or rejection of the authority.

Authority exercised by these individuals and groups, external to the enterprise, is always an extremely important factor in the direct determination of the behavior of the managers of the enterprise.[30]

## Influence and the Decisions of Managers

In making decisions, managers can also be indirectly affected by the influence of many individuals and groups. The information supplied by

---

[28] For examples, see Neil W. Chamberlain, *The Union Challenge to Management Control* (New York: Harper & Brothers, 1948), chap. 4 and appendixes A–D; and Robert M. C. Littler, "Managers Must Manage," *Harvard Business Review*, vol. 24, pp. 367–370, Spring, 1946.

[29] For a discussion of the degrees of authority available to an impartial umpire in labor disputes, see Sumner H. Slichter, *The Challenge of Industrial Relations* (Ithaca, N.Y.: Cornell University Press, 1947), pp. 60 f.

[30] For an excellent discussion of the problem of managerial adaptation to these individuals and groups, see Philip Selznick, "Foundations of the Theory of Organization," *American Sociological Review*, vol. 13, pp. 25–35, February, 1948.

these individuals and groups can add to or change the relevant factors (means or ends) which managers otherwise would take into account in arriving at decisions. It must be remembered that the individual or group which exercises influence may offer advice, make suggestions, enter into discussions, use propaganda, and the like; but they do not thereby exercise authority.

As in the case of authority, there are individuals who are members of the formal organization of the enterprise who exercise influence with respect to managers. First, nearly all managers, as managed, are subject to the influence of their managerial superiors. This relationship, also, was probed in the preceding section. What is important here is that this exercise of influence indirectly affects, among other things, the decisions made by the subordinate manager to affect the behavior of his own subordinates. Second, managers are subject to the influence of their subordinates. In this connection, it is useful to see that a manager can subdivide the work related to the decisions which he must make, holding subordinates responsible for the making of preliminary decisions (involving recommendations to him) which enter into his making of the final decision.[31] In this manner the manager can be provided with information with respect both to relevant behavior alternatives and to the consequences attendant upon specific behavior alternatives. The organizational device of the staff is a specialized unit whose function is to provide information to the manager to whom it is attached.[32] Through the channels of upward communication and such devices as suggestion systems, information also flows to managers.

Many individuals and groups who are not members of the formal organization of the enterprise also exercise influence with respect to managers. These include, among others, governmental agencies; suppliers of productive services; customers; cartels, trade associations, and other business associations; and consultants (including accountants, lawyers, engineers, and similar specialists). Few decisions are made by managers which are not indirectly affected by the influence of such individuals and groups.

[31] See Simon, *op. cit.*, pp. 221–228.
[32] Lewis C. Sorrell has commented upon this fact, as follows: "While much confusion obtains regarding the proper functioning of a staff in business concerns . . . , essentially it is coming to mean one or more persons charged with the responsibility of ascertaining the important trends internal and external to the business, determining their incidence upon the enterprise or some important division thereof, observing the methods employed by others for coping with similar situations, selecting the several alternatives of policy that appear to be most practical under all the circumstances, and presenting all this to the proper executives—but without authority to direct or order anything into execution" ["The Role of Management in the Organization of Resources for Production," in William N. Mitchell (ed.), *Management's Adjustment to the Changing National Economy* (Chicago: University of Chicago Press, 1942), p. 37].

## MANAGERS AND REGULATORS DIFFERENTIATED

In the preceding chapter it was concluded that managers are those who use formal authority to organize, direct, or control responsible subordinates in order that all service contributions be coordinated in the attainment of an enterprise purpose. The use of formal authority for these purposes is the essence of management.

The practice is currently prevalent on the part of many writers and speakers to refer to individuals and groups (external to the formal organization of the enterprise) exercising authority and influence with respect to the managers of the enterprise as participating or sharing in management.[33] These individuals and groups do not participate or share in management, and they are not managers (except, perhaps, of the enterprises to which they belong). They regulate managers (through authority and influence), but they do not manage.[34] In our view, if one attempted a definition of the manager broad enough to include these individuals and groups (the regulators), the result would be a concept of the manager which would be so lacking in content and sharpness as to be of little theoretical or practical value.

The point is simply this: managers head groups (either of other managers or of nonmanagers) in formal systems of coordination. They use formal authority to manage responsible subordinates. The individuals constituting each group are guided by an enterprise purpose, and their specialized service contributions are coordinated by their manager in the attainment of that purpose. On the other hand, the regulators, who are external to the formal organization of the enterprise, are not a part of the formal system of coordination. They use authority (but not formal authority) and influence to regulate (i.e., directly and indirectly to affect) the behavior of others. They and the managers are not guided by the same purpose, nor is coordination of specialized service contributions toward the attainment of an enterprise purpose involved in the relationship between them.

To differentiate clearly between managers and regulators is to provide an extremely useful frame of reference for dealing with many problems, including those of public policy. To fail to make the differentiation can lead to confusion and misunderstanding, the effects of which, in our judgment, can only be an incorrect approach to those problems.

---

[33] An example of this usage is to be found in Chamberlain, *op. cit., passim.* See a review of this book by Robert Tannenbaum (*Journal of Business,* vol. 21, pp. 128–132, April, 1948) for comments relating to the implications of such usage.

[34] The term "control" would be preferable, in this connection, to the term "regulate." The former term is not used here because it has been used above with another connotation.

# CHAPTER 17

# Organization in Action: Bureaucracy
# in a Government Laboratory*

Actual bureaucracies seldom conform to the models in the classic litera-ture.[1] Whenever an organization is studied, its unique features must be considered. Some of the features of bureaucracy as they occur in a naval research and development laboratory will be described here. The aim of this paper is to show how a group of professional scientists and engineers has met the partly conflicting demands of bureaucratic pro-cedures, professional standards, and personal values.

In any organization the influence of specific individuals with personal interests and desires is felt. Their influence, together with that of the supervisory training and human relations programs in current use, tends to modify the bureaucratic features. Thus, the rejection of some bureau-cratic features is both recognized and approved by many organizations today. Many officials realize that their actions are not always guided by the "rational" application of bureaucratic rules. Furthermore, in pro-fessional groups, officials often refer to professional standards as the basis for their actions.

* This chapter is a slightly modified version of "Bureaucracy in a Government Laboratory," by Paula Brown, *Social Forces*, vol. 32, no. 3, pp. 259–268, March, 1954.
    [1] We have in mind such characteristics as the organization of specific functions bound by rules; specified spheres of competence; hierarchical structure; the rational application of rules by officials with specialized training; the separation of ad-ministrators from the means of production or administration; absence of appropria-tion of his official position by the incumbent; formulation of administrative acts and decisions in writing; the appointment of officials; and promotion by seniority or achievement. *Cf.* Max Weber, *The Theory of Social and Economic Organization*, translated by A. M. Henderson and Talcott Parsons and edited by Talcott Parsons (New York: Oxford University Press, 1947), especially pp. 329–340.

The demands of bureaucratic procedures, professional standards, and personal values affect many aspects of the social system. The succeeding sections of the chapter will consider (1) problems of structure and function: principles of grouping, tasks and responsibilities, supervisory roles, and staff organization; and (2) social psychological aspects: attitudes toward bureaucracy, and identification with the organization.[2]

The laboratory to be discussed conforms to civil service and naval regulations. In addition, it has a specific technical function which distinguishes it from other kinds of government agencies and allies it to nongovernmental laboratories. While the laboratory may have many unique features, it also has some characteristics which it shares with other groups of professionals, other research and development laboratories, other naval organizations, other civil service organizations, and other bureaucracies.

The laboratory is one department of a naval station. The major facilities of the station are located elsewhere. The department has approximately 400 employees and is organized into staff offices, divisions, branches, and sections. At this location there are units of several other departments which provide services for the entire station and also carry out independent work. The department studied is relatively independent of the station: it works on a different kind of equipment and its separate location allows it considerable autonomy. However, it is a part of a larger bureaucracy consisting of the station and, above that, a naval bureau in Washington. There is exchange of information and cooperation with other naval stations and private firms working on government contracts. Nearly all the members of the department are civilians, but naval officers hold some administrative and advisory positions. The navy provides certain services to the station, such as the use of naval equipment and manpower for testing.

PRINCIPLES OF GROUPING

Bureaucracies are generally thought to be rigid social systems in which functions, responsibilities, and spheres of competence are clearly defined. This has been questioned in empirical studies, and our data tend to support these doubts. In general, professional employees resist rules made for them by persons outside the professional group. Bureaucratic principles may be especially difficult to apply in this laboratory. Large-scale research and development organizations are relatively new.

---

[2] The data upon which this analysis is based consist of interviews, documents, and observations of meetings and discussions in the laboratory. They may be considered suggestive rather than conclusive. Examples are limited by personal confidence and security requirements.

Because of the complexity of the work, no simple grouping of persons or functions solves all problems.

Because the key personnel of the laboratory are scientists and engineers, a somewhat privileged class of professionals in America today, their attitudes concerning the organization of their own work command respect by governmental administrators. Furthermore, the technical personnel of the laboratory would argue that they are able to construct a more "rational" structure because they understand the technical activi-ties better than any administrator could.[3] The department has taken the initiative and obtained administrative support for its internal organization.

In general, the department is concerned with research on, and the development and testing of, a specific kind of naval equipment. Some of its functions and emphases have been modified in the past few years. A series of reorganizations has followed these changes. The possible organizational schemata are numerous, especially when the changing functions are considered. At one time or another groups at different levels have been organized according to a variety of principles. These include the following:

1. By the components of the equipment: specific mechanisms, types of mechanism, segments of the equipment, etc.

2. By the phases through which the equipment and its components must pass: e.g., applied research, feasibility studies, development, testing.

3. By the special skills and training required to accomplish the work: mathematical, mechanical, electrical, electronic, etc.

4. By the location of the objects the groups use: e.g., computers, test ranges, types of laboratory equipment.

5. By the kinds of problems the groups consider: theoretical, experimental, design, etc.

A "functional" organization could be based upon any one of these principles, and many more.[4] There are a number of additional factors which may or may not be considered. For example, a "functional" organization could well be established in which one branch would contain thirty people and another three; however, the position of branch head is expected to carry a certain amount of supervision, and such a small branch does not satisfy this requirement.

Problems arise when the organizational principle in use does not account for all the department's activities. A number of service groups

[3] Many of these administrators are also engineers and scientists. However, the departmental personnel tend to view them as "pencil pushers."

[4] *Cf.* Herbert Simon, *Administrative Behavior* (New York: The Macmillan Company, 1947), chap. 2, pp. 20–45.

must be somehow placed in the department. Some of these serve the entire department, while others serve only some segment of it. Most of these groups have been attached to several different segments at one time or another. Further, the responsibility which service groups should have must be considered: if they are structurally parallel to "operating" groups, do they have equal authority to make decisions about their work? The service groups themselves are of several kinds, so that each presents its own problem of integration into the organization.

Whatever principle is adopted, problems arise. Thus, in this department, organizational lines must be crossed in order to accomplish many specific tasks. In addition, as the departmental functions are modified, its organization often proves cumbersome and inefficient. Whenever the structure is changed, some new, less important anomalies appear.

The relationship between the department and other groups of the station also creates problems. The functions of these latter groups include personnel, libraries, administration of communications (telephone, mail), travel, security, etc. Some parallel in size and responsibilities is expected among the departments of the station.

With the variety of possible arrangements of personnel, departmental management recognizes that it must give some reason for adopting one scheme rather than another. Our inquiries have unearthed a number of justifications for the departmental organization as it has developed. At one time it was "logical" to organize according to components; at another, it was more "logical" to organize by phases. One supervisor stated that specialists prefer to work with persons in their own specialty and that this was his reason for so organizing his groups.

In practice, many special adjustments are made. Fission takes place when a group grows beyond the usual size for units of that level. As functions are modified or new functions develop, groups are re-formed or new units established. The necessity for having certain units within the department, but at a separate location because of the equipment used, creates special cases which are often in conflict with the principles upon which the larger organization is based.

Most of the higher civil service ratings involve supervision. Thus groups are sometimes established to reward an able person with a higher position. Cases of this kind occasionally arise when an ambitious and able man receives, or pretends to receive, an offer of a better job elsewhere. His threat to resign may induce his supervisor to create a higher position for him.

It seems that the structure of subgroups depends on a variety of factors: requirements established by the larger organization; certain rules set up by the management of a subunit; particular, tailor-made principles to fit anomalous situations; and catering to individual ambitions.

## TASKS AND RESPONSIBILITIES

In the literature on bureaucracy, it is often assumed that, once the organization is established, the activities are handled automatically by reference to working rules. In this department, the allocation of tasks to groups presents many problems. The permanent organization provides a setting for the actual research and development activities. The allocation of a task to an individual or group is the end product of a series of management decisions. Since tasks vary in scope, complexity, and urgency, each assignment must be separately evaluated by management.

At the risk of oversimplification, the process of task assignment can be described as follows. The naval bureau directs a request for work to the station. This request often follows discussion with members of the station and general agreement about the project. Requests are passed by the station director to the department in whose scope the project falls. Of course, some requests do not fall clearly into the scope of any one department, and some might fall into the scope of other stations. After the station accepts a project, it may be assigned to one or more departments. When a request is made to a department, the department head makes a similar decision as to the division or branch which should carry out the work. Again, several groups may be involved. Responsibility for the coordination of a task is assigned to an individual whose experience and ability are appropriate to the complexity of the task.

A small-scale task is assigned to a *project engineer,* who must plan, execute, or oversee the work, and prepare a report when it is completed. The limits of authority for project engineers are neither clear nor consistent throughout the department. In many cases, persons who supervise the smaller permanent groups (sections and branches) are at the same time project engineers, but the task group of a project is not necessarily identical with the permanent group under this supervisor. The task group may involve only some of the members of the section or branch, or it may include members of other branches (see Figure 17-1).

A *project manager* is responsible for planning, overseeing the execution of, coordinating, and reporting on large-scale projects which involve many individuals both within and outside the department. These projects may occupy several hundred people at one time or another over a period of years. A project of this size is divided into phases and tasks to be distributed among members of the department. Other departments of the station, other stations, and private contractors may also perform certain tasks. Individual project managers often have a small staff of assistants, but the persons who actually carry out the many tasks report to their permanent supervisors and project engineers for the tasks. The project manager is a staff man, tangential to the

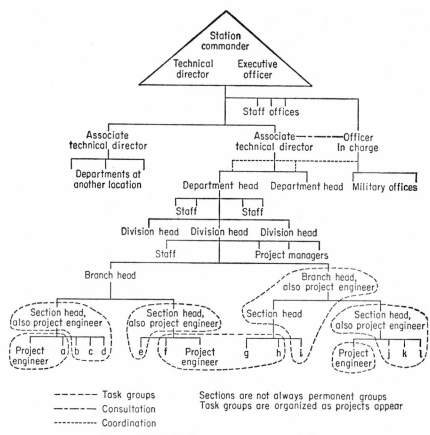

FIGURE 17-1. A schematic organizational chart.

chain of command. He has no authority to order men or work. However, he is responsible for the satisfactory completion of the tasks.

As tasks are defined by project managers and project engineers, often after discussion with division heads, branch heads, section heads, and individual engineers, informal assignments are made to individuals on the basis of personal agreement on the work involved. Formal work orders to the persons doing the work are rarely made. Occasionally, an order is written after the work has started. In general, no formal orders are necessary when the individuals are acquainted, the task personnel are all in one division, no other urgent work is scheduled, and the work is within the normal scope of the group and the individuals involved. But if one or more of these conditions do not hold, the individuals who will carry out the work may be reluctant to proceed without an order. In these cases, the project manager or project engineer makes a formal request to the division head, and the task is then assigned through a branch to an individual.

When the department is viewed as an association of professionals, the informal arrangements seem appropriate. But a bureaucracy should maintain schedules and follow orders. Many of the engineers feel most comfortable with the personal arrangements. Those individuals who prefer to receive direct orders from a single supervisor find it difficult to live with such a system.

Throughout the process of assigning tasks to groups and individuals, problems arise. First, task responsibility must be assigned to the most appropriate group. The urgency of the work must be established. Then a specific decision must be made as to who can or should perform the work. Cooperation between structurally separate groups is often required. Branches and divisions often have different operating customs and rules. Finally, individuals differ in their attitudes toward accepting work without the explicit approval of their branch heads or section heads.

In general, cooperation within divisions has been more common than cooperation between divisions. For several years, the work of each division was relatively self-contained, so interdivisional cooperation was infrequent. The need for interdivisional cooperation became pressing when the department's functions were modified. Then the department was reorganized in order to enlarge the groups which would normally cooperate and to allocate authority accordingly.[5]

The problems which are found in the allocation and execution of assignments seem to be linked to two main factors. First, the work is somewhat unpredictable: many assignments originate outside the department; cooperation with outside groups may cause delays; unforeseen circumstances arise frequently in research and development work; and priorities change. Second, the distribution of responsibility and authority between project engineers and project managers, on the one hand, and permanent supervisors on the other, requires exceptionally complex adjustments of schedules and work assignments. It would be very difficult to specify the rights and duties of project engineers and

---

[5] This process has been termed "cooptation" by Philip Selznick; see his *TVA and the Grass Roots* (Berkeley, Calif.: University of California Press, 1949), especially pp. 259 ff.

project managers. Furthermore, such specification would conflict with the professional code of informal cooperation.

## SUPERVISORY ROLES

The theory of bureaucracy assumes that administrative behavior is bound by rules. We recognize a wide variety of executive activities, even at the same organizational level.[6] Few studies have shown to what extent the executive himself determines the amount of time and effort he will spend on each activity.

Supervisory personnel are responsible for the efficient operation of the units under them. They must handle both administrative and technical problems. Each individual has a "job description" stating his responsibilities in general terms. These are written by the individual and his supervisor. But while the "job descriptions" do not vary greatly from supervisor to supervisor at the same level, or even between levels, the actual emphasis on these activities varies considerably.

At the lowest supervisory level, the section head oversees all the work of his group. At the same time, he may be a project engineer, in charge of a somewhat different group. However, as project engineer, he concentrates on a technical problem; as section head, he is the general supervisor of a group of individuals. These roles are easily confused. The responsibilities of a section head vary with the number of subordinates and the amount of authority delegated by higher management. For example, some section heads give efficiency ratings, assign work, and exercise close control over the members of the section; others serve as technical consultants for the members; in some cases the section consists of one person who carries out a self-contained portion of the technical work of the branch.

The branch is the next larger organizational unit. Branches range in size from five to thirty members. Most branches are divided into sections. Although the activities of branch heads vary considerably, the formal statements of their duties are similar. These duties include technical guidance of work in the branch, coordination of branch work, technical liaison with other groups, organization of the branch, planning and scheduling work, budget preparation and control, receiving and screening station communications for the branch, writing or reviewing

[6] See Robert K. Merton et al., *Reader in Bureaucracy* (Glencoe, Ill.: The Free Press, 1952), especially R. A. Gordon, "The Executive and the Owner-Entrepreneur"; E. H. Dale, "The Daily Life of the Civil Servant"; R. Turner, "The Navy Disbursing Officer as a Bureaucrat"; S. Carlson, "Records of Executive Behavior." See also William E. Jaynes, *An Analysis of Differences among Navy Officer Specialities and among Navy Organizations,* Columbus, Ohio, The Ohio State University Research Foundation, Studies in Naval Leadership, 1952.

technical reports, hiring and evaluating employees, and suggesting promotions. With this range of duties, some branch heads prefer to carry out some technical work themselves; others concentrate on the organization of technical work and serve as consultants to their subordinates, while others are most concerned with administrative or "human relations" problems.

A division contains three to six branches. Division heads are concerned with broad organizational problems, programs, and policies, rather than with direct supervision. They form a planning and policy committee for the department head, although their actual contribution to the making of decisions varies. Both technical and administrative skills are required by division heads when they plan programs, check technical reports, allocate work to and consult with branch heads, section heads, and project engineers. While the division heads are technical experts in their fields and have attained their status largely because of these abilities, their actual participation in the technical work consists of planning, occasional consultation, and review. Most of a division head's time is occupied with administrative problems within the division, among divisions, and outside the department. Personnel decisions concerning high-level hiring, promotions, and evaluation within the division are made by the division head.

There are striking differences in the manner in which the several division heads view their responsibilities and in the time which they devote to the activities listed in their "job descriptions." The diverse interests of these division heads—in creative ideas, in efficient administration, in progress toward technical goals, in group cohesion, or in motivation of subordinates—are reflected throughout their divisions. For example, one division head stresses knowing what the job is and getting it done by the proper combination of skills and experience; another sees that each project engineer understands his part in the total activity and organizes his work efficiently; still another is most concerned with making original research contributions. All these activities, and many others, are within the aims of the department as a whole. These differences in emphasis create conflicts, misunderstanding, and varying perceptions of organizational goals. Divisions also vary in the extent to which administrative functions are delegated to branch heads, section heads, and project engineers.

The modification of major goals through time depends largely upon national policy beyond the department's control. However, many specific decisions regarding department policy and goals have been influenced by individual staff officers and division heads. Thus the differences in the interests and aims of influential individuals have served to define varying group goals. At several periods, parts of the department or the entire department pursued variant ends, reflecting the rise and fall in influence of staff officers and higher supervisors.

While the social organization is bureaucratic, an analysis of sources of influence reveals many charismatic features.[7] These can also be seen when the careers of the higher supervisors are examined; some have experienced a rapid rise, while others have not changed in status for years. Enthusiasm for changes, combined with ability, often leads to promotions.

## STAFF ORGANIZATION

The relations between staff and line managers and the organization of staff functions have been the subject of much theoretical discussion and some empirical study.[8] Staff organization within a department which itself performs a staff function to the Chief of Naval Operations presents a rather more complex problem and has some special features.

While the "operating groups" of the department are hierarchically arranged into divisions, branches, and sections, the department has developed a large staff performing a variety of functions. One group is concerned with the usual staff activities such as planning, budget preparation and control, editing of reports, personnel control, etc. Some of these staff functions are also performed in the divisions. Conflicts occasionally arise between divisional personnel and departmental staff officers. The divisional personnel regard the departmental staff as disproportionately large, thus tending to reduce the funds available for the "real work" of the department. The size of the departmental staff is taken as an attempt to control the divisions.

Many of the staff officials have some engineering training. As technical work carries more prestige than administrative work, some of the technical personnel feel that the staff officers are engineers who failed to "make the grade" technically and have obtained high-level jobs for themselves in administration. Consequently, staff officers are often at great pains to demonstrate their technical knowledge to line personnel. In addition to the distrust of the technical ability of staff officials, there is a running struggle for influence on higher management between ambitious staff officials and line personnel.

[7] By "charismatic features" we mean that the influence wielded by the individual is derived from his personal leadership qualities rather than from the position he holds in the organization.

[8] These discussions are mainly in the field of sociology. See, for example, D. C. Miller and W. H. Form, *Industrial Sociology* (New York: Harper & Brothers, 1951). An empirical study is Melville Dalton, "Conflicts between Staff and Line Managerial Officers," *American Sociological Review*, vol. 15, no. 3, pp. 342–351, June, 1950.

Another staff group is devoted to broad research programs beyond the scope of any one division. This research group fulfills several interesting subsidiary functions. Its members work somewhat independently on projects largely of their own choosing. An "academic" atmosphere of friendly interchange prevails, where supervision is minimal and little pressure is applied to complete urgent work. Also, flexibility in personnel assignments is provided, since these technical specialists (scientists rather than engineers) may be temporarily assigned to work with line groups on specific research problems. Civil service regulations do not provide many high-ranking technical, as opposed to supervisory, positions in the line organization. But skilled scientists obtain a suitable rating here. The group serves as a temporary haven where a person learns the work of the department and is available to fill high-level line positions when they fall vacant.

For various reasons, there is little cooperation between the line groups and the staff scientists except for occasional special assignments. The work of the scientists on the staff is not widely known, for they have few contacts with other parts of the department. Much of their work consists of library research and they identify themselves with scientists in the universities rather than with the engineers in the department. This isolation is partly due to the nature of the work: research is primarily an individual or small-group pursuit; engineering and administration require cooperation and integration with other groups. The research carried on in the divisions has many of the same characteristics as that in the staff office.

Within the line groups, cooperation and group loyalty are encouraged by the supervisors. As civil service policy states that promotions should be made from within the organization whenever possible, members expect to be promoted within the branch or division as vacancies occur. The existence of other technically skilled persons within the department threatens their intrabranch and intradivision promotion hopes. Some of the cases in which individuals moved from staff to line positions have presented problems, but these cases are few and difficult to analyze because personalities and technical qualifications vary considerably.

Some of the difficulties between the staff and the line groups are common to staff-line relations in other types of organization. These include feelings that the problems faced by each group are not appreciated by the others and jockeying for influence on higher management between staff and line officials.

The educational level of staff personnel is higher than that of line personnel. Such an educational difference is often found, but in this case it consists of a larger proportion of persons with Ph.D. and M.A. degrees on the staff than on the line. (In other organizations a higher proportion of persons with a college education on the staff than on the line is usual.) Advanced education fits these staff men for administrative specialization or research work. The engineers in the department, most of whom possess a bachelor's degree, respect higher education, but they also feel uncomfortable in the presence of Ph.D.'s. This ambivalent attitude toward the staff is intensified by the promotion policy.

## ATTITUDES TOWARD BUREAUCRACY

The members of the department believe that they have certain special characteristics which make many of the usual bureaucratic practices inapplicable. The supervisory engineers often feel that, since their subordinates are also professional specialists, they must be treated as equals rather than as subordinates.[9] For example, a supervisor may say that his subordinates are intelligent and highly trained professionals; he expects them to take a problem and work it out without direct supervision. A supervisor often considers himself a senior colleague rather than a boss. Our observations suggest that this attitude may be a stereotype on the part of the professional workers; while some subordinates respond to general problems and enjoy the freedom which this attitude brings, many others need more definite assignments and direct supervision. They also need to be praised and criticized occasionally.

The tendency to allow persons to work out solutions by themselves extends to broader organizational problems as well. The place of a task in the objectives of the department may not be explained. In some cases the persons concerned with an impending change are not informed before a general announcement is made. At such times, rumors circulate, and questions are asked over coffee. The tension increases because the possession of information may be a carefully guarded source of prestige, and the uninformed suspects his colleagues of disregarding his interests.[10] When subordinates attend meetings as deputies for their superiors, they may fail to report all that transpired, either because some things seem irrelevant or because they wish to enhance their prestige by retaining inside information. There is no set policy regarding the proper extent of such communication.

An interesting attitude difference can be drawn, partly along the staff-line dichotomy and partly along the research-development dichotomy. This distinction is based upon the need of the line groups, and especially those concerned with development problems, to plan and

[9] *Cf.* Peter Drucker, "Management and the Professional Employee," *Harvard Business Review*, vol. 30, no. 3, pp. 84–90, May–June, 1952.

[10] The importance of information as a source of prestige in a laboratory was also observed by Herbert A. Shepard, in "Communication and Cooperation in a Physical Science Research Laboratory," unpublished doctoral dissertation, Massachusetts Institute of Technology, 1950.

execute large-scale cooperative projects, whereas the staff and research personnel work more independently. The importance of both types of work is recognized by higher management, but among the groups themselves there are somewhat conflicting views about the importance of the two kinds of work. For example, a development worker may state that his work is vital because it is aimed toward getting equipment to the fleet. A research worker will assert that his work requires higher qualifications and is fundamental to development. Each sometimes claims that management shows favoritism to the other: development personnel believe that they can obtain higher ratings only by accepting supervisory jobs, while high-level "consultant" positions are open to research experts; some of the research personnel feel that advancement is more rapid in development.

Those individuals whose work is not subject to direct supervision, time schedules, or integration with other station activities are more or less indifferent to management problems and desire only the freedom to carry out independent work. Their contact with other groups in the organization is limited, since their need to coordinate their work with others is minimal. On the other hand, those who must coordinate their work with other groups and who depend upon management decisions are highly involved in management problems. The pressure upon them is reflected in violent criticism of the civil service system, department and station management, and various service groups on the station. For example, management at each level above is accused of giving insufficient information and delaying decisions; personnel, supply, and service groups are blamed when information or equipment moves slowly. In some cases the criticism is justified, as each level may avoid making final decisions. But the prevalence of this criticism seems to reflect a tendency to project responsibility upward and away from the immediate group.

While such a tendency may be found in many establishments,[11] it seems especially common to civil service organizations. Where the structure is very large and the ultimate authority distant (both far away and many levels removed) and impersonal, a reluctance to accept the responsibility for making decisions is easily rationalized. Few of the personnel feel that the success of the national defense effort, or even of the station or department, depends on them. Furthermore, responsibility and authority are not coordinate. Thus the projection of blame upward when problems arise affords an easy excuse.

When a specific duty is assigned to a supervisor, he frequently delegates it to a committee. Most committee members see their roles as advisers rather than as administrators. The committee system tends to

[11] This tendency has been noted in Elliott Jacques, *The Changing Culture of a Factory* (London: Tavistock Publications, Ltd., 1951), especially p. 284.

spread responsibility thinly—the supervisor feels relieved of a responsibility, but the committee members do not take it on.[12]

The professionals in this laboratory have some interests and values which conflict with bureaucratic procedures. Those concerned with research seem to hold these most strongly. Many of the engineers in development and testing work have resisted adapting to large-scale bureaucratic organization, although they recognize the need for it more than do the research scientists. Even those who accept the need for bureaucratic procedures show their resistance in attacks on the civil service system, management practices, and committee organization.

## IDENTIFICATION WITH THE ORGANIZATION

A number of groups, subgroups, and classes of individuals serve as reference groups for the members of the department. In varying circumstances, any one of these may serve as a focal point for alignments and factions.[13]

Many alignments take place along organizational lines. These may be at any level. Members of a branch usually work in one area of the laboratory and have close relations. Most people identify themselves with their branches. But when the branches are more permanently sub-

[12] Also noted in *ibid.*, p. 279.

[13] Alignments occurring along lines of status, prestige, and esteem are considered in some detail in an article closely related to the present chapter: Paula Brown and Clovis Shepherd, "Status, Prestige and Esteem in a Research Organization," *Administrative Science Quarterly*, vol. 1, no. 3, pp. 340–360, December, 1956. Among findings of the latter research, conducted in the same setting, are the following: (1) Status groups are defined principally by occupational level attained within the organization (high professionals, middle professionals, low professionals, administrators, etc.) rather than by conventional job titles (chemical engineers, electrical engineers, etc.). (2) Systematic differences in background characteristics (age, experience, education, seniority) appear among status groups. For instance, professionals tend to be young and mobile; clerical employees, while young, tend to have relatively more experience in their field than other occupational groups, presumably because they begin work in their specialty at an earlier age, etc. (3) Systematic differences in behavior and attitudes appear among status groups. For instance, high-status groups tend to have greater numbers of personal acquaintances, among them a substantial number of superiors; committee appointments are differentially assigned to different status groups; professional and official contacts outside the organization markedly reflect status differentials; *dis*satisfaction rises with status, etc. (4) Esteem, as measured by sociometric choices, tends to be related in a curvilinear fashion to status. Esteem measures for various organizational subunits are significantly intercorrelated.

In conclusion, the article notes that systems of stratification in a research organization are subject to the following conflicting stresses: (1) the emphasis on the value of science and the attendant emphasis on objectivity, independent activity, and individual initiative; (2) the need for a functional type of organization which permits flexibility in work relations and yet is a part of a larger bureaucratic structure; and (3) the existence of status groups which are differentiated and stratified in a prestige hierarchy.

divided, the sections may be more cohesive than the branch as a whole. On a broader level, divisional loyalties are found, and there are cases in which the entire department stands together. Often an attack, real or imagined, by an outside group stimulates members of the department to express their cohesion. Recently, the department offered strong resistance when the removal of a staff office to another department was suggested by higher management and by the other department. Divisions stand together when another division threatens their realm of activity or criticizes their methods of operation. Since the groups differ somewhat in their emphases, in-group loyalty is rationalized as conviction concerning principles of organization or procedures.

Because the higher-level personnel of the department help to shape departmental policy, attitudes concerning what are or should be the goals of the organization often serve as the basis of group identification. There have been serious conflicts based upon the definition of research, development, and testing.

As described above, the staff-line and project group–permanent group distinctions may form a basis for factional groupings.

Although station management is somewhat concerned about cooperation between departments and station cohesion, this department is quite isolated from the others. Its detachment can be traced to its relatively self-contained program and distance from the main facilities of the station. All the groups at this location feel that they are "stepchildren" of the station, who receive little attention from station management. Individuals who serve on station committees or whose work is related to that of other groups in the station certainly recognize the wider context of station activities, but the majority of individuals are most concerned with their face-to-face associates within the department.

Some associations seem to be based upon status distinctions. These status groups are of several kinds. Within the civil service system itself, a distinction is made between per annum and per diem employees. This is commonly known as the white-collar–blue-collar distinction. Both of these groups contain a series of positions. Among the per annum employees, further distinctions are made between professionals, subprofessionals, and clerical-administrative-fiscal personnel. While the same grade system exists for all these, ceilings and rates of advancement do vary among them. The salary and grade of supervisors at a given organizational level do not vary more than one step. These status categories cut across organizational lines; under certain circumstances, they may act in opposition to group loyalties. For example, individuals frequently get together on the working level. If two division heads clash over an issue, the branch heads or section heads in these divisions may together work out a suitable arrangement to accomplish a particular job. When questions arise in the course of a project, the project engineer often seeks advice from someone at his own level in another group. The informal arrangements by project engineers and project managers with individuals for specific short-term jobs are another example of this. Secretaries usually help one another when work piles up.

As in so many cases, when questions were asked, the explanation of this "getting together on the working level" appealed to professional preferences. An engineer stated that the people who are actually carrying out the work possess the kind of information about it that he needs, so he goes directly to them. As a part of the professional atmosphere, supervisors encourage informal visiting in order to obtain information about current work.

At the same time, there are many signs of deference to superiors, even when a subordinate is quite certain of his own technical judgment. Perhaps the individuals are more comfortable in working with someone on the same level than with someone of greatly different status.

A number of disagreements can be traced to the attitudes held concerning the importance of different kinds of work. For example, the conflict in values between research and development workers may be the basis of attempts to expand one function at the expense of the other. Many individuals feel that their own contributions are most important. Views of this sort may be expanded into what is locally known as "empire building"; since each branch can be regarded by its members as central to the entire work of the department, many branch heads attempt to convince their superiors that the branch should be a division, if not a department. In this way, personal ambitions for a higher salary and increased authority are given a "technical" basis.

Other alignments and factions are based upon individual values and interpersonal ties. Such factors as education (both the degree obtained and the university attended), professional interests, outside interests, past associations in other organizations, and home friendships fall into this category. Some individuals look to their professional colleagues outside the laboratory for approval. This serves to remove them from internal friction as well as to provide a larger reference group.

As issues arise and problems change, there are different alignments of individuals and groups, on the basis of different subgroups, past associations, personal goals, group goals, and individual attitudes toward the issues themselves. Thus identification with the department as a whole is less frequent than identification with one of its subgroups.[14] Furthermore, the people who exercise influence often stimulate small group loyalty rather than identification with the department or station.

---

[14] We have here another instance of a phenomenon often observed. A study of the determinants of cohesiveness was made by Jay M. Jackson at the Research Center for Group Dynamics, University of Michigan (unpublished manuscript).

CONCLUSION

Our research in a government laboratory shows that there are discrepancies when the classic concept of bureaucracy is applied to a particular bureaucratic structure. The group studied is a department of a government research and development laboratory, so that the personnel of this organization are for the most part scientists, engineers, and technicians. As a privileged professional group, they feel that they·should have authority to make decisions about the internal organization of the department and should participate in policy decisions concerning group objectives. While most of the individuals in the organization admit to having the same personal ambitions and shortcomings as other adults, most of their expressed attitudes are stated in technical terms. Technical reasons are usually given for modification in the organization, although our analysis reveals a wide divergence of opinion, based upon personal as well as technical values. As university-trained scientists and engineers, they seem to feel that their professional standing depends upon the technical reasons that they can advance to support attitudes and decisions. Individuals are criticized in terms of their engineering knowledge or ability, but supervisors are sometimes called to task for their failures in "dealing with people" as well as in technical skills.

It appears that the members of this department think of themselves as "rational" engineers rather than as "rational" bureaucrats. At the same time, interpersonal factors are increasingly recognized as modifying both the bureaucratic ideal and the impersonal engineering ideal.

The observations in this laboratory suggest further work in several areas. Some interesting contrasts might be found in private laboratories, where individuals may not often become as firmly entrenched in their positions[15] and stronger feelings of responsibility to the organization may exist. Other groups of professionals could be studied.[16] We would predict that groups of professionals who had lower national prestige would not be able to control their organizations as completely as these engineers do. In more highly respected professions (e.g., among university groups, doctors, or lawyers), there might be even stronger resistance to bureaucratic principles than at this laboratory.

[15] This is a common belief, but not substantiated by available information.
[16] An interesting study has been carried out by Alvin Zander at the Research Center for Group Dynamics, University of Michigan. See "Some Determinants of Role Relations: A Study of the Relations among Psychiatrists, Clinical Psychologists, and Psychiatric Social Workers," a symposium presented at the 1952 Annual Meeting of the American Psychological Association. Two articles on research organization in Britain are of interest: R. L. Meier, "Research as a Social Process," *British Journal of Sociology*, vol. 2, no. 2, pp. 91–104, June, 1951; and John D. Cockcroft, "The Organization of a Research and Development Establishment," *Occupational Psychology*, vol. 27, no. 3, pp. 152–156, July, 1953.

CHAPTER 18

*Developing Objectives and Evaluation Procedures*
*in Research Organizations**

Today, millions of dollars are being spent on research and development work. Individuals, isolated research teams, and large-scale laboratories are working toward the development of new ideas and methods. When such large sums of money and numbers of people are concerned, the sound formulation of objectives and careful evaluation of progress toward these objectives become of increasing importance. However, the formulation of objectives and the evaluation of performance in the research and development field have involved so many intangibles that the evolution of useful guidelines has proved to be most difficult.

FORMULATION OF OBJECTIVES

At the outset, it becomes necessary to clarify the meaning of the term "objectives." In a broader sense, the term "objectives" is frequently synonymous with the over-all research and development mission of a given organization and of its various subunits. As such, it reflects the *long-range goals* as determined by outside agencies or by top management. For instance, in naval research settings, the mission of one laboratory might be the development and testing of rockets and explosives. Various subunits of the organization also have their unique objectives or missions. These should fall within the scope of the over-all

* This chapter is based on a portion of "Setting a Frame of Reference for the Evaluation of Research and Development," by Robert Tannenbaum, in Irving R. Weschler and Paula Brown (eds.), *Evaluating Research and Development*, Human Relations Research Group, Institute of Industrial Relations, University of California, Los Angeles, 1953, pp. 13–19 and 94–98 (Annotated Proceedings of a Conference of Research Administrators held at the University of California, Los Angeles, on May 10, 1952).

purpose of the larger organization. Thus, in the same naval laboratory, the mission of one department might be to develop ground-to-air rockets; one of its divisions might be responsible for developing certain relevant rocket components; and so on for further organizational subunits down to specific individuals working "on the line" whose positions or job descriptions might be viewed as their "objectives" or missions. What this amounts to is really a chain relationship between objectives. Each of the successively smaller units, with its own objective, contributes toward the attainment of the larger objective of the organization. Each of these objectives or missions is usually very generally stated, marking the limits within which the activities of each organizational unit are to be carried on.

In a narrower sense, the term "objectives" refers to *specific tasks* to be accomplished. In this sense, the objectives specify the results to be attained by given individuals and groups through work performance. Task objectives are set out in a statement of detailed specifications which should answer the following questions: "What should be done?" "Who should do it?" "When and where should it be done?" And, finally and perhaps most difficult to answer: "How should it be done?"

Objectives originate from various sources. The project proposal frequently stems from an outside agency. The people in the laboratory or research organization are told what they are supposed to work on, what tasks they are supposed to accomplish. At other times, the proposal emerges from within the organization. It may come from top management or from one of the several subunits. It may come from the grass roots rather than from the top; someone who is close to a problem sees something worth doing, attempts to define an objective, and then "sells" it to the appropriate power higher in the organization. If the proposal is approved, it will be financed and put into operation. In a research setting, many more of the proposals seem to emerge from lower levels in the organization than, for instance, in a factory or commercial firm.

There are differences among definitions of mission or task objectives for basic research, applied research, development, and testing activities. Although a basic-research mission may be fairly well established, it is typically difficult to specify task objectives implementing this type of activity. Thus a person in the laboratory may know that his job is to expand knowledge in hydrodynamics, but the specific work problems will arise from his hunches and the way in which he approaches the subject. Task objectives for applied research, development, and testing activities seem more readily subject to specification. Further knowledge is needed concerning the problems existing in defining objectives for these different types of functional activities within laboratory or research organization; and there are demands for a clear-cut analysis of the criteria affecting the selection of some objectives as potentially fruitful and the rejection of others as probably sterile.

A complete statement of objectives must be translated into a series of specific instructions: *Who* is to do the job—what individuals, what organizational units? *When* is it to be done—a time specification—that is, on what date is the project supposed to start and on what date is it supposed to be finished? *Where* is it to be done—with reference to a missile- or weapon-testing problem, for instance, on what range is the test to be conducted? And finally, *how* is it to be done? We may know what we want. We may decide on who is to do it, and when and where. Our lack of knowledge with regard to the "how" aspect seems to be the most outstanding single factor responsible for the lack of adequate specification.

Rarely do objectives remain frozen. Often—and necessarily—they are modified during the course of a project. In research, and to lesser degree in development, the ultimate objectives are not always known until exploratory work has been going on for some time. It may be quite difficult to set in advance a completion date for a project or to determine the course of work which will lead to its successful conclusion. Very often there must be continuous feedback, to superiors or peers, with attendant alteration of the objectives. The process seems to run somewhat like this: a hazy objective emerges from the over-all mission; some work is done; the objective seems to require sharpening; new specifications are laid down; further work is undertaken; obstacles are encountered; objectives are again modified; and so it goes, back and forth, until the "last" objective is accomplished or the project is abandoned.

EVALUATION OF PERFORMANCE

The matter of *performance evaluation* concerns the measurement of progress toward objectives. Ideally, evaluation should be based upon objectives which have been established through perfect knowledge of the total performance required to maximize results. Unfortunately, perfect knowledge is not available, and the objectives which are in practice formulated often reflect only hypotheses as to the kinds of performance which will yield optimum results. Thus evaluation, in practice, must be made with reference to those objectives which are formulated in the light of existing knowledge, hypotheses, or reasonable hunches.

If there were full knowledge of the necessary procedures in research, all the factors responsible for the optimum functioning of any given organization could be specified. Once the over-all objective or mission of an organization were known, it would be possible to detail the ideal performances for each individual or group which would lead to the optimum performance of any given task. If one knew, for example, that a basic-research group would be most productive if communications followed a given pattern, if certain people were located in close proximity to each other, or a particular series of operations were required to do a job, then specifications could include all of this. The performance of individuals or group might then be referred to as the *actual performance,* and *the problem of evaluation would be to compare the actual performance with the ideal performance.* Indeed, there is but imperfect knowledge of the nature of this ideal performance.

In practice, evaluation consists of an appraisal of actual performance against a set of specifications which through necessity suffers from lack of knowledge of an ideal, but which makes use of a complex system of hunches, assumptions, and guidelines developed by the evaluator.

The process of the evaluation of individuals or groups can perhaps best be made clear by means of the following illustration. Assume that you are in charge of a graduate seminar at a university and that one of your tasks is to grade your students on their over-all performance during the term. Your job is not an easy one, and you are likely to go through three distinct processes in making your evaluations. First, you are going to determine the *kinds of performance* on which you will judge your students. For example, you might require a term paper, an examination, a panel appearance, participation in a group research project, and the like. These kinds of performances help to define the objectives for your students. They do not include everything that might be relevant, but seem to offer a fair sample of performances. Second, when a student turns in his first term paper, you have to consider the *characteristics* or *attributes* of the term paper which you feel can be evaluated. You might think of such characteristics as its organization, use of the literature, coverage of the subject, originality, perhaps length, bibliography, and footnoting. If you are a good teacher, you probably will have told your students in advance what attributes of a term paper you are planning to evaluate. Finally, you have to decide on the specific *techniques* which you have available *for getting a quantitative measure* with reference to these characteristics. For instance, you might count the number of pages, make a content analysis of the main themes, check the bibliography, and so on. Some of the characteristics may not lend themselves to a quantitative analysis, and you are interested to learn which ones, and why, and have to decide what qualitative judgments you are prepared to substitute. The evaluation of research performances involves similar considerations. A suggested evaluation check list for individual and/or group performance follows.

A Preliminary Check List for the Evaluation of Individual
and/or Group Performance with Reference to Objectives

| Kinds of performance to be evaluated | Characteristics of performance | Specific techniques for measuring characteristics |
|---|---|---|
| Research proposals | Number | Counting |
| | Quality of proposals | Ratings by peers, panel of superiors, customers, etc. Content analysis of key ideas[1] Readability, i.e., intelligibility check with Flesch formulas[2] |
| | Feasibility of proposals | Ratings by organizational superiors Calculated risk formulas (Vaughn, etc.)[3] Equivalent cost of success formulas (Reeves)[4] Merit $=$ probability of success $\times$ value of project if successful/cost of development (Shepard)[5] |
| | Realism of proposals: relative to objectives, mission | Ratings by customer; by superiors on behalf of customer |
| Research methodology | Originality of procedures | Ratings by peers, superiors |
| | Systemization of procedures | Ratings by peers, superiors Evaluation check lists Flanagan's "critical incidents"[6] |

[1] B. Berelson: *Content Analysis in Communications Research* (Glencoe, Ill.: The Free Press, 1952).

[2] R. Flesch: "A New Readability Yardstick," *Journal of Applied Psychology*, vol. 32, pp. 221–233, 1948.

[3] T. H. Vaughn: "Calculated Risk: Its Place in the Selection, Control and Termination of Research Projects," in *Proceedings of the Fourth Annual Conference on the Administration of Research* (Ann Arbor, Mich.: Engineering Research Institute, University of Michigan, Sept. 11–13, 1950), pp. 1–10.

[4] E. D. Reeves: "Calculated Risk: Its Place in the Selection, Control and Termination of Research Projects," in *Proceedings of the Fourth Annual Conference on the Administration of Research* (Ann Arbor, Mich.: Engineering Research Institute, University of Michigan, Sept. 11–13, 1950), pp. 10–13.

[5] H. A. Shepard, as quoted by E. A. Walker, in *Summary of the Addresses and Discussions of the Second Annual Conference on the Administration of Research* (State College, Pa.: Pennsylvania State College, Oct. 13–15, 1948).

[6] J. Flanagan: "Measuring Research Effectiveness," *Proceedings of the Conference on Scientific Manpower* (Washington, D.C.: Office of Naval Research, Department of the Navy, December, 1951), pp. 74–80.

A PRELIMINARY CHECK LIST FOR THE EVALUATION OF INDIVIDUAL
AND/OR GROUP PERFORMANCE WITH REFERENCE TO OBJECTIVES
(*Continued*)

| Kinds of performance to be evaluated | Characteristics of performance | Specific techniques for measuring characteristics |
|---|---|---|
| Operating procedures | Effective planning, scheduling, budgeting, and control | Ratings of adequacy of procedures<br>Flanagan's "critical incidents"<br>Evaluation check lists<br>Gantt charts, linear programing, operations research[7] |
| | Effective utilization of manpower: selection, placement, training, evaluation, etc. | Organizational surveys<br>Evaluation check lists<br>Manpower charts, etc. |
| | Effective utilization of facilities: availability, adequacy, maintenance, etc. | Organizational surveys<br>Evaluation check lists |
| | Effective communications:<br>Amount of new, usable information in files | Amount of information added per unit of time |
| | Extent, adequacy, and use of library facilities | Ratings<br>Evaluation check lists |
| | Existence of established patterns of communication within and between organizational units | Number of committee meetings, conferences<br>Amount and content of written communications |
| | Clarity of written and oral communications | Ratings<br>Flesch readability formulas<br>Content analysis |
| | Accessibility of key individuals within and outside the organization | Indices based on surveys, interviews, etc. |
| Leadership toward objectives | Acceptance by subordinates | Attitude surveys, Multi-relational Sociometric Survey (MSS), etc.[8] |
| | Appropriate personality traits: empathy, flexibility | Personality tests[9] |

[7] P. M. Morse and G. E. Kimball: *Methods of Operations Research* (New York: John Wiley and Sons, Inc., 1951).

[8] I. R. Weschler, R. Tannenbaum, and E. Talbot: "A New Management Tool: The Multi-relational Sociometric Survey," *Personnel*, vol. 29, pp. 85–94, July, 1952; also Chapter 22.

[9] A. Roe: "A Psychological Study of Physical Scientists," *Genetic Psychology Monographs*, vol. 43, pp. 123–235, May, 1951.

A Preliminary Check List for the Evaluation of Individual
and/or Group Performance with Reference to Objectives
(*Continued*)

| Kinds of performance to be evaluated | Characteristics of performance | Specific techniques for measuring characteristics |
|---|---|---|
| Leadership toward objectives (*continued*) | Administrative skills | Biographical records<br>Flanagan's "critical incidents"<br>Administrative aptitude tests[10] |
| | Technical competence | Biographical records<br>Aptitude and achievement tests[11] |
| | Understanding by members of objectives | Ratings by superiors<br>Open-ended interviews<br>Per cent deviation in understanding of objectives through time<br>Content analysis of deviations in understanding |
| | Agreement among members concerning desirability of attainment | Attitude surveys<br>Open-ended interviews<br>Data on turnover, tardiness, absenteeism, job satisfaction, and morale |
| | Amount of effort toward attainment of objectives | Time sampling of productive activities[12] |
| | Cooperation and/or lack of conflict | Attitude surveys, MSS, etc.<br>Ratings<br>Participant observation |
| Progress reports | Approach to objectives | Evaluation of progress against plans, schedules, budgets |
| | Clarity of presentation | Flesch readability formulas<br>Ratings |
| Technical reports | Quantity, in terms of difficulty of accomplishment | Number of reports, weighted by difficulty, per unit of time (ratings) |

[10] M. M. Mandell and D. C. Adkins: "The Validity of Written Tests for the Selection of Administrative Personnel," *Educational and Psychological Measurement*, vol. 6, pp. 293–312, Autumn, 1946.

[11] M. M. Mandell and S. Chad: "Tests for Selecting Engineers," *Public Personnel Review*, vol. 11, pp. 217–222, October, 1950.

[12] C. L. Brisley: "How You Can Put Work Sampling to Work," *Factory Management and Maintenance*, July, 1952, pp. 84–89.

A PRELIMINARY CHECK LIST FOR THE EVALUATION OF INDIVIDUAL
AND/OR GROUP PERFORMANCE WITH REFERENCE TO OBJECTIVES
(*Continued*)

| Kinds of performance to be evaluated | Characteristics of performance | Specific techniques for measuring characteristics |
|---|---|---|
| Technical reports (*continued*) | General significance | Ratings by peers, customers, etc. Publications, reports at professional meetings |
| | Cost of accomplishment | Cost per objective: time, manpower, facilities utilized per objective |
| | Applicability of results | Ratings by customers Time required to translate ideas into "hardware" |
| | Approach to objectives | Ratings by superiors |
| "Hardware" | Quantity, in terms of difficulty of accomplishment | Amount of "hardware" produced, weighted by difficulty, per unit of time |
| | Approach to specifications | Per cent accomplishment per objectives (ratings) |
| | Cost of accomplishment | Cost per objective: time, manpower, facilities; economic formulas[13] |
| | Usefulness | Ratings by customers Evaluation check lists |
| | General significance | Olsen's broad-gauge values: economic, political, and cultural[14] |

[13] A. Abrams: "Appraising Returns from Research," *Mechanical Engineering*, August, 1950, pp. 645–646.

[14] F. Olsen: "Methods for Evaluation of Research," in *Proceedings of the Third Annual Conference on the Evaluation of Research* (State College, Pa.: School of Engineering, Pennsylvania State College, Sept. 12–14, 1949).

The evaluation of individual and group performance may be affected by such factors as (1) different types of products, such as component parts, reports, models, and engineering designs; (2) the organizational level at which the evaluation is made—is it, for instance, in navy terms, made at the branch, division, department, or station level; (3) the competence of the evaluator—does he have to be technically competent to do a job before he can be qualified to evaluate it; and finally, (4) whether the evaluator is a member of the organization—does he have to experience the particular conditions in the laboratory, or can he come in as a member of an outside consulting firm, for instance, to give a valid appraisal?

The necessity for more and better "research on research," particularly with reference to the setting of research objectives and concerning the evaluation of research performance, remains a major challenge to scientific social inquiry.

CHAPTER 19

# The Impact of Altered Objectives: Factionalism
# and Organizational Change in a Research Laboratory*

This chapter will describe what happened when a naval bureau in
Washington changed the objectives of one of its laboratories on the
west coast. The change was, in essence, from applied research to development. If the personnel of the department had behaved as "obedient
employees," they would simply have changed their behavior to conform
to the new policy. But these employees were engineers and scientists who
had professional opinions about their work and about the organization.
The change in policy produced a sharpening of factions, a power
struggle, an extensive reorganization, and the resignation of a number of
persons. In this series of changes the actors were mainly the scientists
and engineers in top staff and line positions. Each man had a set of
beliefs about his professional work, about the organization and its goals,
and about the other persons in the organization. The alignment and
conflict of persons holding these beliefs produced a number of changes
in the organization which had little to do with the purported aims of the
policy change.

The data for this study were collected over a period of two years
(1952–1953) of regular visits to the laboratory. Methods of study were
for the most part informal: They included interviewing members in
private, entering into casual conversations in offices and corridors, attending meetings, and a brief questionnaire.

* This chapter is a slightly modified version of "Factionalism and Organizational
Change in a Research Laboratory," by Paula Brown and Clovis Shepherd, *Social
Problems*, vol. 34, pp. 235–243, April, 1956. An earlier version, entitled "The Reaction of Engineers to Organization," was presented as a paper at the annual meeting of the American Sociological Society, September, 1954.

## FORMATION AND DEVELOPMENT OF THE DEPARTMENT

The laboratory was originally composed of three separate groups, two of which were once connected with a university. In 1945, the laboratory became one department of a naval research and development station. By 1950, the department contained five divisions: three original groups, and two additional divisions which were first established as service groups to design and build equipment needed by the others. The department had grown to about four hundred members organized into the five divisions, into branches and sections with staff offices attached at both the department and division levels. After the laboratory became a part of the naval station, basic policy and objectives were set by a naval bureau and by the station. The department had to conform to these policies and objectives and to civil service regulations. Within this framework, the department itself determined much of its action.

While the department included clerical and technical personnel, the largest group of its members were civilian professionals. The persons in supervisory positions, of whom we shall speak most, had at least a bachelor's degree in engineering or one of the physical sciences. Another important group of relatively high rank were technical specialists. Among the 175 professionals, 61 per cent had bachelor's degrees, 24 per cent had master's degrees, and 7 per cent had doctor's degrees. The distinction between research and development work and interests was not directly linked with the distinction between science and engineering training, or with that between persons with advanced degrees and persons with bachelor's degrees.

Until 1952, the work done in the laboratory was largely applied research. The higher-level professionals suggested projects which were approved by the naval bureau if they fitted into the research interests of this agency. This resulted in a large number of independent activities. During this time each of the three divisions which did research work was more or less autonomous: divergent technical interests and administrative procedures were pursued, and each division had its own standards and measures of effectiveness. As new division heads took over, they modified the divisions according to criteria which their "engineering judgment" considered most appropriate. These changes included establishing and abolishing branches, initiating projects, and shifting personnel. When a new department head was appointed, there were changes in the departmental structure as well. The department was seen by its members as a collection of individuals and subgroups pursuing a variety of goals and interests. Past associations and friendships cut across some of these ties, but few occasions arose to sharpen factional groupings.

## CHANGES IN ORGANIZATIONAL OBJECTIVES
### BY EXTERNAL AUTHORITIES

This pattern of three independent applied research divisions and two service divisions existed for some years. As the Navy clarified and changed its interests, it began to give the department specific requests for equipment development. Because of the kind of work, responsibility for most of these was given to the service division concerned with development. The entire department became responsible to the naval bureau for a number of large-scale projects. Two important changes were involved: increased cooperation among the divisions in the department, and an increased emphasis upon equipment-development and testing activities. One expression of this was a decrease in the funds available for research and an increase in development funds. In attempting to meet these requirements, department management gradually modified the jobs of individuals and subgroups. Further personnel increases were largely restricted to groups performing the new functions. The cumulative effect of these changes was great, as the groups which became most important in equipment development were the two divisions which had been originally established as service groups. The groups which had been the core of the department saw these service groups become equal, and then superior, to them (the research divisions) in funds, manpower, and project assignments.

These changes met resistance by many people in the other three divisions. Much of it was phrased in terms of professional values. Such comments as the following were quite common: "It's ridiculous to drop a project just when it's beginning to show results." "I know all there is to know about A and now they want me to drop it and start working on B." "We can't possibly carry out these tests unless the statistical criteria are more specific." "They want us to take on a new job, but no one tells what to do or when to do it." "They expect us to have the tests completed by September 1, but they haven't given us all the equipment yet."

Some of these objections may be expected to arise in any period of technological change; that is, a man may feel that his competence in a particular area is being ignored, and that he is being required to develop a new skill. Here, the idea that a professional is the best judge of his own progress supported these objections. Furthermore, the professional atmosphere gave a person the right to complain to anyone in the organization. To the extent that the argument was convincing, management might alter its decision. In contrast to industry generally, both supervisor and subordinate were professional engineers. Differences in age and experience were small: 77 per cent of the professionals were under forty years old, 53 per cent had less than eight years' experience, and 82 per cent had less than fifteen years' experience. In many ways, the professional members of the department regarded themselves as a society of equals, any one of whom could exert influence on the others. Thus, they often allowed professional values to override traditional organizational practice (see also Chapter 18).

As the need for coordination between divisions developed, certain staff functions became more important. Some of these staff functions had to be discharged by engineers who were able to set up schedules and analyze results. The position of "project manager" was created for the coordination of the large-scale projects which involved groups from different divisions. This function was not highly regarded. Some typical remarks by the members of the department were the following: "The staff doesn't realize that they're here only to help the line organization; this expansion of staff is due to overspecialization and civil service red tape." "A project manager is just an errand boy." People who accepted these positions were faced with a personal conflict in that they agreed with the line people that an engineer should work "on equipment" rather than "on paper." But once he became familiar with the requirements, the project manager replied, "They don't appreciate all the detailed work of coordination that a project manager has to do." Each project manager had a time schedule for every phase of his project. Many things could interfere with this schedule, as equipment and manpower were under the control of line supervisors who had time schedules of their own to meet. In an attempt to justify the staff role, and to force others to recognize the significance of the coordination function, the project managers demanded greater status and authority. Since many of them were from the service divisions, such attempts were interpreted by many people as a further wresting of authority from the research divisions. Thus, this attempt to coordinate the work of the divisions was resented by those who felt that they were losing prestige and power.

THE APPEARANCE OF FACTIONS

As a result of these changes there was confusion, since people could not decide how to divide their time and efforts. Conflicts among individuals and groups for services were common. The department management attempted to meet the change in Navy policy by minor internal changes, such as shifting the work of individuals and groups and transferring some small groups to the service divisions. The ideal of professional independence was being threatened by the demands of the naval bureau and attempts of local management to meet the new requirements. Control of basic policy and specific requirements was now more clearly located outside the department. Many of the older members of the department resented this. The major conflict within the department was between some older leaders and those who, for one reason or another, supported the new policy of emphasis upon equipment development. A number of factional splits appeared, the most striking of which was that between the "old guard" and the new leaders supporting development.

The "old-guard" faction wished to continue research in their fields of special interest. The strongest position, taken by a few, was that they were better qualified to establish goals than the "pencil pushers" in Washington. They regarded the new policy as unwarranted interference with scientific work.

The group supporting the change had a choice of several reasons for doing so. Firstly, they could be professionally interested in development rather than in research. Secondly, they could accept the naval bureau's right to set the policy of the department and their own duty to make the necessary changes. And thirdly, they could expect personal gains in rank, salary, and control of personnel in the new policy.

The leaders of the factions were at approximately the same level in the organization. Most of them were division heads and staff officials. But the equality of formal status did not lead to equal influence or authority. Leaders of the development faction had achieved their status only recently. Their rapid rise was due to a combination of ability, ambition, adaptability, loyalty to the organization, and support of the new organizational objectives. Leaders of the "old-guard" faction had long occupied their positions. Many of them had been in the laboratory since it was established. These "old-guard" leaders had, in the past, often conflicted with one another. They were forced together to oppose the new leaders. But even in coalition, they were overshadowed by the new leaders.

As these factions were developing, the department tried to meet the naval requirements within the existing structure. The department head had a long history of difficulties with the heads of the older divisions. In his attempt to satisfy his superiors, he tended to side with the development faction. In time, the agreement of this faction with the naval bureau allowed the faction to promote a reorganization of the department which destroyed the independence of the divisions and removed the most vociferous of the "old guard" from positions of power.

## THE STRUCTURAL CHANGE

The new organizational structure was proposed as a means of delimiting responsibilities and providing coordination for large-scale projects. It was a widespread opinion in the laboratory that the previous organizational structure could have been adapted to the new policy, and that the reorganization added greatly to the adjustments which all persons had to make to the new objectives. Furthermore, the policy change did not require all groups to change their activities. The change in structure was the result of the increased power of the development faction. It introduced a new set of positions to coordinate three divisions. These positions were taken by members of the development faction, who thereby gained control of the majority of the department's personnel. Two other divisions were given the functions of research and testing. The five divisions established in this reorganization were only in part a continuation of the previous five divisions.

The heads of these divisions and the new level of management were appointed by the department head, and the assignment of individuals to these groups proceeded. The composition of some work teams was not changed, although some modification of function was expected. For the majority of persons, however, assignment was in doubt for various reasons. No clear statement of the boundaries between research, development, and testing had been agreed upon. The members of this department have not been the first to find such definition difficult. But in this case there was another reason for conflict. In order to enhance the scope of his division and attract borderline individuals, each division head used the broadest definition possible. Everyone recognized that these definitions overlapped, but none of the division heads would limit his definition. The greatest conflict was between research and development. A number of persons went into the development group on the promise that they could continue their work, although its classification as development was questionable. The head of the newly established research division found himself with some of his former subordinates, a group previously attached to the department staff, and a few persons from other divisions.

Among the factors involved in the making of personnel assignments were the following:

1. The need to distribute "experts" throughout the organization; thus when two men were of approximately equal skill in a given field, if one of them chose to go to division R, the other was more or less forced to join division F.

2. The personal desires of division heads for certain men; many promises were made concerning future types of work.

3. Identification of the individuals to be relocated with a faction.

4. Expectations of higher status or increased authority by joining one division rather than another; while no promotions in rank could be made during the organizational change, promises of future promotions were a common way of winning over doubtful persons.

The final allocation of personnel demonstrated even more clearly the triumph of the development faction. Because of the broad definitions used and the changes in organizational goals, the scope of development expanded at the expense of other functions. While future requirements could not accurately be predicted, many people believed that this expansion was greater than that needed to meet the policy change.

The results of the structural changes were (1) to strengthen greatly and enlarge the development group; (2) to give the development group

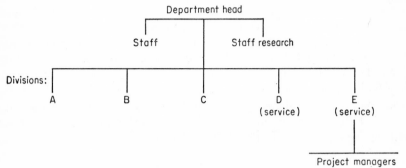

FIGURE 19-1. Organization in 1950.

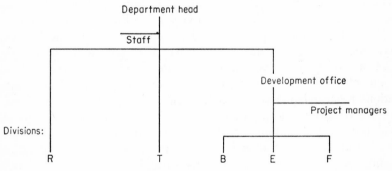

FIGURE 19-2. Organization in 1953.

a large measure of control over the testing group and its "old-guard" leader; (3) to set off the research group, under another "old-guard" leader, from the others with independent authority but greatly decreased personnel and funds. Thus the development faction, by its control of funds, personnel, and activities, became the central focus of the department. In 1952, Divisions C and D were combined into testing division (T). The structural changes of 1953 were as follows:

¶ Division A divided between research division (R) and new development division (F).

¶ B and E continued with few changes.

¶ Staff research joined research (R).

¶ Some members of T joined research (R).

¶ New level of management, development office, created and included project managers.

The new power situation was so strikingly different from that which had held in the past that the leaders and some members of defeated factions left the organization. They gave as their reasons for leaving that a vital function (theirs) was being disregarded, or that their groups could not properly perform their work without certain facilities (testing sites, equipment, etc.) which were now under the direction of others. Other persons left during or after the reorganization period because they did not want to go through the extensive readjustments necessary. A number of these people had been considering other positions, and they took this occasion to leave. A few of the men who left did so because they felt that the new policy did not allow them to do the work in which they were interested. Still others left because they did not wish to engage in the factional struggle.

ANALYSIS OF FACTIONS

The issues involved in this example of factionalism may be classified into three categories: objectives, in-group loyalties, and personal relationships. There was a pair of problems connected with the first category. One was the acceptance of the naval bureau's and station's right to set or modify objectives. Many of those who participated in the development of the original organizational objectives and in later modifications regarded themselves as the scientific experts best qualified to plan the department's program. The assertion of this authority by the naval bureau and station management was regarded as an unwanted intrusion in their realm of influence. Other members of the department accepted the naval bureau's authority to make these decisions and attempted to meet the modified objectives. Some of these people supported the new objectives because they thought that development was more important than research. Thus, there were two sources of disagreement: (1) who should set objectives; (2) which objectives were best. Either of these questions could bring individuals into a faction. Eight months after the structural change took place, 58 per cent of the department members felt that the department *should* be devoted to development rather than research, and 71 per cent of the department members felt that the department *would* emphasize development rather than research. Compared with those who chose research as the goal which the organization should pursue, those who preferred development were more confident of their ability to handle their positions and were interested in higher positions within the organization.

The second problem connected with objectives is that of the *personal* goals of the members of the department. In responding to a questionnaire each professional answered this question: "If you could achieve a wide reputation for just one thing, would you prefer to be known for: (a) a general research idea; (b) being a good fellow to work with; (c) developing useful equipment; (d) an original formula; (e) organizing the work of a successful group; or (f) applying a known principle to a new and important use?" It is interesting to compare these goals of individuals to their reference groups. Persons with reference groups outside the station tended to have pure and applied research goals (a, d, and f). With both reference groups and personal goals located outside the organization and its primary aims, these persons could hardly be expected to ally themselves with current organizational policy. In contrast, a significant proportion of persons whose reference group was within the station had supervisory goals (e), and those with their occupation as a reference group tended to have development goals (c). Persons in these last two groups might be expected to identify with the organization and its current objectives, but for different reasons. Personal goals also varied with position: the lower levels of professionals had more pure research goals (a and d); middle levels had more applied research and development goals (c and f); and higher levels had more supervisory and research goals (a, d, e, and f). The interpersonal goal (b) was chosen by only 4 per cent of the professionals.

The second category of issues arising from factionalism is that of in-group loyalty. In the laboratory, work teams attempted to protect their membership and functions from the inroads of others. This was seen in the conflicts which arose about the allocation of responsibility and personnel for specific projects. It occasionally took the form of failure to cooperate with other groups. Communication between work teams was often difficult and sometimes broke down completely. On the whole, work teams were kept intact when structural changes were made, because of a feeling that the team members should remain together if possible. Some time before the reorganization described here occurred, two divisions were combined. However, no attempt was made to redistribute members; rather, the component branches remained separate. There was some antagonism between the component groups. Later, at the time of the major structural change, one division was divided between two of the newly created divisions. Many supervisors objected to the breaking up of their groups, and when possible, the sections of a branch were kept intact in the transfer. In theory, the reorganization should have involved a similar segmentation of another division, but in-group loyalty and compromises made in the definition of functions allowed the entire division to be included in the development group. When a supervisor transferred to another division, many of his subordinates accompanied him. The branch heads, though interested, did not all take strong positions in the dispute, and many tried to keep their personnel out of the struggle. One branch head told us, "I held a meeting in my branch and explained the reorganization as well as I could. I suggested that they talk to anyone they like about it, and decide what they wanted to do. Then when I had another meeting some weeks later, none of them had decided. They asked me what I wanted them to do, while I had tried to get them to decide for themselves."

The third category of issues is that of personal relationships. Many people found in the department, but not in their work groups, former schoolmates, neighbors, bridge partners, car-pool members, fellow members of clubs, sportsmen, etc. By their participation in these groups some people were influenced in their choice of assignment. Our analysis of observational records, interviews, and sociometric responses shows that this participation was sometimes a decisive factor.

Hence, each person was influenced by his attitude toward the objectives of the organization, by his group loyalties, and by his personal relationships. Some persons had little difficulty in deciding which group they preferred. For others, their affiliations resulted in conflict. Their final decision was based upon the superior strength of certainties. For example, one section head preferred research work and had ties with others in research, but joined development because of the pressure applied by higher management and because of his friendship with a branch head in the development group.

The factional split was based upon clash of attitudes and beliefs of different kinds. Some of the attitudes and beliefs were probably acquired in the professional schools. Still others developed from the separate interests of the five original divisions. While diverse attitudes about the purpose of the organization, or of parts of it, could exist as long as the parts remained somewhat independent, the need for a unified organization brought these differences into conflict. In the course of the conflict, new leaders, who were not loyal to the "old guard" or to the old way of doing things, could succeed. If there had been in the department a general willingness to accept the new objectives and modify behavior accordingly, the structural changes might have been unnecessary. Authority could have been more equitably distributed among the former leaders. In addition to the desired effect of bringing about greater coordination, a job first attempted by the project managers, the reorganization had the further effect of making many individuals so uncomfortable in their new positions that they left. Some persons who increased their status as a result of the change left within the year to accept positions in other organizations which promised less strain and conflict.

CONCLUSION

The process of change in this laboratory has been shown in three phases:

1. From 1946 to 1952 the department was a relatively stable group in which divergent objectives and activities were pursued.

2. The imposition, from outside, of new demands on the organization required the modification of organizational objectives and the increased coordination of activities. At first, minor changes were made. However, the modification of objectives and the rising importance of different functions and activities threatened the power and independence of older groups. These changes were resisted by the older groups for a variety of reasons.

3. A structural reorganization, proposed as a more efficient way of achieving the new objectives, resulted in grealy increased power for one faction, and the resignation of some former leaders.

The differences of objectives within the organization were of minor importance while the subgroups were relatively autonomous. But as the organizational requirements changed, these differences became the basis of sharply conflicting factions. A faction composed of leaders of former service groups rose to power. This faction, in agreement with external authority, became strong enough to promote a structural reorganization and thereby further increase its power. The "old-guard" group had to change their activities to some extent. But their greatest loss, and the one to which they objected most, was their loss in power and independence. Thus their professional interests were combined with their feelings about the organization and their positions in it.

The official explanation for the reorganization was that it would better meet the current objectives. This explanation was accepted by the station and by the naval bureau. But an analysis of events and attitudes within the organization suggests that the modification of objectives and need for coordination were conditions which brought the underlying differences into conflict. The factions, rather than the policy, appeared to produce the organizational change.

CHAPTER 20

# Problems of Evaluation: The Impact
# of Interpersonal Relations on Ratings of Performance*

Many administrative decisions, of necessity, are based upon evaluations of performance. These evaluations, involving judgments concerning individuals or groups, are usually formalized as performance ratings. Some factors which influence performance ratings, such as the "halo effect," "errors in central tendency," and "judgments of leniency," have been identified,[1] and various methods have been proposed to reduce the effect of these factors. Few studies, however, have directly investigated the effect of the interpersonal relationship between the superior and his subordinates upon the former's ratings of the latter's performances.

The formulation of valid, reliable criteria of effectiveness in a research and development setting is particularly complex and raises a number of problems. An approach to this evaluation problem was made in May, 1952, when a day-long invitational conference of leading research administrators was held on the UCLA campus. This conference was largely devoted to eliciting those criteria which research administrators actually use in evaluating the work of their subordinates or

* This chapter is a slight modification of "The Impact of Interpersonal Relations on Ratings of Performance," by Verne J. Kallejian, Paula Brown, and Irving R. Weschler, Public Personnel Review, vol. 14, no. 4, pp. 166–170, October, 1953. This journal is published by the Public Personnel Association, which has granted permission for our use of the indicated article.
[1] For a discussion of some of these factors, see Donald G. Paterson, "Rating," in D. H. Fryer and E. R. Henry (eds.), Handbook of Applied Psychology (New York: Rinehart & Company, Inc., 1950), vol. 1, p. 153. For a different critical investigation of the rating process, see Irving R. Weschler, Fred Massarik, and Robert Tannenbaum, "Experimenting with Federal Efficiency Ratings: A Case Study," Journal of Social Psychology, vol. 36, pp. 205–222, 1952.

subunits. Unfortunately, few criteria emerged which can be described as objective.[2] Analysis of the conference proceedings supported the following conclusions:

1. At present, evaluation of performance is based primarily upon the subjective judgments of "competent individuals."

2. A wide variety of characteristics of performance are used in the evaluation of research and development.

3. There is no substantial agreement as to which of these characteristics is most valid in evaluating performance, nor are the circumstances specified which favor the use of one criterion as against another.

A PRELIMINARY FIELD STUDY

In order to examine these conclusions in a field setting, a preliminary study was undertaken to determine what characteristics of performance superiors actually use in evaluating their units, and to determine what conditions, if any, favor the use of one characteristic as against another.[3] One department of the research and development laboratory was studied. At the time of the investigation, this department consisted of approximately 425 people, organized in five divisions, each of which was subdivided into four or five independently functioning branches. Some of these branches were in turn subdivided into sections.

The superiors in this department rated the groups they supervise in terms of their *over-all effectiveness of performance*. Next, they were asked to state what criteria of performance they used in arriving at these over-all ratings. Then, the raters were presented with a list of *seventeen specific characteristics of performance* (such as general technical competence of personnel in the group, communications within the group, administrative competence of the group leader, quantity of work accomplished, etc.), and were asked to rate their units again, independently, on each of these. Each item was defined and explained to the subjects. A scale ranging from 0 (very poor performance) to 10 (outstanding performance) was used. These ratings are referred to as the "actual ratings." Finally, the supervisors were asked to indicate the relative importance they attached to each of the items. The following findings emerged:

[2] See Irving R. Weschler and Paula Brown (eds.), *Evaluating Research and Development*, Human Relations Research Group, Institute of Industrial Relations, University of California, Los Angeles, 1953 (annotated proceedings of a conference of research administrators held at the University of California, Los Angeles, on May 10, 1952). See also Chapter 18.

[3] A more detailed description of this research can be found in Weschler and Brown (eds.), *ibid.*, pp. 87–94.

1. The criteria of performance which superiors stated they had actually used in the over-all evaluation of the groups they supervise can be readily grouped into four major categories: output, skills, supervision, and group variables (morale, cooperation, accepting group objectives). Within each of these categories, however, there is no significant agreement as to which specific characteristics are to be emphasized.

2. The ratings on the seventeen characteristics of performance show some agreement as to the importance or lack of importance of certain specific items. Superiors at all levels within the department placed emphasis on four items: general technical competence of the personnel in the group, proper utilization of the personnel, technical competence of the head, and effectiveness of the head as a leader. There was a tendency to minimize the importance of such factors as planning, scheduling, and control procedures, systematic work methods, potential for group "growth," and conformity of the product to specifications.

3. The reliability of ratings, in those cases where two or more individuals rated the same groups on the seventeen items, ranged from $-0.60$ to $+0.94$. This range was to be expected in view of the lack of agreement concerning the relative importance of specific characteristics in evaluating performance. The effect of this divergence of attitudes is also reflected in a lack of agreement with regard to the over-all ratings of performance, in those cases where two or more superiors rated the same groups.

## A CLINICAL INVESTIGATION OF THE RATING PROCESS

The results from the preliminary study clearly indicate that the evaluation of performance is subject to wide individual variation. This finding suggests that the problems associated with ratings of performance might profitably be studied in much the same way as other instances of interpersonal judgments. Since few guidelines exist for the evaluation of performance in research and development settings, it is likely that situational and interpersonal factors operate to influence ratings of performance. Considerable evidence is available which indicates that, particularly in ambiguous situations, the personality characteristics of the judge are also important determinants of his evaluations.[4]

One division of the department in which the preliminary study had been conducted was selected for further investigation. This division contained five branches, four of which had two or more sections.

[4] See J. S. Bruner, "Personality Dynamics and the Process of Perceiving," in Robert R. Blake and Glenn V. Ramsey (eds.), *Perception, An Approach to Personality* (New York: The Ronald Press Company, 1951).

A clinically skilled interviewer, who had no previous contact with the laboratory or the data obtained in the preliminary study, interviewed members of subordinate groups regarding their relationships with coworkers and superiors. After the interviews with subordinates, the interviewer formulated a diagnostic personality evaluation of the superiors who rated each group. From this personality evaluation of the superior and the interviewer's obtained knowledge of the group and the leader of the group being evaluated, he then attempted to predict the superior's actual ratings for the group. These are called "predictive ratings." They were made for the over-all ratings of performance as well as for all the seventeen specific characteristics of performance. The actual ratings of eleven superiors were predicted in this way. In addition, the interviewer gave his own impressions of each group by completing a set of "evaluative ratings."

Thirty-two people were interviewed. These included every member of two sections in each of two branches, all the branch heads and their assistants, and the division head and his assistant. The fifty-minute interviews were conducted in a private office at the laboratory and were recorded. The subjects were assured that the interviewer had no official connection with the laboratory and that no one at the laboratory would have access to any information obtained during the interview. After interviewing the subordinates of a given group, the predictive and evaluative ratings were completed and an interview was held with the group's superior.

The evaluative ratings made by the interviewer were primarily based upon his evaluation of variables found within the group itself, i.e., the maturity and adjustment of the subordinate leader (e.g., the section head), the effectiveness of each leader-subordinate relationship, the general level of job satisfaction and morale, and the degree of cooperative effort among members of the group. The interviewer based his judgments primarily on interpersonal factors and was not acquainted with the technical work.

The predictive ratings were based upon three classes of variables, i.e., the personality characteristics of the superior making the rating, his relationship with the persons being rated, and situational factors. The following assumptions served as a basis for the formulation of these predictive ratings:

1. Superiors will react to, and place greater importance on, those characteristics of performance which are related to their personal needs.

2. The quality of the relationship between the superior and the subordinate is a determinant of the superior's perception of that subordinate's performance. Those individuals who behave in such a way as to satisfy the personal needs of the superior will generally be rated higher.

Those subordinates who interfere with the satisfaction of the personal needs of the superior will generally be rated lower. The specific ratings of superiors are likely to be determined by the more global, conscious or unconscious reactions to subordinates.

3. Superiors will be differentially influenced by the following situational factors: the actual performance itself, the nature of the rating task, the organizational setting (e.g., the structure of the work group, the attitudes and interests of higher echelons of management, the mission of the laboratory). Effects of these influences are reflected in the performance ratings.

The interviews were structured to obtain the information necessary to evaluate these variables. Some of the factors which were investigated included a consideration of the extent to which the following conditions were true:

1. Subordinates had favorable reactions to the superior.

2. Subordinates felt that the superior is aware of the effect which he has on the group.

3. The superior followed a consistent behavior pattern in dealing with his group.

4. The superior was able to adapt his behavior to the different personality characteristics of individuals in the group.

5. The superior was perceived as being aware of the needs of his subordinates.

6. Subordinates felt that they understood the objectives established by their superiors.

7. Subordinates felt that they have contributed to decisions relevant to their particular jobs.

8. Subordinates were aware of the relationship between their objectives, the objectives of the next higher unit, and the over-all mission of the laboratory.

9. Subordinates felt at ease in discussing their problems, personal and technical, with their superior.

10. Subordinates felt that differences in opinion between their superiors and themselves are expressed, understood, and accepted.

11. Subordinates felt that the attainment of objectives, as they saw them, was worthwhile.

12. Subordinates were willing to supplement each other's skills and knowledge.

13. Subordinates felt satisfied with their own performance in relation to the over-all objectives.

14. Subordinates were aware of the superior's attitudes toward the performance of the group.

15. Job satisfaction and morale were related to actual job activities, rather than to other aspects of the work situation, such as location and civil service employment.

When the interview protocols concerning various superiors were analyzed, sharp contrasts appeared in the way in which subordinates reacted to their superiors. For example, the following remarks made by various subordinates all describe superior A:

¶ He gives orders indiscriminately and changes them without notice.
¶ I talk to him as little as possible.
¶ He may know his job, but we pay a high price to get it done.
¶ I'm not sure he really knows what we are doing.
¶ I don't think he knows my name.
¶ I never ask questions, and he rarely asks for my opinion.
¶ Even if something is really wrong with work based on his orders, I have a tough time convincing him.
¶ For a long time he would give orders to my group without telling me.
¶ I don't think he respects anyone around here.

A similar set of subordinate responses for superior B follows:

¶ It's a real pleasure working for him.
¶ He doesn't always do the things I like, but I respect his judgment.
¶ He is the best man around.
¶ I think other people may know more than he does, but he knows how to help you think through a problem.
¶ If anything goes wrong, I know I can tell him about it and he'll look into it.
¶ He is easy to talk to.
¶ I think he knows everything that goes on.
¶ He keeps on top of the operation.

From an analysis of all the interview material relating to superior A, it was concluded that he was relatively unaware of his effect upon subordinates. His primary concern was with production and the promotion of his own ideas. He discouraged initiative among his subordinates and considered almost any deviation from his orders as a personal insult. He was very little concerned with the welfare of his subordinates and bolstered his own insecurities by maintaining rigid control, primarily by withholding information and depreciating the efforts of his subordinates. When predicting the ratings for superior A, it was relatively easy to determine what characteristics of performance he would consider important and what factors would influence the level of his ratings.

The ratings for superior B were more difficult to predict. From interviews with his subordinates it was possible to conclude that he was conscious of his effect upon people and also seemed to be aware of the needs of his subordinates. He actually delegated responsibility and encouraged his subordinates to communicate freely with him. He seemed concerned about maximizing the performance of each subordinate and promoting cooperative efforts toward common goals. Subordinates in his group were aware of what was going on and where they fitted into the total activity. It was concluded that superior B would evaluate his subordinates in much the same way as an impartial observer. Thus, in this instance, the interviewer's predictive ratings were not greatly different from his evaluative ratings. For superior B, the interviewer's predictions were not as accurate with regard to the technical items, since B's ratings on these items were less influenced by interpersonal factors.

The following illustrations show how many of these conclusions were substantiated by interviews with the superiors themselves after the evaluative and predictive ratings had been made. Consider these edited samples of two interviews with superiors A and B. First, superior A:

INTERVIEWER: Tell me about Joe White.
SUPERIOR A: He is a good worker, fast, a good engineer.
INTERVIEWER: Is there anything else about him you consider important to keep in mind as his supervisor?
SUPERIOR A: No, he has had good training.
INTERVIEWER: How do you get along with him?
SUPERIOR A: All right. He doesn't give me any trouble.
INTERVIEWER: You mentioned Jim Blue. How about him?
SUPERIOR A: He is a slow worker. He is working on a new job, and always griping about something. As an engineer, he is fair.
INTERVIEWER: What sort of person is he?
SUPERIOR A: What do you mean?
INTERVIEWER: Well, what is he like as a person?
SUPERIOR A: Oh, I guess he is all right.
INTERVIEWER: How about John Black?
SUPERIOR A: He is a good man.

Next, a comparable interchange with superior B:

INTERVIEWER: Tell me about Bill Green.
SUPERIOR B: He is coming along rather well. Some of the others don't quite understand his temperament. He is methodical. I try to give him jobs that require care and precision, and try to keep him away from work that requires a lot of decisions or new methods. He is very stable and consistent in his work. It took me a long time to learn that he needs time to think out an answer. Some people think he doesn't know very much because he is quiet. I ask him to give his reports in written form, and I pass them around. This has helped a lot.
INTERVIEWER: Anything else?
SUPERIOR B: Well, I could tell you a lot about him personally, his background and family.

INTERVIEWER: How about Frank Brown?

SUPERIOR B: He is a key man in the group. He is well liked by the other people. If I can get him interested in a project, the others seem to go along. Things were a little strained for a while as he wanted a promotion and I couldn't get it for him, but he knows I'm trying, so that's disappeared. He needs to ask questions and talk over every aspect of the problem before he feels comfortable about going ahead. I usually bring the group together when we start something new and his questions stimulate the others to do a lot of thinking.

INTERVIEWER: Anything else?

SUPERIOR B: He's been having some trouble. I suspect it's financial. Sometimes he slows down for a week or two. I leave him alone, and he pulls out of it.

In comparing these two sample interviews, the differences in personality, which were already brought out in the interviews with the subordinates, were dramatically substantiated in a number of ways. Superior A seems to have little, if any, awareness of the personality differences between subordinates, while superior B thinks in terms of relationships and personalities. Superior A sees people primarily as engineers with certain work habits, while superior B is able to differentiate "engineers" by personal characteristics. Also, superior A talks as though his reactions are determined exclusively by the nature of the subordinate. Superior B, on the other hand, is aware that some of his reactions are determined by his own personality make-up rather than by the characteristics of his subordinates, and he is aware of his effect upon subordinates.

## RESULTS AND CONCLUSIONS

The interviewer's predictive ratings, when compared with the superiors' actual ratings with regard to *over-all effectiveness of performance,* were accurate at the 3 per cent level of confidence.[5] With the exception of one case, the predictions were thus accurate in terms of relative rankings of groups, the amount of difference between groups, and their absolute standing on the rating scale.

The interviewer's predictive ratings, when compared with the superiors' actual ratings with regard to the *seventeen specific characteristics of performance,* were accurate at the 5 per cent level of confidence.[6]

It was also found that there was a much closer relationship between the interviewer's predictive ratings and the superiors' actual ratings

[5] Determined by point binomial for the number of correct predictions.

[6] Determined by product-moment correlation.

than between the interviewer's evaluative ratings and the superiors' actual ratings. Thus, the predictive ratings were accurate not only when they coincided with the evaluative ratings, but also when they failed to coincide.

*On the basis of these results, we conclude that the interviewer was able to account for a significant portion of the variance of performance ratings on the basis of his clinical evaluation of personal, interpersonal, and situational factors.*

The personality characteristics of the superior which influence his ratings consist of those attitudes and personal needs that determine the way he sees himself and responds to the world around him. The components of the relationship between superior and subordinate which affect the superior's ratings are, for example, tensions, likes, and dislikes. Among the situational variables which influence performance ratings are the actual performance itself, the nature of the rating task, and the organizational setting.

Most superiors are unaware of the factors which reduce the validity of their performance ratings. Their recognition of these factors should result in more objective judgments of individuals and groups. In addition, individuals whose administrative decisions are based upon performance ratings would do well also to recognize the limitations of this kind of information as a basis for action.

# CHAPTER 21

# Assessing Organizational Effectiveness: Job Satisfaction, Productivity, and Morale*

As part of a larger project on the role of interpersonal relations in a local naval research laboratory, an attempt was made to determine the relationship between job satisfaction, perceived productivity, and perceived morale in two comparable divisions of the laboratory.

Two divisions of the same department, A and B, with twenty-eight and thirty-eight members respectively, were studied. The two divisions differed from one another in the style of leadership under which they operated and in the "atmosphere" which appeared to prevail in each. Division A, the smaller of the two, was headed by a brilliant young scientist, who directed the division along restrictive lines. Division B was headed by an older man, a fatherly type, who directed his division along permissive lines. The employees in these two divisions were physicists, engineers, and scientific aides, with supporting clerical personnel.

All subjects from these two divisions, who participated primarily in an intensive sociometric investigation,[1] were also asked (1) to indicate their level of job satisfaction, their work group, and their *perception* of the level of productivity and of morale of their own work group, of their division, and of the laboratory as a whole, and (2) to specify their choices for leaders in research, administration, and popularity for the two divisions, as well as for the laboratory.

The sociometric portion of the questionnaire focused attention on interpersonal relationships in a number of activities—both job-oriented (e.g., efficiency rating, order giving, advice and assistance in work) and

* This chapter is a slight modification of "Job Satisfaction, Productivity and Morale," by Irving R. Weschler, Murray Kahane, and Robert Tannenbaum, *Occupational Psychology*, vol. 26, no. 1, pp. 1–14, January, 1952.
[1] See Chap. 22.

non-job-oriented (e.g., eating lunch together, socializing after working hours). Intensive interviews with the respective division heads, their superiors, and administrative assistants, as well as with key staff people, provided clues about the internal operations as well as about the effect of differing leadership styles upon the productivity, morale, and job satisfaction of these two divisions.

BASIC FINDINGS

*Job satisfaction* referred to the individual's personal satisfaction with his position, as evaluated by himself on a five-point scale, from "very high" (scale value 1) to "very low" (scale value 5) (see Table 21-1). In division B, headed by the permissive leader, 63.2 per cent of the members considered themselves satisfied with their position, as compared with only 39.3 per cent of the members in division A, headed by the restrictive leader. (Satisfied members included all those who rated themselves either as "very well satisfied" or "well satisfied" with their positions; that is, those who rated their job satisfaction either 1 or 2.)

With regard to *productivity,* all subjects were asked to evaluate the level of productivity of their own work group, of their division, and of the laboratory as a whole. In a scientific organization the evaluation of productivity represents a difficult and still more or less unsolved problem. Intangible, unstandardized mental "products" lend themselves to evaluation much less readily than do tangible, standardized physical products. In the former case, evaluation criteria (standards) are difficult to define, performance is difficult to measure, and a comparison of performance with standard is difficult to make.

In view of the above, *ratings of productivity* at present represent as meaningful an alternative device as can be found. All individuals in the two divisions were asked to rate the productivity of their own work group, of their division, and of the laboratory as a whole.

As far as the individual's perception of his work group was concerned, the following points should be noted. The smallest operating unit at the laboratory is a group; several groups make up a section; several sections a branch; a few branches a division; several divisions a department; and a few departments, plus supporting smaller service units, the laboratory. Although the organizational chart places people at a specific level in the organization as related to their formal positions, the individuals concerned did not always identify themselves with these organizational units.

The findings indicate (see Table 21-1) that the majority of individuals in both divisions rated the productivity of their perceived work groups as above average; that is, 57.1 per cent in division A and 57.8 per cent in division B viewed the productivity of their perceived work groups as either "very high" or "high" (scale value 1 or 2). In evaluating the productivity of their respective divisions, 55.2 per cent in division B considered its productivity above average, as compared with 28.6 per cent in division A. Finally, the productivity of the laboratory as a whole was rated above average by 26.3 per cent of the members of division B, as compared with 7.1 per cent in division A.

The determination of *morale* for the various work groups, for the divisions, and for the laboratory as a whole represented another difficult

TABLE 21-1. JOB SATISFACTION, PERCEIVED PRODUCTIVITY, AND PERCEIVED MORALE (DIVISIONS A AND B)

| Division | Job satisfaction | | Perceived productivity | | | | | | Perceived morale | | | | | |
|---|---|---|---|---|---|---|---|---|---|---|---|---|---|---|
| | | | Work group | | Division | | Laboratory | | Work group | | Division | | Laboratory | |
| | Per cent | No. | Per cent | No. | Per cent | No. | Per cent | No. | Per cent | No. | Per cent | No. | Per cent | No. |
| **A:** | | | | | | | | | | | | | | |
| Very high (1) | 21.4 | 6 | 7.1 | 2 | 3.6 | 1 | 0.0 | 0 | 10.7 | 3 | 0.0 | 0 | 0.0 | 0 |
| High (2) | 17.9 | 5 | 50.0 | 14 | 25.0 | 7 | 7.1 | 2 | 25.0 | 7 | 21.4 | 6 | 7.1 | 2 |
| Average (3) | 42.8 | 12 | 28.6 | 8 | 32.1 | 9 | 39.3 | 11 | 35.7 | 10 | 21.4 | 6 | 28.6 | 8 |
| Low (4) | 10.7 | 3 | 3.6 | 1 | 10.7 | 3 | 25.0 | 7 | 17.9 | 5 | 35.7 | 10 | 53.6 | 15 |
| Very low (5) | 3.6 | 1 | 0.0 | 0 | 17.9 | 5 | 7.1 | 2 | 0.0 | 0 | 17.9 | 5 | 3.6 | 1 |
| Other (−) | 3.6 | 1 | 10.7 | 3 | 10.7 | 3 | 21.5 | 6 | 10.7 | 3 | 3.6 | 1 | 7.1 | 2 |
| Total | 100.0 | 28 | 100.0 | 28 | 100.0 | 28 | 100.0 | 28 | 100.0 | 28 | 100.0 | 28 | 100.0 | 28 |
| **B:** | | | | | | | | | | | | | | |
| Very high (1) | 18.5 | 7 | 13.1 | 5 | 13.1 | 5 | 2.6 | 1 | 23.7 | 9 | 26.3 | 10 | 2.6 | 1 |
| High (2) | 44.7 | 17 | 44.7 | 17 | 42.1 | 16 | 23.7 | 9 | 57.9 | 22 | 55.3 | 21 | 34.2 | 13 |
| Average (3) | 26.3 | 10 | 29.1 | 11 | 31.6 | 12 | 44.7 | 17 | 10.5 | 4 | 15.8 | 6 | 50.0 | 19 |
| Low (4) | 5.3 | 2 | 2.6 | 1 | 5.3 | 2 | 7.9 | 3 | 5.3 | 2 | 2.6 | 1 | 5.3 | 2 |
| Very low (5) | 2.6 | 1 | 2.6 | 1 | 2.6 | 1 | 5.3 | 2 | 0.0 | 0 | 0.0 | 0 | 0.0 | 0 |
| Other (−) | 2.6 | 1 | 7.9 | 3 | 5.3 | 2 | 15.8 | 6 | 2.6 | 1 | 0.0 | 0 | 7.9 | 3 |
| Total | 100.0 | 38 | 100.0 | 38 | 100.0 | 38 | 100.0 | 38 | 100.0 | 38 | 100.0 | 38 | 100.0 | 38 |

problem. Most of the so-called objective indicators of morale, such as absenteeism, employee turnover, or spoilage, do not provide the kind of needed information. Although these variables appear related to what may be identified as morale, the nature of the relationship is still too obscure to permit meaningful interpretations.

In a doctoral dissertation, Bernberg[2] noted that the collective rating of a group of employees concerning their own morale was the most meaningful single variable related to various other criteria of morale. In our investigation, the subjects were asked to rate the "level of morale"

[2] R. E. Bernberg, *An Objective Analysis of Some of the Socio-psychological Factors in Industrial Morale,* unpublished doctoral dissertation, University of California, Los Angeles, 1950.

of their group, of their division, and of the laboratory on a five-step scale, from "very high" (scale value 1) to "very low" (scale value 5). Although the specific interpretation of the concept "morale" was left to each individual as he saw it, the question implied a group concept as distinguished from individual job satisfaction.

Since the classic studies of Lewin, Lippitt, and White,[3] evidence has accumulated to show that permissively led groups tend to have higher morale over the long run than restrictively led groups. In this instance (see Table 21-1), 81.6 per cent of the members in division B

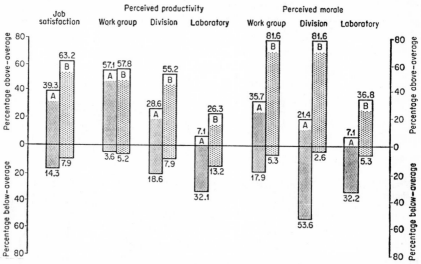

FIGURE 21-1. Bar chart comparing above-average [very high (1) and high (2)] ratings with percentage below-average [low (4) and very low (5)] ratings for job satisfaction, perceived productivity, and perceived morale (divisions A and B).

(permissive), as compared with 35.7 per cent in division A (restrictive), perceived the morale of their work groups as either "very high" or "high." In evaluating the morale of their respective divisions, 81.6 per cent of division B and only 21.4 per cent of division A provided above-average ratings. As far as the perception of the morale of the laboratory as a whole was concerned, the difference in above-average ratings of 36.8 per cent in division B and 7.1 per cent in division A was also significant.

The data which have been reported with regard to job satisfaction, perceived productivity, and perceived morale can best be viewed with the aid of Figure 21-1. This diagram not only compares the two divi-

[3] K. Lewin, R. Lippitt, and R. K. White, "Patterns of Aggressive Behavior in Experimentally Created Social Climates," *Journal of Social Psychology*, vol. 10, pp. 271–299, 1939.

sions with respect to their above-average ratings (scale values 1 and 2) on all these variables, but it also shows meaningful differences with regard to their below-average ratings (scale values 4 and 5). In summary, with one exception (perceived productivity, work group), the members of division B provided the higher ratings. With regard to productivity and morale, both divisions rated their work groups as highest, as compared with their respective divisions or the laboratory as a whole.

There is no evidence that the productivity and morale of the laboratory, as viewed by competent observers, are lower than those of either of the two divisions. It seems, therefore, that organizational distance— that is, the number of levels between the individual's perceived work group and various other, higher echelons—is inversely related to ratings of perceived productivity and morale. Thus, people generally tend to have a more favorable opinion of groups to which they psychologically belong.

RATINGS OF SUPERIORS

The data which have so far been reported concerned themselves with the job satisfaction, productivity, and morale *perceptions* of the members of both divisions. These data are largely subjective and reflect the individual employees' experiences, hopes, and aspirations.

In order to get a more objective appraisal which would permit a critical comparison of these two divisions, intensive interviews were held individually with five superiors and two staff people, all familiar with the objectives and performance of both divisions.

At the beginning of the interviews, the above seven informants were asked to fill out five-step rating scales concerning the job satisfaction, productivity, and morale of the two divisions, the answers to which served as steppingstones to the discussion which followed. Although these ratings covered many of the identical dimensions that were rated by the individual division members themselves, it should be noted that the situation provided a different set of stimuli. The superiors found it difficult, for instance, to distinguish between job satisfaction and morale—something which was not too difficult for the individual division members. To remedy this situation, the respondents were told that the job-satisfaction rating was to reflect their evaluation of the job satisfaction for all individuals combined in each division, while morale was to refer to the functioning and *esprit de corps* of each group as a whole. As far as productivity was concerned, they were asked to give their evaluation of the effectiveness of each division in meeting the objectives of the laboratory.

The average ratings of these key superiors and staff people showed some similarity to the ratings of the division members themselves (see Table 21-2). Again, the job satisfaction and morale ratings were considerably lower for division A, the restrictive group, than for division B, the permissive group. On the other hand, with regard to productivity, division A rated slightly higher than division B.

It is interesting to compare more fully the ratings of these seven key persons with the collective ratings of each division on the three variables under discussion. With regard to the restrictively led division A, the superiors underestimated the job satisfaction of the individual members, but rated higher by a wide margin the level of productivity. There was

TABLE 21-2. COMPARISON OF MEAN RATINGS ON JOB SATISFACTION, PRODUCTIVITY, AND MORALE OF SEVEN KEY STAFF PERSONNEL AND ALL DIVISION MEMBERS (DIVISIONS A AND B)

| Division | Job satisfaction | | | | Productivity | | | | Morale | | | |
|---|---|---|---|---|---|---|---|---|---|---|---|---|
| | Staff personnel | | Division members | | Staff personnel | | Division members | | Staff personnel | | Division members | |
| | Mean | S.D. | Mean | S.D. | Mean | S.D. | Mean | S.D. | Mean | S.D. | Mean | S.D. |
| A | 3.29 | 0.78 | 2.46 | 1.12 | 2.71 | 0.78 | 3.22 | 1.17 | 3.43 | 0.24 | 3.42 | 1.08 |
| B | 2.43 | 0.24 | 2.27 | 0.92 | 2.86 | 0.12 | 2.37 | 0.90 | 2.00 | 0.86 | 1.95 | 0.72 |

no difference in the evaluation of the level of morale. In the permissively led division B, the superiors underrated somewhat the level of job satisfaction, to a considerable extent the level of productivity, and to less extent the level of morale.

The findings with regard to productivity were especially significant. If the standards set by the superiors can be considered as meaningful criteria, then division A was performing an adequate job in spite of the restrictive leadership, a better job, as a matter of fact, than the group gave itself credit for. On the other hand, the superiors rated the performance of division B considerably poorer than the division members did.

The intensive interviews with the seven key individuals, as well as with the two division heads and their administrative assistants, provided part of the answer for these discrepancies. The interviews placed special emphasis on such topics as the nature of leadership in research organizations, the establishment of criteria for effective scientific work, and the determination of productivity in this type of setting.

Both division heads exercised considerable influence in determining objectives for their respective divisions. It appeared that the objectives which the superiors assumed for division A were more or less identical with those set by division head A, who was able to lead his group in that direction in spite of low morale and job satisfaction. However, the objectives set by division head B did not correspond too closely with those assumed by his superiors. He thus utilized the services of a high-morale group and of satisfied people in the performance of tasks which his superiors did not consider of highest importance to the laboratory.

## RELATIONSHIP BETWEEN KEY VARIABLES

Inspection of the ratings which have so far been reported suggests the existence of certain relationships which are due either to a "halo" effect in the raters' perceptions or to other variables yet to be determined. The Survey Research Center of the University of Michigan has conducted research at various industrial establishments on the relationship between job satisfaction, productivity, and morale.[4] Their investigations at the Prudential Insurance Company, the Detroit Edison Company, and the Chesapeake & Ohio Railroad have yielded numerous valuable findings, some of which may be directly relevant to this study.

One of the most important hypotheses which has been largely substantiated by the Michigan group holds that high productivity is not necessarily a function of job satisfaction or morale.[5] If we distinguish between organizational goals and personal goals, then those people who find satisfaction of their own personal needs by meeting the goals of the organization for which they work are more likely to be highly productive. It is, however, possible for people to be satisfied with their jobs although they contribute little toward meeting the goals of their organization. It is also possible for a group of employees to have high morale because they are able to accomplish important group goals, although these are not necessarily related to productivity. Thus, a unit which has been striving to set a community chest record may get its gratifications through this type of success rather than through a spectacular showing in productivity.

There may be many other factors which account for negligible correlations between job satisfaction, productivity, and morale. Each situation must be examined separately before any causal relationships can be inferred.

In this study we shall first look at the relationship between job satis-

[4] Institute for Social Research, University of Michigan, *Human Relations Program of the Survey Research Center: First Three Years of Development*, September, 1950.
[5] D. Katz, *Morale and Motivation in Industry*, Survey Research Center, University of Michigan, 1949. Mimeographed.

faction and perceived productivity. The data at hand show low or even negative correlations for division A and moderate correlations for division B, providing support for the contention that these two variables are not necessarily related (see Table 21-3).

In division A, the low negative correlation between job satisfaction and perceived work-group productivity permits some interesting speculations. The distribution of ratings for job satisfaction followed a more or less normal curve (see Table 21-1), while the productivity ratings were considerably skewed toward the favorable end of the distribution. Thus, the explanation suggests itself that a relatively high level of

TABLE 21-3. CORRELATION BETWEEN PERCEIVED PRODUCTIVITY AND JOB SATISFACTION (DIVISIONS A AND B)

| | Perceived productivity | | | | | | | | |
|---|---|---|---|---|---|---|---|---|---|
| | Work group | | | Division | | | Laboratory | | |
| | Div. A | Div. B | C.R. A vs. B | Div. A | Div. B | C.R. A vs. B | Div. A | Div. B | C.R. A vs. B |
| Job satisfaction.. | −0.08 | 0.67 | $t = 3.26$ $p < 0.01$ | 0.44 | 0.57 | $t = 0.62$ $p$ not significant | 0.13 | 0.46 | $t = 1.27$ $p$ not significant |

perceived productivity can emerge in spite of the pressures and strains created by a restrictive leadership. At the division level, ratings of job satisfaction tended to be more closely related to ratings of productivity, accounting for the somewhat higher correlation. At the laboratory level, the low correlation between job satisfaction and productivity was due primarily to the poor evaluation of the laboratory's productivity.

In division B, the moderate correlations between job satisfaction and productivity can be accounted for as follows: the distribution of job satisfaction ratings was skewed toward the favorable end of the scale; that is, most division members indicated a liking for their job. At the same time, those people who were satisfied tended to have a good opinion of their productivity, while those who did not feel satisfied also failed to find their units productive. This relationship held for all three levels of evaluation. The fact that some of the superiors disagreed concerning the productivity of this division has no bearing on the above relationships.

The relationship between job satisfaction and perceived morale is positive at all three organizational levels (see Table 21-4). In division A the correlation is especially strong between job satisfaction and perception of morale of the division. It seems that those individuals who were satisfied with their jobs in spite of, or even because of, the restrictive climate saw their division as a high-morale organization, while those who were personally unhappy in their jobs tended to have the opposite reaction. The one low correlation between job satisfaction and perceived morale for the whole laboratory, as rated by the members in division A, can be explained by the fact that the division members did not identify themselves with the laboratory per se. Instead, they saw

TABLE 21-4. CORRELATION BETWEEN PERCEIVED MORALE AND JOB SATISFACTION (DIVISIONS A AND B)

| | Perceived morale | | | | | | | | |
|---|---|---|---|---|---|---|---|---|---|
| | Work group | | | Division | | | Laboratory | | |
| | Div. A | Div. B | C.R. A vs. B | Div. A | Div. B | C.R. A vs. B | Div. A | Div. B | C.R. A vs. B |
| Job satisfaction.. | 0.54 | 0.47 | $p$ not significant | 0.74 | 0.41 | $t = 2.6$ $p < 0.02$ | 0.12 | 0.60 | $t = 2.1$ $p < 0.05$ |

the laboratory as a large, bureaucratic structure, whose lack of purpose and success resulted in generally low morale. This situation existed in spite of the fact that the superiors were fairly well satisfied with the division's performance in carrying out the objectives of the laboratory. Division B, on the other hand, participated freely in the laboratory's activities, identified itself more or less with the *general mission* and program of the laboratory, as it saw it, and attached its own conception of success to that of the laboratory. As a result, the considerable degree of high job satisfaction in the division, combined with the perception of relatively high morale for the laboratory as a whole, gives the positive correlation.

The consistently moderate correlations between perceived productivity and perceived morale in a scientific setting (see Table 21-5) suggest a common factor. The highest correlation between these two variables can be found at the division level—that is, fairly close agreement exists between the productivity and morale ratings of the division, regardless of whether they are high or low. This type of agreement is not nearly so pronounced at the work-group or laboratory level.

Although the correlations for the work-group, division, and laboratory levels are similar for divisions A and B, the reasons for their moderate size vary for the two divisions. In the case of division A, the moderate correlations are primarily due to the fact that the productivity ratings were considerably higher than the morale ratings; while in division B, the morale ratings were relatively higher than the productivity ratings. An analysis of the ratings on job satisfaction, perceived productivity,

TABLE 21-5. CORRELATION BETWEEN PERCEIVED MORALE AND PERCEIVED PRODUCTIVITY (DIVISIONS A AND B)

| Perceived productivity | Perceived morale | | | | | | | | |
|---|---|---|---|---|---|---|---|---|---|
| | Work group | | | Division | | | Laboratory | | |
| | Div. A | Div. B | C.R. A vs. B | Div. A | Div. B | C.R. A vs. B | Div. A | Div. B | C.R. A vs. B |
| Work group..... | 0.32 | 0.49 | p not significant | | | | | | |
| Division......... | .... | .... | ......... | 0.67 | 0.62 | p not significant | | | |
| Laboratory...... | .... | .... | ......... | .... | .... | ......... | 0.48 | 0.45 | p not significant |

TABLE 21-6. AVERAGE RATINGS OF SUPERVISORS AND SUBORDINATES ON JOB SATISFACTION, PERCEIVED PRODUCTIVITY, AND PERCEIVED MORALE (DIVISIONS A AND B)

| | Division A | | | | | | Division B | | | | | |
|---|---|---|---|---|---|---|---|---|---|---|---|---|
| | Supervisors | | | Subordinates | | | Supervisors | | | Subordinates | | |
| | Av. rating | No. | S.D. | Av. rating | No. | S.D. | Av. rating | No. | S.D. | Av. rating | No. | S.D. |
| Job satisfaction......... | 3.20 | 9 | 0.87 | 2.19 | 15 | 0.92 | 2.11 | 9 | 1.20 | 2.32 | 28 | 0.80 |
| Perceived productivity: | | | | | | | | | | | | |
| Work group.......... | 2.33 | 9 | 1.26 | 2.47 | 15 | 0.50 | 2.11 | 9 | 1.20 | 2.38 | 26 | 0.68 |
| Division............. | 3.22 | 9 | 1.31 | 3.21 | 14 | 1.10 | 1.89 | 9 | 1.20 | 2.54 | 26 | 0.69 |
| Laboratory........... | 3.50 | 7 | 1.00 | 3.38 | 13 | 0.62 | 2.89 | 9 | 0.99 | 2.87 | 23 | 0.80 |
| Perceived morale: | | | | | | | | | | | | |
| Work group.......... | 2.89 | 9 | 0.87 | 2.67 | 15 | 0.87 | 1.88 | 8 | 0.59 | 1.96 | 29 | 0.81 |
| Division............. | 3.89 | 9 | 0.99 | 3.31 | 16 | 1.04 | 1.78 | 9 | 0.79 | 2.03 | 29 | 0.72 |
| Laboratory........... | 3.33 | 9 | 0.47 | 3.83 | 15 | 0.75 | 2.63 | 8 | 0.48 | 2.67 | 27 | 0.67 |

and perceived morale of all individuals in supervisory positions and of their subordinates in the divisions was made. It showed the ratings of the supervisors in restrictively led division A to be considerably lower than the equivalent ratings of the supervisors in permissively led division B (see Table 21-6). On the other hand, the discrepancies generally were not nearly so large between the ratings of the two groups of subordinates, and in one instance (job satisfaction) the subordinates in division A as a group gave the higher ratings.

One way to account for the considerable differences in the supervisory ratings might be in terms of the personal influence of the two division heads. In both divisions, almost all supervisors were directly under their respective division heads in the chain of command. The manner in which these two individuals operated was more or less known through interviews and comments included in the completed sociometric questionnaires—that is, the behavior of the restrictive division head had been operationally identified through a collection of specific incidents which characterized his activities, and the same held true for the permissive leader. The personality characteristics of their respective subordinate supervisors were less known, although the hypothesis might be tested that supervisors tend to choose as their immediate subordinates individuals "in their own image."

In this instance, the low ratings of the supervisors in division A may have been due to the type of leadership exerted directly upon them by the division head, whereas the subordinates were more removed from the center of power and therefore less under its influence. On the other hand, our sociometric survey[6] reveals that division head A was rejected as a leadership choice for a number of job-oriented activities primarily by members of the rank and file who were supposed to have little direct contact with him rather than by the supervisors directly under his authority. As yet, the meaning of this discrepancy escapes us. Other outside variables, such as the perceived lack of support for the division's efforts on the part of responsible authorities, both inside and outside the laboratory, may well have been primarily responsible for the depressive effect upon the supervisors in this division. In division B, the supervisors were known to be well satisfied with the accomplishments of their division as well as with their own techniques of administration and supervision, a fact which is reflected in their relatively high ratings. These techniques were not completely successful in view of the fact that the subordinates generally gave lower ratings, especially with regard to job satisfaction and perceived productivity, than did their supervisors.

## LEADERSHIP CHOICES

A number of questions included in the questionnaire were designed to determine the chosen leaders in research, administration, and popularity for the two divisions, as well as for the laboratory. The degree of acceptance of the division heads can be inferred from the number of

[6] See Chap. 22.

times they were chosen as best researcher, best administrator, or best-liked person in their respective divisions (see Table 21-7). Division A, which generally had a favorable view of its productivity, selected its division head in 39.3 per cent of the total choices as the best researcher in the division; 39.3 per cent of the choices were given to other members in the division; and 21.4 per cent were unspecified. The unspecified category includes such responses as "don't know," no answer, or "no particular choice." In view of the importance of research success to the activities of this division and in view of the technical competence of its head, the relatively high estimate of its productivity was not surprising. With regard to the low ratings on job satisfaction and morale,

TABLE 21-7. DIVISION "LEADERSHIP" CHOICES

| Chosen individuals | Best researcher | | | | Best administrator | | | | Best-liked | | | |
|---|---|---|---|---|---|---|---|---|---|---|---|---|
| | Division A | | Division B | | Division A | | Division B | | Division A | | Division B | |
| | Per cent | No. | Per cent | No. | Per cent | No. | Per cent | No. | Per cent | No. | Per cent | No. |
| Division head... | 39.3 | 11 | 15.8 | 6 | 7.1 | 2 | 26.4 | 10 | 0.0 | 0 | 31.6 | 12 |
| Other.......... | 39.3 | 11 | 50.0 | 19 | 71.4 | 20 | 57.8 | 22 | 92.8 | 26 | 52.6 | 20 |
| Unspecified..... | 21.4 | 6 | 34.2 | 13 | 21.4 | 6 | 15.8 | 6 | 7.2 | 2 | 15.8 | 6 |

the data on the role of the division head as best administrator or best-liked person again provide some helpful clues. In this instance, division head A was chosen by only 7.1 per cent of his subordinates as best administrator and by no one as best-liked person in the division. The picture is reversed in division B, which was characterized by comparatively moderate estimates of its productivity and high ratings on job satisfaction and morale. Division head B was chosen by only 15.8 per cent as best researcher, but by 26.4 per cent as best administrator, and by 31.6 per cent as best-liked person in the division.

An analysis of the choices for top spot in research, administration, and popularity for the laboratory as a whole concerned itself with a comparison of choices of people *within* any division against outside or unspecified choices (see Table 21-8). In division A, 32.2 per cent chose a member of their own division, in most instances the division head, and 21.4 per cent chose someone outside the division as best researcher in the laboratory compared with 7.9 per cent inside and 13.2 per cent outside choices for division B. All other choices were unspecified. This provides supporting evidence of the high caliber of research talent found in division A. In division A, 3.6 per cent of the members chose one of their own people as best administrator, while 7.9 per cent in division B did likewise. Outside choices totaled 57.1 per cent for division A and 31.6 per cent for division B. Finally, for the best-liked person in the laboratory, only 3.6 per cent inside and 53.6 per cent outside choices characterized the selections of division A, compared with 15.8 per cent inside and 28.9 per cent outside choices in division

TABLE 21-8. LABORATORY "LEADERSHIP" CHOICES

| Division | Best researcher | | | | | | Best administrator | | | | | | Best-liked | | | | | |
|---|---|---|---|---|---|---|---|---|---|---|---|---|---|---|---|---|---|---|
| | Inside division | | Outside division | | Un-specified | | Inside division | | Outside division | | Un-specified | | Inside division | | Outside division | | Un-specified | |
| | Per cent | No. | Per cent | No. | Per cent | No. | Per cent | No. | Per cent | No. | Per cent | No. | Per cent | No. | Per cent | No. | Per cent | No. |
| A | 32.2 | 9 | 21.4 | 6 | 46.4 | 13 | 3.6 | 1 | 57.1 | 16 | 39.3 | 11 | 3.6 | 1 | 53.6 | 15 | 42.8 | 12 |
| B | 7.9 | 3 | 13.2 | 5 | 78.9 | 30 | 7.9 | 3 | 31.6 | 12 | 60.5 | 23 | 15.8 | 6 | 28.9 | 11 | 55.3 | 21 |

B. These latter findings indicate the greater degree of cohesiveness and identification found among the members of the permissively led division B than among the members of the restrictively administered division A.

This investigation was primarily aimed at exploring the relationship between two diverse leadership patterns (restrictive and permissive) and job satisfaction, perceived productivity, and perceived morale in two comparable divisions of a naval research laboratory. Although this study was unable to eliminate the influence of many outside variables upon the factors under consideration, it yielded some findings whose proper interpretation and application might lead to the more effective operation of various formal organizations.

# CHAPTER 22

# Assessing Organizational Effectiveness: The Multi-relational Sociometric Survey *

The Multi-relational Sociometric Survey (MSS) is concerned with the measurement of interpersonal variables associated with organizational effectiveness. Specifically, it involves an expansion of sociometric method to the study of *several* activities and relations at a given time and the development of indices, derived from the resulting patterns, that may serve as useful measures of effective organizational functioning.[1]

The MSS grows from the context of theory distinguishing informal from formal organization. The literature continues to show considerable disagreement concerning the meaning of these two concepts. In defining formal organization, for example, some writers stress the rational, prescribed relations between positions—the blueprint or organization-chart approach—while others stress the rational, prescribed relations between specific persons.[2] On the other hand, in defining informal

* This chapter is a modified version of "Sociometric Choice and Organizational Effectiveness: A Multi-relational Approach," by Fred Massarik, Robert Tannenbaum, Murray Kahane, and Irving R. Weschler, *Sociometry*, vol. 16, no. 3, pp. 211–238, August, 1953. The research was reported in more popular form in "A New Management Tool: The Multi-relational Sociometric Survey," by Irving R. Weschler, Robert Tannenbaum, and Eugene Talbot, *Personnel*, vol. 29, no. 1, pp. 85–94, July, 1952.

[1] Our research was conducted in a laboratory, wherein effectiveness often had to be inferred indirectly from supervisors' ratings and from measures of morale, job satisfaction, and productivity *perceptions*.

[2] The following illustrate some shades of meaning in the use of the concept "formal organization":

1. "A formal, rationally organized social structure involves clearly defined patterns of activity in which, ideally, every series of actions is functionally related to the purposes of the organization. In such an organization there is an integrated series of offices, of hierarchized statuses, in which inhere a number of obligations and privileges closely defined by limited and specific rules," Robert K. Merton,

organization, some include *all* relations that are not formally prescribed; some, only spontaneously developed, affective relations; some, only those relations which are extraorganizational in character (i.e., those not clearly directed toward organizational goals).[3]

From these various definitions, the main point emerges that the people who constitute any organization are necessarily related to each other in numerous ways. Further, it may be hypothesized that the degree of congruence between specific relations may have some implications for organizational effectiveness. The research problem is to analyze selected types of relations and develop the appropriate indices showing their interrelations. Although this problem will be discussed more fully below, consideration of some key concepts must precede.

Interpersonal activities among people who make up any organization may be divided into two main types: those clearly directed toward the attainment of organizational goals, and those not so directed. For the sake of brevity, we shall speak of the first type as "goal-directed" and of the second type as "nongoal-directed."

The first type incorporates those activities which specifically are necessary (as seen by persons in authority) to the achievement of the purposes of the organization. Order giving, efficiency rating, and the giving of advice and assistance in work are examples of this type. The second type incorporates those activities not directly essential to the achievement of organizational purposes. Socializing after working hours and lunching are illustrative.

Each activity includes a number of *relations*. For each of the goal-directed activities, five relations are postulated. These are the *prescribed,* the *perceived,* the *actual,* the *desired,* and the *rejected.*

---

"Bureaucratic Structure and Personality," in his *Social Theory and Social Structure* (Glencoe, Ill.: The Free Press, 1949), p. 151.

2. " . . . the most useful concept for the analysis of experience of cooperative systems is embodied in the definition of a formal organization as a system of consciously coordinated activities or forces of two or more persons," C. I. Barnard, *The Functions of the Executive* (Cambridge, Mass.: Harvard University Press, 1947), p. 73.

[3] The following illustrate some shades of meaning in the use of the concept "informal organization":

1. "Informal organization is the network of personal and social relations which are not defined or prescribed by formal organization," Delbert C. Miller and William H. Form, *Industrial Sociology* (New York: Harper & Brothers, 1951), p. 863.

2. Informal organization "is composed of the animosities and friendships among the people who work together," *ibid.,* p. 146.

3. "By informal organization I mean the aggregate of the personal contacts and interactions and the associated groupings of people. . . . Though common or joint purposes are excluded by definition, common or joint results of important character nevertheless come from such organization . . . informal organization is indefinite and rather structureless . . . ," Barnard, *op. cit.,* p. 115.

The *prescribed relations* are defined by the official sanction of the duly constituted leaders of the organization. X has been delegated authority by his superior to give orders in work to Y. These relations are either explicitly specified or implicitly accepted by persons in authority. They are explicit when they are defined by oral or written directive; they are implicit when their existence within the organization is accepted by those in authority although such existence is not based upon directive. By way of example, in most organizations prescribed order giving is explicit; in many, however, prescribed giving of advice and assistance is implicit.

The *perceived relations* are defined by persons' perceptions of the prescribed relations. For example, Y perceives Z as having authority to give him orders in work—even though it is, in fact, X who has such authority.

The *actual relations* are defined by the interactions which in fact take place among persons. For example, Y regularly receives orders in work from X. Operationally, these relations can be revealed by two methods—by observation of behavior as it occurs, or by asking individuals to indicate the person(s) with whom they interact.[4] When the latter method is used, the replies represent perceptual data which probably correlate positively, although imperfectly, with data that might be obtained by direct observation.

The *desired relations* are defined by persons' preferences regarding interactions with other persons (positive affect). For example, Y *would like to* receive orders in work from W.

It is possible here to include *all* preferred interactions or only the one (or ones) *most* preferred. For operational purposes, a choice between these alternatives must be made.

The desired relations are equivalent to the "choices" as used in sociometry.

The *rejected relations* are defined by persons' adverse reactions regarding interactions with other persons (negative affect). For example, Y *would not like* to receive orders in work from X.

It is possible here to include *all* rejected interactions or only the one (or ones) *most* rejected.

The rejected relations are equivalent to "rejections" as used in sociometry.

---

[4] Thus we might distinguish an "actual actual," designating a relation for which data were obtained by direct observation, and a "perceived actual," for which data were obtained by asking individuals to indicate the person(s) with whom they interact. In the pilot investigation, the "perceived actual" was used, but for the sake of brevity, we shall frequently speak simply of the "actual" when referring to the "perceived actual."

In comparing the five relations discussed above, we may view the prescribed relations as organizational norms and the perceived relations as the psychological corollaries of these organizational norms. The desired and rejected relations may either support these norms (if the prescribed is desired) or contravene these norms (if the prescribed is rejected). The actual relations may be resultants, dependent, among other things, upon the norms, awareness of these norms, and desires and rejections.

For each of the nongoal-directed activities, only three relations are postulated. These are the actual, the desired, and the rejected. Clearly, the prescribed and the perceived relations are not relevant to nongoal-directed activities.

## DEVELOPMENT AND ADMINISTRATION OF THE RESEARCH INSTRUMENT

### The Setting

The pilot investigation was conducted in a research and development laboratory. The subjects were primarily engineers, physicists, chemists, draftsmen, and supporting administrative and clerical specialists. Specifically, they were the members of two divisions, characterized by presumably contrasting styles of leadership. Division A was headed by an apparently restrictive leader, while division B was more permissively led.

Prior to the MSS study, other human relations research projects had been conducted in the laboratory, and continuing contact had been maintained with its formal leadership. Thus, a degree of rapport already had been established when the current project was initiated.

### Specifying the Principal Activities

In planning the MSS, it became necessary to specify for research purposes a sensibly small number of activities. The selection was made on a common-sense basis, buttressed by interviews with key personnel in the laboratory.[5] The following activities were chosen:

1. Goal-directed activities
   a. Being efficiency-rated
   b. Turning to others for advice in work
   c. Being given directions or orders
   d. Presenting major grievances

[5] This is essentially a type of sampling problem. One might imagine a large universe of all possible activities between individuals in a particular setting from which a representative sample must be drawn.

e. Being designated for a promotion

f. Having one's mistakes in work pointed out

g. Spending time with others during working hours[6]

h. Discussing annoyances arising from work

2. Nongoal-directed activities

a. Socializing after working hours

b. Having lunch with others

c. Discussing personal problems

*Obtaining the Data*

*The Prescribed Relations.* Two sources were utilized to secure information about the prescribed relations of the goal-directed activities: (1) organizational charts and manuals; (2) interviews with top administrators and personnel specialists. These data describe what often is referred to as the "formal organization."

*The Perceived, Actual, Desired, and Rejected Relations.* To secure facts about relations other than the prescribed, a questionnaire was constructed and administered to persons at all levels of the hierarchy. This questionnaire is the basic instrument of the MSS. The following may serve as a prototype to indicate the kinds of questions used:

*Goal-directed.*

THE PERCEIVED. "Who is *supposed* to give you directions (or orders) in your work?"

THE ACTUAL. "Who *actually* gives you directions (or orders) in your work?"

THE DESIRED. "If it were up to you to decide, *whom would you* choose to give you directions (or orders) in your work?"

THE REJECTED. "*Whom would you least want* to give you directions (or orders) in your work?"

*Nongoal-directed.*

THE ACTUAL. "With whom *do* you usually have lunch?"

THE DESIRED. "With whom would you *like to be able* to have lunch?"

THE REJECTED. "With whom would you *least like* to have lunch?"[7]

No constraints were imposed on the subjects to limit the number or nature of their responses. More than one answer was permitted, organizational units could be used as choices, and qualifying or qualitative comments could be appended to any reply. The questionnaires were completed by the respondents at their homes and mailed unsigned to

---

[6] Some activities, such as this one, are difficult to classify, as they may vary in terms of goal-direction and nongoal-direction.

[7] In some cases, the rejection relation was not included, even though it did apply. At the time of the field study, this was done for the sake of economy; but it was realized subsequently that the relevant questions should have been included.

the university address of the research team.[8] Code numbers were used so that only the members of the research team could identify individuals. Out of a population of sixty-eight, sixty-six completed questionnaires were obtained.

The need for a virtually complete return of replies in a sociometric investigation is apparent. High nonresponse would leave such gaps in the matrix as to diminish greatly the value of the data. An instrument such as the MSS may represent a threat to the security of some of the respondents. Therefore, straightforward, satisfactory interpretation of the research project's objectives is essential. Feedback of data must be handled with caution, for it too may represent a threat. In the pilot investigation, it was emphasized that the survey results would *not* be used as a basis for any sort of administrative action. In fact, it was made clear that no management person would see individual replies; all findings would be available only in such form as to protect the individuals concerned by making identification impossible.[9]

### Coding and Preparing the Data for Analysis

A number had been assigned to each of the respondents, and these numbers became part of the code. Most replies did mention specific individuals, but responses such as "no one," "anyone," "people near my desk," and "my superiors," also appeared with some frequency and were added to the code.[10]

---

[8] This was done as a further safeguard against the operation of direct or subtle interpersonal pressures such as might be generated by face-to-face contact among the respondents during the filling out of the questionnaire.

[9] There are certain differences between the use of the MSS as a tool of management and as a research device. When used as a managerial tool, action is a logical consequence of the MSS. In academic research, on the other hand, considerable stress is laid on the fact that *nothing* will happen within the organization to modify existing regulations directly as a result of the findings. Clearly, this implies a different type of motivation to cooperate than if change, and particularly change for the better, is promised. There is no reason to believe, however, that the sort of motivation elicited by a promise of action necessarily results in more honest or more valid data than the motivation that exists when it is emphasized that the research results will not be used directly as an instrument for change. Change, brought about indirectly by interest aroused in topics raised by the MSS, may nevertheless be a by-product of the research.

[10] The following illustrates some of the categories that were developed to deal with choices other than those for specific individuals:

A. Unnamed persons, e.g., (1) anyone, (2) all, (3) many, (4) some, etc.
B. Self-reference, e.g., (1) myself, (2) alone, etc.
C. "Formal" organizational units within the laboratory, e.g., (1) power plant division, etc.
D. "Informal" groups, e.g., (1) my car pool, (2) the bridge group, etc.
E. Status units, e.g., (1) my superiors, (2) my subordinates, etc.
F. Functional units, e.g., (1) people who can help me, (2) people who are qualified . . . , (6) anyone else who can help me. etc..

In the pilot investigation, IBM procedures were not used, although this might have been done successfully. Rather, the code designations were transferred to large general-purpose tables from which they could be converted into matrix form.

In order to facilitate analysis and interpretation, a method for organizing the raw data was needed. The method that was developed for this purpose is considered in the next section.

## A METHOD FOR ORGANIZING THE DATA

Let us recapitulate the basic concepts. We distinguish two major categories of activities: the goal-directed and the nongoal-directed.[11] For each of the former, five relations are postulated: the prescribed, the perceived, the actual, the desired, and the rejected. For each of the latter type, three relations are postulated: the actual, the desired, and the rejected. The following symbols will prove useful for putting the data into matrix form:

$'$ to indicate an instance of a prescribed relation
$o$ to indicate an instance of a perceived relation
$x$ to indicate an instance of an actual relation
$+$ to indicate an instance of a desired relation
$-$ to indicate an instance of a rejected relation

In conventional sociometric matrices, each cell contains information about a particular choice or relationship between two individuals in a particular activity.[12] However, in an MSS matrix cell, for any goal-

---

G. Physical-arrangement units, e.g., (1) people near my desk, (2) people in my office, etc.

Also, qualifying remarks were coded, using categories such as the following:

H. Frequency of interaction, e.g., (1) always, (2) sometimes, (3) usually, etc.

I. Feeling tone of interaction, e.g., (1) friendly, (2) unfriendly, etc.

Following is an example of how a particular response may be coded:

Smith, code number 123, might have replied as follows to the question, "To whom do you turn for advice in your work?": " . . . to Jones; but sometimes I go to other people in the power plant division, or to anyone else who can help me." This would be coded as follows:

Jones—code number for specific individual: 124.

"Other people in power plant division" (formal organizational unit)—see *C* above: *C-1.*

"Sometimes" (qualifying remark for power plant division)—see *H* above: *H-2.*

"Anyone else who can help me" (functional unit): *F-6.*

The reliability of the coding was checked, and although no coefficients were calculated, it was apparent that only a trivial number of disagreements between coders appeared.

[11] The goal-directed and the nongoal-directed activities studied in the pilot investigation are listed in full on pages 349 and 350.

[12] Conventional sociometric usage frequently employs the word "criterion" for what we call "activity." For example, see Charles H. Proctor and Charles P. Loomis,

directed activity, such as order giving, it is possible to indicate all, some, or none of the five relations shown above. Thus, an MSS matrix cell contains some variant of the pattern shown in Figure 22-1.[13] Each symbol is placed in the appropriate position within the cell. Thus, ′ always appears in the upper left-hand corner, *o* in the upper right-hand corner, etc.

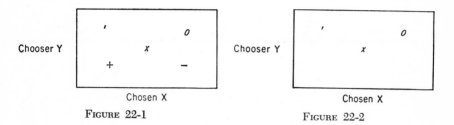

|  | Chosen X |  | Chosen X |
|---|---|---|---|
| FIGURE 22-1 | | FIGURE 22-2 | |

For example, the pattern of relations shown in Figure 22-2 may be found for the order-giving activity. According to this figure, Y is supposed to take orders from X (prescribed), he believes that X is supposed to give him orders (perceived), and indeed X does give him orders. However, on the affective level, Y neither desires nor rejects X as an order giver, for we find neither a plus (+) in the lower left-hand corner of the cell, nor a minus (−) in the lower right-hand corner (see positions of symbols shown in Figure 22-1).

A cell that is completely blank indicates that, for a particular activity, no relations link the individuals concerned.

For each activity an entire matrix may be formed with the choosers arranged along the ordinate and the chosen along the abscissa.[14] In practice, it may be that more cases will fall along the abscissa than along the ordinate. This is so because a given chooser may select persons outside his own group or organizational unit; he may choose "unnamed persons" (e.g., "my friends"), or entire groups (e.g., "my division"), which, of course, cannot directly reciprocate the choice.

---

"Analysis of Sociometric Data," in Marie Jahoda, Morton Deutsch, and Stuart W. Cook, *Research Methods in Social Relations, Part Two: Selected Techniques* (New York: The Dryden Press, Inc., 1951), p. 562.

[13] Actually, it is unlikely that all five of the relations will be found in any one cell. Typically, one person will not be both desired and rejected by the same chooser. This is not to deny the existence of ambivalence as a personality dynamic, although most sociometric methods have not made use of this concept.

[14] Actually the terms "chooser" and "chosen" are not entirely accurate, but will be used in lieu of neologisms, for no adequate terms seem to exist. The inaccuracy stems from the fact that when X is prescribed for Y, Y does not necessarily do any choosing—the relevant prescription simply is thrust upon him. Nor is a perception of a prescribed or actual relation really a "choice" in the usual sense of the word. The only genuine choices are the desired and the rejected.

One can visualize an array of matrices similar to the one just discussed, with each matrix dealing with one particular activity. Figure 22-3 shows what this total scheme might look like.

In summary, the MSS scheme indicates the relations (entries in cells) between individuals (*x* axis and *y* axis) for a number of activities (*z* axis).

Among research questions generated by this are the following:

1. For any activity, what relational patterns characterize various organizational units? We shall construct some indices concerned with such patterns. These we shall call *intra-activity indices*. The relevant basic data are the entries in various cells of *any one matrix* defined by the *x-y* plane in the three-dimensional scheme.

2. What patterns are found in various organizational units as we trace any *one* relation from activity to activity? We shall construct some indices concerned with this. These we shall call *interactivity indices*. The relevant basic data are the entries for *any one relation*, such as the prescribed, perceived, actual, desired, or rejected, as they appear in a horizontal array of cells along the *z* axis, from one matrix to another.


INTRA-ACTIVITY INDICES

Intra-activity indices are constructed on the basis of relation patterns in any one activity. They use as data the cell entries of any one matrix in the *x-y* plane.

Intra-activity indices provide information about various aspects of group functioning and about the functioning of the individual in the group. This section will consider the following indices:

¶ *Indices of understanding*, that measure the extent to which the prescribed relations are correctly perceived.

¶ *Indices of normative conformity*, that measure the extent to which actual behavior conforms to the prescribed and/or to perceptions of the prescribed.

¶ *Indices of affective conformity*, that measure the extent to which actual behavior conforms to desires and rejections.

¶ *Indices of satisfaction and dissatisfaction*, that measure the extent to which prescribed, perceived, or actual relations also are desired or rejected.

¶ *Indices of affective atmosphere*, that measure the state of balance that exists in an organizational unit between affectively positive choices (desired) and affectively negative choices (rejected).

¶ *Indices of centralization*, that measure the extent to which choices (prescribed, perceived, actual, desired, or rejected) are concentrated in a particular person or in a particular group of persons.

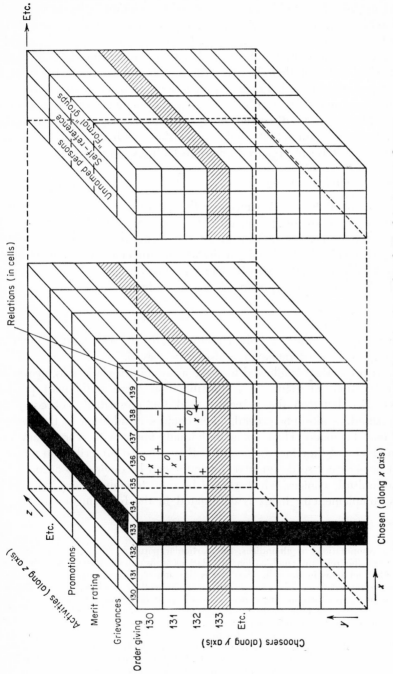

FIGURE 22-3. A three-dimensional scheme for the Multi-relational Sociometric Survey.

The hypothesis was formulated that some systematic variations in index magnitudes would be associated with variation in leadership style and with certain criteria of organizational effectiveness. As has been noted before, the two divisions, A and B, of the laboratory were chosen because there was some indication that they varied considerably in the leadership styles of their heads, with A being restrictively led, and B being permissively led. Further, perceptions of productivity, job satisfaction, and morale were obtained from the members of the two divisions. The example discussed later indicates some expected covariations between intra-activity indices, on the one hand, and leadership styles and criteria of organizational effectiveness, on the other.

## Indices of Understanding

Indices of understanding measure the extent to which the prescribed relations are correctly perceived. They measure the degree to which people have an accurate idea about the formal organization in which they are involved. By definition, indices of understanding always have the prescribed and the perceived in the numerator.

The following is one possible index of understanding:

$$\Sigma'o/\Sigma' \qquad (1)[15]$$

In words, "Of the prescribed relations (for a given activity such as order giving), what percentage also is perceived?"

Each respondent is allowed to make a number of choices in answer to each question. Therefore, it is possible that there could exist perfect congruence between the perceived and the prescribed; yet complete understanding may not prevail, since choices in addition to the correct one may be made. Thus, some individuals know with whom they are to interact, yet they may believe that they are also prescribed to interact with persons not so designated. An index can be devised to account for these multiple choices, which should be used to complement index (1). This complementary index is designated in the following manner:

$$\Sigma'o/\Sigma o \qquad (2)$$

[15] In computations of all indices, the particular patterns, such as $'o$, are counted whenever the relevant combination of relations appears, whether or not there are any other relations in the cell. Thus $\Sigma'o$ is the sum of all cell entries which contain $'o$, including $'ox$, $'o+$, $'ox+$, $'o-$, $'ox-$, etc., as well as $'o$ alone. Indices, as used in the pilot investigation, are concerned with percentages of relations rather than with percentages of individuals. Since multiple responses were permitted, this raises some questions of weighting. One individual with numerous choices exerts a relatively greater influence upon an index than an individual with a single choice. What implications this may have empirically would have to be determined by the construction of another set of measures in which the responses of individuals, regardless of number, would be weighted equally. For another possible solution of this problem, see Weschler, Tannenbaum, and Talbot, *op. cit.*, footnote 7, p. 91.

Thus, there are two different indices of understanding. Index (1) answers the question: "What percentage of prescriptions is perceived correctly?" Index (2) answers the question: "What percentage of the perceived is also prescribed?"

An analysis of understanding by organizational units or by individuals may demonstrate gaps in the comprehension of formal structure which may affect the functioning of these units.

*Indices of Normative Conformity*

Indices of normative conformity measure the extent to which reported actual behavior conforms to the prescribed and/or to perceptions of the prescribed. These indices measure the degree to which people report that they do what they are supposed to do, or do what they *think* they are supposed to do. By definition, the actual always appears in the numerator.

As one measure of the degree of normative conformity (with the prescribed as the norm) one may use the proportion of all the prescribed relations which are actual relations as well. This is represented symbolically as

$$\Sigma'x/\Sigma' \tag{3}$$

A problem concerning multiple responses exists here similar to that encountered with the indices of understanding. This problem can be resolved by using the total number of actual as the base in determining the proportion of actual relations which are prescribed. Symbolically,

$$\Sigma'x/\Sigma x \tag{4}$$

Thus, we have two measures of normative conformity with the prescribed as the norm. Index (3) answers the question: "What percentage of all prescribed relations is also actual?" Index (4) answers the question: "What percentage of all actual relations is also prescribed?"

Further, it is possible to measure normative conformity to relations *perceived* as being prescribed. The relevant indices would be the following:

$$\Sigma ox/\Sigma o \tag{5}$$

$$\Sigma ox/\Sigma x \tag{6}$$

Index (5) answers the question: "What percentage of all perceived relations is also actual?" Index (6) answers the question: "What percentage of all actual relations is also perceived?"

Still another set of measures of normative conformity is concerned with the extent to which an activity that is both prescribed and perceived is also reported as being acted upon:

$$\Sigma'ox/\Sigma'o \tag{7}$$

Index (7) answers the question: "What percentage of all relations that are both prescribed and perceived (understood) is also actual?"

And similarly,

$$\Sigma' ox / \Sigma x \qquad (8)$$

Index (8) answers the question: "What percentage of all actual relations is also perceived and prescribed (understood)?"

We might consider some of the psychological meanings of these three sets of measures of normative conformity. The first set, indices (3) and (4), regards conformity as determined by the extent to which behavior corresponds to the organizational blueprint, regardless of any other circumstances. In the second set, indices (5) and (6), conformity is concerned with the individual's own view of the organization in which he operates, whether or not this perceptual structuring corresponds to the blueprint. Finally, the third set, indices (7) and (8), is designed to judge conformity against the correctly perceived (or understood) relations only.

If, upon examination of indices (3) and (4), it is found that some persons show relatively little conformity to what is prescribed, then it should be ascertained whether these persons act in accordance with their perceptions of the prescribed [see indices (5) and (6)]. If they do, then better communication of the prescribed relations becomes the solution, providing it is agreed that organizational goals will be attained most effectively if prescriptions are followed. Another point to note is that when individuals are found to interact with persons neither prescribed for them nor perceived by them, this may be due to the lack of availability of the prescribed or perceived individuals or to hostilities with them.

### Indices of Affective Conformity

Indices of affective conformity measure the extent to which reported actual behavior conforms to desires and rejections. They indicate the degree to which people's behavior is in accord with their preferences for interpersonal contact. By definition, the actual always appears in the numerator. These measures are somewhat similar in purpose to the indices of satisfaction which will be taken up in the next section.

The principal measure of affective conformity is concerned with the following question: "What percentage of all desired (or rejected) relations is also actual?" Symbolically,

$$\Sigma + x / \Sigma + \qquad (9a)$$
$$\Sigma - x / \Sigma - \qquad (9b)$$

*Indices of Satisfaction and Dissatisfaction*

Indices of satisfaction and dissatisfaction measure the extent to which prescribed, perceived, or actual relations are also desired or rejected. Thus, these indices measure relative satisfaction or dissatisfaction with formal organization and/or with the existing interactions. By definition, indices of satisfaction always have the desired in the numerator; indices of dissatisfaction always have the rejected in the numerator.

One pair of relevant indices may be symbolized as follows:

$$\Sigma' + / \Sigma' \tag{10a}$$

$$\Sigma' - / \Sigma' \tag{10b}$$

Indices (10a) and (10b) are concerned with the question: "What percentage of all prescribed relations is also desired (or rejected)?"[16]

A pair of indices focusing on the perceived instead of the prescribed may be represented symbolically as follows:

$$\Sigma o + / \Sigma o \tag{11a}$$

$$\Sigma o - / \Sigma o \tag{11b}$$

Indices (11a) and (11b) answer the question: "What percentage of all perceived relations is also desired (or rejected)?"

Variants of these indices, which perhaps are more relevant to management, are the following:

$$\Sigma' o + / \Sigma' o \tag{12a}$$

$$\Sigma' o - / \Sigma' o \tag{12b}$$

Indices (12a) and (12b) use the understood relations as the base. They answer the question: "What percentage of all relations that are perceived *and* prescribed (understood) is also desired (or rejected)?"

Still another type of satisfaction and dissatisfaction measure may focus on the actual relations:

$$\Sigma x + / \Sigma x \tag{13a}$$

$$\Sigma x - / \Sigma x \tag{13b}$$

In a sense, indices (13a) and (13b) are the converse of the affective conformity measures (9a) and (9b). Indices (13a) and (13b) answer

---

[16] These indices measure satisfaction and dissatisfaction with reference to relations that are prescribed but *not necessarily* perceived. However, it may be of interest to find out to what extent prescribed relations are desired or rejected, regardless of the extent to which they are also perceived. For example, it may be that superiors designated to fulfill specific functions, such as order giving, are well liked in the roles which they are to fulfill according to the organizational blueprint, but few people are aware that these superiors are indeed assigned these roles. Clearly, the remedy for this kind of situation (which also would be indicated by some of the indices of understanding) would be more effective communication of the organizational prescriptions.

the question: "What percentage of all actual relations is also desired (or rejected)?," while indices (9a) and (9b) answer the question: "What percentage of all desired (or rejected) relations is also actual?"

Indices of satisfaction and dissatisfaction may point to morale problems in various organizational units. When satisfaction indices between activities are compared, the comparisons may indicate those interactions that might be at the root of organizational difficulties.

## Indices of Affective Atmosphere

An index of affective atmosphere measures the state of balance that exists in an organizational unit between affectively positive choices (desired) and affectively negative choices (rejected). If all affective choices are positive, the index figure will be 100; if the number of desired relations is the same as the number of rejected relations, the index figure will be 50; and if all affective choices are negative, the index figure will be 0. Thus, this index may provide some measure of the extent to which a pleasant emotional state characterizes the group.

Symbolically, the index may be stated as follows:

$$\Sigma(+)/[\Sigma(+) + \Sigma(-)]^{17} \qquad (14)$$

A variant of this index is concerned not merely with the balance between positive and negative choices, but also with the extent to which such choices are accompanied by actual relations. It provides information on the ratio of desired-actual relations to the total number of actual relations with positive or negative affect. The following is a symbolic representation of this index:

$$\Sigma(+x)/[\Sigma(+x) + \Sigma(-x)] \qquad (15)$$

## Indices of Centralization

An index of centralization measures the extent to which choices are concentrated in a particular person or in a particular group of persons.[18]

[17] The plus sign in the denominator indicating addition of $\Sigma(+)$ and $\Sigma(-)$ should not be confused with our symbol for the desired relation which, of course, is also a plus sign.

[18] Indices discussed so far have focused on relations existing within given organizational units. Here the emphasis shifts to choices received by specific persons. Thus it becomes important to count the total number of times *one particular type* of choice is received by a given person. For example, X may receive the following choice patterns from five people: $'ox$, $'ox$, $'+$, $'-$, $'x-$. This would yield the following summary of choices when $\Sigma(')_x$, $\Sigma(o)_x$, $\Sigma(x)_x$, $\Sigma(+)_x$, and $\Sigma(-)_x$ are the respective totals of the prescribed, perceived, actual, desired, and rejected choices given to X:

$$\Sigma(')_x \quad \ldots \quad 5$$
$$\Sigma(o)_x \quad \ldots \quad 2$$
$$\Sigma(x)_x \quad \ldots \quad 3$$
$$\Sigma(+)_x \quad \ldots \quad 1$$
$$\Sigma(-)_x \quad \ldots \quad 2$$

Let us take an activity such as order giving. For a hypothetical organizational unit, we note that there are 100 instances of prescription. By simple count, we find that 80 of these instances involve one person as the order giver. Only 20 prescriptions are designated for other members of the group. It is clear that here the power inherent in order giving is concentrated in that one person.

One such index of centralization may be calculated for each relation, and the group of indices of centralization can be symbolized as follows:

$$\Sigma(')_x/\Sigma' \tag{16a}$$
$$\Sigma(o)_x/\Sigma_Q \tag{16b}$$
$$\Sigma(x)_x/\Sigma x \tag{16c}$$
$$\Sigma(+)_x/\Sigma+ \tag{16d}$$
$$\Sigma(-)_x/\Sigma- \tag{16e}$$

Each index (16a) through (16e) answers a question of this form: "What percentage of a given relation in a particular organizational unit involves a particular person or group of persons?"

A profile may be drawn, showing indices (16a) through (16e) for a specific superior; such a profile may summarize key aspects of that superior's leadership role. This will be further illustrated in the section describing an example.

## OVERLAP BETWEEN INTRA-ACTIVITY INDICES

A consideration of the intra-activity indices suggests that a certain systematic overlap exists between various of the indices.[19]

For the sake of simplicity, we select three of the five relations: the actual, prescribed, and perceived. Representing each as a circle, we note the existence of certain overlapping areas. Each of these areas represents a particular relational pattern. In order to avoid repeating the entire symbolism, we can designate each area by a capital letter. Thus,

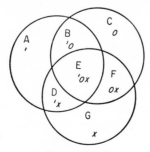

FIGURE 22-4

[19] We are indebted to Dr. Leon Festinger for suggesting this matter.

Translating several of the indices into the capital-letter notation, we obtain the following:

Index (1): $\Sigma'o/\Sigma'$ $= B + E/A + B + D + E$

Index (2): $\Sigma'o/\Sigma o$ $= B + E/B + C + E + F$

Index (3): $\Sigma'x/\Sigma'$ $= D + E/A + B + D + E$

Index (4): $\Sigma'x/\Sigma x$ $= D + E/D + E + F + G$

Index (5): $\Sigma ox/\Sigma o$ $= E + F/B + C + E + F$

Index (6): $\Sigma ox/\Sigma x$ $= E + F/D + E + F + G$

Index (7): $\Sigma'ox/\Sigma'o =$ $E/B + E$

Index (8): $\Sigma'ox/\Sigma x =$ $E/D + E + F + G$

Rewriting index (6) as $(E/D + E + F + G) + (F/D + E + F + G)$, we note that, in fact, index (8), which is $(E/D + E + F + G)$, is an important component of index (6). Specifically for division A, index $(8) = 63.64$. Obtaining index (6), we find that it yields the figure 78.79. Thus, 15.15 points only $(63.64 + 15.15 = 78.79)$ are accounted for by the component $(F/D + E + F + G)$. It is clear that many of the indices, although of varying psychological meaning, systematically overlap one another.

## INTERACTIVITY INDICES

In the previous section, we considered a number of measures that used as basic data the entries in the cells of any one matrix in the $x$-$y$ plane (see Figure 22-3). Next, we shall select specific relations, such as the prescribed, perceived, actual, desired, or rejected, and observe them as they appear when we focus on the $z$ axis, along which the various activities are arrayed.

### Indices of Pervasiveness

An index of pervasiveness measures the extent to which any one relation connects a pair or pairs of specific individuals in a number of activities. In other words, this index tells us how pervasive ties between two individuals are, as we examine several activities in which the persons may interact. It is possible to construct one index of pervasiveness for each relation. There exists an index of prescribed pervasiveness, perceived pervasiveness, actual pervasiveness, desired pervasiveness, and rejected pervasiveness.

Let us assume that an MSS is designed which covers twenty activities —ten goal-directed and ten nongoal-directed. The following might be one way of arranging the results showing the relations between individuals X and Y, in which Y is the chooser and X is the chosen. Each $f$

represents the number of activities in which a particular relation exists for the individuals concerned.

| | Goal-directed activities $(n_G = 10)$ | | Nongoal-directed activities $(n_{NG} = 10)$ | | Total $(n = 20)$ | |
|---|---|---|---|---|---|---|
| Y − X | $f_G/n_G$ | (17a) | $f_{NG}/n_{NG}$ | (17b) | $f/n$ | (17c) |

In a hypothetical case, $f_G = 7$, and $f_{NG} = 1$. If the relation used happens to be actual, this would mean that Y indicates that in seven of the ten goal-directed activities he is in actual contact with X, and that in one of the ten nongoal-directed activities he is in contact with X. Stating these frequencies in percentages for each group of ten, we would say that the pervasiveness index for Y to X in the actual relation is 70 for the goal-directed activities and 10 for the nongoal-directed activities. This would suggest that Y sees himself as actually relating to X primarily in areas of behavior related to work, and considerably less in activities that are oriented toward off-job and personal-need satisfactions. For *all* activities, the pervasiveness index would be 55; i.e., Y has actual relations with X in eleven of the twenty activities studied.[20]

## A *Direct Approach to Interactivity Indices*

Instead of constructing measures such as the pervasiveness indices, it is possible to proceed simply by direct observation. We might look at the MSS data, noting the combinations of activities in which a specific relation appears for any pair of individuals. For example, it might be that persons who are actual order givers frequently also are individuals with whom personal problems are discussed and from whom advice is solicited. Thus, order giving, advice seeking, and discussing personal problems may form a cluster, as defined by the appearance of the actual relation.

## AN EXAMPLE

Tables 22-1, 22-2, and 22-3 contain certain summaries of data, taken from the sociometric matrices, that were obtained in the pilot investigation at the laboratory. These summaries furnish the raw material for the calculation of the *intra*-activity indices. The data were not sufficient to permit calculation of any meaningful *inter*activity indices.

Table 22-1 summarizes the relational patterns for one goal-directed activity, order giving, and for one nongoal-directed activity, socializing after

[20] To justify the calculation of an index for all relations, some assumptions have to be made regarding the exhaustiveness or representativeness of the relations included in the study.

TABLE 22-1. A SUMMARY OF RELATIONAL PATTERNS†

| Relation | Symbol | Frequency of patterns for | | | |
|---|---|---|---|---|---|
| | | Order giving in | | Socializing in | |
| | | Division A | Division B | Division A | Division B |
| **One:** | | | | | |
| Pattern code 1.1 ‡ | ′ | ... | 3 | None | None§ |
| 1.2 | o | ... | 1 | None | None |
| 1.3 | x | 3 | 9 | 21 | 15 |
| 1.4 | + | 7 | 9 | 20 | 17 |
| 1.5 | — | 10 | 9 | 21 | 17 |
| **Two:** | | | | | |
| Pattern code 2.1 | ′o | 1 | 2 | None | None |
| 2.2 | ′x | 1 | 1 | None | None |
| 2.3 | ′+ | 1 | 1 | None | None |
| 2.4 | ′— | ... | 1 | None | None |
| 2.5 | xo | 4 | 8 | None | None |
| 2.6 | +o | ... | 2 | None | None |
| 2.7 | o— | ... | 1 | None | None |
| 2.8 | +x | ... | 7 | 4 | 21 |
| 2.9 | x— | 3 | 1 | .... | .... |
| 2.10 ¶ | +— | ... | ... | .... | .... |
| **Three:** | | | | | |
| Pattern code 3.1 | ′xo | 9 | 6 | None | None |
| 3.2 | ′+o | 1 | ... | None | None |
| 3.3 | ′o— | 1 | ... | None | None |
| 3.4 | ′+x | ... | ... | None | None |
| 3.5 | ′x— | ... | ... | None | None |
| 3.6 ¶ | ′+— | ... | ... | None | None |
| 3.7 ¶ | +o— | ... | ... | None | None |
| 3.8 | xo— | ... | 1 | None | None |
| 3.9 | +xo | 1 | 10 | None | None |
| 3.10 ¶ | +x— | ... | ... | .... | .... |
| **Four:** | | | | | |
| Pattern code 4.1 | ′+xo | 11 | 22 | None | None |
| 4.2 | ′xo— | 1 | 1 | None | None |
| 4.3 ¶ | ′+o— | ... | ... | None | None |
| 4.4 ¶ | ′+x— | ... | ... | None | None |
| 4.5 ¶ | +xo— | ... | ... | None | None |
| **Five:** | | | | | |
| Pattern code 5.1 ¶ | ′+x—o | ... | ... | None | None |

† All figures for choices within division.

‡ The patterns are grouped by number of relations in the pattern. The first numeral of each pattern code designates the number of relations in that group of patterns; the second numeral designates the particular pattern within the group. For example: 1.1, one relation, pattern 1; or 3.10, three relations, pattern 10.

§ "None" indicates that no such pattern exists for the particular activity. The dots indicate that a pattern exists, but that in the pilot investigation no instances of this were found.

¶ Denotes inconsistent pattern, which includes both most desired and least desired (rejected).

working hours. As is demonstrated by the formula for the total number of combinations of $n$ different things (the sum of the number of combinations of $n$ things taken 1, 2, . . . $n$, at a time), $2^n - 1$, there are thirty-one possible combinations (or relational patterns) for the goal-directed activity (number of relations, $n = 5$), and seven different combinations for the nongoal-directed activity ($n = 3$). However, certain patterns are psychologically inconsistent because they contain both "most desired" ($+$) and "most rejected" ($-$). These patterns are marked by symbol ¶. Excluding these, the number of patterns drops to twenty-three for the goal-directed activity, and to five for the nongoal-directed activity. In fact, for order giving, only fourteen patterns actually were found in division A, and nineteen patterns in division B. For socializing, four patterns were found in each of the two divisions.

TABLE 22-2. A SUMMARY OF RELATIONAL TOTALS: ENTIRE DIVISION

| Symbol | Order giving | | Socializing | |
|---|---|---|---|---|
| | A | B | A | B |
| ' | 26 (0.93)* | 37 (0.97) | None | None |
| o | 29 (1.04) | 54 (1.42) | None | None |
| x | 33 (1.18) | 66 (1.74) | 25 (0.88) | 36 (0.95) |
| + | 21 (0.75) | 51 (1.34) | 24 (0.86) | 38 (1.00) |
| − | 15 (0.54) | 14 (0.37) | 21 (0.75) | 17 (0.45) |

* Figures in parentheses indicate "relations per individual." In division A, 28 persons responded; in division B, 38 persons responded. Thus, for example, 26/28 = 0.93. There are 0.93 prescriptions per person in division A.

Table 22-2 summarizes relational *totals* for the divisions. The average number of choices per person for each relation is shown in parentheses. Table 22-2 may be derived directly from Table 22-1. For example, the total of prescribed relations for division A in order giving is found by summing the frequencies of all patterns in which the prescribed (') appears. Specifically, it is the total of patterns 1.1, 2.1, 2.2, 2.3, 2.4, 3.1, 3.2, 3.3, 3.4, 3.5, 3.6, 4.1, 4.2, 4.3, 4.4, and 5.1.

Table 22-3 is an extract from the matrices, analogous to Table 22-2, except for the fact that the summary of relational totals is shown for the two division heads only. A similar summary could be prepared for any other person in the organization.

Table 22-4 is a summary of the intra-activity indices for the two divisions. By way of illustration, let us trace the process by which index (1), an index of understanding ($\Sigma'o/\Sigma'$), was calculated for division A. To find the numerator, Table 22-1 is scanned for all patterns containing the combination 'o. These are patterns 2.1, 3.1, 3.2, 3.3, 4.1, 4.2, 4.3,

TABLE 22-3. A SUMMARY OF RELATIONAL TOTALS:
RECEIVED BY DIVISION HEADS ONLY

| Symbol | Order giving | | Socializing | |
|---|---|---|---|---|
| | Div. head A | Div. head B | Div. head A | Div. head B |
| ' | 7 | 7 | None | None |
| o | 9 | 13 | None | None |
| x | 12 | 16 | 4 | 3 |
| + | 4 | 13 | 2 | 2 |
| − | 11 | 3 | 6 | 4 |

TABLE 22-4. INDEX SUMMARY

| | Order giving | | | | Socializing | | | |
|---|---|---|---|---|---|---|---|---|
| | Division A | | Division B | | Division A | | Division B | |
| | Ratio | Per cent | Ratio | Per cent | Ratio | Per cent | Ratio | Per cent |
| Understanding: | | | | | | | | |
| (1) $\Sigma'o/\Sigma'$ | 24/26 | 92.31 | 31/37 | 83.78 | | | | |
| (2) $\Sigma'o/\Sigma o$ | 24/29 | 82.76 | 31/54 | 57.41 | | | | |
| Normative conformity: | | | | | | | | |
| (3) $\Sigma'x/\Sigma'$ | 22/26 | 84.61 | 30/37 | 81.08 | | | | |
| (4) $\Sigma'x/\Sigma x$ | 22/33 | 66.67 | 30/66 | 45.45 | | | | |
| (5) $\Sigma ox/\Sigma o$ | 26/29 | 89.66 | 48/54 | 88.89 | | | | |
| (6) $\Sigma ox/\Sigma x$ | 26/33 | 78.79 | 48/66 | 72.73 | | | | |
| (7) $\Sigma'ox/\Sigma'o$ | 21/24 | 87.50 | 29/31 | 93.55 | | | | |
| (8) $\Sigma'ox/\Sigma x$ | 21/33 | 63.64 | 29/66 | 43.94 | | | | |
| Affective conformity: | | | | | | | | |
| (9a) $\Sigma+x/\Sigma+$ | 12/21 | 57.14 | 39/51 | 76.47 | 4/24 | 16.67 | 21/38 | 55.26 |
| (9b) $\Sigma-x/\Sigma-$ | 4/15 | 26.67 | 3/14 | 21.43 | 0/21 | 0 | 0/17 | 0 |
| Satisfaction and dissatisfaction:* | | | | | | | | |
| (10a) $\Sigma'+/\Sigma'$ | 13/26 | 50.00 | 23/37 | 62.16 | | | | |
| D (10b) $\Sigma'-/\Sigma'$ | 2/26 | 7.69 | 2/37 | 5.41 | | | | |
| (11a) $\Sigma o+/\Sigma o$ | 13/29 | 44.83 | 34/54 | 62.96 | | | | |
| D (11b) $\Sigma o-/\Sigma o$ | 2/29 | 6.89 | 3/54 | 5.56 | | | | |
| (12a) $\Sigma'o+/\Sigma'o$ | 12/24 | 50.00 | 22/31 | 70.98 | | | | |
| D (12b) $\Sigma'o-/\Sigma'o$ | 2/24 | 8.33 | 1/31 | 3.23 | | | | |
| (13a) $\Sigma x+/\Sigma x$ | 12/33 | 36.36 | 39/66 | 59.09 | 4/25 | 16.00 | 21/36 | 58.33 |
| D (13b) $\Sigma x-/\Sigma x$ | 4/33 | 12.12 | 3/66 | 4.55 | 0/25 | 0 | 0/36 | 0 |
| (14) $\Sigma+/[\Sigma(+)+\Sigma(-)]$ | 21/36 | 58.33 | 51/65 | 78.46 | 24/45 | 53.33 | 38/55 | 69.09 |
| (15) $\Sigma(+x)/[\Sigma(+x)+\Sigma(-x)]$ | 12/16 | 75.00 | 39/42 | 92.86 | 4/4 | 100.00 | 21/21 | 100.00 |
| (16a) $\Sigma(')_x/\Sigma'$ | 7/26 | 26.92 | 7/37 | 18.92 | | | | |
| (16b) $\Sigma(o)_x/\Sigma o$ | 9/29 | 31.03 | 13/54 | 24.07 | | | | |
| (16c) $\Sigma(x)_x/\Sigma x$ | 12/33 | 36.36 | 16/66 | 24.24 | 4/25 | 16.00 | 3/36 | 8.33 |
| (16d) $\Sigma(+)_x/\Sigma+$ | 4/21 | 19.05 | 13/51 | 25.49 | 2/24 | 8.33 | 2/38 | 7.14 |
| (16e) $\Sigma(-)_x/\Sigma-$ | 11/15 | 73.33 | 3/14 | 21.43 | 6/21 | 28.57 | 4/17 | 23.53 |

* Indices of *dis*satisfaction, for which low values indicate satisfaction, are marked with a D

and 5.1. The figure obtained is 24. To find the denominator it is necessary simply to examine Table 22-2, the line marked ʹ. The figure is 26.
Thus index (1) for division A is 24/26, or 92.31.

A set of criteria against which the indices may be evaluated is provided by a series of responses regarding perceptions by the people in
each division of morale, productivity, and job satisfaction. Table 22-5
summarizes some of the findings.

Thus it is indicated that division B consistently exceeds division A
in high or very high ratings in job satisfaction, perceived productivity,
and perceived morale. This finding becomes more meaningful when we

TABLE 22-5. A SUMMARY OF PERCEPTUAL RATINGS OF JOB SATISFACTION,
MORALE, AND PRODUCTIVITY†

| Division | Job satisfaction of each person in division | | Productivity of division | | Morale of division | |
|---|---|---|---|---|---|---|
| | % rating high or very high | % rating low or very low | % rating high or very high | % rating low or very low | % rating high or very high | % rating low or very low |
| A | 39.3 | 14.3 | 28.6 | 18.6 | 21.4 | 53.6 |
| B | 63.2 | 7.9 | 55.2 | 7.9 | 81.6 | 2.6 |

† Adapted from I. R. Weschler, M. Kahane, and R. Tannenbaum, "Job Satisfaction, Productivity and Morale: A Case Study," *Occupational Psychology*, vol. 26,
p. 5, January, 1952, appearing here as Chap. 21.

consider the MSS results. In the sociometric indices of satisfaction, indices (10a), (11a), (12a), and (13a), division B ranks higher. On all
the indices of dissatisfaction, (10b), (11b), (12b), and (13b), division
A ranks higher. Thus, it would seem that at least as far as order giving
is concerned, the various measures of satisfaction and dissatisfaction
vary concomitantly with the measures of job satisfaction, perceived
productivity, and perceived morale. The indices of affective conformity,
(9a) and (9b), and of affective atmosphere, (14) and (15), show a
similar relationship. Here, too, the indices for division B suggest the
more harmonious social situation.

On the other hand, in understanding of prescription, higher indices
(1) and (2) are found in division A. Similarly, for five of the six
indices of normative conformity, (3), (4), (5), (6), and (8), measures
for division A are somewhat higher than those for division B, although
the differences generally are slight. Only in index (7), which measures
conformity to the understood ($\Sigma'ox/\Sigma'o$) does the index figure for division B exceed that of division A.

These findings indicate greater understanding of prescription and a
somewhat higher degree of conformity to prescription in division A than

in division B. But division B ranks higher than division A in satisfaction with interpersonal relations, in conformity of behavior (actual) to the desired, and in affective atmosphere. These results make sense in light of the following: 1. Division B provides higher ratings in job satisfaction, perceived morale, and perceived productivity. 2. As indicated by a broad a priori analysis of the two divisions, division A appears to have certain attributes associated with restrictive leadership, while division B has attributes associated with permissive leadership.

Further evidence is furnished by the indices of centralization. The prescribed, perceived, and actual relations are more centralized in the head of division A than in the head of division B [see (16a), (16b), (16c)]. On the other hand, the head of division B receives a greater proportion of desired choices than the head of division A [see (16d)], while conversely, and significantly, a much greater proportion of the rejected relations is concentrated in the head of division A, who heads the division characterized by restrictive leadership.

In examining indices for affective conformity, satisfaction, and affective atmosphere [see (9a), (13a), and (14)] for the activity of socializing after working hours, we observe that again the more harmonious social situation exists in the permissively led division B. For indices (9b), conformity of actual to rejected, and (13b), dissatisfaction with actual relations, both divisions reveal zero scores. This is not hard to understand in view of the fact that usually, although not necessarily, people will not seek voluntary social intercourse with those they reject. An exception to this may be provided by instances in which socializing is oriented toward an end, such as the influencing of a superior regarding a promotion, even though, in fact, that superior may be rejected. Analogously, the scores for both divisions on index (15), which measures the extent to which socializing interactions with positive affect predominate over those with negative affect, are 100. Again, this is plausible because social contacts outside the job setting will be primarily with those people who are desired as social companions rather than with those who are rejected in that role.

So far, order giving has been the only goal-directed activity that we have considered, but we may inquire how the several indices compare when calculated for a number of other activities. Some relevant data are shown in Table 22-6.

For all activities but determination of promotions, understanding of prescription, as measured by index (1), is greater in the restrictively led division A. Conversely, for all relations, satisfaction, as measured by index (10a), is greater in the permissively led division B. However, in efficiency rating, determination of promotions, and pointing out mistakes, normative conformity in division B exceeds corresponding measurements for division A. At first glance this is puzzling, because, as indeed is the case for order giving and grievance handling, we would have expected higher conformity in the restrictively led division. This lack of conformity can be explained, however. Indices of centralization (not shown here) indicate that the head of division A assumes much more responsibility for efficiency rating, promoting, and pointing out mistakes than is prescribed for him. Thus, the index of conformity is lowered, because the division head himself has gone beyond the limits set for him by organizational fiat.

Looking at Table 22-6 from a different standpoint, it is apparent that some activities more often rank high on certain indices than others. For example, in understanding and satisfaction, order giving and efficiency

TABLE 22-6. A COMPARISON OF SELECTED INDICES FOR SEVERAL
GOAL-DIRECTED ACTIVITIES IN DIVISIONS A AND B

| Activities | Understanding index$(1)\Sigma'o/\Sigma'$ | | Normative conformity index$(3)\Sigma'x/\Sigma'$ | | Satisfaction index $(10a)\Sigma - /\Sigma'$ | |
|---|---|---|---|---|---|---|
| | Div. A | Div. B | Div. A | Div. B | Div. A | Div. B |
| Order giving................ | 92 | 84 | 85 | 81 | 50 | 62 |
| Efficiency rating.............. | 96 | 76 | 29 | 68 | 54 | 61 |
| Grievance handling............ | 86 | 61 | 74 | 58 | 36 | 45 |
| Determination of promotions.... | 59 | 63 | 45 | 50 | 22 | 45 |
| Pointing out mistakes.......... | 79 | 74 | 71 | 80 | 43 | 55 |

rating typically exceed the other indices in magnitude. Thus, the interpersonal networks for order giving and efficiency rating are understood more clearly, and accepted somewhat better, than corresponding networks for grievance handling, for the determination of promotions, and for pointing out of mistakes. Normative conformity is highest for order giving.

In most instances, indices of understanding for the various relations have the greatest magnitudes. They are followed by indices of normative conformity and by indices of satisfaction in that order.

In the pilot investigation, only eleven activities were studied. Thus, the data obtained did not lend themselves to an adequate construction of interactivity indices. A hypothetical example, demonstrating the use of these indices, was given in the section on interactivity indices.

## SUMMARY

The Multi-relational Sociometric Survey is an extension of sociometric methodology to a variety of interpersonal activities and relations. Activities may be clearly directed to the attainment of organizational goals (goal-directed, e.g., order giving), or they may not be so directed (nongoal-directed, e.g., socializing after working hours). Five relations are distinguished: (1) the prescribed, which resembles the organizational blueprint; (2) the perceived, which corresponds to the extent to which persons in the organization are aware of the blueprint; (3) the actual, which indicates the reported interactions among the members of the organization; (4) the desired, which indicates preferences regarding interactions; and (5) the rejected, which indicates aversions to interactions. For goal-directed activities all five of these relations are relevant; for nongoal-directed activities, only the last three are relevant.

A pilot investigation was conducted in a research and development laboratory. Sixty-six subjects, from two contrasting divisions, were studied. The data were organized in the form of a series of matrices, one for each activity. Information on the specific relations was entered in the cells of each matrix. Using the cell entries of any one matrix as raw data, a series of *intra-activity* indices was constructed: (1) indices of understanding, (2) indices of normative conformity, (3) indices of affective conformity, (4) indices of satisfaction and dissatisfaction, (5) indices of affective atmosphere, and (6) indices of centralization. Systematic overlap among intra-activity indices was discussed. Using entries dealing with a given relation as it appears in various activities as raw data, some *interactivity* indices were also constructed.

Chapter 21, using the data obtained in the pilot investigation, suggests that there are some significant relationships between intra-activity index results, on the one hand, and perceived morale, perceived productivity, job satisfaction, and leadership style, on the other. For example, indices of satisfaction were higher in the more permissively led of the two divisions, which also had higher ratings from its members on morale, productivity, and job satisfaction. Understanding of the organizational blueprint was shown to be higher in the more restrictively led division.

The MSS technique requires considerable further theoretical examination and empirical testing. Indices other than those proposed here may ultimately prove more useful, and various refinements or simplifications are no doubt possible. However, it is suggested that by making the sociometric method multi-relational through the systematic examination of several activities and relations, desirable dimensions of depth and realism are added to the sociometric study of social structure.

CHAPTER 23

# Relations with the Host: Social Research
# Faces Industry*

Social research in America has become a million-dollar business. From time to time it has changed its emphasis and method, but the work of management consultants and university research groups has become an established part of the industrial scene.

The most familiar kind of social research in industry is applied research. Management consultants are frequently called in to examine a specific situation and to recommend solutions to certain problems. The consultant interviews individuals, studies documents, or carries out whatever other investigations seem appropriate, and states his recommendations as guides to managerial action.

In contrast, the programs of basic social science research, established during the past few decades by universities, government organizations, and private institutions, have different aims and interests. These programs are concerned with a fundamental understanding of social life. Their objective is general knowledge rather than specific policy recommendations.

The relationship between applied and basic social research is parallel to this relationship in natural science: applied natural science research uses the general findings of basic natural science research to solve spe-

* This chapter is based upon the following: "Social Research Faces Industry," by Fred Massarik and Paula Brown, *Personnel*, vol. 30, no. 6, pp. 454–462, May, 1954; and "Human Organizations Research Faces Industry: An Exercise in the Public Relations of Science," paper presented by Fred Massarik before the annual meeting, American Association for the Advancement of Science, St. Louis, 1952. A portion of this chapter is adapted from *An Evaluative Focus on Human Relations*, by Robert Tannenbaum, miscellaneous publication (mimeo, 1954) of the Institute of Industrial Relations, University of California, Los Angeles.

cific technological problems. In the same way, management consultants use basic social science findings to obtain specific, uniquely applicable solutions to industrial problems. Their task is more difficult because basic social science knowledge upon which they can draw is limited.

## SECURING BACKING AND A RESEARCH SETTING

A practical difference between these two types of research is commonly found in their respective sources of financial backing. While interested managements directly support applied research conducted in their own firms, the social scientist who conducts basic research receives financial support from outside the research setting. Here the social scientist takes the initiative in selecting a topic for investigation, and it is he who applies for a grant from a university, private research foundation, or government agency. Usually a committee screens the applications and supports those investigations which conform best to the standards of the institution.

After having obtained the necessary financing, one of the social researcher's immediate problems is to gain entry into an organization in which he may carry out basic research. Often he finds that this is not easy. Managers do not always understand the nature of basic social research, or its role in the economy. Researchers are not always skilled in interpreting to managers the functions of fundamental social science. When confronted by social scientists seeking research settings, managers often have doubts and objections. These typically have their foundations in fact. Offering an organization as a "guinea pig" is not necessarily an appealing prospect. Yet the "guinea-pig" analogy is not quite valid. While a laboratory animal is passively at the mercy of an experimenter, human organizations are never passively at the mercy of social scientists. In fact, mutually beneficial relationships can be developed between basic social research and industry if both parties recognize their mutual responsibilities, as well as the potential advantages of working together.

## APPLIED RESEARCH IS NOT ENOUGH

Applied research typically is instituted when a manager recognizes an organizational difficulty which he believes can be solved by a consultant or expert. Unrecognized difficulties, and difficulties which the manager believes insoluble, are not considered. Few of these issues are likely to come to the attention of the social scientist unless he himself attempts to ferret them out.

If most social research in industry is to be directed toward solving specific human and organizational problems *recognized by manage-*

*ment,* there is serious danger that a distorted view of industry will be obtained. If laws and generalizations are based upon a biased sample of industrial situations, in the long run scientific understanding of social structure and the derivable answers to management problems can never be complete.[1] Representative samples of organizations are needed, and not fortuitous accumulations of information drawn largely from situations conspicuously beset by recognized organizational problems. It is apparent, then, that to obtain a balanced and comprehensive overview of the human dynamics of industrial organizations, the widest variety of firms must cooperate with social researchers. Thus the manager who is in a position to permit or deny entry in a very real sense influences social research progress.

## SOCIAL RESPONSIBILITY AND BASIC RESEARCH

The paths of science are not always direct. A penny spent on research is not always followed immediately by two pennies earned. Still, American industry spends immense sums on physical science research. The Bell Telephone Laboratories, General Electric, and the Du Pont Company are among the many large firms supporting such research. Over the years a single finding may justify all the time and effort that may have appeared fruitless.

Industry's direct financial support of basic social research has been limited, though the ultimate rewards of increasingly effective human organization in industry may be considerable. Yet even if actual financing is disregarded, management shares social responsibility for facilitating such research. For many years universities and foundations have devoted energy to investigating fundamental principles of social functioning. Studies of group process, of participation in decision making, of counseling and interviewing are illustrative.[2] Many of the ideas de-

---

[1] Another kind of social research—laboratory experiment with small groups—is now producing interesting analyses of some social phenomena. At present, these experiments are limited to artificially simplified social situations. Observations in industry are necessary to test the agreement between laboratory results and the findings drawn from actual industrial situations. For accounts of laboratory research, see R. F. Bales, *Interaction Process Analysis: A Method for the Study of Small Groups* (Reading, Mass.: Addison-Wesley Publishing Company, Inc., 1950); A. Bavelas and D. Barrett, "An Experimental Approach to Organizational Communication," *Personnel*, vol. 27, pp. 366–371, March, 1951; and Mary E. Roseborough, "Experimental Studies of Small Groups," *Psychological Bulletin*, vol. 50, no. 4, pp. 275–303, July, 1953.

[2] Robert Tannenbaum and Fred Massarik, "Participation by Subordinates in the Managerial Decision-making Process," *Canadian Journal of Economics and Political Science*, vol. 16, pp. 408–418, August, 1950; Carl R. Rogers, *Counseling and Psychotherapy* (Boston: Houghton Mifflin Company, 1942); D. Cartwright and A. Zander, *Group Dynamics: Research and Theory* (1st ed.; Evanston, Ill.: Row, Peterson & Company, 1953).

veloped by university and foundation scientists have already found application in supervisory training, selection, and plans for streamlining formal organization. In this way management shares the benefits of social science. Through time, the further expansion of basic knowledge bears promise of ever-increasing service to practical managerial situations. Thus, there are good reasons for aiding the work of social researchers. There is need for true give and take between the social scientist in search of a field setting and the manager who plays the role of gatekeeper. Frank facing of the problems that may arise when a firm plays host to basic social research and a clear understanding of respective purposes and goals would do much to facilitate such projects in industry.

In attempting to find suitable industrial organizations for social research, we have encountered various resistances. While these resistances are undoubtedly based in part upon real concerns, they are due also in part to vague uneasiness and to misunderstanding. It may be well to consider a few in some detail.

EXPRESSED RESISTANCES:
  SOME QUESTIONS AND STATEMENTS

*"Will a study mean trouble?"* Frequently the manager views the researcher as a possible source of trouble, and he asks many questions in order to ascertain the nature, extent, and implications of the anticipated disturbance. For example, such comments as the following are characteristic:

To tell you the truth, everything is going so well that we don't need any help here. We just don't have any problems, and we don't see how you can ask a lot of questions in the factory without making the men wonder what's going on.

A top executive of a firm planning to open a new Los Angeles branch spoke more unequivocally when a researcher asked why repeated letters to his eastern office, proposing a study, had remained unanswered:

Well, wasn't my silence answer enough? What do you think we are trying to do here? We can't be a bunch of guinea pigs for you fellows. We don't want people asking us a lot of silly questions. Frankly, we are moving out here to run a factory, and we just can't be bothered with this sort of thing.

Yet "trouble" is not a necessary concomitant of research. Indeed, it is to the researcher's advantage to be as unobtrusive as possible. Especially when he intends to continue his research within a given organization for a period of time, he will not want to alter the existing interpersonal or attitudinal characteristics of the firm. Since he is merely a measuring instrument, he will want to minimize his own impact upon the situation he is measuring.

Still, for practical reasons, managers may ask researchers to avoid "danger spots," such as a department in which the pressure of work or internal tensions might hinder both research and organizational effectiveness.[3] Research may have unforeseen consequences by drawing attention to unrecognized problems. Some of these problems are not serious while they are latent, but demand resolution when recognized, thus diverting energy from other areas of work. In the long run, however, facing up to slumbering problems may well pay off in heightened organizational effectiveness.

Social researchers are currently being trained in the human relations skills necessary for effective relations with others during the research process. This training, too, attempts to help the researchers to be more adept, and thus nondisruptive, while collecting data in organizations.[4]

This is not to claim that all those who wish to carry out research have acquired these skills. A theoretically oriented social researcher may be unfamiliar with the requirements of field work. The manager retains his prerogative of judging the possible effects caused by any particular researcher.

In a sense, the researcher enters into an informal contractual relationship with the manager, whereby the researcher agrees that the research will not be disruptive. If, as the study progresses, disruption can be clearly traced to the research work, there is no question that the manager can terminate the relationship.

"*Will a study mean expense?*" Many managers are quite concerned about financial commitments that a research project might entail. They are occasionally suspicious of a project which, superficially at least, seems to give something for nothing.

It is true that university-sponsored or grant-supported basic research rarely makes any direct demands upon the firm for financial support. We have already noted that in this respect it differs from "consulting" research, which is usually financed by the organization which hopes to benefit from it. However, even basic research does involve expense to the host organization—a less direct cost consisting of the time which employees on all levels spend cooperating with the research staff, and overhead.

[3] An avoidance of such danger spots would not affect the validity of all research projects. But unless we examine some of these problems, perhaps with special techniques, we may end up with serious gaps in knowledge.

[4] See "Social Relations Skills in Field Research," *The Journal of Social Issues,* vol. 8, no. 3, 1952.

Inquiring about such costs, one executive put it this way:

Let's suppose that you go ahead with the study. This means that you will be spending a lot of time talking to people around the plant and giving them all sorts of tests and questionnaires. That sort of thing is going to cost us a lot of money because we will be paying for the time that is spent on other things besides production. Just how much time do you think it will take for each employee?

Lack of clarity about costs may lead to confusion and misunderstandings. Whenever possible, the manager should obtain some estimate of the time demands the researcher will make upon members of the organization. This does not mean that the figures should be inflexible, but that adequate estimates will make possible optimal scheduling and realistic planning.

Over the years, time and overhead costs resulting from basic social research may well pay for themselves. The benefits that may emerge later from basic social science—benefits analogous to those accruing from basic physical science—have already been mentioned. It is yet early in the history of large-scale fundamental social inquiry. Though the ultimate gains still are not certainties, current evidence surely suggests that these expenditures are worthwhile investments in future social and industrial well-being.

*"How will a study benefit the firm?"* In general, a manager expects a direct return for time and effort. When he is asked to cooperate with basic social research, he may doubt whether it can lead to tangible financial gains or improved morale. For the manager of a corporation, these doubts may be heightened by awareness that he may have to answer to the stockholders for the time and overhead costs involved.

An executive of a large Los Angeles manufacturing plant expressed this feeling:

I've never been sure about the sort of thing (basic social research) that you've been suggesting. We had consultants in a year ago, and had just a little success with their work. I'm not at all sure that the Board of Directors would let me authorize a study. I think they would balk because, with production pressures being what they are, all the time that the workers would spend in the project just would not pay off as far as we are concerned.

Of course, it is true that the benefits may be long run rather than immediate, and that no single basic investigation can be viewed as necessarily having an immediate, clear-cut economic reward for the host organization. Still, relevant aspects of fundamental social science projects can be "fed back" into the organization. This feed back, by way of staff meetings, training programs, and memoranda, may not concern crucial trouble spots, and it may not "solve problems." But it can provide some useful insights into the host organization's day-by-day operation. When employers and employees understand the social environment in which they live and work, tensions and barriers to communication can be reduced more easily. The research may provide a healthy stimulant in a quest for constructive self-criticism.[5]

From a practical standpoint, it is possible for the social researcher to incorporate within the frame of a basic investigation some hypotheses of *immediate* interest to management. Indeed, such hypotheses or hunches for investigation also may be meaningful parts of the broader study. At any rate, it is not unreasonable for management to ask the social scientist to integrate some subsidiary "applied" phases within the design of the fundamental inquiry. Significant direct gains, as well as long-run benefits, may thus be provided.

*"How will the employees feel about this?"* Whether it is a rationalization or a fact, some managers express the fear that the employees will regard the study as an imposition or threat. For example, one company president said:

I think your study is a good idea. But the workers here are hired to do a job. They don't care about science, and they don't want to fill out questionnaires or worry about interviews. I think we'll have a tough time getting them to cooperate.

There is much evidence that the cooperation of employees is readily obtained if two conditions are met: first, if the management and any unions that may exist take an interest in the project and encourage cooperation; and second, if the researcher assures the employees that their confidences, represented by the information they furnish, will be fully respected.

Research rapport is determined largely by the attitudes toward the investigation held by the management, the formal union organization (if any), the social researcher, and the employee himself. If these attitudes create an atmosphere of understanding and free interchange of opinion, positive results have a good chance of emerging.

For example, basic social research may even serve a function akin to that of counseling or morale surveys. The data-gathering methods often provide the employee with an opportunity to vent feelings about his job, his fellow workers, and his superiors, which he cannot easily express during his daily work. Responding to a basic research questionnaire or interview often creates less anxiety than is aroused when, in applied social science or counseling, employees suspect that their responses may lead to adverse managerial action, despite assurances to

[5] See F. Mann and R. Likert, "The Need for Research on the Communication of Research Results," *Human Organization,* vol. 11, no. 4, pp. 15–19, Winter, 1952.

the contrary. Of course, in basic social research the individual still has the right to refuse to cooperate, though nonresponse does reduce the value of the findings.

*"What will happen to the findings?"* Some managers are quite concerned about the possibility that confidential information may spread to competing organizations. Similarly, in some instances managers express fears that negative publicity may result from a general dissemination of findings. One vice-president put it this way, for example:

> Now you may know that we are in a pretty tough competitive position. We certainly don't want the other outfits to get any inside dope about the way we've been operating. We don't want them to know our plans either. . . . Just what are you going to do with the results of your research?

Or, as another company officer said:

> Will you mention the name of the firm in your reports? Will we have an opportunity to look over your materials before you write them . . . just in case there is some aspect that we don't feel we should be publicizing right now?

No competent researcher wishes to communicate confidential information to his host organization's competitors. Most articles for the technical journals consist of general statements about social processes rather than potentially harmful case material. Still, managers should clearly understand the implications of the publication of research findings. While in many cases no mention is made of the host organization's real name, identification is sometimes possible. Researchers agree that not all findings are publishable, particularly if damaging or truly confidential facts may be laid bare. Experience has shown, however, that in most cases a technical report dealing with a basic research project is oriented in such a way that the problem of disseminating confidential information to unauthorized personnel is minimal.

UNEXPRESSED RESISTANCES: UNDERCURRENTS

The manager who is asked to make his firm available for a study occasionally has feelings and attitudes which prevent him from recognizing or expressing openly all his misgivings about the project. He may not want to state all his doubts. Some of these "hidden" questions seem to be the following:

*"Can science be applied to social phenomena?"* The researcher is cast in the role of scientist when he speaks to the manager. This is legitimate, because the researcher's primary interest is obtaining scientifically valid conclusions. Furthermore, this role emphasizes the impartiality

of the research process and thus may remove some elements of suspicion from the manager's mind. This role is not an unmixed blessing, however. While few managers would say so, they may doubt that any sort of social investigation can be "scientific." The associations that go with the word "science" stem largely from the realm of natural science in general and from physics in particular. In fact, it is the *method*, not the *data*, that determines what is scientific.[6] While the complexity of social events makes their scientific analysis more difficult, research already has shown that such analysis is feasible. Researchers at MIT, Ohio State, Harvard, Yale, and Michigan, among others, have provided outstanding examples of the effective application of scientific method to complex social problems.

*"Will the study show management in a bad light?"* Perhaps unrecognized, there may be fears that some phase of the research may point to errors for which particular managers can be held responsible. The crux rests not in a basic management policy of covering up for mistakes, but rather in a general fear that managers are not performing their jobs most effectively. Such lack of confidence is very common but is rarely expressed.[7]

In a sense this is the unstated counterpart of the question: "What will happen to the findings?" The central concern here, however, is with the protection of individual managers, rather than with broader questions relating to competitive strength or organizational reputation. Again, though research reports do not identify individuals, unique circumstances still may make it possible for persons familiar with the situation to do so. Furthermore, criteria of organizational effectiveness or ineffectiveness, which frequently are necessary to research projects, may suggest success or failure on the part of specific managers. The atmosphere in which such indirect "fault finding" takes place is crucial. With adequate understanding and with a willingness to learn, such recognition of shortcomings can prove extremely valuable in enhancing managerial and organizational effectiveness.

*"Just who is behind this study?"* We have found that the interactions between researcher and manager are influenced somewhat by the manager's opinion of the agency that is sponsoring the research. If the sponsoring agency is a university, a manager may hold preconceptions about the social or political beliefs of the faculty members or, in fact, about

---

[6] *Cf.* Otakar Machotka, "Is Sociology a Natural Science?" *American Journal of Sociology*, vol. 54, February, 1949.

[7] See the analysis of apprehension and fear of failure in executives by William E. Henry, "The Business Executive: A Study in the Psychodynamics of a Social Role," *American Journal of Sociology*, vol. 54, pp. 286–291, January, 1949; and Robert N. McMurry, "The Executive Neurosis," *Harvard Business Review*, vol. 30, no. 6, pp. 33–47, November-December, 1952.

universities in general. He may have confidence in the university for its contributions to research and industrial progress. Similarly, some managers may believe that a private foundation sponsoring research may have a special interest in the results, especially if the foundation happens to be supported by a large business organization. And, at the semantic level, "socialism" and "social science" may be confused, with obviously disastrous consequences for the possibilities of conducting social research.

The manager has every right to know who is backing a particular research proposal. He should make it his business to find out. Almost always, he will find that the motives of the social researcher are sincere, and devoted to the progress of interpersonal and industrial harmony.

## TOWARD BETTER RESEARCHER-MANAGER UNDERSTANDING

We think that these resistances to basic social research in industry can be overcome. The social scientist needs to gain greater insight into the nature of the manager's attitudes. Similarly, the manager needs to learn more about the motives and functions of social scientists. Basic to such heightened mutual awareness is a real knowledge of the specific beliefs and attitudes that are held by the people who are "management" and by those who are "social science." Research in this area, however, is limited.[8]

Indeed, we have much to learn about what social scientists and managers are like. But some steps can now be taken to break down the barriers that stand in the way of good working relationships, for we do have some knowledge, drawn from the literature and from commonsense observation, which provides a starting point.

### Cross-fertilization of Ideas

Increasingly, business executives and social scientists find that they have something in common. The separate ivory towers of both business and science are disappearing. There is growing participation by managers in university programs, including teaching, and university people frequently serve as management consultants. More and more student groups are visiting industrial plants as a part of their social science training, and industrial employees are receiving further training at universities. With increased contacts between university and industrial personnel, those who are interested in conducting basic social research in industry have greater opportunities to meet their potential research

[8] See Anne Roe, "Psychological Study of Eminent Psychologists and Anthropologists, and a Comparison with Biological and Physical Scientists," *Psychological Monographs*, vol. 67, no. 2, 1953.

subjects and the managers who can open the doors. At the same time, industry people are becoming acquainted with the social scientists who may wish to study them. Managers have issued open invitations to us after becoming familiar with our interests and aims.

In addition to an increase in personal contacts in general, some special techniques can be employed to further mutual understanding between researchers and managers.

## Community Relations Programs

Both businessmen's groups and universities frequently sponsor conferences, round tables, and conventions. Often these get-togethers concentrate on technical topics of interest primarily to "the fraternity." At other times, however, energetic efforts are directed toward obtaining wide participation, and some university activities of this sort attempt to bring about closer liaison between industry and university. The inclusion of subject matter on the relationships between social inquiry and industrial functioning in conference programs sponsored by universities and industrial groups would be desirable to bridge the gap between managerial and research values. Furthermore, universities and business associations well might consider planning community conferences around such topics as "Social Science and the Goals of Management," or "Industry Meets Social Research."

## Publications

Another aspect of the researcher's public relations problem involves the communication of research results through publications. One management respondent, after mentioning a number of basic social science contributions, stated:

> These researches have hardly been felt in industry . . . their chief effect to date is to make managers generally aware that there is a growing body of social knowledge. But just now industry is beginning to wonder what it's all about and how it can be applied.

Judging from the comments of managers, social researchers are not imparting knowledge as skillfully as possible. When research reports are labeled "jargonesque," vague, and involved, when technical language and terminology are viewed as obscuring meaning, the social researcher must seriously consider more effective means of interpretation.

Of course, many of the results of social research are available to management, both in social science journals and in management journals. However, there is a greater need for popularized, nontechnical handbooks, pamphlets and compendiums of basic knowledge summarizing the approaches of social research in the language of business rather than in the formal terminology of science. There is need for a greater number of "social science writers"—individuals with both writing skill and an ability to popularize without changing meaning. Additional cross-fertilization of ideas could be achieved through the technical journals. For example, it might be valuable for social science journals to publish relevant writings by business executives more frequently, while social scientists might do well to write more often for the less academic, practical trade publications. There is an increasing number of examples of two or more reports being written on a given piece of research—one for professional colleagues and the other, a more popular version, for potential users.

## PROSPECTS

Much research in industrial settings has been made possible despite the resistances discussed in this chapter. But the organizational manager holds the key to social research in industry, for without his cooperation and interest social science cannot obtain the data it needs.

As science learns more about what *really* happens when human beings join in productive endeavors, managers will have less and less reason to criticize university research for being "too theoretical." If one is permitted a judgment of faith, a wider basic knowledge of social phenomena ultimately will result in a more effective economy and in more satisfactory working relationships.

# CHAPTER 24

# Relations with the Subject: Problems in the Use
# of Indirect Methods of Attitude Measurement*

The use of indirect methods of attitude measurement has recently come into vogue, and a number of new techniques have been developed which supposedly get at those "deeper-level" attitudes which a person may be internalizing and unwilling to reveal.[1] These indirect devices conceal from the individual the intent of the measurement and allow him to produce responses which would not be freely forthcoming if he were fearful of becoming personally involved. The purpose of this chapter is to raise several as yet unresolved questions relating to the use of these new techniques.

Indirect methods of attitude measurement may be constructed and used for a number of purposes. They are used to explore and test various psychological theories, especially those related to problems of learning and perception. They are used to construct reliable and valid test instruments which may be valuable in the clinical situation as part of a test battery for the assessment of the total personality. Finally, indirect attitude-measurement devices are applied in the actual field situation for the measurement of attitudes held by the members of various groups.

* This chapter is primarily based on "Problems in the Use of Indirect Methods of Attitude Measurement," by Irving R. Weschler, *Public Opinion Quarterly*, vol. 14, no. 1, pp. 133–139, Spring, 1951. The last paragraphs of the original article have been replaced by the section entitled "The Researcher's Values," which is based on a portion of *An Evaluative Focus on Human Relations*, by Robert Tannenbaum, miscellaneous publication (mimeo, 1954) of the Institute of Industrial Relations, University of California, Los Angeles.

[1] See D. T. Campbell, "The Indirect Assessment of Social Attitudes," *Psychological Bulletin*, vol. 47, no. 1, pp. 15–38, January, 1950; also I. R. Weschler and R. Bernberg, "Indirect Methods of Attitude Measurement," *International Journal of Opinion and Attitude Research*, vol. 4, pp. 209–229, Summer, 1950.

A CASE STUDY

Typical of these studies, perhaps, is "The Personal Factor in Labor Mediation," utilizing the "error-choice" technique for the measurement of attitudes toward labor and management.[2] Some of the ethical and public relations problems which arose during this study's progress are probably encountered in any kind of investigation using indirect methods of attitude measurement.

The "error-choice" technique, developed for attitude testing by Professor Hammond,[3] utilizes an information test which forces the respondent to choose between two alternative answers, each of which is by intent factually wrong, or controversial, or of such a nature that the correct answer is not easily accessible. This kind of test situation provokes the respondent to select pseudo facts from memory, and the "direction" of the error is measured as an indication of the respondent's attitude.

Using the "error-choice" technique, a test was developed which was designed to measure information as well as attitudes in the field of labor relations. The test was validated on a group of students, as well as on active union and management people, and was later incorporated as part of the test battery in the study on "The Personal Factor in Labor Mediation."

The results were, in general, as expected. Union members and students who classified themselves as "prolabor" scored high in the "prolabor" direction, as measured by the test, while the management representatives and students declaring themselves to be "promanagement" scored low. When the test was administered to the labor mediators, many mediators who were rated high by their colleagues in terms of their ability to do the job tended to score in the "neutral zone," that is, near the sample population mean, while those who were rated as "poor" by their colleagues scored either in the "promanagement" or in the "prolabor" zones of the attitude range.

There was no difficulty in validating the first form of our Labor Relations Information Inventory with the help of UCLA students and various labor and management groups, especially since the hypotheses and workings of the technique were explained after each administration of the test. Trouble came for sundry reasons from the labor mediators who were not ready to accept the results which had been obtained. A labor mediator usually sees himself as a "neutral" agent who, through

[2] See I. R. Weschler, "The Personal Factor in Labor Mediation," *Personnel Psychology*, vol. 3, pp. 113–133, Summer, 1950.
[3] See K. Hammond, "Measuring Attitudes by Error-Choice: An Indirect Method," *Journal of Abnormal and Social Psychology*, vol. 43, pp. 38–48, 1948.

his personal skill, is able to bring labor and management together in a settlement of mutual satisfaction. Although many "biased" mediators, as measured by the test, were rated "good" by their colleagues on performance, the fact that most of them scored far from neutral on the test apparently became a threat to their personal security. The following excerpt from a letter by one mediator is an indication of the feeling which many others may have shared:

I tend to agree with those mediators who participated in your survey who feel that our confidence was violated and abused when conclusions were reached and publicized which were based to some degree on "loaded" questions. Those of us who agreed to be "guinea pigs" in your survey were assured that our replies would be held in strict confidence, and although I may not disagree very much with the conclusions which you have reached, I am questioning the propriety of using the materials which you have collected.

It should be mentioned in passing that none of the individuals participating in the survey could in any way be identified.

## TRICKERY OR SCIENTIFIC METHOD?

When the attitude surveyor presents his subjects with materials and instructions which are not related to the stated purpose of his investigation, it becomes difficult to distinguish between honesty of purpose and deception. Members of the public who are misled into offering a glimpse into "the hidden crevices of their soul," to use one of the timeworn clichés, are not likely to appear enthusiastic on discovering the hoax, even though it may have been carried out for the noble scientific goals of obtaining knowledge and learning truth. The "error-choice" method and many other indirect attitude-measurement techniques keep the respondent in the dark about the true purpose of the test; or, putting it in less elegant terms, they use an element of deceit to trick the respondent into answers which the experimenter considers more honest.

The widespread use of various indirect methods of attitude measurement creates a series of problems with ethical as well as public relations implications, and any investigator who makes a decision about using these indirect methods might well consider these two related aspects. Although many of us may have rationalized our use of these indirect methods with the maxim "truth regardless of consequences," the time has come to analyze the consequences that are involved.

From an *ethical* point of view, the social scientist must be concerned primarily with the interests of his subjects and should view with suspicion any attitude investigation which endangers the subjects' security.

This is, in essence, a "client-centered" point of view, which places the investigator under a moral obligation to protect the goals and objectives of his subjects and not to undertake any course of action which is harmful to their social, economic, or psychological well-being.

From a *public relations* point of view, the social scientist is obliged to consider only those practical aspects of his investigation which concern the smooth functioning of relations with his subjects or the general public. Public-relations-minded, he has an "experimenter-centered" point of view which looks primarily to the creation of a permissive atmosphere that makes possible the orderly progress of long-range research. A research activity may prove to be unwise from an ethical point of view, but if the researcher concerns himself mainly with the public relations aspects of his investigation, he should be prepared to deal with some of the following problems: how to treat subjects who discover that they have been duped into revealing their attitudes on one of the new measurement devices; how to deal with the rising distrust of the public toward the techniques as well as the findings of social research; how to reach the public which discovers the manner of operation of these indirect devices; how to prevent possible misuse of the techniques which he is inventing; how to encourage the public to participate in the increasing number of projects which he is contemplating for the future.

## QUESTIONS THAT NEED ASKING

Every experimenter who considers utilizing indirect methods of attitude measurement in his investigation might profitably ask himself a series of questions whose answers will help him to deal with some of the ethical and public relations problems which he may have to face.

### The Right to Investigate

The first question, basic to any kind of attitude investigation, might perhaps look something like this: "Do I have the right to investigate other people's attitudes?" A democratic society presumably protects the right of the individual to his personal privacy, and there is no law, other than the census law or perhaps some local ordinance, which forces him to participate in a polling activity. If the respondent who recognizes the intent of the investigator refuses to take a stand on an issue which the social researcher is interested in, it illustrates a public relations rather than an ethical problem. Without full participation by his subjects, the social scientist cannot hope to get results which accurately reflect the attitudes of his total population. His job, therefore, is to encourage participation through an active educational program among the general public.

The investigator who is unable to get the subject's permission to test his attitude may find it appropriate to utilize some of the indirect techniques to which reference has been made. In this instance, the investigator gets cooperation by involving the subject in a situation which does not reveal to him the true intent of the investigation. The subject fails to give the experimenter permission to examine his attitudes, but agrees to participate because he is unable to discern the true nature of the investigator's intentions.

## The Propriety of Deception

This raises a second vital question that might be posed by the social scientist at this time: "Do I have the right to deceive people in order to get at their attitudes?" It must be understood that the social scientist is in a different situation than the clinician who uses a variety of projective techniques for the purpose of helping the individual make a better, more healthy adjustment. The projective tools which the clinician applies are part of his diagnostic kit, similar to the many other devices which the regular physician uses in his practice. The client knows the intent of the therapist, and even though he may not understand or be convinced of the validity of the various projective techniques, he feels that the therapist has his best interests at heart.

This relationship of trust and confidence is usually not the case when the social scientist uses indirect methods to get at the attitudes of individuals who are quite likely unwilling to divulge their opinions through the use of any of the more direct techniques. The violent anti-Semite, the latent radical, the arch conservative usually cannot be identified in the experimental test situation unless devices are used which penetrate the protective cover with which these individuals surround themselves.

It should be kept in mind that indirect methods of attitude measurement vary greatly in the effectiveness of their disguise. Some of these tools hide only the purpose of their utilization, and a sophisticated subject can easily see the many ways in which the results can be utilized. In this respect, the degree of indirectness of the attitude-measurement device is a function of the subject's sophistication and depends greatly upon the frame of reference which the subject brings to the testing situation. Thus, the differential perception of the degree of indirectness produces a variable which partly accounts for the various degrees of tolerance and resistance with which the "duped" subjects react to their discovery of the real purpose of these testing devices. An analogy can be taken from the field of mental testing. Although an intelligence test usually uses straightforward direct manipulations, many subjects are un-aware—at least while taking the test—that their intelligence is being measured. Through the eyes of the unsophisticated subject, the intelligence test appears as an indirect method, although the examiner may consider the intent of the investigation quite obvious.

Even if we decide that we do have the right to deceive people in order to get at their attitudes, there is still an additional point which should be considered. It may not take long before the public in general "catches on" to the operation of the various indirect techniques of attitude measurement. When this occurs, the usefulness of these techniques will be greatly impeded, because they depend for their effectiveness upon hiding the purpose for which they are used. Furthermore, unless precautionary measures are taken to prepare the public for the type of investigations in which the social scientist expects it to cooperate, it may look upon all operations of social science with rising scorn, distrust, or perhaps even fear.

## Misuse of Indirect Techniques

The third question which the social scientist should ask himself is: "Do I have the right to report on new indirect attitude-measurement devices, at a time when these can be misused by unscrupulous politicians or other selfish interests?"

It is quite easy to imagine that some of the new indirect attitude-measurement devices might be discovered by people in various kinds of inquisition movements, and used by them for evil purposes. Although it will undoubtedly take a long time before any of these techniques is valid for prediction at the individual level, we are sure that before too long enthusiastic and unscrupulous practitioners may find these techniques ideally suited for prying into the attitudes of people whom they regard as dangerous.

The "error-choice" test is a good case in point. No doubt instruments using the "error-choice" technique might be constructed which could be applied to eliminate allegedly "disloyal" citizens from jobs of confidence and trust, to spot so-called "troublemakers" and "agitators" in industrial concerns, or, in effect, to discover "nonconformers" in many other important social areas.

## Misinterpretation of Results

Finally there is a fourth question whose pertinence is not limited necessarily to the use of indirect methods of attitude measurement: "What is my responsibility for seeing that the findings which I report are properly interpreted?"

The danger of misinterpretation is especially great in those investigations which utilize the various indirect methods of attitude measurement. The general public, unfamiliar with the background and assumptions of these methods, is likely to read something into the results which may not even be implied in the investigator's formal report. An illustration of this sort of thing comes again from the study of "The Personal Factor in Labor Mediation." A reporter for one of the large industrial trade publications learned, through personal contact, about the "error-choice" test which was devised to test the mediator's knowledge as well as his so-called "impartiality." He asked permission to see the study, and to quote from it prior to its publication in one of the professional journals. The request was granted, but he was warned to check any conclusions or statements of which he might not feel sure. No more was heard until his story appeared in print, with the headline "Heads-or-Tails Odds Beat Mediation," followed by a grossly inaccurate statement of the findings. This reporter undoubtedly felt that he had given an accurate account of the mediator study; his misinterpretations may have been due to a lack of clarity with which the assumptions were originally expressed.

## THE RESEARCHER'S VALUES

In conclusion, one may consider a question implicit in the researcher's use of the "error-choice" method or of similar indirect approaches: his *own* value orientation. It would seem that the researcher cannot divest himself of valuations. Certainly, his choice as to what he is going to work on involves a value judgment. When he is engaged in basic research, his purpose is to test hypotheses in order to add to knowledge; even then, his valuative frame of reference has an impact on the way he formulates his problems and on the methods he selects. When he undertakes applied research, by definition he typically adapts findings and methods of basic research in seeking answers to practical short-run problems.

The major difficulties arise when his research objectives are not liked by others, and such a reaction is not unusual. For instance, a union leader has pointed out that, in his opinion, some human relations researchers exist solely to create labor relations plans designed to develop a docile work force and to obtain acceptance of a paternalistic attitude by management toward workers.

But there does exist a distinction between science and values. Science is method—making observations, drawing and testing inferences. A subject matter is treated scientifically if the scientific method is followed, regardless of the objectives for which the method is being used. So even if a researcher is interested in discovering effective means for defeating union organization or for overcoming management resistance to such organization, it is still possible for him to be scientific in the discovery of these means, though his values inevitably accompany him in his quest.

The "error-choice" method then, as other methods, may be regarded as a scientific tool that is subject to use and misuse. The researcher surely must be aware of his own values and of a system of ethical assumptions in the application of this tool.

# PART FOUR

*Commentaries*

The following three independent commentaries assess the work of the HRRG from the point of view of a social psychologist and therapist, of a sociologist, and of a management theorist and consultant. The discussants were given complete freedom to present their personal views and candid evaluations.

# Scientific Concern for the Human Factor in Industry

BY GEORGE R. BACH*

This book documents the evolution of creativity in a group of psychological researchers who have worked together for a decade to develop principles and methods for improving group production in industrial organizations.

Taken as a whole, this book provides a model illustration of how a group of behavioral scientists and consultants can, over a period of many years, build a structure of concepts, methods, and values, which is here presented as a unit of achievement. For criticism's sake, a critique of this structure is made superfluous by the fact that on practically every page of this book the reader will find a word, if not a whole paragraph, of continual self-evaluation. The authors are indeed practicing what they are preaching. They carefully and self-critically assess every step they take in their self-assertive bid to make their mark. Their sincere efforts will undoubtedly have an impact on the complex and competitive area of human relations consultantship, and will serve to introduce the subject to students of business administration.

What the authors have done here is to take human relations in industry, management, and business leadership seriously enough to subject the human factor to academic and research scrutiny and to come forth with valuable ideas and procedures. They have thus elevated this much lip-serviced area above the slick common-sense con artistry and the double talk so typical of the public relations field. The generalities, the one-dimensional thinking, and the journalistic stereotypes peddled by the Madison Avenue jesters to the courts of corporation chairmen now have to face the competition of scientific consultantship. The authors are aware that reeducation of management has to precede its eventual

* Institute of Group Psychotherapy, Beverly Hills, Calif., and the Claremont Graduate School, Claremont, Calif.

acceptance of a behavioral science approach to industry. Their approach is multidimensional, field-theoretical, or system-oriented, in contrast with the tradition which it is replacing, which was unifactorial, segmental, and component-oriented. To make these new values more palatable, the authors' style of writing is tender rather than tough. Perhaps this is the smart way of getting into the mansion of American industry, a house into which academic psychologists do not as yet feel officially invited. For my taste, this kind of writing is a little too defensive. The significance of several novel contributions may escape many readers because of the self-critical context in which they are overcautiously presented and underplayed.

The authors do to themselves the very thing that they ask of the executive, the manager, the trainee. "Confront yourself with what you are doing. Sort out the deeper meaning of your behavior. Provide for feedback and listen to it." Now look at the bibliography of papers on which this book is based. Coauthors, coauthors, coauthors! Teams are here, searching, re-searching, creating, writing, developing, growing—together.

This book is a documentation of our *Zeitgeist*—the spirit of the times in which creative productivity emerges, not from brilliant individuals working in isolation, but from teams and groups. This is especially true in the sciences and industry, and most clearly in world government. The need to know all one can about human relations is due to the historical emergence of organizational creativity in industrial societies. The creative genius must make his individual impact within the interpersonal interactions of the task-relevant reference groups in which he functions. For example, designers of complex systems are no longer able to create a new system on their own, since their individual creativity is deeply interdependent with team effort and group creativity. Today the group is the vehicle of creativity, and only those individuals who are able to play their part in helping to create what may be called "synthetic geniuses"[1] are truly effective in modern progressive industries. Industrial progress no longer need await the emergence or selection of individual geniuses, as up-to-date management acquires the human relations skills to train and develop teams which are able to integrate the creative productivity of its members. This is a new challenge to enlightened management. To meet this challenge, the manager will need to become sophisticated and sensitized to the psychodynamic and group-dynamic factors involved in the group approach to creative productivity. This is not only new, but it threatens old, well-rooted expectancies and criteria for gaining narcissistic individual satisfactions.

[1] I am indebted to Mr. M. Andrew Haladej, Bendix Corporation, Computer Division, for this term.

This book is a real help to present and future managers for mastering the new human relations skills involved here. Our age can be characterized as an age in which human factors are no longer viewed in the restrictive Marxian and/or capitalistic terms of economic-need satisfactions, or power-need satisfactions, or status-need satisfactions, or dependency-need satisfactions, or any other single need of single individuals. Rather, ours is the age in which the survival of each individual man in good mental and physical health very directly depends on the survival and the good material and spiritual health of the human group or interpersonal system to which the individual belongs. The basic questions are: "How can large and small groups work together productively rather than destructively? How can an individual who has to live and work in groups be stimulated to individual productivity and creativity? What is to replace old concepts of materialistic need satisfactions?"

Tannenbaum, Weschler, and Massarik face this challenge of the urgency for more knowledge in the areas of industrial relations with three conceptual weapons: (1) leadership constructs; (2) empathy (sensitivity training); and (3) organizational dynamics. The concept of participative and flexible leadership as a functional role aiding in decision-making processes is welcome reorientation away from the traditional cult of the policy-setting leader personality in industry. Most significant from the standpoint of individual and group mental health is the only apparently paradoxical idea that good leaders sometimes lead by "defaulting" (Bion), denoting refusal to fulfill the dependent person's nonconstructive expectancies to be shown the way. The current leader concept entitles the follower to services from the expert only in terms of being shown how to find the way by himself eventually. My critique here is that the authors have not given enough specific attention to the management of tensions, frustrations, and resistances which, in my experience, invariably arise when clients are disappointed in their traditional expectations of what experts and leaders should do. Since these traditional expectancies are so smoothly filled by dozens of ever-ready Madison Avenue public relations consultants, the regressive needs of followers for charismatic leadership and the tendency of managers to respond to these basically destructive needs deserves much further exploration than is presented here. This would mean that the authors might well have to expand their conceptual frame of reference as far as leadership is concerned to include the effect of the follower-leader relationship on the intrapsychic structure of both, such as Schutz[2] has attempted.

[2] William C. Schutz, "Leader Ego and FIRO Theory," unpublished manuscript, presented at Louisiana State University, Mar. 4, 1959.

In view of the authors' participative frame of reference, I had expected that they would give more emphasis to the concept of the leader as a "programmer of whole systems." It is not quite clear whether the authors' concept of leadership includes the function of cultural innovation, such as aggressively introducing new ways of interaction and new values within an organization. How much would a leader who is expertly trained along Tannenbaum-Weschler-Massarik lines actively try to change the culture of his group? There seems some conceptual confusion here concerning such forms of leader impact on the whole group system. A good leader's impact is, in actual practice, often in the nature of innovation rather than simple reflection. In the conceptual handling of this matter, the authors seem to be limiting themselves by holding on to the weak side of Carl Rogers' original theory of nondirectiveness. Is not the leadership of this very book definable as "introducing new information into an existing system" rather than just reflecting its state of affairs?

From a clinician's standpoint, a clearer exposition of the various forms of both overt and covert personal satisfactions which people derive from leading and/or from following behavior would be a welcome expansion. It is recognized that resistance to change in leadership and followership patterns occurs because leading and following fulfill deep intrapsychic needs, which on the surface are supposed to be irrelevant to work productivity. Thus leading and following can be conceptualized as an interpersonal game between personifiers of basic human strivings for fulfillment, as, for example, in the parent-child relationship. The interpersonal-games theory (e.g., Eric Berne's *Transactional Analysis* and Bach's "Set-up Operations")[3] and the older transference concept are relevant here. The authors, by ignoring these and other alternate levels of conceptualization of the leadership phenomenon, invite the criticism that they are engaged in constructing an "inbred" system of internally integrated constructs unrelated to overlapping ideas of neighboring workers.

As a practicing psychotherapist, I am understandably most interested in Part 2, "Sensitivity Training: A Personal Approach to the Development of Leaders." Here is a practical, corrective approach to one of the basic evils in industrial corporate life, the misunderstandings, tensions, and conflicts due to misperceptions and lack of reality orientation. Many psychotherapists have seen business executives and managers who have come to them privately for psychotherapy and specialized leadership training. Their clinical observations confirm the value and the validity of sensitivity training procedures as described in this book.

[3] E. Berne, *Transactional Analysis in Psychotherapy*, in press, and George R. Bach, *Intensive Group Psychotherapy* (New York: The Ronald Press Company, 1954).

The authors again are overmodest here. They do not tell the reader a very interesting sociological fact, which I happen to know because of my geographical proximity to the center of the authors' work. Many graduates of sensitivity training groups have formed long-term post-training associations designed to maintain the great awakening that these participants experienced in the course of their sensitivity training. Is this not a validating item worth mentioning in a scientific evaluation? I can testify without reservation to the practical utility and pragmatic helpfulness of this approach to train people to be more realistic in their interpersonal relationships. Even more significant for business managers is the opportunity that sensitivity training presents for the participative learning about the nature of group processes.

Conceptually, the sensitivity training laboratory simulates the world of the manager's work groups. What is learned can be transferred directly to the job. Critically, I would say that one needs more decisive research data on this factor of transfer of training from lab group to on-the-job application. What procedures would make this transfer more efficient? New observations of the relationship of simulated to real situations in professional training, such as are currently made by Robert Boguslaw at System Development Corporation,[4] would be relevant here.

As is, alas, so often true in the field of the clinical arts, the practical excellence of sensitivity training stands on its own pragmatic grounds without having a respectable conceptual clarification to back it up theoretically. It works because it works. That is the pragmatic level of many therapies (*cf.* drug and shock therapies). The conceptual level of sensitivity training is not too much more sophisticated than this. The operation is clear enough. Managers want to be better executives; executives have to be effective leaders; effective leaders are more sensitive and more accurate perceivers of how others really think and feel than less effective leaders.

The first step in learning to be a sensitive perceiver is to have a chance to find out what kind of perceiver one is in the first place: participation in a sensitivity training group is indicated. There one will actually be told when his perceptions are accurate—*touché*—or when one is "seeing things" because of subjective tendencies and/or idiosyncratic factors.

Thus the sensitivity training consultant provides a most peculiar group atmosphere, one in which people actually respond honestly to each other, overtly and safely. This comes about because a professional psychologist-trainer injects his value system of what a training group in leadership should be like. He intervenes, sometimes by defaulting on traditional leadership attitudes, to create a setting in which every

[4] R. Boguslaw and G. Bach, " 'Work Culture Management' in Industry: A Role for the Social Science Consultant," *Group Psychotherapy*, June, 1959, pp. 134–142.

participant can explore the true, usually private, attitudes of every participant and their view of each other. This occasion provides the opportunity, the only one I know of in our society outside of actual group psychotherapy, for normally functioning people, and especially for "leaders," to get an honest feedback and an honest confrontation of what the impact of their personality is on their environment. They can also learn what kind of distortions in person and group perceptions need to be corrected.

The kinship of sensitivity training and group psychotherapy is obvious on this practical level. What is the conceptual relationship? The authors are not explicit enough on this important question of the theoretical relation of what they are doing and what psychotherapists are doing. I think we are doing very similar things, except that one is called to help people in real despair, while the other offers to assist already fairly well-functioning people to improve themselves.

When a person enters sensitivity training, he has available the defense that he is educating himself rolewise, e.g., to be a better manager. Then he finds out that to be a better manager means he must become a more realistically oriented and a more emphatically understanding person. When a patient seeks help for his psychosomatic, characterological, and/or sociopathic symptoms, he enters with the defense that the therapist will cure him by some therapeutic technology which, if he follows it obediently, will set him free. Soon, however, the patient finds out that respectable psychotherapists (as distinguished from quacks) are not too interested in doing anything directly about the presenting symptoms. Instead they ask the patient to "know thyself" *in toto*. Perhaps the conceptual difference between sensitivity training and intensive group psychotherapy is a quantitative one. How much of the total organism is the focal concern of each method? Sensitivity training gets the person started, turned around, switched in orientation from preoccupation with segmental perceiving (role, leader technique, symptoms, etc.) to organismic or systemwise perceiving (the private phenomenological total world of people, their life space, group processes, etc.). Group psychotherapy does the same type of gear shift. But, whereas sensitivity training shifts from neutral or reverse to first gear, group therapy goes full speed ahead to the fullest exploration of the self. Sensitivity training, as the name implies, improves perceptual skills, while group psychotherapy is really an action-training process. The authors leave the performance level of this first-gear speed conceptually unanswered. Clinical experience shows that many people can get where they want to go by first-gear operations, but many others need more.

I would venture to say that sensitivity training is an eye opener or an explanation which makes its participants aware of the hidden nine-tenths of the iceberg. What does sensitivity training have to do with this awakening, this awareness of hidden agendas, subjective projections, irrational motives? What is the responsibility of the sensitivity trainer who exposes initially unsuspecting subjects, who come expecting "leadership" techniques only to find that a mirror is stuck in their faces?

I believe the sensitivity training program has great therapeutic-practice potentialities, both for individual managers and for the improvement of the value system of whole organizations. However, a conceptual clarification of what is really going on here is overdue. Parenthetically, I am disappointed that the authors failed to take notice of my own research on "Specific Group Cultures as Release Mechanisms for Individual Behavior Patterns,"[5] in which I had something to say about the integration of training and therapy groups.

I have used up my allotted space in this book, and I have still not covered the authors' important studies on organizations. This is regrettable, because improvement in organizational-level thinking is undoubtedly most crucial to human survival. Did not the German culture demonstrate that a majority of sane individuals can be caught up overnight in an insane society? You can labor all your professional life to improve the mental and physical health of individuals, and yet find them embroiled in various forms of group pathology.

As a summary comment concerning this last section of the book, I have three issues to raise. First, on the conceptual level, the authors' helpful distinction between formal organizational plans and the actual interpersonal channel system seems just a starting point on the road to a purer concept of what a man-to-man (as well as man-machine) system actually does psychologically rather than economically. Secondly, in this section, the authors seem at times to forget or abandon their systems orientation, and they seem to regress to old-fashioned "component thinking," as in their exploration of single-variable problems, such as status, leadership styles, rating conditions, and others. They have failed to integrate these into a total theory of organizational functioning. Third, and last, may I suggest that future evaluations of organizations do not rest content on traditional criteria of organizational efficiency (such as productivity), but fathom the state of mental health of the organization as a whole. The Multi-relational Sociometric Survey described by the authors is a valuable step in this direction. But the whole topic of group pathology (see Bach, 1956)[6] remains a challenge for future research.

In conclusion, I wish to reiterate, in view of the critical self-appraisal

[5] G. R. Bach, "Specific Group Cultures as Release Mechanisms for Individual Behavior Patterns," *Group Psychotherapy*, December, 1957, pp. 277–286.
[6] G. R. Bach, "Pathological Aspects of Therapeutic Groups," *Group Psychotherapy*, August, 1956, pp. 133–148.

by the authors, that the above critique is meant to reinforce further interest in research to clarify the issues opened up by the authors' courageous pioneering in a new and complex field.

The present work takes a significant step in better understanding of human relations in industrial settings. This book provides useful tools for business managers and students of business administration for more effective solving of human problems which have become focal concerns of progressive management.

# Psyche, Sensitivity, and Social Structure

BY ROBERT DUBIN[*]

This critique of the work of the UCLA Human Relations Research Group is illuminated by an orientation that needs to be stated at the outset. My preferences guide the nature of this analysis, and statement of them will put these comments in proper perspective for the reader.

My first belief is that theory and empirical research are inextricably interwoven. Research is designed to test theory. This means that any research has to have its theoretical models laid bare so determinations can be made of the relevance of empirical tests for the models being tested. I will do this in linking some of the theory and empirical findings of the HRRG.

My second assumption is that an adequately worked out theoretical model generates a set of analytical problems. This will also be examined from the standpoint of the models used in the HRRG research. I will call attention to the analytical problems flowing from the models dealt with by the group, and also suggest some other problems that have not yet been in the group's focus of attention.

My third preference is to consider any theory as tentative, suggestive, and developed as a stage leading to even more sophisticated models. Theory can be viewed as a way of organizing experience. The expectation is that once initial sense is made out of experienced environment, the way is cleared for an even more adequate organization of this experience. Thus, theory is a set of successive models that make sense of man's world. Each theoretical model is a new starting point for a more adequate successor. I will suggest some of the advances that seem possible, going beyond the present state of theorizing about human behavior in organizations as formulated in this volume.

* Department of Sociology, University of Oregon. This critique was written while on leave as Ford Visiting Professor of Behavioral Sciences, School of Commerce, University of Wisconsin.

Finally, a personal note. I have known the senior member of the HRRG, Professor Tannenbaum, for more than a decade. When he invited me to undertake this review, he unreservedly extended the privilege to be constructively critical. The work of the HRRG has been highly respected by students of organizations. This respect I share. Consequently, the reader will understand that Professor Tannenbaum invited these comments fully anticipating critical appraisal, and that my regard for his work and that of his associates is underscored by accepting his invitation " . . . to evaluate, assess, and comment on the viewpoint, methods, and subject matter presented." You have already read this book and know its many valuable contributions. I do not need to call them specifically to your attention.

## THEORETICAL MODELS USED BY THE HRRG

The fundamental characteristics of the *person,* in the view of the group, are that his behavior is goal-oriented; that his central goal is defense of his own personality integrity; and that he requires strong motivation to maintain pursuit of his goals. The underlying dynamic process that keeps the person behaving in meaningful relationship to his social environment is the constant stress to maintain congruence between his intellectual understandings and his emotional reactions. Where any disparity between intellectual understanding and emotional reaction occurs, the person's distress is the driving force that initiates actions to reduce or eliminate such disparity. Thus, tension generated by failures of intellectual understandings and emotional reactions to coincide becomes both the source for motivation of behavior and the mechanism by which personal goals and supporting behaviors are chosen.

The HRRG view of an *organization* is this: it is a finite or closed social system having concrete institutional goals; these goals are independent of the personal goals of its participating members; each organization member has only specialized demands made on him for contribution to organization goals, which generates the need for adjustive mechanisms in internal structure and operations to make individual effort and organization aims compatible. This model of an organization focuses primary analytical attention on the problems internal to the system—essentially personnel problems of fitting people into jobs, positions, and offices of the organization in order to maximize their individual contributions to organization goals.

The HRRG model of the *person as organization member* contains these salient features: each person is confronted with three adjustive needs: (1) to establish compatibility between personal goals and organization goals, (2) to defend personality integrity from attack by peers, subordinates, and *especially* superiors, and (3) to maintain motivation in socially acceptable directions in the face of these problems. Thus, the person as organization member is modeled out of the conjunction of the two preceding theories of personality dynamics and organization characteristics.

CENTRAL ANALYTICAL PROBLEM OF THE HRRG

One major analytical problem, derived directly from these models, has been the principal focus for the writing and research of the group. The problem is this: to what extent are the face-to-face, interpersonal relations among organization members determinant of organizational effectiveness? More particularly, and in an even narrower context, to what extent are leader-follower relations the most critical variable in organization effectiveness?

In dealing with this central analytical problem of the consequences of leader-follower relations, the authors distinguish only two polar types of leaders, "authoritarian" and "permissive." While this typology is compatible with their starting models, it is scarcely exhaustive of leadership types. A more extensive typology of leadership can well provide grounds for further empirical testing of the theories used by the HRRG.

The authors have value preferences for "permissive" leadership styles based on two principal contentions. 1. "Permissive" leadership behavior is more likely to preserve the personality integrity of followers than is "authoritarian" leadership. 2. "Permissive" leadership leads to maximum self-realization by subordinates of their productive capacities and, therefore, contributes significantly to organization effectiveness. I deliberately call these value preferences, or hypothetical predictions, since I find no empirical data supporting either contention in this volume (nor, for that matter, in an extensive literature oriented to the same conclusion —a literature whose discussion is beyond the scope of this critique). Indeed, some of the research findings of the group seem to challenge these predictions, as will be pointed out below.

From these predictions the authors' principal argument of Part 1 is logically derived. They contend that leaders should be "permissively oriented" in the interests of organizational effectiveness. My own values as a citizen accord with this conclusion, but my interests as a student of organization behavior keep demanding an answer to the nagging question: "What is the evidence to support this prediction?"

An unanticipated consequence of this point of view is the reasonable conclusion we can draw (but not strongly emphasized by the authors) about the result of permissiveness *for the leader*. It seems reasonable to expect (again without supporting evidence as yet marshaled) that the *leader's* personality integrity may be sustained by his permissive behavior, and that *his* psychic comfort may be enhanced by acting permissively towards subordinates. If this insight turns out to be supported by research, then those readers of this volume who are operating executives and who accept this conclusion will be more than repaid their investment in reading time.

Sensitivity training is also derived from the authors' predictions about the value of "permissive" leadership. A major share of the technique of sensitivity training involves encouraging free-flowing, uninhibited interactions among trainees. For real organization leaders who are so trained, the experience presumably opens their eyes to the hidden potentialities that can be unearthed in their real working associates and subordinates. There remains the moot question of what consequences are in store for the real subordinates, whose inhibitions are reduced by sensitivity training, if they return to their operating situations with a freewheeling approach to interpersonal relations. They may behave "permissively" towards their own subordinates, but what about their relationships with their own bosses? Is there some jeopardy involved here? Is this perhaps one of the critical points needing immediate investigation, since it may account for the authors' observation that sensitivity training is believed to have only short-run behavioral consequences for some trainees after they return to their work situations.

## ADDITIONAL ANALYTICAL PROBLEMS FLOWING FROM HRRG MODELS

There are four additional analytical problems derived from the HRRG models of organization behavior worthy of consideration. These are illustrative of directions in which it might be profitable to pursue further the study of organization within the HRRG framework.

### Types of Working Behaviors

We have pointed out above the assumption made by the HRRG that interpersonal relations are a major determinant of organizational effectiveness. This is a most legitimate assumption, but one clearly unsupported by research. It seems to me that a question logically prior to this assumption is: "How are actual working behaviors distributed among interpersonal relations and other categories of behavior?" It is a truly amazing fact that we do not have any systematic studies of this simple descriptive problem. I have suggested, for example, that working behavior can be classified into four systems: technological, formal, nonformal, and informal.[1] There are other types of classifications possible.

---

[1] Robert Dubin, *The World of Work* (Englewood Cliffs, N.J.: Prentice-Hall, Inc., 1958), especially chap. 4.

Studies directed at determining the volume of activities for each type of working behavior, the volume of interpersonal relations involved in each, and their consequences for output (by whatever criteria measured) seem to be an essential step to pin down the assumption that interpersonal relations constitute a major determinant of organization effectiveness.

If we look at the secular trend of productivity in American manufacturing industries, there appears to be an annual increment of about 3 per cent in productivity per man hour. This is such a widely accepted notion that it has been given institutional recognition in collective bargaining through automatic annual wage increases to share such productivity increases with workers. It is generally recognized that this is a technological improvement factor, presumably operative independently of interpersonal relations in getting work done. Does this broad phenomenon suggest that organization effectiveness, measured in output per man hour, may be largely a product of technological behaviors involving the basic determination of working activities by machines and technical processes? What impact, if any, would modifications in the climate of interpersonal relations have on raising or lowering the rate of increase in productivity? We simply do not know. This seems to be a thoroughly worthwhile issue to examine, for it will provide an empirical test of the assumption that interpersonal relations are a major determinant of organization effectiveness.

### Inner-directed versus Other-directed Leaders

Implicitly the authors argue that the "authoritarian" leader is too "inner directed," to use Riesman's characterization.[2] They propose a stronger "other-directed" orientation for leaders which will presumably result in developing "permissive" leadership styles. This is best illustrated in their discussion of the "restrictive" leader in Chapters 21 and 22, and some of the anonymous illustrations used in the first eight chapters.

This highlights a fundamental analytical dilemma. Does the actual process of sensitivity training primarily develop "inner-directedness," "other-directedness," or both simultaneously? What is the evidence for any of these consequences of sensitivity training?

Does self-insight and self-understanding, both in process and in consequence, tend to make the person more "inner directed"? This is really the operational meaning we give to "inner-directedness"—to know your own mind and to act this knowledge out. Furthermore, we usually add to the notion of "inner-directedness" the idea that emotional support for

---

[2] David Riesman et al., *The Lonely Crowd* (New Haven, Conn.: Yale University Press, 1950).

intellectual insights (especially about the self) comes from within the personality rather than from people in the social environment.

If these are some of the characteristics of being an "inner-directed" personality, and if sensitivity training is specifically designed to develop these characteristics, then such training, when successful, will result in "inner-directed" leadership styles. Such leaders would be mature personalities, knowing their own minds and feelings, and capable of realistically orienting them to the social environment. This also implies inner strength to maintain poise, detachment, and patient indifference to attacks from the less mature personalities in the environment. Thus, one of the hopes for sensitivity training is that people so trained will become mature personalities capable of genuine objective detachment from their operating environment, from which vantage point they can better understand the social relations in which they are constantly immersed. This orientation could be consonant with an authoritarian-leadership stance.

The other side of the sensitivity training coin is the insistence that such training is crucial for developing the individual's ability to take the role of the other, to use Mead's happy phrase.[3] This is particularly well illustrated in the fictionalized account of managers in transition contained in Chapter 11. Taking the role of the other means figurative projection into another person's intellectual views of the world and emotional states. This process of projection is maximized to the extent that one's own feelings and thoughts are temporarily set aside. To put it most bluntly, taking the role of the other means becoming "other directed" at the expense of "inner-directedness," either temporarily or, possibly, permanently.

If sensitivity training serves to maximize skills in "other-directedness" at the expense of "inner-directed" maturity, then one of its major consequences may be to produce dependent, immature leaders and/or dependent and subservient followers. Could it be that sensitivity training can produce the conformist that Whyte so tellingly inveighs against[4] and which is the very consequence that the authors of this volume find distasteful?

I ask this question with due attention to the seriousness of its implication because of considerable disturbance about the evidence dealing with the consequences of sensitivity training. There is a *mystique* here, summed up in the paraphrase of statements in this volume that trainees "feel it's good, but can't explain why." I am convinced that

[3] George Herbert Mead, *Mind, Self, and Society* (Chicago: University of Chicago Press, 1934).

[4] William H. Whyte, Jr., *The Organization Man* (New York: Simon and Schuster, Inc., 1956).

these feelings of goodness are genuine. We must then ask: "What is the cause of the satisfactions being expressed?" It is conceivable that trainees find joy and satisfaction in learning techniques of dependence on the enfolding comforts of the intimate, face-to-face group (perhaps even as a symbolic equivalent of the Freudian "return to the womb"). This seems to me to warrant a very tenable hypothesis: "sensitivity training is an efficient technique for developing abilities to become 'other-directed' in the interests of organization effectiveness whether or not accompanied by personality maturity."

Let me be clearly understood on two points. 1. I am *not* asserting that the conditions leading to the mature personality are in question. The preceding highly abbreviated description of personality maturation is accepted as a viable model. 2. I am *not* trying to dismiss sensitivity training because I interpret it as having a possible consequence other than that attributed to it by its developers.

What I am saying is this: the evidence so far adduced for the consequences of sensitivity training on those subjected to it could equally support the hypothesis that it is an admirable training device for achieving an "other-directed" orientation. There may accompany this a side effect jeopardizing the personality maturity of trainees. Note, for example, the data of Chapter 12, in which the observer of two sensitivity trainers constantly highlights the "inadequacies" of trainer II because he has personal goals for the training outcome that "interfere" with group development. The feedback to trainer II is in the form of making him see the need for setting aside his personal standards of judgment in favor of something that would presumably promote group welfare. Since trainer II had situationally relevant goals, and some significant reasons for them, it could, perhaps, be argued that the insights fed to him could have had the effect of driving him into the group fold, at the expense of his own ideas.

We owe a great deal to the HRRG for development of sensitivity training and the various attempts to evaluate its consequences against a model of how it works. Such data as is displayed from their studies suggests the viability of an alternate formulation of the dynamics of sensitivity training. If either alternative can be sustained by further research, we will have advanced still another step in understanding organization behavior, even if the results are not as originally predicted.

## Consideration as an Adjustive Mechanism

It has been suggested above that the HRRG model of an organization has built into it the need for adjustive mechanisms in internal structure and operations to make individual effort and organization aims compatible. At the level of interpersonal relations, the authors' primary focus of attention, this adjustive mechanism can be described by the term "consideration."

For the authors, consideration means that each person is sensitive to the needs of those in his environment to support their own personality integrity. Each person can maximize his considerate behavior toward others by learning techniques that do not threaten the personality integrity of people with whom he is interacting. Consideration for others is asserted to be a principal product of sensitivity training after insight about the self is developed. The authors particularly emphasize the crucial character for organization effectiveness of considerate behavior of leaders toward subordinates and of organization peers toward each other.

It might well be worthwhile to consider "congruence" as an equally important adjustive mechanism in organizations. By congruence is simply meant that the individual fulfilling an office in an organization behaves, in fact, consistently with respect to the socially determined expectations of that office. For example, if principal executives of a company are expected to be decisive, then occupants of top executive offices must behave decisively to be congruent with the social expectations surrounding their organization position.

It is important to distinguish the reference group that generates the social expectations for an organization office. In the authors' view, this reference group consists almost wholly of those in face-to-face relationship with the occupant of an office. (Chapters 15 and 16, by the way, depart significantly from this position, in directions I will immediately suggest.) It seems reasonable to broaden the scope of reference groups determining the behavioral expectations of an office to include all institutional participants, and even the larger society in which the institution is embedded. When we do this, it becomes clear that there are possibilities of conflicts between the expectations of organization behavior derived from immediate working associates and those coming from a broad and anonymous group of institutional participants.

For example, in Chapter 17 the authors highlight the fact that many of the professional participants in the organization derive their notions about the importance of their own work from a society of professional associates, the bulk of whom are not organization members. Again, in the same chapter, it is pointed out that there are structural strains coming from the way the organization is set up that affect methods chosen for departmentalizing work and the forms used for making work assignments. These and other examples marshaled by the authors from their own research suggest that the society of face-to-face associates may determine only a portion of the total behavioral expectations surrounding an organization office.

Chapter 10, even though an incomplete set of protocols of college-student diaries about participation in a sensitivity training group, clearly reveals the impact of the larger culture of a university in determining the students' image of the teacher's office. To be a teacher, for example, may mean grading down a poor performance by a student, even though student and teacher are close to each other because sensitivity training has sharpened the perceptions of each and maximized their consideration for each other. A number of diary entries deal specifically with this conflict between expectations about teacher behavior flowing from experience in the face-to-face class group and behavioral standards derived from the larger culture of the university in which the class was conducted.

The authors tend to attribute the perception of this conflict between behavioral standards derived from different reference groups, and the distressed reaction to the conflict, to immaturity on the part of the students. There is no denying such conflict always exists in all formal organizations. The critical issue is whether the most successful resolution of this conflict, from the standpoint of organization effectiveness, is always in favor of the primacy of the behavioral expectations of the face-to-face reference group.

I would argue that the behavioral expectations for an organization office derived from reference sources other than the group of face-to-face associates are the most salient for organization effectiveness. This then raises the central issue: "What is it that one becomes sensitive to in receiving and internalizing sensitivity training?"

The answer to this question seems clear-cut. Sensitivity training teaches its students to recognize the personal, idiosyncratic behaviors of people that stand in the way of matching the culturally determined behavior expectations of the positions occupied. Thus, if a boss is experienced as being arbitrary and vindictive in his treatment of subordinates, the sensitized observer can separate the idiosyncratic quality of this behavior unique to the particular boss, from the culturally legitimatized behaviors of bosses in general.

One of the derived consequences of this conclusion is the possibility of a pathological outcome for sensitivity training. If sensitivity training results in the *substitution* of the behavioral expectations of the face-to-face group for culturally determined standards of behavior for an office, then the organization may become historically unique and suffer real threats to its existence with any turnover of its personnel. Every established primary group has its unique behavior standards. Such groups are modified with turnover in membership; with such changes may come different standards of conduct for group members. A group of company executives may become a primary group through long-time association. If their behavior standards as executives are solely determined by their unique face-to-face associations, then the removal of one or more participants (through death, retirement, resignation, discharge) may not only rupture personal ties, but can also play havoc with executive action. Chester Barnard recognized this issue when he posed the problem of a catastrophe requiring immediate replacement of top executives of New Jersey Bell Telephone Company.[5] He pointed out that the unrecorded understandings among the "lost" executives would disappear with their passing and this would lower the immediate effectiveness of successors. He also pointed out that the culturally determined behavioral expectations for executives in this industry would make feasible immediate substitution of executives drawn from other Bell-system companies, or even from other industries. It is this latter which may be jeopardized by misconstruing the goal of sensitivity training as being that of substituting primary group standards of behavior for broader standards of organization behavior.

We may then conclude that sensitivity training can well sharpen the perceptions of trainees about the degree of congruence between idiosyncratic fulfillment of an organization office and the culturally determined standards of behavior for that office. If, through sensitivity training, the organization participant is led to substitute standards of behavior governing the former for those governing the latter, then an organization pathology, in the form of threat to continuity, may result.

## Leadership at a Distance

An aspect of executive action not within the purview of the HRRG research can be described as leadership at a distance. This is the realm of decision making in which the actions of the leader, and the consequences of his decisions, are divorced from any interpersonal relations with those affected by the decision. Examples of leadership in this area include the decisions to initiate the Manhattan project for the development of the atom bomb, where even the feasibility of the outcome was in doubt while great sums were expended on the undertaking; the development of the Edsel car, which became an admitted business mistake even though men of vast experience made the decisions in the light of highly rational considerations; and the decision to drop the first atom bomb, still considered controversial, although militarily significant. There is a large realm of decisions comparable to this in which leadership operates at a distance from those affected by the decisions.

It seems clear that bringing this kind of leadership behavior into view suggests still another limitation of the HRRG model of leader-

[5] Chester I. Barnard, *Organization and Management* (Cambridge, Mass.: Harvard University Press, 1948), pp. 201–202.

follower relations. Their model applies to the circumstance of face-to-face interaction and would have to be significantly modified to make sense out of leadership at a distance.

Granting the models with which the authors started, two general conclusions emerge. The first is that the empirical research marshaled to test their theories is incomplete, and at points nonconforming to the predictions of their theory. The second is that there are analytical problems still to be dealt with in exhausting the predictive power of their models. Both of these results are to be expected in any scientific study.

It would be a rash person who asserted that the individual psyche should not be fully developed. By this is usually meant that the individual has real insight into his own personality, and the formative influences that have shaped his character. So far as sensitivity training, *first,* contributes to a greater awareness of one's impact in social relations and serves to modify these behaviors to reduce friction with the social environment and, *second,* generates self-probing of past experiences to find the roots of friction-creating behaviors, such training would appear to contribute to the maturity of the psyche. Furthermore, the authors' contention that intellectual insight must be coupled with affective reaction to it accords with a fundamental assumption of many schools of psychotherapy. So far as sensitivity training produces this affective reaction (emotional involvement, in the authors' words), it becomes a worthwhile technique for developing the mature personality.

Beyond a congress of mature personalities (assuming we could ideally recruit only mature personalities as personnel of an organization), is there more to organization behavior than interpersonal relations? The answer seems to be clearly affirmative. The social system of an organization does generate constraints, restraints, and limitations on behavior that lie beyond the reach of personal, idiosyncratic behavior. This has been the contrapuntal framework against which I have examined the models, analytical problems, and research results of the HRRG.

## SOME ALTERNATE MODELS OF ORGANIZATION BEHAVIOR

To illustrate what happens when we change some of the assumptions of a theoretical model in order to make sense of an existing body of empirical facts, I will suggest, very briefly, two alternatives. The first deals with motivation, the second with influence.

### Motivation and Organization Behavior

It is one of the widely acclaimed and accepted precepts of work in modern capitalism, stemming from the classic analyses of the Protestant ethic by Weber and Tawney,[6] that strong motivation is essential for adequate work performance. One modern guise of this belief is to be found in the group-dynamics movement, partially divorced from religious-ethical values and centered on the virtues of group participation. The fundamental precept of the group-dynamics movement is that group output, and individual satisfaction, will both be highest under conditions of maximum personal involvement in group activity. In this view, participation in group activity and involvement are intimately associated, and both are often measured by the perceived degree of "say-so" each individual has in determining group goals and functioning. This is clearly a position compatible with that of the authors of this volume.

A rather considerable number of studies of group output, including the one reported in Chapters 21 and 22 of this volume, seem to call into question the group-dynamics expectation that output (measured in volume or more generally by "effectiveness") will increase with increased personal involvement of group members. Indeed, the studies tend to make a good case for "restrictive" leadership (read "authoritarian" if you prefer a more loaded term for this style of leadership) *if* the desired outcome is high productivity. This has then led to the need for restricting the predicted impact of involvement to the realms of personal satisfaction and morale.

The model now predicts, in the light of empirical research testing its adequacy, as follows: as involvement in group processes increases, satisfaction with group membership and morale of members will also increase. Thus, involvement, as the mechanism for "carrying" individual motivation, is seen as the major independent variable determining individual satisfaction with participation in group experiences, and morale of the group as a whole. In this more restricted model, the maximization of motivation is still viewed as desirable, when high satisfaction and morale are the hoped-for outcomes.

If, however, we examine the data of Chapter 19 (and a number of similar studies) dealing with factionalism and organizational change, it becomes apparent that maximum involvement, in the sense meant by the group-dynamics stance, may constitute a significant barrier to organizational change. It will be recalled that, in the study reported in Chapter 19, considerable resistances were generated against organization changes demanded by a distant-headquarters directive. These resistances were grounded in unwillingness to rupture social ties, the product of group participation. This data is used to argue that formal

---

[6] Max Weber, *The Protestant Ethic and the Spirit of Capitalism* (London: George Allen & Unwin, Ltd., 1930). Richard H. Tawney, *Religion and the Rise of Capitalism* (Baltimore, Md.: Penguin Books, 1926).

organization is never fully and predictively responsive solely to direction by rule and fiat. Well and good: the evidence supports this conclusion.

But the other side of the coin must also be examined. Can we conceive of situations where organization changes are deemed necessary, and where the decisions must be made at a distance from the affected organization members? If we can, and I think this is a most realistic situation, we come to the conclusion that maximum involvement by personnel may be dysfunctional in circumstances of required organization change. This results because the changes are resisted as personnel remains stubbornly attached to present settings of established social relations and to present associates.

This now suggests the need for a modified model of the impact of involvement in group behavior on organization change. The new model would predict that optimal involvement in group activities will be less than maximum involvement where significant organization change is necessary or deemed desirable. Furthermore, the minimal point of involvement is that amount just sufficient to make retention of organization membership desirable to the individual. This revised model, derived from that with which the HRRG started, seems to make sense of more of the empirical facts than its parent.

This conclusion about the difference between maximum involvement and optimal involvement is tangentially supported by the analysis of phases of group development (Chapter 13), wherein it is found that there is a cyclical variation in extent of personal involvement in the group. Indeed, it might be argued, as the authors do, that continuous, maximum involvement generates exceptional strains on group members, probably related to the high demand for emotional investment in group participation. Emotion can be mobilized only periodically (due, perhaps, both to resistance to its emergence and the wear and tear involved in its expression), and any group pressure to maintain a high pitch of emotional investment may be inimical to group stability.

I have suggested, then, that maximum involvement, and hence maximum motivation, by organization participants in the social groups found in the work place may not be the most desirable goal in organizations that are undergoing modifications. This seems to be the most typical condition of most of the business and other organizations on the American scene.

*Authority and Influence*

Some of the most difficult aspects of organization to conceptualize are the relationships between authority and influence. In Chapter 15 and 16 particularly, the authors make the general point that authority is grounded in the consent of the governed. In Chapters 7 and 16, much is made of the fact that subordinates may influence superiors by being the source of information necessary to decisions. Indeed, influence in this context is equated to feeding information into the decision process.

By this definition of influence, the direction of flow is immaterial. That is, superiors can presumably also influence subordinates by feeding information into their decisional steps. Yet, as in Chapter 12, when precisely this kind of influencing is attempted by trainer II, it is viewed with alarm by the analyst, because it interferes with group development.

I would argue that there is a logical contradiction involved here. Either influence means what it is defined to mean and is a process available to leaders and subordinates alike, or the term is reserved to describe the upward flow of information affecting decisions and a new concept has to be developed to describe the downward flow of information, or influence. The formulation of Chapter 5 does not help on this problem, nor does the discussion of Chapter 2 in which leadership is defined as "interpersonal influence, exercised in situation and directed, through the communication process, toward the attainment of a specified goal or goals." In Chapter 2 the authors constantly maintain that leadership is the exercise of influence on the behavior of followers, and they even point out that one of the four coordinate goals of such influence is to attain organization ends, as distinct from work-group goals and personal goals.

In this context, influence of leader has a much broader meaning than influence of follower. Any behavioral change induced in a subordinate that can be traced to a prior act of a leader is defined as the product of the leader's influence. But the subordinate's influence comes to be defined as the extent to which information controlled by the subordinate is used when the leader makes an organization decision. There are then three logical possibilities, if we reserve the term influence to include only the control of information necessary to decisions: (1) the influence process is primarily (or exclusively) available to subordinates; (2) it is primarily (or exclusively) available to leaders; or (3) it is available to both. The authors at various points in this volume favor (1), strongly argue against (2), and are of two minds about (3). In pleading for "permissive" leadership styles and in illustrating its virtues, the authors seem to be constantly arguing for restraint by leaders in using influence. Yet their broad definition of leadership as influence presumably encompasses the control of information flowing to subordinates as one of the legitimate behaviors of leaders.

I suspect here, as elsewhere, the authors' distaste for "authoritarian" leadership has led them into an extremist position that fails as a theoretical model of what takes place in leader-follower relations. Leaders do exert influence, downward, upward, and horizontally in an organization. Indeed, it may turn out that one of the best tests of leadership may be the ability to monitor information (and hence influence) in order to keep it: relevant to a situation; of satisfactory volume (neither too little nor too much at a time); properly timed (for both the phase of group behavior, and the distance from the outcome of group action); and legitimate (as to source, and degree of "privilege" surrounding it).

Influence is a complex component of leadership. To argue that the leader should minimize his influence (defined narrowly as monitoring information useful in decisions) may be to ask him to walk only on the one leg of benevolent authority, and a game leg at that.

The stock-taking of theory and research contained in this volume is desirable and eye-opening. It took exceptional maturity on the part of the authors (at least they practice what they preach) to permit colleagues like myself the privilege of critical appraisal within the same covers as their report on a decade of work. The significant successes in modeling the reality of organization behavior should be a source of permanent satisfaction for the members of the HRRG. The happy circumstance of the relative youthfulness of the staff means rich opportunity to benefit by this stock-taking so as to turn disturbing and controversial findings already available into the analytical problems of the next decade of studies.

# Management and Human Relations

BY LYNDALL F. URWICK*

Students of management all over the world owe a great debt of gratitude to the United States of America for the initiative and vigor with which, during the present century, they have developed a substantial apparatus for teaching this new branch of knowledge. Whereas in 1898, there was in the United States but a single university with a department or division of business administration,[1] today, there are some 600.[2] These cater to the needs of more than 300,000 undergraduate students and of smaller numbers studying for second and third degrees. It has been estimated that by 1970 this figure will have risen to 600,000.[3] As far as my knowledge goes, this achievement in developing educational facilities in a previously unrecognized "discipline" is unique in the history of education anywhere in the world.

To this debt has been added a second. The development of foreign-aid programs under the stimulus of the Marshall Plan and their support both from federal resources and by private foundations have placed the state of learning thus gathered together at the disposal of other nations, and particularly of economically underdeveloped peoples. With a completeness and a generosity also unprecedented in human history, American "know-how" has been mobilized in the service of a distracted world.

In the face of so considerable an achievement and so high an ideal of intellectual and material cooperation, criticism may well appear graceless and redundant. But the United States itself has been the first to

* Urwick, Orr, and Partners, Ltd., London.
[1] The Wharton School of Finance and Commerce, University of Pennsylvania.
[2] Robert Aaron Gordon and James Edwin Howell, *Higher Education for Business* (New York: Columbia University Press, 1959), p. 26.
[3] *Faculty Requirements and Standards in Collegiate Schools of Business*, New York, American Association of Collegiate Schools of Business, 1955, p. 3. See also Gordon and Howell, *op. cit.*, p. 24, on this estimate.

recognize that the speed with and the scale on which academic facilities for the study of management have been developed have their dangers. Quite recently two of the most important private foundations have financed inquiries into management education, and the respective reports have been frankly critical in a number of directions.[4]

In particular three potential dangers may be indicated.

1. Managing, whether in business or in other fields, is a practical art. The final test of whether any system of education in this subject is of value, to the United States and to the world, is not whether this or that proposition is intellectually defensible, but whether it is accepted and applied by those who have the responsibility of conducting enterprises of all kinds. The development of teaching apparatus, on the other hand, has been due almost entirely to academic initiative. It has owed little to practical business, which even in the United States has only begun to treat executive development as a serious issue within the last dozen years.[5] The social esteem attaching to business as a career and the general material belief in education brought students and parents together in a demand which the universities met.

But, in the development of knowledge about a practical art, it is of importance that theory and practice should keep in step. The art of medicine is a case in point. In medicine the most elaborate researches and the most advanced laboratory work are of little value unless they become incorporated in general medical practice and contribute to the relief of human suffering. The analogy with medicine is of special pertinence to management: both are among the few practical arts which deal all the time with human beings.

It implies no criticism of business or of the universities to suggest that hitherto this essential union of the two points of view has not been achieved. It is certainly far less developed than, in my experience, it is in medicine. The universities have done their best to keep their teachers of management in touch with practice by encouraging them to undertake consulting work, by organizing executive development programs, and so on. If business was indifferent to what the universities were doing, it must be remembered that, up to the end of the 1930s, very few businessmen in positions of responsibility had themselves received

[4] Gordon and Howell, *op. cit.;* this inquiry was sponsored by the Ford Foundation. Frank C. Pierson et al., *The Education of American Businessmen* (New York: McGraw-Hill Book Company, Inc., 1959); this inquiry was sponsored by the Carnegie Corporation.

[5] In 1946, the National Industrial Conference Board set out to make a study of company training programs for executives. It discovered that "there were not enough such programs to form the basis for a report." The report appeared in 1950. Stephen Habbe, *Company Programs of Executive Development*, National Industrial Conference Board, Studies in Personnel Policy, no. 107, New York, 1950, p. 3.

any formal education in management subjects. The idea that managing is "an intelligent occupation" which can, in part, be taught and learned rather than acquired unsystematically from the chance impact of experience,[6] was novel. And new ideas take time to create any deep impression on a developing society.

In consequence, there has been a tendency for academic research in the field of management to "get its feet off the ground," to develop techniques which, however objective in intent and ethical in application, are in no shape for practical application under the pressures of everyday business. It is no accident that the authors' concluding chapters, "Relations with the Host: Social Research Faces Industry" and "Relations with the Subject: Problems in the Use of Indirect Methods of Attitude Measurement," touch on this difficulty.

But neither of them appears to face squarely what seem to me to be the two major obstacles to be overcome:

*a.* The point where theory and practice meet most frequently and most realistically is in the work of management-consulting undertakings. The records of any consulting firm, which maintains records properly, are a mine of information as to actual situations and as to the results of applying modern techniques of management. But the obligation of professional confidence which management consultants very properly observe immobilizes the great proportion of such information and renders it inaccessible to research workers. A method of overcoming this barrier between clinical experience and basic research is an urgent requirement.

*b.* In almost every instance in which an institution employing human beings is changed or reorganized, someone gets hurt. There is a loss of status or prestige, real or imagined, of the nature of those discussed in Chapter 17. Much of the art of managing well consists in implementing essential changes while minimizing the adverse effects on morale due to the hurt feelings of individuals. For this reason any contemporary record of any reorganization is, almost invariably, misleading and inaccurate. Good policy and ordinary human kindliness demand that it should be. It is traditional that accurate history seldom is written till a century or so after the event, when the feelings of those concerned and of their descendants have become irrelevant. Fear that the scientific research worker will ignore the fictions and rip off the "cover story" and recognition that, if he doesn't, his work will lose much of its value

---

[6] *Cf.* "Up to the beginning of this century any success obtained by industrial leaders was commonly attributed to natural aptitude, inheritance or accident," *Developing a National Pattern for Education and Training of Managers,* Report to the XII International Congress for Scientific Management (C.I.O.S.) by Rolf Nordling and the French National Committee for Scientific Management (C.N.O.F.), Melbourne, Australia, 1960.

are two of the most serious handicaps to the extension of social research, especially in the field of organization.

For all these reasons there appears to be a widening gap in the United States between theory and practice, between what academic people are thinking and the problems which preoccupy them and what business people are thinking and doing. Such a tendency is gravely to the disadvantage of both parties and of the art of administration. The gap should be closed.

The other dangers resulting from the very rapid development of educational facilities in management may be indicated more briefly.

2. It has undoubtedly placed a great strain on the national resources in persons competent to teach at university level. In this particular field of knowledge the more exciting opportunities and the larger remuneration offered by business are a serious competitor with the universities for the services of the more brilliant students. That this competition is effective is shown by the figures. A smaller percentage of the graduates with a second degree in business administration proceed to a doctorate with a view to taking up teaching as a calling than of those in any other subject.[7] It is open to question whether the universities, in this particular field, would not be wise to place less emphasis on a doctorate and more emphasis on good practical experience and teaching ability as qualifications for admission to and advancement within their faculties of business administration.

3. It has tended to emphasize the occupational characteristics popularly associated with the academic calling. These are well known. They include a preference for the abstract rather than the concrete, a tendency to proliferate jargons, overspecialization, internecine wars between faculties, and so on.

There are traces of all these tendencies in this book and, in parallel with them, signs that they are being resisted. If for no other reason, it is greatly to be welcomed on this account. It demonstrates within the compass of a single volume the contrast between discussions of management intended for use by businessmen and discussions of technical problems aimed at fellow academic workers in the same or parallel fields. Being a compendium of work extending over a decade, it naturally presents many different approaches. This is a strength rather than a weakness. The preface frankly admits that the component elements were "addressed to different audiences, from knowledgeable professional colleagues to hardware-oriented, practicing executives."[8]

---

[7] In 1955–56 only 2.8 per cent of those taking a master's degree in business or commerce proceeded to a doctorate as compared with 5.3 per cent in education, the next lowest, and more than 50 per cent in the physical and biological sciences. Gordon and Howell, *op. cit.,* p. 23, Table 2.

[8] P. xii.

On the other hand, this fact is likely to limit its appeal to business-men, which is a pity. I would much like the authors to consider a companion volume, in which the portions addressed to "knowledgeable professional colleagues" are rewritten in the simple form adopted in those chapters which have already appeared in the *Harvard Business Review.*[9] I am strengthened in the idea that this would be desirable by the whole of Part 2. The technique of "sensitivity training" developed by the Human Relations Research Group appears to me an important practical invention, indeed one of the few developments known to me which holds out some hope of developing more acceptable leadership behavior in those destined to occupy positions of responsibility in business.

While, as appears from Chapters 12 and 14, it is at present too soon for a scientific assessment of such problems as the selection and de-velopment of trainers or the detailed impact of the training process, enough appears to have been done to show clearly that here is a method of training individuals which gives them direct experience of the emo-tional consequences of behavior in and with groups. It is my experience that, in the development of awareness of the effect of behavior on others, it is only processes which involve the emotions which really teach. A "talking-to" which appeals to logic alone remains "mere words." Indeed, one of the great handicaps in convincing "practical" men that management can, in part, be taught is their conviction that such teaching must necessarily be a purely intellectual process. They know, from their own experience, that many of the most important lessons they have learned were emotional and not intellectual.

With the general theory underlying the book I find myself less at ease. This, not because I disagree violently with any particular phase of this theory, but because I fail to see the need of yet another theory which merely expresses in somewhat different form concepts with which most students of the subject are in general agreement.

Thus Chapter 1 states categorically, "when we view human relations as a scientific discipline, with both basic and applied branches, there is little reason to doubt that it is here to stay." But is such a view de-sirable in the interests of the study of management or, indeed, of the progress of industrialized societies? I suggest that it is not. With the authors' general contention that the study of inter- and intrapersonal phenomena must be multidisciplinary, I am in complete agreement. Their effort to make headway against the tendency to fragment the study of the human side of management into a whole series of "be-

[9] For example, Chap. 5, "How to Choose a Leadership Pattern," Chap. 8, "The Management of Differences," and Chap. 11, "Sensitivity Training for the Manage-ment Team."

havioral" sciences deserves every support. So far as they are protesting against those who see "business units as essentially economic and technological entities (which certainly they are), but not important as social organizations (which certainly they also are),"[10] I am equally in agreement with them.

Surely, however, the day is past when it is necessary to insist that understanding of people, whether individually or in groups, is a necessary part of management? If, in the effort to combat obsolete concepts of economics, we try to divorce the study of people from the purposes for which they try to cooperate, shall we not fall out of the frying pan into the fire? Practical men who are trying to administer groups of their fellow human beings for this purpose or that will not accept this division of the subject. To them it seems academic and unrealistic. The better leaders they are, the more will their minds be concentrated on the common purpose of the system of cooperation for the whole or a part of which they are responsible. The first function of a leader is representation —to represent the purpose of the group he leads both to the outside world and to those collaborating with him.[11]

In other words, from my standpoint, the unifying "discipline" is *management, not* human relations. The study of human relations is an important part of management, but it is only a part. Managing, to be sure, is getting things done *through people*, or, more elaborately, the executive aspect of the art of government; and some specialization may be inevitable in bringing to bear on that art the various underlying disciplines which deal with human behavior, both individually and in groups. But those who specialize in human behavior will forget or minimize the "things," the work which human systems of cooperation are created to do, at their peril.

If they do, they will find themselves in the position of a medical man who, because he is specializing in psychopathology, forgets that human beings have also an anatomy and a physiology. His diagnoses will inevitably become biased and inaccurate. In his enthusiasm for and interest in functional disorder, he will omit the elementary precaution of examining for organic causes of discomfort or disease.

The specialization of human relations in theory has had, too, an unfortunate influence on practice. It has led to the idea that the right way to look after the well-being of people employed in business is to have a specialized officer, a vice-president for personnel or director of industrial relations, who makes a full-time job of taking care of this aspect of operation.

[10] For both quotations in this paragraph, see p. 11.
[11] *Cf.* Paul Pigors, *Leadership or Domination* (Boston: Houghton Mifflin Company, 1935), particulrly chap. 10, "The General Function of Authority: Representation."

This weakens the whole function, because it undermines its importance in two directions. From the point of view of the chief executive, it tends to reduce care for personnel to one of a group of functions which he has to coordinate. He has many other preoccupations; he has appointed a competent official; why should he worry? In fact, care for personnel is a good half, and many people think the most important half, of his job. From the standpoint of the departmental manager, personnel management, where thus specialized, has nothing to do with the work in hand. As Drucker has pointed out, the relation between manager and employee is fundamentally a working relationship. A job which is not focused on work is bound to lose relative status in his eyes and to degenerate into a position in which it performs, maybe useful, but necessarily incidental, chores.[12]

This is not to say that in a large-scale undertaking there may not be enough of such services—employment, salary administration, trade-union relations, medical care, and the like—to be conveniently centralized and which justify the appointment of an important officer to administer them. But such appointments are no substitute for personnel management properly interpreted. That involves that those holding positions of authority at all levels should feel a sense of responsibility issuing in a concern for the well-being of individual subordinates, *not* as an exercise in altruism, but as an essential condition of successful operation.

Indeed, one of the factors which so often renders bureaucracy as a system of government "wooden" and humanly intolerable is its tendency to rely on detailed establishment regulations rather than on individual concern for human beings as people to adjust its relations with those it employs. Ordway Tead made this point a good many years ago: "that is what bureaucracy essentially means, a reliance upon procedures and precedents and a distrust of the exercise of personal power of true leadership caliber."[13]

The organization theory on which the book is based is logical and rational enough. The authors' argument starts with the proposition that managerial functions are "those performed exclusively by managers."[14] After considering a wide range of theories, they come to the conclusion that "all managerial activities are included in three functions: organiza-

---

[12] *Cf.* Peter F. Drucker, *The Practice of Management* (New York: Harper & Brothers, 1954), chap. 21, "Is Personnel Management Bankrupt?" "Personnel administration looks upon the management of worker and work as the job of a specialist rather than as part of the manager's job. It is the classical example of a staff department and of the confusion the staff concept causes" (p. 277); and "Human Relations also lacks an adequate focus on work. Positive motivations must have their center in work and job" (p. 278).

[13] Ordway Tead, *The Art of Leadership* (New York: McGraw-Hill Book Company, Inc., 1935), p. 51.

[14] P. 243.

tion, direction, and control."[15] There is little objection to this, since the function of planning is clearly included under the term *direction*.

Here again, we encounter the danger of confusing practical men by the multiplication of academic arrangements of the same material. Sixty years ago, the French industrialist Henri Fayol, who was in fact the originator of the scientific study of organization, defined management[16] as consisting of five, or rather six, functions:[17] forecasting, planning, organizing, directing,[18] coordinating, and controlling. It will be seen that he agrees with the authors' three, but adds three more: forecasting, planning, and coordinating.

As explained in footnote 17, the term used by Fayol involved the conceptions of both forecasting and planning. I feel that these two concepts should be kept distinct in the minds of students. It is one thing to try to arrive at a calculated estimate of what is likely to happen in the future. It is another to make arrangements of men and materials designed to meet such projected events. To conclude that the population of a particular sales area is likely to increase by 50 per cent in the next five years is one kind of decision; to project an increase of the sales force in that area by 10 per cent per annum and corresponding increases in manufacturing facilities is a decision of a different order.

Whether both forecasting and planning should be included under directing is a matter of taste. From my standpoint, planning so frequently precedes organization—there is no point in building up organization unless and until there is a plan to do something with it—that it is desirable to treat planning and directing as separate activities. Frederick Winslow Taylor's principle of separating planning from performance has been exaggerated. But basically his contention that the two functions should be kept distinct was well founded. Where planning is

---

[15] P. 254.

[16] The original title of Fayol's book in French was *Administration industrielle et générale*. It was first published as a paper in the *Bulletin de la Société de l'industrie minérale*, in 1916. But Fayol had outlined his theory of administration as early as 1900 in a paper to the *Congrès des mines et de la metallurgie*. There is no word in the French language exactly corresponding with the English term "management." But it is clear from his context that Fayol meant by *administration* exactly what Anglo-American writers of today mean by *management*. The word was so translated in the standard English translation of Fayol's book ( Henri Fayol, *General and Industrial Management*, translated by Constance Storrs [London: Sir Isaac Pitman & Sons Ltd., 1949]).

[17] Fayol listed only five functions. But the word he used for the first, *prévoyance*, means both to foretell the future and to provide for it. It can only be translated into English by the two words "forecasting" and "planning."

[18] The French word used by Fayol was *commander*. But "to command" or "to order" have an unpleasant tone in American ears ("pushing people about"). Again it is clear from the context that Fayol meant exactly the same by *commander* as the authors mean by "to direct."

mixed up with the actual directing of operations it tends to be done badly.[19]

As for coordination, the authors say "coordination is not properly a function; it is something to be achieved. And it is achieved by adequate organization, direction and control."[20] To be sure coordination is the purpose of organization, as Mooney and Reiley[21] pointed out in 1931. But to say that it is achieved by adequate organization, direction, and control is to fail to identify the activities which are specifically necessary to secure it. The authors, for instance, are clearly advocates within limits of what they describe as "permissive management," or at least of the manager who makes "a continuing effort to confront his subordinates with the challenge of freedom."[22] But confronting subordinates with "the challenge of freedom" is no part of the purpose of an economic enterprise. The argument in favor of, for example, consulting subordinates before coming to a decision is that such methods, which may be very time consuming, will nevertheless incline subordinates to submit to the manager's formal authority. They will operate with higher morale and be less inclined to refuse to accept his communications. In the long run less time will be expended on argument *after* communications have been issued. Such methods are therefore directly aimed at coordination—unity of effort.

Mary Parker Follett identified four principles designed to secure coordination.[23] In fact, many business executives spend a great proportion of their time attending conferences, committees, etc. The purpose of all such activities is to improve coordination. Theoretically the written or verbal communications of superior managers should suffice. Actually they do not. That they do not suffice may be due to a variety of causes. But to say that "adequate direction and control" will make *all* activities directed specifically to coordination unnecessary seems to me an unjustifiable assumption. The failure to identify coordination as a separate function

---

[19] What Taylor was thinking of was the clerical work connected with the planning of a machine shop and the confusion which usually ensues when a foreman tries to do everything himself, trusting to a well-thumbed notebook, which he may or may not keep systematically. A proper planning room is, of course, infinitely more effective. The principle has been attacked on the ground that it is inhuman and merely turns the worker into an adjunct of a machine. But this is a consequence of pushing the principle too far, of not seeing, as Drucker has pointed out, that "one cannot . . . do only; without a trace of planning his job, the worker does not have the control he needs even for the most mechanical and repetitive routine chore" (*op. cit.*, p. 284).

[20] P. 263.

[21] "When we call *coordination* the first principle, we mean that this term expresses the principles of organization in toto; nothing less," J. D. Mooney and A. C. Reiley, *Onward Industry* (New York: Harper & Brothers, 1931), p. 19.

[22] P. 78.

[23] H. C. Metcalf and L. Urwick (eds.), *Dynamic Administration: The Collected Papers of Mary Parker Follett* (New York: Harper & Brothers, 1941), p. 297.

frequently leads to a failure to provide for it or to appreciate the volume of work involved in taking care of it. An example appears in Chapter 19 of this book—"they don't appreciate all the detailed work of coordination that a project manager has to do."[24]

Chester Barnard has pointed out that many executives who are able leaders find difficulty in explaining verbally how and when they lead. This is due, primarily, to the fact that the activities involved in leading cannot be isolated for purposes of verbal expression. The leader is constantly doing two or more things at the same time. Consequently he finds difficulty in isolating and expressing, even to himself, those elements in these composite actions which constitute leadership.[25]

The same seems to me to be true of coordination. Many executives agree with the authors in questioning its existence as a separate function. But the fact that those activities which secure coordination are difficult to identify and express does not mean that there is no separate function. I would therefore urge the view that Fayol's analysis of the functions of management is of long standing, logical, accurate, and convenient. It should be allowed to stand and only altered on the strongest proof that it can be improved.

Finally, I am dubious about the authors' definition of "leadership." This reads: "Interpersonal influence, exercised in situation and directed, through the communication process, toward the attainment of a specified goal or goals." This definition, they say, "treats leadership as a process or function rather than as an exclusive attribute of a prescribed role."[26]

I would agree immediately that leadership as a concept cannot be limited to those in a prescribed role, that is, occupying a position of authority. There are far too many instances of leadership being exercised by those initially occupying no role at all.

> One man with a dream, at pleasure,
> Shall go forth and conquer a crown;
> And three with a new song's measure
> Can trample a kingdom down.[27]

[24] P. 316.

[25] "I shall attempt here to say generally what leaders do, dividing their work under four topics. . . . Unfortunately it is necessary to discuss these topics separately. This is misleading unless it is remembered that, except in special cases or when specially organized, these kinds of action are not separated but closely interrelated, interdependent, and often overlapping or simultaneous. Therein lies one reason why it is so difficult for a leader to say what he does or to avoid misrepresenting himself. He does not know how to untangle his acts in a way suitable for verbal expression," Chester I. Barnard, "The Nature of Leadership," in *Organization and Management, Selected Papers* (Cambridge, Mass.: Harvard University Press, 1949), p. 85.

[26] Pp. 24, 25.

[27] Arthur William Edgar O'Shaughnessy (1844–1881), Ode: "We Are the Music Makers."

The critical acts of leadership often occur before, rather than after, any formal role is acquired. This is sometimes described as "informal leadership." But it is too common and too important to be relegated, as it were, to a subsidiary position. Indeed, much of the confusion which has surrounded the discussion of leadership may be traced to the tendency to confuse it with authority—"the formal right to require action of others."

On the other hand, to treat the abstract term *leadership* as describing a "process or function" appears to me to be confounding the abstract with the concrete.[28] A person engaged in a process or function is active. He is doing something. And the active form of the verb "to lead" is *leading*. To lead means to go in front of, be ahead of, guide. What a person is doing who leads is leading; leadership is the kind of behavior which enables an individual to lead others. It may be defined formally as *the kind of behavior by an individual which inclines others to accept his/her guidance.*[29]

If this definition of leadership is accepted, much of the difficulty of reconciling it with authority disappears. The two concepts are seen as complementary and, in a sense, antithetical to each other.

They are complementary for two reasons. The first is that any individual occupying any position of authority must behave in some way or other. That behavior will incline others to accept communications from the position, or it will disincline them to do so. In the second case, the authority will evaporate. But because the individual does occupy a position of authority, he/she is bound to "go through the motions" of leading. The problem becomes one of quality. He/she is a good or a bad leader. It is frequently said of a man who has failed in a position of authority, "he was no leader" or "he lacked leadership." In this context leadership is the kind of behavior which makes formal authority effective.

The second reason is that individuals participating in a system of human cooperation are often inclined to accept the communications of those occupying positions of formal authority in the system and to act upon them without too much thought as to whether they are positively motivated so to act or not. There is what Barnard has described as "the zone of indifference." A poor leader may therefore secure some of the effect at which he aims merely because of his position. But he is

---

[28] The tendency to use abstract terms to describe concrete actions is responsible for much of the confusion which attends discussions of management. An example is the use of the term "management" itself when what is meant is "managing." See L. Urwick, "The Problem of Management Semantics," *California Management Review*, vol. II, no. 3, pp. 76–82, Spring, 1960.

[29] *Cf.* Chester I. Barnard, "the quality of the behavior of individuals whereby they guide people or their activities in organized effort," *op. cit.*, p. 83.

unlikely to do so over a prolonged period; and, at no stage, will he enlist the positive enthusiasm of those collaborating with him. Because he is merely "going through the motions" of leading, they will merely "go through the motions" of following.

They are antithetical because a position of authority usually connotes some superiority of status. In any democracy there is normally a healthy and widespread suspicion of any attempt to assert superiority of status by any individual. In themselves self-assertiveness and superiority breed resistance. Thus the kind of behavior which inclines others to accept the guidance of an individual is precisely the kind of behavior which does *not* emphasize that individual's formal right to require action of them or his consequent superiority of status. Mary Parker Follett's discussion of "depersonalizing orders" and highlighting "the law of the situation" recognizes this principle.[30]

For this reason, I find difficulty in accepting the authors' expansion of their definition of leadership—"leadership always involves attempts on the part of a *leader* (influencer) to affect (influence) the behavior of a *follower* (influencee) or followers in *situation*."[31] This appears to make the behavior appropriate in a position of authority far too deliberate and self-conscious.[32] In many individuals the mere suspicion that they are being influenced, that they are being "sold" something, generates resistance. It is, of course, true that any person in a position of authority has a defined duty to try to influence those associated with him towards reaching the objectives of the undertaking. But his success in so doing will depend far more on what he is than on what he does or says. Those associated with him will form their judgment of what he is, on the cues offered by his overt behavior. But the fact that they are associated with him in work means that that judgment will probably be both more accurate and more intimate than he is prepared to imagine.

A former chief of staff of the United States Army once said, "The leader must be everything that he desires his subordinates to become. Men think as their leaders think, and men know unerringly how their leaders think."[33] Field-Marshal Sir William Slim, Commander in Chief

---

[30] *Dynamic Administration*, pp. 58–62.

[31] P. 24.

[32] *Cf.* "The sorts of acts or behavior by which executives 'persuade' to coordinated action are innumerable. . . . Why do they vary? Some obvious differences of combination in leaders, in followers, in organization, in technology, in objectives, in conditions, will occur to you. But the effective combinations are often so subtle and so involved in the personalities of both leaders and followers that to be self-conscious about them, or for others to examine them when in process, would disrupt them," Chester I. Barnard, *op. cit.*, p. 90.

[33] General Charles P. Summerall, quoted in Mooney and Reiley, *op. cit.*, pp. 33 and 34.

of the 14th Army in World War II and, more recently, Governor General of Australia, said that five qualities are necessary in a leader: courage, will power, flexibility of mind, knowledge and "the last quality, on which all the other qualities have to be based, is integrity—the thing that makes people trust you."[34] This view is confirmed from the business angle by Peter Drucker, who, in a single volume, refers to integrity more than twenty times as *the* quality essential in a manager.[35]

The individual who aims deliberately at convincing others that he possesses integrity is foredoomed to failure, because the very attempt to convey such an impression is an almost certain indication that he is in doubt either as to the validity of his own code of ethics or as to his ability to live up to it. On the other hand, the individual with an understandable and simple standard of personal conduct who is clearly devoted to the task in hand and puts it in front of personal interests of any kind, almost invariably attracts the adherence and commands the loyalty of other people. If he is in a position of authority, that authority is accepted because it is manifestly directed to the common purpose and does not challenge resistance by raising doubts whether followers are being asked to serve that purpose or merely to minister to the leader's egotism or ambition.

Possibly it is this element of self-forgetfulness, of unconsciousness of role, which is so common an element in successful leaders, which, in addition to the difficulty of isolating and expressing actual activities of leading, renders so many of them inarticulate about the subject. They do influence people, but largely because they do not attempt to do so. Indeed, many of them would appear to share the philosophy expressed in Robert Browning's lines:

> 'Tis an awkward thing to play with souls,
> And matter enough to save one's own.[36]

This discussion of points raised in my mind by reading the manuscript of this book must necessarily appear more critical than is its intent. It concentrates on possible areas of misunderstanding rather than on those portions of the work which tempted me "to beat happy applause." As a whole, the ten years' work of the Human Relations Research Group, as here partially recorded, is a notable contribution to the study of management and to the efforts of those who are striving to improve their understanding of the problems involved.

[34] Field-Marshal Sir William Slim, G. C. B., etc., *Leadership,* an address to the Sydney Division, Australian Institute of Management, Nov. 25, 1953. Published as a pamphlet by the Institute, p. 3.
[35] Peter F. Drucker, *op. cit., passim;* see pp. 146, 157, 158, 345, 348, 349, etc.
[36] Robert Browning, "A Light Woman," in *Dramatic Romances.*

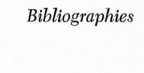

*Bibliographies*

# Publications of the Human Relations Research Group, 1950–1960

## STUDIES IN METHODOLOGY

Weschler, Irving R., and Raymond E. Bernberg: "Indirect Methods of Attitude Measurement," *International Journal of Opinion and Attitude Research*, pp. 209–228, Summer, 1950. Reprinted in Robert Ferber and Hugh G. Wales, *Motivation and Market Behavior* (New York: Richard D. Irwin, Inc., 1958). (Institute of Industrial Relations unnumbered reprint.) *

Weschler, Irving R.: "An Investigation of Attitudes toward Labor and Management by Means of the Error-choice Method," *Journal of Social Psychology*, pp. 41–62, August, 1950. Reprinted in Milton L. Blum, *Readings in Industrial Experimental Psychology* (Englewood Cliffs, N.J.: Prentice-Hall, Inc., 1952), pp. 140–148. (Institute of Industrial Relations Reprint no. 17.) *

Weschler, Irving R.: "A Follow-up Study on the Measurement of Attitudes toward Labor and Management," *Journal of Social Psychology*, pp. 63–71, August, 1950.

Weschler, Irving R.: "Problems in the Use of Indirect Methods of Attitude Measurement," *Public Opinion Quarterly*, vol. 14, no. 1, pp. 133–139, Spring, 1951. (Institute of Industrial Relations unnumbered reprint.) *

Weschler, Irving R., Robert Tannenbaum, and Eugene Talbot: "A New Management Tool: The Multi-relational Sociometric Survey," *Personnel*, vol. 29, no. 1, pp. 85–94, July, 1952. (Institute of Industrial Relations Reprint no. 25.)

Massarik, Fred, Robert Tannenbaum, Murray Kahane, and Irving R. Weschler: "Sociometric Choice and Organizational Effectiveness: A Multi-relational Approach," *Sociometry*, vol. 16, no. 3, pp. 211–238, August, 1952. (Institute of Industrial Relations Reprint no. 34.) *

Massarik, Fred, and Paula Brown: "Social Research Faces Industry," *Personnel*, vol. 30, no. 6, pp. 454–462, May, 1954. (Institute of Industrial Relations Reprint no. 41.) *

* Out of print.

Tannenbaum, Robert: "The Methods and Techniques of the Science of Human Relations," *Hospital Administration,* vol. 1, no. 1, pp. 22–28, Fall, 1956.

Massarik, Fred: "A Definitional Model for Behavioral Research," *Pacific Sociological Review,* vol. 2, no. 2, pp. 81–86, Fall, 1959.

STUDIES IN MANAGEMENT, LEADERSHIP,
AND HUMAN RELATIONS

Tannenbaum, Robert: "The Manager Concept: A Rational Synthesis," *The Journal of Business,* vol. 22, no. 4, pp. 225–241, October, 1949. (Institute of Industrial Relations Reprint no. 8.)

Tannenbaum, Robert: "Managerial Decision-making," *The Journal of Business,* vol. 23, no. 1, pp. 22–39, January, 1950. Reprinted in Eugene J. Kelley and William Lazer, *Managerial Marketing* (New York: Richard D. Irwin, Inc., 1958). Reprinted in part in Robert Dubin, *Human Relations in Administration* (Englewood Cliffs, N.J.: Prentice-Hall, Inc., 1951), pp. 206–211, and in Max D. Richards and William A. Nielander, *Readings in Management* (Cincinnati: South-Western Publishing Company, 1959). (Institute of Industrial Relations Reprint no. 9.)

Tannenbaum, Robert, and Fred Massarik: "Participation by Subordinates in the Managerial Decision-making Process," *The Canadian Journal of Economics and Political Science,* August, 1950, pp. 408–418. Reprinted in part in Robert Dubin, *Human Relations in Administration* (Englewood Cliffs, N.J.: Prentice-Hall, Inc., 1951), pp. 223–228. Also reprinted in I. L. Heckmann and S. G. Huneryager, *Human Relations in Management: Text and Readings* (Cincinnati, Ohio: South-Western Publishing Company, 1960), pp. 378–391. (Institute of Industrial Relations Reprint no. 14.)

Tannenbaum, Robert: "Overcoming Barriers to the Acceptance of New Ideas and Methods," in *Proceedings of the Fourth Annual Industrial Engineering Institute of the University of California,* Los Angeles, Feb. 4–5, 1952. Reprinted in Richard G. Canning, *Electronic Data Processing for Business and Industry* (New York: John Wiley and Sons, Inc., 1956). With adaption this appeared as "When It's Time for a Change," *Supervisory Management,* July, 1956. Reprinted in Supervisory Management (eds.), *Leadership on the Job* (New York: American Management Association, 1957). (This latter article appears as an Institute of Industrial Relations unnumbered reprint.)

Tannenbaum, Robert: *An Evaluative Focus on Human Relations,* a working paper presented in May, 1954, at the Tenth Annual Industrial Relations Research Conference of the Labor Market Research Committee, Social Science Research Council. Institute of Industrial Relations, University of California, Los Angeles. Mimeographed.

Tannenbaum, Robert, and Fred Massarik: "Leadership: A Frame of Reference," *Management Science,* October, 1957, pp. 1–19. Reprinted in Austin Grimshaw and John W. Hennessey, Jr, *Organizational Behavior: Cases and Readings* (New York: McGraw-Hill Book Company, Inc., 1960), pp. 427–447, and in *Revista di Psicologia Sociale,* Fascicolo III, pp. 235–259, Luglio-Agosto-Settembre, 1959. (Institute of Industrial Relations Reprint no. 68.)

Tannenbaum, Robert: "The Introduction of Change in Industrial Organizations," in *Improving Managerial Performance,* American Management Association, General Management Series, no. 186, 1957. (Institute of Industrial Relations unnumbered reprint.)

Tannenbaum, Robert, and Warren H. Schmidt: "How to Choose a Leadership Pattern," *Harvard Business Review,* vol. 36, no. 2, pp. 95–102, March-April, 1958. Reprinted in Harvard Business Review (eds.), *Successful Patterns for Executive Action.* (Institute of Industrial Relations Reprint no. 69.)

Tannenbaum, Robert: "Some Basic Issues in Human Relations," in Robert D. Gray (ed.), *The Frontiers of Industrial Relations* (Pasadena, Calif.: Industrial Relations Section, California Institute of Technology [copyrighted], 1959). Also published as "Some Current Issues in Human Relations," *California Management Review,* vol. 2, no. 1, pp. 49–58, Fall, 1959. (Institute of Industrial Relations Reprint no. 92.)

Schmidt, Warren H., and Robert Tannenbaum: "Management of Differences," *Harvard Business Review,* vol. 38, no. 6, pp. 107–115, November-December, 1960.


STUDIES IN SOCIAL SENSITIVITY AND IN
SENSITIVITY TRAINING

Kallejian, Verne J.: *Interpersonal Perception in the Informal Group,* doctoral dissertation, University of California, Los Angeles, 1953.

Tannenbaum, Robert, Verne Kallejian, and Irving R. Weschler: "Training Managers for Leadership," *Personnel,* vol. 30, no. 4, pp. 254–260, January, 1954. (Institute of Industrial Relations Reprint no. 35.)

Weschler, Irving R., Marvin A. Klemes, and Clovis Shepherd: "A New Focus in Executive Training," *Advanced Management,* vol. 20, no. 5, pp. 17–22, May, 1955. Reprinted in C. G. Browne and Thomas S. Cohn (eds.), *The Study of Leadership* (Danville, Ill.: The Interstate Printers and Publishers, Inc., 1958), pp. 439–449, and in Keith Davis and William G. Scott (eds.), *Readings in Human Relations* (New York: McGraw-Hill Book Company, Inc., 1959), pp. 318–327. (Institute of Industrial Relations Reprint no. 48.)*

Kallejian, Verne, Irving R. Weschler, and Robert Tannenbaum: "Managers in Transition," *Harvard Business Review,* vol. 33, no. 4, pp. 55–64, July-August, 1955. (Institute of Industrial Relations Reprint no. 47.)

Gebel, Arnold S.: *The Impact of a Change Setting on Different Levels of Personality,* doctoral dissertation, University of California, Los Angeles, 1955.

Tannenbaum, Robert: "Sensitivity Training—Useful Implement in Developing Leaders?," in *Research Developments in Personnel Management,* Proceedings of the First Conference, held on the campus of the University of California, Los Angeles, June 7–8, 1956, pp. 29–37. (Available from the Institute of Industrial Relations.)

Massarik, Fred: *Socio-perceptual Accuracy in Two Contrasting Group Settings,* doctoral dissertation, University of California, Los Angeles, 1957.

* Out of print.

Tannenbaum, Robert: "Dealing with Ourselves before Dealing with Others," *Office Executive*, vol. 32, no. 8, pp. 29–30 and 35, August, 1957. Reprinted in I. L. Heckmann and S. G. Huneryager, *Human Relations in Management: Text and Readings* (Cincinnati, Ohio: South-Western Publishing Company, 1960), pp. 605–610.

Weschler, Irving R., Robert Tannenbaum, and John H. Zenger: "Yardsticks for Human Relations Training," *Adult Education*, vol. 7, no. 3, pp. 152–168, Spring, 1957. Reprinted with bibliography in Adult Education Association, *Adult Education Monograph* no. 2, 1957. (Institute of Industrial Relations Reprint no. 66.)

Weschler, Irving R., and Jerome Reisel: *Inside a Sensitivity Training Group*, Institute of Industrial Relations, University of California, Los Angeles. Industrial Relations Monograph no. 4, 1959.

Massarik, Fred, and Irving R. Weschler: "Empathy Revisited: The Process of Understanding People," *California Management Review*, vol. 1, no. 2, pp. 36–46, Winter, 1959. (Institute of Industrial Relations Reprint no. 77.)

Reisel, Jerome: *A Search for Behavior Patterns in Sensitivity Training Groups*, doctoral dissertation, University of California, Los Angeles, 1959.

Lohmann, Kaj, John H. Zenger, and Irving R. Weschler: "Some Perceptual Changes during Sensitivity Training," *Journal of Educational Research*, vol. 53, no. 1, pp. 28–31, September, 1959. (Institute of Industrial Relations unnumbered reprint.)

## STUDIES IN THE ASSESSMENT OF ORGANIZATIONAL EFFECTIVENESS

Massarik, Fred, Irving R. Weschler, and Robert Tannenbaum: "Evaluating Efficiency Rating Systems through Experiment," *Personnel Administration*, vol. 14, no. 1, pp. 42–47, January, 1951. (Institute of Industrial Relations Reprint no. 20.)*

Weschler, Irving R., Murray Kahane, and Robert Tannenbaum: "Job Satisfaction, Productivity and Morale: A Case Study," *Occupational Psychology*, vol. 26, pp. 1–14, January, 1952. Translated and reprinted in *Tecnica ed Organizzazione*, May-June 1952, pp. 73–79. (Institute of Industrial Relations Reprint no. 23.)*

Kallejian, Verne, Paula Brown, and Irving R. Weschler: "The Impact of Interpersonal Relations on Ratings of Performance," *Public Personnel Review*, vol. 14, no. 4, pp. 166–170, October, 1953. (Institute of Industrial Relations Reprint no. 33.)*

Weschler, Irving R., Robert Tannenbaum, and Fred Massarik: "Experimenting with Federal Efficiency Ratings: A Case Study," *Journal of Social Psychology*, vol. 36, pp. 205–222, November, 1952. (Institute of Industrial Relations Reprint no. 26.)

Shepherd, Clovis: *Bureaucratization in the Supermarket Industry*, doctoral dissertation, University of California, Los Angeles, 1957.

Shepherd, Clovis, and Irving R. Weschler: "The Relation between Three Interpersonal Variables and Communication Effectiveness: A Pilot Study," *Sociometry*, vol. 18, no. 1, pp. 103–110, May, 1955.

* Out of print.

## STUDIES IN RESEARCH AND DEVELOPMENT

Henderson, Norman B.: *The Relationship between the Attitudes of Scientific Research Workers toward the Components of Scientific Work and Their Performance Rating,* doctoral dissertation, University of California, Los Angeles, 1953.

Weschler, Irving R., and Paula Brown (eds.): *Evaluating Research and Development* (Los Angeles: Human Relations Research Group, Institute of Industrial Relations, University of California, 1953). (Annotated Proceedings of a Conference of Research Administrators, held at UCLA, May 10, 1952.)

Brown, Paula: "Bureaucracy in a Government Laboratory," *Social Forces,* vol. 32, pp. 259–268, March, 1954. (Institute of Industrial Relations Reprint no. 36.)

Brown, Paula, and Clovis Shepherd: "Factionalism and Organizational Change in a Research Laboratory," *Social Problems,* vol. 3, no. 4, pp. 235–243, April, 1956. (Institute of Industrial Relations Reprint no. 60.)

Shepherd, Clovis, and Paula Brown: "Status, Prestige and Esteem in a Research Organization," *Administrative Science Quarterly,* vol. 1, no. 3, pp. 340–360, December, 1956.

## MISCELLANEOUS STUDIES

Weschler, Irving R.: "Who Should Be a Labor Mediator?," *Personnel,* November, 1949. (Institute of Industrial Relations unnumbered reprint.) *

Weschler, Irving R.: "The Personal Factor in Labor Mediation," *Personnel Psychology,* vol. 3, no. 2, pp. 113–132, Summer, 1950. Reprinted in Milton L. Blum, *Readings in Experimental Industrial Psychology* (Englewood Cliffs, N.J.: Prentice-Hall, Inc., 1952), pp. 148–158. (Institute of Industrial Relations unnumbered reprint.)

## STUDIES IN INTERPERSONAL INFLUENCE AND THE NURSING FUNCTION

Meyer, Genevieve Rogge: "The Attitude of Student Nurses toward Patient Contact and Their Images of a Preference for Four Nursing Specialties," *Nursing Research,* vol. 7, no. 3, pp. 126–130, October, 1958. (Institute of Industrial Relations unnumbered reprint.)

MacAndrew, Craig, and Jo Eleanor Elliott: "Varying Images of the Professional Nurse: A Case Study," *Nursing Research,* vol. 8, no. 1, pp. 33–35, Winter, 1959. (Institute of Industrial Relations Reprint no. 78.)

Meyer, Genevieve Rogge: "Conflict and Harmony in Nursing Values," *Nursing Outlook,* vol. 7, July, 1959. (Institute of Industrial Relations unnumbered reprint.)

Meyer, Genevieve Rogge: *Tenderness and Technique: Nursing Values in Transition* (with a chapter by Bruce Gordon, Joan Butler, Jeanne Quint, Marilyn Folck, Phyllis Nie, and Martha Adams), Institute of Industrial Relations, University of California, Los Angeles, Industrial Relations Monograph no. 6, 1960.

* Out of print.

# Selected and Annotated Bibliography
# of Works by Other Authors*

Argyris, Chris: *Personality and Organization* (New York: Harper & Brothers, 1957). An attempt is made to integrate much research on human behavior in organizations within a systematic framework. Argyris discusses individual personality and formal organization, and the influence of formal organization on the employee. He holds that the organization is in conflict with the individual and that this conflict prevents self-actualizing on the part of the individual. The conclusions are set forth as a series of propositions about organizational behavior.

Argyris, Chris: *Understanding Organizational Behavior* (Homewood, Ill.: Dorsey Press, 1960). Argyris develops conceptual and methodological approaches to the study of organization and presents the results of an empirical research program guided by his theoretical model. Of particular interest are the author's proposals for the quantitative investigation of self-actualization and his hypotheses concerning the impact of organizational change.

Bach, George R.: *Intensive Group Psychotherapy* (New York: The Ronald Press Company, 1954). Bach covers both the practice and theory of intensive group therapy in the treatment of personality disorders. Part I deals with clinical technique; Part II explores the nature of the therapeutic process that is fostered by group therapy participation; Part III examines the group dynamic forces that influence the therapeutic process in the individual.

Bass, Bernard M.: *Leadership, Psychology and Organizational Behavior* (New York: Harper & Brothers, 1960). The author develops a comprehensive theory of leadership and group behavior from a logical-positivistic point of view. His definitions, constructs, postulates, and theorems are based upon and supported by empirical data from the social sciences, industrial management, and history. Bass covers such topics as group effectiveness

---

* This bibliography, which complements, supplements, extends, or otherwise closely relates to the work of the Human Relations Research Group, was prepared by Iris Tan and Gerald Fogelson.

and attractiveness, leadership motivation, leadership evaluation and measurement, coercive and permissive leadership, status, and esteem. The book is written from the viewpoint of social psychology and includes an extensive bibliography on leadership.

Blake, Robert R., and Jane Srygley Mouton: *Training for Decision-making Groups* (Austin: University of Texas, 1958). The authors describe the ways in which members of "development groups" form themselves into decision-making organizations. Key chapters deal with the reasons for studying group development, ways of learning in a development group, problems of agenda building and goal setting, the nature of decision making, language aspects of communication, the role of the trainer, and the kind of learning possible from group development experiences.

Blau, Peter M.: *The Dynamics of Bureaucracy: A Study of Interpersonal Relations in Two Government Agencies* (Chicago: The University of Chicago Press, 1955). This volume investigates the activities of lower officialdom in a bureaucratic setting. Part I traces the "operating adjustments" which followed the introduction of performance records" in a small department of a state agency. Part II examines the relations between colleagues, informal status, and productive efficiency. Part III includes the author's theoretical work and a summary. Blau holds that bureaucracy is not necessarily opposed to change; this opposition only occurs under certain conditions—chiefly under conditions of status insecurity.

Bradford, Leland P. (ed.): *Theory of T-group Training* (Washington, D.C.: National Training Laboratories in Group Development, in preparation). One of the best collections of papers on human relations training, presenting the theoretical framework and experiences of various staff members of the National Training Laboratories in Group Development. In addition to Bradford, contributors include Kenneth D. Benne, Warren G. Bennis, Robert R. Blake, Jack R. Gibb, Murray Horwitz, Herbert A. Shepard, Roy Whitman, Jerome D. Frank, and Dorothy Stock. A good summary of research conducted on training groups is included.

Browne, C. G., and Thomas S. Cohn (eds.): *The Study of Leadership* (Danville, Ill.: The Interstate Printers and Publishers, Inc., 1958). This volume contains a broad sampling of published studies cutting across many areas of leadership activity. The approach taken avoids adherence to any specific theory of leadership; rather the authors present a broad view of the current thinking on leadership by psychologists and sociologists. The four parts deal with various conceptual and analytic issues, including the measurement of leadership through observational and participant techniques; the criteria of leadership; the dynamic aspects of leader personality, perception, and behavior; and approaches to leadership training. References cited in the original articles are included in this reprinting and constitute a valuable source of materials related to many aspects of the study of leadership.

Cantor, Nathaniel: *The Learning Process for Managers* (New York: Harper & Brothers, 1958). Cantor takes a skeptical look at existing management development programs, while attacking the "fads for training." He describes the functions of a manager and suggests that the quality of management performance cannot be separated from the quality of the people who are managers. The author sees the "teaching-learning process" as a way to personal development for individual managers.

Cartwright, Dorwin: *Studies in Social Power* (Ann Arbor, Mich.: University of Michigan Press, 1959). In this book, power is viewed as the ability of one person (or group) to influence or control some aspect of another person (or group). The studies deal with such phenomena as the ability of one person to influence the attitudes and behavior of another, the abilities of individuals to influence the decision of a group, and the ability of one person to determine whether or not another reaches his goal. The book includes a chapter on power as a neglected variable in social psychology. The closing chapters are concerned with the theory of social power and include the formulation of a rigorous mathematical model of power.

Cartwright, Dorwin, and Alvin Zander (eds.): *Group Dynamics: Research and Theory* (2d ed.; Evanston, Ill.: Row, Peterson & Company, 1960). A collection of studies on group functions and group patterns. The studies have been organized into six sections: an introduction (which includes a theoretical treatment of the whole subject area and presents research methods used on groups); group cohesiveness; group pressures and group standards; individual motives and group goals; leadership and group performance; the structural properties of groups. The editors provide an introduction to each section; they break down the problem area, indicate what research has been performed and what research needs to be done, and relate the studies to each other. The contributors include many key persons in the field of group dynamics and related areas.

Corsini, Raymond J.: *Methods of Group Psychotherapy* (New York: McGraw-Hill Book Company, Inc., 1957). The first part of this book is devoted to describing various therapeutic techniques and methods applied to people in groups. Corsini acknowledges that the theories of Freud, Adler, Moreno, and Rogers are the major foundation for many therapeutic group techniques. He distinguishes eight different types of group psychotherapy by means of the triple dimensions of *directive-nondirective*, *verbal-actional*, and *superficial-deep*. The last section of the book is set aside for excerpts from protocols of four representative methods of group therapy: nondirective therapy, family counseling, psychoanalytic therapy, and psychodramatic group therapy.

Coser, Lewis A.: *The Functions of Social Conflict* (London: Routledge & Kegan Paul, Ltd., 1956). The author provides an excellent clarification of the concept of social conflict. Through an examination of a number of propositions distilled from theories of social conflict, and in particular from the work of Georg Simmel, attention is called to the conditions under which social conflict may contribute to the maintenance, adjustment, or adaptation of social relationships and social structures. In the examination of the sixteen propositions set forth by Coser, the reader will find many ideas having important implications for various areas of human activity.

Dalton, Melville: *Men Who Manage* (New York: John Wiley & Sons, Inc., 1959). Using the participant-observer research approach, Dalton provides new and enlightening observations on the "nonofficial" behavior within organizations. He analyzes a number of commercial and industrial firms, including several factories, a drug chain, a department store, and a research firm. His still uncommon method provides additional evidence for the frequently made observation that formal social systems provide imprecise guides for action and for the prediction of behavior.

Davis, Keith: *Human Relations in Business* (New York: McGraw-Hill Book Company, Inc., 1957). A broad view of human relations in business. The author gives extensive consideration to the problem settings of human relations in business and to management action to improve human relations. A variety of case materials is presented from the author's management-consultant experience.

Davis, Keith, and William G. Scott (eds.): *Readings in Human Relations* (New York: McGraw-Hill Book Company, Inc., 1959). This volume presents a balanced selection of recent developments reported in the human relations literature. It includes readings on topics such as morale, motivation, leadership, communication, formal and informal organization, and human relations training.

Driver, Helen Irene: *Multiple Counseling—A Small-group Discussion Method for Personal Growth* (Madison, Wis.: Monona Publications, 1958). Multiple counseling uses a small-group discussion activity as the learning medium for personal growth of the participant. Individual counseling with the group leader is an inherent part of the process. The theoretical description of multiple counseling is followed by examples of application in a variety of settings.

Dubin, Robert: *The World of Work: Industrial Society and Human Relations* (Englewood Cliffs, N.J.: Prentice-Hall, Inc., 1958). This volume is "devoted to what people do while they are working, and the reasons for their behavior." Dubin emphasizes the importance of work in modern society. He discusses such topics as the structure of organization, behavior systems, automation, motivation and morale, and individual mobility. He also develops an approach to a theory of human interaction in industry.

Fromm, Erich: *Escape from Freedom* (New York: Rinehart & Company, Inc., 1941). An insightful investigation into the meaning of freedom for modern man. The role of the psychological factors underlying social processes is stressed. The development of freedom is interpreted as having root in man's awareness of himself as a significant separate being. Fromm speaks pointedly of the suppression of spontaneity and the sense of isolation and impotence which are caused by modern culture and which threaten to force culture back to authoritarianism.

Gibb, J., G. Platts, and L. Miller: *Dynamics of Participative Groups* (St. Louis: Swift, 1951). One of the first successful handbooks or "study guides" for people interested in improving the effectiveness of groups of which they are a part.

Goffman, Erving: *The Presentation of Self in Everyday Life* (Edinburgh: Social Science Research Centre Monograph no. 2, 1956). Also available in paperback (Garden City, N.Y.: Doubleday-Anchor, 1959). This book may be considered a qualitative guide for analyzing various subtle aspects of social situations. The author emphasizes the "roles" an individual must play in everyday life. For this purpose, he utilizes the thought-provoking framework of the theatrical performance.

Gordon, Thomas: *Group-centered Leadership* (Boston: Houghton Mifflin Company, 1955). An excellent presentation of a theory of leadership which is based on "the application of true democracy to small as well as to large groups." Direction is seen as something different from the mere development of techniques of control or of tricks by which one person may dominate others in a social situation. The book describes the efforts of a "collection" of people, at first passively dependent upon their leader, to develop into a "group" of active and creative participants who can establish their own objectives and work effectively toward their attainment.

Grimshaw, Austin, and John W. Hennessey, Jr.: *Organizational Behavior: Cases and Readings* (New York: McGraw-Hill Book Company, Inc., 1960). The authors provide a collection of cases in organizational behavior, supplemented by selected readings. The book is designed "to present a broad variety of situations and problems in which administrative decisions must be made and to offer some general insights about key administrative processes."

Haire, Mason (ed.): *Modern Organization Theory* (New York: John Wiley & Sons, Inc., 1959). In this collection of papers by well-known authors, a number of approaches related to organization theory are presented. Current research developments in the area are considered. The papers were presented at a symposium held by the Foundation for Research in Human Behavior at Ann Arbor, Mich., in February, 1959. Among the contributing authors are Chris Argyris, E. Wight Bakke, Dorwin Cartwright, R. M. Cyert, Robert Dubin, Rensis Likert, S. G. March, Jacob Marschak, Anatol Rapoport, and William Foote Whyte.

Haney, William V.: *Communication: Patterns and Incidents* (Homewood, Ill.: Richard D. Irwin, Inc., 1960). This book conceives of communication as a serial process, involving the phases of encoding, sending, medium, receiving, and decoding. The focus is on the encoding and decoding phases, since it is felt that these two phases are the least understood, and perhaps the most important causes of miscommunication. Examples of miscommunication are given and an extensive bibliography is included.

Hare, Paul A., Edgar F. Borgatta, and Robert F. Bales (eds.): *Small Groups: Studies in Social Interaction* (New York: Alfred A. Knopf, Inc., 1955). A collection of papers, representing several disciplines, focusing on social interaction in small groups. The book is divided into four parts. The first part is concerned with the early historical and theoretical background of the field. In the second, studies are presented which analyze the process of social interaction from the standpoint of the individual in a social setting. The third section presents papers which view the social setting from without. The final section contains an excellent annotated bibliography of approximately 580 titles. This bibliography serves as a survey of the status of work in the field.

Heckmann, I. L., and S. G. Huneryager: *Human Relations in Management: Text and Readings* (Cincinnati, Ohio: South-Western Publishing Company, 1960). The basic purpose is "to present an integrated view of the fundamental and foundational aspects of human relations." Major topics include human relations as an emerging discipline, leadership, motivation, organization, communication, participation, resistance to change, and human relations in perspective.

Heider, Fritz: *The Psychology of Interpersonal Relations* (New York: John Wiley & Sons, Inc., 1958). This work represents a preliminary analysis of a variety of concepts and phenomena that are seen as playing important roles in interpersonal relations. Theoretical notions are often implicitly developed out of unsystematic observation and intuitive thinking about interpersonal behavior. The author views this work as the development of a "pretheory" of interpersonal behavior, which, it is hoped, can serve as a common-sense basis for more rigorous theorizing.

Homans, George C.: *The Human Group* (New York: Harcourt, Brace and Company, Inc., 1950). Homans attempts a synthesis of sociological theory by beginning at the small-group level. Not much new experimental material is introduced, but Homans carefully reviews, analyzes, and integrates portions of several well-known studies, including the Hawthorne studies, *Street Corner Society* and *We, the Tikopia*. The book is a suitable, vigorous text in small-group behavior and provides many interesting, testable hypotheses for the advanced researcher.

Jennings, Eugene E.: *An Anatomy of Leadership: Princes, Heroes, and Supermen* (New York: Harper & Brothers, 1960). This is an exposition concerning types of leaders and their place in society. The author subdivides leaders into three categories: "princes, heroes, and supermen." Jennings defines, traces the history of, and relates each type to modern organizational life. The basic tenet of this book is that "ours is a society without leaders," and the major blame for this is placed on the large organization which tends to inhibit leadership ability.

Knowles, William H.: "Human Relations in Industry: Research and Concepts," *California Management Review,* vol. 1, no. 1, pp. 87–105, Fall, 1958. A critical survey of various trends in human relations is presented. Knowles believes that much of the current controversy in human relations results from the different attitudes of scientifically oriented and evangelical, mystically oriented researchers. He also reviews major concepts used in human relations research.

Koontz, Harold, and Cyril O'Donnell: *Principles of Management: An Analysis of Managerial Functions* (New York: McGraw-Hill Book Company, Inc., 2d ed., 1959). An orderly presentation of the principles and techniques of management developed out of the experience and observations of the authors and drawing freely upon the formulations and researches of others in the field. The work is characterized as an attempt to summarize the principles and techniques of the managerial functions of organization, staffing, direction, planning, and control.

Leavitt, Harold J.: *Managerial Psychology: An Introduction to Individuals, Pairs and Groups in Organizations* (Chicago: University of Chicago Press, 1958). Utilizing research from the areas of communication and personality and the approach of psychology, Leavitt systematically discusses the problems of management ranging from the single individual through the large organization. The author skillfully combines the theoretical and practical and offers management useful bases for action.

Malamud, Daniel A. *Teaching a Human Relations Workshop,* Center for the Study of Liberal Education for Adults, Chicago, Notes and Essays on Education for Adults, no. 10, 1955. This summarizes the author's experiences in teaching a course on the psychology of interpersonal relations by means of "discussion methods which are aimed at helping the students arrive at their own insights."

March, James G., and Herbert A. Simon: *Organizations* (New York: John Wiley and Sons, Inc., 1958). A conceptual, well-reasoned, dynamic approach to the theory of formal organizations. Such topics as "classical" organization theory, motivational constraints, conflict in organizations, cognition and planning, and innovation are covered.

Marrow, Alfred J.: *Making Management Human* (New York: McGraw-Hill Book Company, Inc., 1957). This book considers the uses of psychology in industry with emphasis on human nature and its relationship to productivity on the job. The author attempts to answer the charge that human relations represents an effort to manipulate people through techniques that offer the form but not the substance of self-determination. He also points out serious flaws in the "economic man" model. The theoretical framework is heavily influenced by the work of Lewin and his associates.

McGregor, Douglas: *The Human Side of Enterprise* (New York: McGraw-Hill Book Company, Inc., 1960). This volume deals with policies and practices in the management of human resources in business and industrial organizations. The author discusses two sets of assumptions upon which management theory may rest. The first covers those assumptions upon which traditional organizations are based; these assumptions are held to be inadequate for the full utilization of human potentialities. The second considers those assumptions proposing the necessity of stimulating higher motivation, and realization of both individual and organizational goals. The ideas are examined in the light of present knowledge in social science.

McNair, Malcolm P.: "Thinking Ahead: What Price Human Relations?," *Harvard Business Review*, vol. 35, no. 2, pp. 15–22, 1957. The author views current human relations activity in business and business education skeptically. McNair feels that there are large segments of practice in human relations which constitute definite dangers; he is concerned with the "vicious circle" stemming from overemphasized human relations tending to create the very problems that it seeks to solve. He feels that by overemphasizing the nonlogical aspects of behavior, there is a great danger that the crucial processes of analysis, judgment, and decision making will be underemphasized.

Miles, Matthew B. *Learning to Work in Groups* (New York: Horace Mann Institute of School Experimentation, Teachers College, Columbia University, 1959). A comprehensive book bringing together what is known about helping people to learn better in groups. The chapters on specific training activities, problems in assuming the trainer role, and difficulties inherent in the evaluation process are especially interesting.

Moreno, J. L. (ed.): *Sociometry and the Science of Man* (New York: Beacon House, Inc., 1956). This volume, issued as the last number of the journal *Sociometry* prior to its transfer to the American Sociological Association, is a collection of papers concerned with a wide variety of sociometric methods and ideas. Papers contributed by the editor discuss the role of sociometry in the development of social science, and a theory of spontaneity and creativity. Included also are sections on the history of sociometry and approaches to sociometric measurement and research. The volume serves as an excellent overview of sociometric thinking and practice.

National Training Laboratory in Group Development: *Explorations in Human Relations Training: An Assessment of Experience, 1947–1953* (Washington, D.C.: National Education Association, 1953). Reports on the major accomplishments in research, training, and consultation of the National Training Laboratory in Group Development during its first six years of existence.

Riesman, David, with Nathan Glazer and Reuel Denney: *The Lonely Crowd: A Study of the Changing American Character* (New Haven, Conn.: Yale University Press, 1950). Also available in paperback (Garden City, N.Y.: Doubleday-Anchor, 1953). The underlying theme of this book holds that "there has been a change in the character of the American people." Where once the "inner-directed," rugged individualist dominated our society, now the peer-influenced, "other-directed" person is in power. The authors contrast these and other personality types in activities such as work, play, politics, and education. Supporting data are broadly empirical rather than experimental.

Rogers, Carl R.: *Client-centered Therapy* (Boston: Houghton Mifflin Company, 1951). An outstanding presentation of the nondirective point of view in counseling, teaching, and administration, with an analysis of its implications for psychological theory.

Rubenstein, Albert H., and Chadwick J. Haberstroh (eds.): *Some Theories of Organization* (Homewood, Ill.: The Dorsey Press, Inc. and Richard D. Irwin, Inc., 1960). This is a text which seeks to integrate scientific studies of organization from many of the traditional scholarly disciplines. The "unifying thread is not the practice of management in organization, but rather *the process of research in organizations.* The various theories are presented as results of research or as the impetus for research."

Ruesch, Jurgen, and Gregory Bateson: *Communication: The Social Matrix of Psychiatry* (New York: W. W. Norton & Company, Inc., 1951). Communication is treated as a central problem in human relations. It is seen as the basis for shared understanding, while lack of communication often results in social confusion and mental disease. The book contains a particularly insightful chapter on communication and American values.

Ruesch, Jurgen, and Weldon Kees: *Nonverbal Communication* (Berkeley, Calif.: University of California Press, 1956). This book presents a largely pictorial documentation of nonverbal communication. The authors skillfully combine text and photography to illustrate the various effects that action, objects, and words can produce. The last chapter is devoted to the development of a theory of nonverbal communication.

Sayles, Leonard R.: *Behavior of Industrial Work Groups: Prediction and Control* (New York: John Wiley & Sons, Inc., 1958). The author examines a wide range of informal work-group behaviors, based upon field investigation. The types of leadership and membership characteristics which make it possible for informal work groups to meet their needs are discussed. The implications of group activity for management, union, and research on work groups are examined.

Schutz, William C.: *FIRO: A Three-dimensional Theory of Interpersonal Behavior* (New York: Rinehart & Company, Inc., 1958). The author presents an inclusive theory in the area of interpersonal behavior. FIRO, an abbreviation for *fundamental interpersonal relations orientation,* is both a theory and method. The theory is concerned with the interpersonal needs of two or more persons. These interpersonal needs are *inclusion, control,* and *affection:* they are based on factorial type of studies which have been conducted in the areas of parent-child relations, personality types, group behavior, and other investigations. Although the test instruments are admittedly still crude at present, this work is both ambitious and promising.

*Scientific American,* September, 1958 (entire issue). The entire issue is concerned with innovation in science. J. Bronowski sets the keynote by pointing out the similarities between science and art, postulating that innovation in both fields can only occur when a single mind perceives a new and "depthful" unity in disorder. Various articles deal with innovation in mathematics, physics, biology, and technology. An article of particular interest is "The Psychology of Imagination," which gives an account of an investigation into the characteristics of creative individuals. Its companion article, "The Physiology of Imagination," deals with the neurological and physical processes underlying creativity.

Shartle, Carroll: *Executive Performance and Leadership* (Englewood Cliffs, N.J.: Prentice-Hall, Inc., 1956). A well-integrated discussion of many aspects of executive and leadership performance. This volume draws in part from an extensive leadership study program carried out at the Ohio State University. The book provides practical interpretations of research results and presents examples from research and observation. Comparisons are made between types of organizations to illustrate how administrative performance varies as a function of organization purpose and climate.

Shepard, Herbert A., and Warren G. Bennis: "A Theory of Training by Group Methods," *Human Relations,* vol. 9, pp. 403–414, 1956. An attempt to apply the theoretical formulations of Sullivan and Lewin to human relations training. It includes a comparative analysis of group therapy and group process.

Stewart, David A.: *Preface to Empathy* (New York: Philosophical Library, Inc., 1956). The author formulates a concept of empathy, traces its psychogenesis, and examines its implications, chiefly for ethics, for psychology, and for group therapy. Empathy is viewed as a basic action of human behavior. The work also includes chapters dealing with the creative role of empathy in art and with the development of a personal psychology grounded in empathy.

Stock, Dorothy, and Herbert A. Thelen: *Emotional Dynamics and Group Culture* (New York: New York University Press, 1958). This book reports on numerous research projects carried out at summer sessions of the National Training Laboratory at Bethel and at the Human Dynamics Laboratory of the University of Chicago. It contributes knowledge as well as methodology about the study of group interaction.

Stogdill, Ralph M.: *Individual Behavior and Group Achievement* (New York: Oxford University Press, 1959). A sociopsychological theory is developed to explain what happens inside the group. From a sociological viewpoint, this theory attempts to explain how member roles emerge in the social group. From a psychological viewpoint, it seeks to explain the influence that members exert upon the group. Stogdill hopes to be able to derive testable hypotheses from the theory.

Tagiuri, Renato, and Luigi Petrullo (eds.): *Person Perception and Interpersonal Behavior* (Stanford, Calif.: Stanford University Press, 1958). These twenty-three papers from the 1957 Harvard Symposium on Person Perception represent an attempt to lay a framework for further study and research. Many of the contributors, such as Fritz Heider, Solomon Asch, Lee Cronbach, and Theodore Newcomb, are well known for their previous writings in the area of social perception. The essays include a discussion of the verbal connections between physical and psychological events, a consideration of the self image of the scientist, and an essay on the analytic treatment of social perception scores.

The International Sociological Association, in collaboration with Jessie Bernard, T. H. Pear, Raymond Aron, and Robert C. Angell: *The Nature of Conflict* (Paris: UNESCO, 1957). This book presents a "survey and evaluation of research by sociologists and social psychologists into the nature, conditions and implications of human conflict," particularly conflict among nations. Three of the chapters deal with conflict from the viewpoints of sociology, especially historical sociology, and psychology. The fourth chapter is concerned with discovering paths to peace. An excellent bibliography is included, covering such topics as intergroup conflicts, international relations, racial conflicts (colonialism), and industrial and agrarian conflicts.

Thelen, H.: *The Dynamics of Groups at Work* (Chicago: University of Chicago Press, 1954). A major work which analyzes concepts useful in group activity regardless of its social purposes or particular membership. The author illustrates the practical application of these concepts in such areas as citizen participation, classroom teaching, in-service professional training, administration and management, human relations training, and public meetings.

Thibaut, John W., and Harold H. Kelley: *The Social Psychology of Groups* (New York: John Wiley & Sons, Inc., 1959). An attempt is made to organize the data of the field of social psychology into a theory of interpersonal relations and group functioning. The presentation is built upon a conceptual structure beginning with rather simple assumptions and adding to them as additions become necessary. The dynamic interactive social process is developed as the central focus.

University of Michigan, Institute for Social Research (numerous publications). Much of the research of the Institute for Social Research, directed by Rensis Likert and located at the University of Michigan, bears on topics considered in the present volume. In lieu of a single publication that may adequately summarize these many investigations in the areas of human relations, social organizations, group process, etc., the reader is referred to bibliographic sources such as the following: *Institute for Social Research, 1946–1956; Publications of the Institute for Social Research*, Fall, 1956; *Supplementary Publication List, Institute for Social Research*, September, 1956–January, 1960, all published by the sponsoring institution, University of Michigan, Ann Arbor, Mich.

Urwick, Lyndall F.: *The Pattern of Management* (Minneapolis: University of Minnesota Press, 1956). This book presents five lectures given by the author in April, 1955, as a guest at the University of Minnesota. The author's concern for the development of management is evident in this wide-ranging discourse. The lectures consider the principles and patterns of management, government, and leadership.

Viteles, Morris S.: *Motivation and Morale in Industry* (New York: W. W. Norton and Company, Inc., 1953). This volume is devoted to a comprehensive description and critical evaluation of American and British experimental studies and attitude surveys concerning the sources of motivation and the determinants of morale in industry. Emphasis is placed upon application of findings in increasing productivity, job satisfaction, and morale.

Whyte, William F.: *Money and Motivation: An Analysis of Incentives in Industry* (New York: Harper & Brothers, 1955). This book explores the relationship between incentives and increases in industrial production. Whyte sets out to build a new model of the workingman. He substitutes the notion of socioeconomic man for the inadequate classical economic-man concept. On the basis of theory and supported by the field work of Donald Roy, Melville Dalton, and Orvis Collins, Whyte concludes that group incentives are more effective than individual incentives. The field work reports provide a significant picture of the workers' reaction to incentive plans, to management practices, and to other workers.

Zaleznik, Abraham, C. R. Christensen, and F. J. Roethlisberger: *The Motivation, Productivity, and Satisfaction of Workers: A Prediction Study* (Boston: Harvard University Division of Research, Graduate School of Business Administration, 1958). True to its title, this study reports the results of research on factors influencing the motivation, productivity, and satisfaction of industrial workers. The research design combines analytical and clinical tools. The researchers state theories, derive hypotheses, and test these hypotheses in relation to a body of predicted and actual outcomes.

# Name Index

447

# Subject Index